The Employee Recruitment and Retention Handbook

OTHER BOOKS BY DIANE ARTHUR

Recruiting, Interviewing, Selecting & Orienting New Employees
(New York: AMACOM, 1986; also published in Colombia in 1987)

Managing Human Resources in Small and Mid-Sized Companies
(New York: AMACOM, 1987)

*Recruiting, Interviewing, Selecting & Orienting New Employees,
Second Edition* (New York: AMACOM, 1991)

Workplace Testing: An Employer's Guide to Policies and Practices
(New York: AMACOM, 1994)

*Managing Human Resources in Small and Mid-Sized Companies,
Second Edition* (New York, AMACOM, 1995)

The Complete Human Resources Writing Guide (New York: AMA-
COM, 1997)

*Recruiting, Interviewing, Selecting & Orienting New Employees,
Third Edition* (New York: AMACOM, 1998; also published in The
People's Republic of China in 2000)

ALSO BY DIANE ARTHUR

*Successful Interviewing: Techniques for Hiring, Coaching, and Per-
formance Meetings* (American Management Association Self-Study
Division, 2000)

Success Through Assertiveness (American Management Association Self-Study Division, 1980)

The Employee Recruitment and Retention Handbook

DIANE ARTHUR

AMACOM
American Management Association

New York • Atlanta • Boston • Chicago • Kansas City • San Francisco • Washington, D. C.
Brussels • Mexico City • Tokyo • Toronto

This publication is designed to provide accurate and authoritative information in regard to the subject matter covered. It is sold with the understanding that the publisher is not engaged in rendering legal, accounting, or other professional service. If legal advice or other expert assistance is required, the services of a competent professional person should be sought.

Library of Congress Cataloging-in-Publication Data

Arthur, Diane.
   The employee recruitment and retention handbook / Diane Arthur.
      p.   cm.
   Includes bibliographical references.
   ISBN 0-8144-0552-5
   1. Employee retention.   2. Employees—Recruiting.   3. Employee selection.   4. Personnel management.   I. Title.
   HF5549.5.R44 A748   2001
   658.3'111—dc21   00-049581

Printing number

10   9   8   7   6   5   4   3   2   1

To
Warren, Valerie, and **Victoria**

Whose encouragement and support
Enhanced my powers of retention

Contents

Preface

S tep back in time twenty years or so. If you were a human resources practitioner, recruitment specialist, manager whose responsibilities included recruitment, executive, or small business
owner, you would probably have turned to employment agencies,
newspaper ads, and employee referrals to fill most of your job
openings. And if some of your best employees resigned, you might
have conducted exit interviews, asked them why they were leaving, then noted and filed their responses.

Now fast forward to the present and what is projected to be
the future employment picture for some time to come. To attract
qualified workers, progressive employers are rejecting a steady diet
of reactive recruitment methods, such as agencies and ads, as well
as sources that could result in charges of systemic discrimination,
like word of mouth. Instead, they are implementing more proactive, creative recruitment techniques, such as cyberspace job banks
and mobile recruiting vans. What's more, the focus has extended
beyond hiring to creating a retention environment that will keep
employees satisfied and less inclined to resign. This includes encouraging employees to develop individual approaches to achieving business plans and redefining, as well as enhancing, jobs to
make them more rewarding.

Increasingly, employers are acknowledging that the recruitment and retention pictures have changed: Applicants are demanding more, competition for good workers is often fierce, and
employees are seeking greater incentives to stay. It's become hard
to know just how to attract and recruit the best workers, in addition
to what factors are required for a successful retention environment.

All of this points to *The Employee Recruitment and Retention
Handbook*, a comprehensive source that analyzes the changing
employment picture and offers a combination of new as well as

proven methods designed to recruit and retain top performers. Each chapter provides a helpful mix of how-to guidance, checklists, and best practices. The last chapter focuses on future workplace trends and challenges. In addition, there are two comprehensive appendices on Employee Benefits Terms and Legal Issues, respectively.

This information will prove helpful to employers as they look beyond existing methods of attracting applicants and keeping employees from leaving, regardless of the type of work environment—corporate or nonprofit, union or nonunion, technical or nontechnical, large or small. In addition, trainers and instructors can use this book when teaching recruitment and retention in a workshop or college classroom setting.

Readers are advised on three points. First, any reference made to specific publications, services, or institutions is for informational purposes only and is not to be considered an endorsement. Second, this book is not intended to provide legal advice. Third, all of the examples and best practices contained herein are, to the best of my knowledge, accurate as of the time of this writing.

Finding and keeping good employees has become increasingly challenging. However, by letting go of some old practices, reshaping others, and embracing new methods of attracting and retaining workers, your organization can be a highly competitive and maximally productive place in which to work.

ACKNOWLEDGMENTS

My sincerest thanks go to AMACOM's very talented executive editor, Adrienne Hickey, who excels at sharpening my prose.

*The
Employee
Recruitment
and
Retention
Handbook*

CHAPTER 1

Profile of a Changing Workforce

"The future ain't what it used to be."
—Yogi Berra

In 1980, Peter Drucker, the man considered by many to be the most influential and widely read authority on management, wrote the book *Managing in Turbulent Times*. In it, he prophetically described what was likely to occur in the workforce at the turn of the new century. His projections included a labor force that would become increasingly heterogeneous and a trend toward continuous fragmentation, especially with respect to age and gender. Specifically, he anticipated that people would work well past the point traditionally considered retirement age and that many retirees would be "knowledge workers," seeking a second career in their sixties, seventies, and beyond. He calculated that the supply of young people entering the labor force would be exceedingly tight and that they would come with high expectations at variance with what would be offered. Women, he noted, would no longer be content to work part-time at lower-paying, less prestigious jobs; their experiences as mothers and homemakers would translate into credit or experience for work-related skills.

Drucker further suggested that people would look upon their jobs as places to hone skills, especially technical skills. Increasingly, then, workers would view their employers as little more than "facilities" or temporary worksites. Loyalty and allegiance, he surmised, would be to one's craft, as opposed to a particular company. Hence, length of service at any one job would be shorter than in the past.

Drucker also addressed the issue of migration and its impact on employment. He projected that the United States could expect continued large-scale migration from countries characterized by substantial labor surpluses and high unemployment, such as Mexico. This would endow U.S. manufacturing with competitive strength, as well as exacerbate ethnic tensions and impact the known cultural composition of the U.S. workforce. Accordingly, Drucker suggested that productivity and morale issues would develop if companies refused to become more responsive to the demands of a diverse workforce. As a step toward more diversity-driven work environments, he suggested that we put aside thoughts of a labor force and think instead of "labor forces," each with different needs and characteristics. He urged organizations to acknowledge these differences, rather than treat all employees as a homogeneous entity in connection with work policies, training programs, benefits, and styles of management.

Drucker's insights, dating more than twenty years ago, have proved to be accurate in many instances. The workforce has changed: Previously, seven out of every ten hours worked was by a white male under the age of 60; currently, diversity-driven work environments have become, of necessity, commonplace. Further, employers are scrambling to come up with ways to cultivate a sense of loyalty on the part of what seems to be a rather fickle collection of workers.

The fact that Drucker was so accurate with many of his projections is significant: The present labor market evolved over a period of decades; it did not suddenly materialize. In spite of the signs, warnings, and signals along the way, many employers seem unnerved by these changes and feel unprepared to cope with them.

In this connection, the contents of Chapter 1 characterize the composition of today's workforce, discuss the necessity for diversity-driven work environments, and describe the new form of employee loyalty. In addition, you will learn how to lessen worker overload and reduce its impact on your ability to recruit and retain a talented group of employees.

COMPOSITION OF THE NEW WORKFORCE

Today's workforce reflects a change in the age mix, gender, ethnic composition, immigrant status, and volume of workers with disabilities. Employers are also turning increasingly to previously untapped resources, such as welfare recipients and prison labor.

Older Workers

In the year 2000, there were more than twice as many adults at the traditional retirement age of 65 as there were thirty years earlier, representing nearly 25 percent of the entire U.S. population. That's because some 77 million people were born during the baby boom era (1946–1964). In addition, life expectancy has risen to nearly eighty years. Compare these figures with a mere 45 million young workers, and it's clear why, increasingly, employers are asking older employees to stay past retirement age, as well as coaxing retirees to return to work. Such workers are being offered continuing employment on a full- or part-time basis, on-site or as telecommuters, or as consultants, mentors, or volunteers. The roster of organizations recognizing aging Americans as valuable assets includes such giants as American Express Financial Services Inc., Amoco Corp., The Gillette Co., H.J. Heinz Co., and Hewlett-Packard Co.

Are these employers merely settling, or is older better? According to a 1999 study conducted jointly by the Society for Human Resource Management (SHRM) and the American Association of Retired Persons (AARP, a Washington, D.C.–based national organization of Americans over the age of 50), seniors have longer job tenure than their younger counterparts at the same companies and are at least as productive. These conclusions were supported in the "Emerging Workforce Study" done by Interim Services, the nation's fifth largest employer in the private sector. This study reported that workers in the older-than-fifty-three category are more likely than younger workers to give higher ratings to job satisfaction and enthusiasm.

Other studies reveal that older workers experience fewer on-the-job accidents, fewer avoidable absences, less stress on the job, a lower rate of illegal drug use, and a lower rate of admission to psychiatric facilities. Factor in an older worker's years of knowledge and experience, and it's hard to understand why every organization with staffing issues doesn't simply contact places like AARP, Unretirement (a Kentucky-based employment consulting organization), the Senior Employment Service, local senior citizen community centers, and Michigan's National Retiree Volunteer Coalition (NRVC). When recruiting volunteers through such places as the latter, there is minimal work and cost for the company. The result is a win-win situation for everyone: The volunteering retirees feel a sense of value and reconnection; the company has the benefit of low- or no-cost labor with a bank of skills as well as knowledge to offer.

While older workers are a great source of experienced and qualified labor, employers may want to offer retirees some help in readapting to the workplace. One way of accomplishing this is through a teaming of older and younger workers in programs that expose the returning workers to new ideas in addition to fresh perspectives. Through these relationships, the younger workers can also benefit from the guidance and experiences of the older employees. These mentoring programs can translate into substantial savings for companies, according to a joint study by the Saratoga Institute and Interim Services. They reported that 35 percent of employees who do not receive mentoring opportunities seek other employment within twelve months, as compared with only 16 percent of employees who receive regular mentoring. For every one thousand employees, this translates into 160 who will leave jobs where mentoring practices are in place, in contrast to 350 who will leave where mentoring practices are not in place, a rate that is more than double! At an average turnover cost per employee estimated to be $50,000, the differences calculate to a potential extra cost (or savings) of $9.5 million. (Additional information on mentoring appears in Chapter 9.)

Younger Workers

The 45 million young workers referenced earlier reflect a shortage of employees under the age of 35 that is expected to continue. In 1996, younger workers represented 35 percent of the labor force; in 2005, that number is projected to drop to 30 percent; in 2015, it is expected to go down again, significantly, to a mere 20 percent. This population—commonly referred to as baby busters, Generation Xers, yiffies (young, individualistic, freedom-minded, and few), and 13ers (in reference to the fact that they are the thirteenth generation to know the U.S. flag and the Constitution)—presents unique recruitment challenges to American businesses. Young workers expect to be able to balance fulfilling careers with family responsibilities, as well as actively pursue personal interests. Work for them must be interesting and reflect leading-edge technology. Not wedded to one job or even one field, young workers are open to alternatives and look for exciting and entertaining opportunities that will expand their skills, knowledge, and interests. More are graduating from high school than ever before (nearly 83 percent as compared with 54 percent thirty years ago). And as rewards for those with more schooling continue to rise, more young people are attracted to college: 24 percent have obtained a bachelor's or more advanced degree. This is a dramatic increase over thirty years ago, when fewer than 10 percent completed college.

Young workers, while offering an enticing package of skills and knowledge, are so few in number that employers must avoid relying on them as a primary labor source. At the same time, organizations need to develop creative and competitive techniques to attract and retain young workers.

Gender

Employment rates differ significantly between men and women, and while those differences will likely continue into the future, men's rates are declining, to a current 75 percent, down from 86 percent fifty years ago. In contrast, the trend for women in the workforce is on the rise. The Department of Labor reports that six in ten women are currently in the labor force, as contrasted with two in ten fifty years ago.

This increase in the proportion of working women has been one of the most important social and economic trends in modern U.S. history. With it comes increased demands on employers to provide childcare and eldercare programs, since 80 percent of all caregivers are women. Indeed, over half of all mothers with young children now work, and the percentage is even larger for mothers of school-age children.

In the past two decades, a significant number of women have entered high-technology industries and nontraditional fields such as engineering and construction, in addition to professions such as medicine and law. For example, the proportion of women physicians has doubled from 7.6 percent to 16.9 percent; the percentage of women lawyers and judges has grown from 5.8 percent to 22.7 percent; and in engineering the percentage has increased from 1.3 percent to 8.6 percent. Among federal contractors required to meet affirmative action goals, the proportion of women holding official and managerial jobs has increased from 18 percent to 25 percent.

Despite these gains, women workers are still clustered in a narrow range of low-paying, low-status occupations, and they are excluded from many jobs. The number of women firefighters, police officers, college presidents, and corporate heads is still low: Women comprise only 3 percent of firefighters, 8 percent of police officers, 11.8 percent of college presidents, and 5 percent of senior-level positions in major companies. In the federal government, 56 percent of women workers are clustered in clerical jobs.

Significant gender-based wage gaps also persist. Overall,

women make only 75 cents to a white man's dollar, even when women have the same training and educational credentials as their male counterparts. For example, a study of the Class of 1982 Stanford MBAs found that ten years later, 16 percent of men held CEO job titles, while only 2 percent of women were CEOs. In addition, 23 percent of the men worked as corporate vice presidents and 15 percent served as directors, compared with 10 percent of women who were vice presidents and 8 percent who held director positions. On average, the women Stanford MBA graduates from the Class of 1982 made only 73.1 percent of the salaries of the men graduates.

Ethnicity

African-Americans, Hispanics or Latinos, Asian-Americans, Native Americans, and other ethnic groups are projected to represent 37 percent of the labor market in 2020, and over 50 percent in 2060. Although these groups represent a large percentage of the changing workforce, relatively few have been targeted for professional positions; those that have often earn less than nonminorities. Consider the status of executive branch white collar employees in the federal civilian workforce, as reported in the "Federal Civilian Workforce Statistics Demographic Profile of the Federal Workforce." Professional nonminority men earned an average of $4,500 more than professional minority men. The gap between white collar minority women and nonminority women was reportedly more than $3,200. And white collar nonminority men earned more than $16,500 more than nonminority women.

Despite the employment difficulties employers currently face, independent audits reveal continued discrepancies in the treatment of nonminorities and minorities. In the 1995 report of the Glass Ceiling Commission, only six-tenths of 1 percent of senior management positions in the nation's largest companies were held by African-Americans, four-tenths of a percent by Hispanics, and three-tenths of a percent by Asian-Americans. White males made up 43 percent of the workforce but held 95 percent of the senior management jobs. Today, the overall corporate professional composition throughout the United States remains pretty much the same.

Immigrants

Immigration will play the largest role in the growth of the United States through midcentury, increasing the U.S. population by 80 million people. Two out of every three immigrants will be of working age upon arrival. High immigration numbers from Mexico are expected to continue, and we can expect increased immigration from the Philippines, China, Cuba, India, and Vietnam. Also, Congress's passage, on October 4, 2000, of a bill to increase the number of visas for foreigners to fill specialized high-technology jobs will contribute to the increased immigration population.

This influx of immigration means employers must tap a greater pool of applicants for whom English is a second language and who arrive lacking concrete job skills. Others will be trained professionals with qualifying credentials from a foreign country that may not be valid in the United States.

People with Disabilities

The most recent figures reveal that approximately 50 million Americans have disabilities—that is, roughly 26 percent of the potential workforce. Of these, 45 percent have physical disabilities; 32 percent suffer from heart disease, cancer, diabetes, or respiratory disease; 13 percent have visual, hearing, or speech impairments; and 6 percent have mental disabilities. The remaining 4 percent have "miscellaneous" disabilities, such as smoke sensitivity or obesity. All in all, there are more than one thousand impairments identified as disabilities under the American with Disabilities Act of 1990.

People with disabilities have the highest unemployment rate of any other group in the United States. As compared with the non-disabled, those with moderate disabilities are nearly twice as likely to be looking for work or have been laid off, and those with severe disabilities are nearly three times as likely to be out of work. Education seems to make some difference: People with disabilities who have college degrees are more likely to find employment than those without degrees.

Additional information on people with disabilities appears in the Appendix.

Welfare Recipients

In 1999, welfare caseloads dropped by a record 6.5 million people since 1993, falling by half or more in twenty-nine states, and 46 percent nationwide.[1] The rolls have declined by 38 percent in 1999 since President Bill Clinton signed the Welfare Reform Law in 1996. Companies in the Welfare-to-Work Partnership have hired over 400,000 welfare recipients, and the federal government has hired nearly 12,000, exceeding its goal of 10,000.

One of the most unique efforts to hire welfare recipients was implemented by New York City's Human Resources Administration. In 1999, it began training and hiring people on welfare to work for a company called Psychic Network as telephone clairvoyants. Applicants were trained to read tarot cards and paid a minimum of ten dollars per hour plus a bonus for their efforts. The program was short-lived, however, after receiving bad publicity.

More women have turned to the labor force for income since welfare reform policies established time limits on public assistance.

Prison Labor

Currently, 6 percent of the 1.1 million state prisoners and 19 percent of the 120,000 federal prisoners in the U.S. correctional system hold jobs in a prison joint venture with American businesses, and use of this largely untapped labor source is on the rise. The Private Sector/Prison Industry Enhancement Program (PIE) allows correctional agencies to engage in interstate shipping of prison-made goods for private business use, as long as the inmates producing the goods are paid the local market wage and local unions are consulted. PIE does, however, prohibit the use of prison labor to displace employed workers outside the prison, the impairment of existing contracts for services, or the failure to use a surplus of workers in the labor market.

The public seems to be generally supportive of prison labor. A recent poll indicated that 56 percent of Americans view the use of prison labor positively, and 46 percent say they would rather have inmates perform meaningful work than be merely punished. Labor unions, on the other hand, are supportive only as long as the programs prohibit use of prison labor to replace strikers or to provide services that may prolong a strike.

There also exists a legitimate concern that employees could lose jobs to low-cost inmates. For example, an Austin, Texas company laid off 150 employees and moved its operations to a local prison.

Businesses that have used prison labor include Travel Wholesalers International to staff an airline reservations center; Escod Industries, a division of the *Fortune* 500 company Insilco Corporation, to assemble electronic cables; and Jostens Inc., another *Fortune* 500 company, to sew, inspect, sort, and package graduation gowns. In addition, TWA has used hundreds of prisoners from the California Youth Authority's Ventura Training School for Juvenile Offenders.

As of this writing, a bill was to be introduced in Congress that would allow state and federal prisons to launch a large-scale effort to promote prison labor to private companies.

DIVERSITY-DRIVEN WORK ENVIRONMENTS

In a memo sent to each Procter & Gamble employee, then-Chairman of the Board John Pepper wrote, "Our success as a global company is a direct result of our diverse and talented workforce. Our ability to develop new consumer insights and ideas and to execute in a superior way across the world is the best possible testimony to the power of diversity any organization could ever have." His successor, Durk Jager, followed up with this message: "We have talked many times about how important it is that we build and leverage the diverse backgrounds, experiences, and cultures of Procter & Gamble people. This is going to be much more important as we move ahead in tomorrow's world. In fact, diversity will be even more important as we strive to accelerate innovation and stretch for bigger, more discontinuous ideas."

These messages underscore two key ingredients for successful diversity-driven work environments: (1) support by senior management for the link between diversity and performance results, and (2) a commitment by the entire organization to diversity as an ongoing strategic business imperative.

Currently, more than 75 percent of major American companies have diversity programs in place, complete with mission statements and employee-friendly objectives. At Kraft Foods Inc., for instance, the company uses common metaphors to describe its commitment to diversity: "A stellar meal requires contrasting and complementing textures and tastes." "A winning sports team depends on the different talents of its members." "A first-class orchestra needs many varied instruments." ". . . a successful business team requires a variety of thought, energy, and insight to attain and maintain a competitive edge." "Kraft Foods is comprised of people . . . with different ways of thinking. We invite these differences. We seek them out. And we know that our business teams and the individuals thrive as a result."

Unlike Procter & Gamble and Kraft Foods, however, there are

still organizations that do not "get" diversity. They ask, "What is it and why do we need it, especially since we already have affirmative action?" But diversity is not the same as affirmative action. By definition, diversity encompasses dimensions of similarities and differences. These include factors such as gender, race, national origin, religion, skills, abilities, interests, goals, talents, communication, work styles, education, experiences, customs, values, personality, physical characteristics, health, language, and mental abilities.

Diversity and affirmative action differ in several ways:

1. Affirmative action is government initiated. Diversity is voluntary.
2. Affirmative action is legally driven. Diversity is productivity-driven.
3. Affirmative action is reactive and meant to redress discrimination suffered by particular groups. Diversity is proactive and benefits the organization overall.
4. Affirmative action is quantitative. Diversity is qualitative.
5. Affirmative action focuses on redressing problems. Diversity seeks out opportunities.
6. Affirmative action requires that employees fit into an existing work culture. Diversity acknowledges, supports, values, and utilizes peoples' differences and adjusts the work culture accordingly.

Successful diversity programs are founded on three key assumptions:

1. All people must be treated with equal regard.
2. The ability to incorporate different talents, skills, interests, abilities, etc., enhances an organization.
3. A diversity-driven work environment results in increased productivity and profits.

Diversity initiatives include recruiting employees with varying backgrounds and holding leaders in the organization responsible for proactive hiring, promotion, and retention at every level. Companies often benchmark against diversity recruitment programs in other organizations to identify best practices. Employees are also expected to interact without bias in dealings with colleagues and customers. In return, they can expect the organization to promote an environment that is inclusive and free from prejudice. Diversity-driven work environments usually offer comprehensive training that focuses on managing behaviors rather than changing employee beliefs, a comprehensive career development plan for each employee, and frequent surveys pertaining to how well the company manages its diverse workforce.

Allstate Insurance Co.'s efforts in elevating diversity to a strategic priority have garnered the company numerous awards, including being placed on the lists of the "1999 Best Companies for Hispanics to Work," the "1998 Top 10 Companies for Minority Managers," and the "1997 Best Companies for Working Mothers."

Organizations need diversity-driven work environments to attract better talent, boost morale, increase a company's access to new markets, increase consumer purchasing, help build a corporate image, and enhance operational efficiency. Diverse teams also tend to be more creative problem solvers; hence, diverse companies have the potential to be more innovative. In addition, companies with diverse boards are considered less risky for stock market investors. Focusing on diversity as a strategic advantage providing greater business leverage should encourage companies that are still resistant to providing diverse work environments.

Global Diversity

Even organizations that have implemented comprehensive diversity programs in the United States have not historically devoted substantial energy to international diversity efforts. In many instances, existing U.S. plans are merely rolled over and plugged in. At best, the results have been mixed. U.S. businesses have more than $600 billion of direct investment in foreign markets, and the number of Americans working in foreign countries is rising steadily. A survey conducted by the London-based Employment Conditions Abroad reports that two-thirds of companies have increased their expatriate population in the past five years, and two-thirds expect to increase the population additionally over the next five years.[2] Since the cost of placing U.S. workers into overseas assignments is, on average, nearly two and one-half times as costly as a domestic assignment, companies need to ensure a cross-cultural fit. In addition, progressive global advances increasingly mean multinational teams working on multinational projects.

Companies that have had the greatest success with global diversity programs are those actively searching for ways to learn from their colleagues around the globe and to share information with them. These organizations treat diversity as an ROI-focused business venture, measuring success in this area as they measure other business factors. For instance, the CEO of Novo Nordisk, based in Switzerland, expects his managers to "buy" and "sell" three best practices to managers in other parts of the world annually.

Many of these companies have also learned, through embarrassing experiences, that being culturally ignorant can be costly. One American company sent a business proposal to Saudi Arabia bound in pigskin; since pigs are an insult to Muslims, the proposal remained unopened. And it took McDonald's over a year to realize that their burgers were not selling in India because Hindus do not eat beef.

If your company has global interests, consider these key diversity-related questions:

1. How do the principles of our U.S. diversity efforts need to be amended to have relevance in foreign nations?
2. Are we learning from the nations with which we have ties and integrating their value systems into our foreign diversity efforts, as opposed to trying to make them more like us?
3. What can our organization glean from the experiences of those returning from overseas assignments?
4. How can these experiences be integrated into our business practices?
5. Are we committed to a marriage between our corporate expectations and foreign norms?

These and other questions can be addressed by a cultural diversity assessment committee, including representatives from all employee levels and backgrounds. Their analysis of domestic diversity policies and practices, as well as feedback from expatriates, can help develop or hone a global program.

Best Practice: BankBoston

While a growing number of companies are treating diversity as a business imperative, a handful stand out as model best practices. One of these is BankBoston, the sixteenth largest bank holding company in the United States, with 26,000 employees and assets totaling $74 billion. This bank understands the potential costs of failing to manage workforce diversity—high turnover, high absenteeism, and low productivity—and appreciates the benefits of diversity— increased creativity, greater productivity, increased employee satisfaction and loyalty, larger market share, and enhanced shareholder value. Its basic philosophy is that "paying attention to diversity issues is really paying attention to managing everybody well." Accordingly, instead of a director of diversity, the bank employs a director of workforce effectiveness, whose responsibilities extend beyond traditional diversity issues to include work/life strategies and performance management.

BankBoston's Workforce Effectiveness program focuses on three main areas: (1) investing in leadership and education, (2) listening to employees, and (3) holding managers accountable.

1. *Investing in leadership and education.* This includes a Diversity Leadership Conference, an intensive five-day program required of all senior managers and other nominated employees. Between 1997 and 1999, 850 people have participated. There are also three workshops in the Diversity Series on Respect, Diversity Beyond 2000, and HIV/AIDS Education. Additional courses under consideration at the time of this writing include Diversity and Decision Making and Diversity and Conflict Management.

2. *Listening to employees.* There are six resource groups for African-Americans, Latinos, Asian-Americans, gays and lesbians, parents, and people with disabilities. Participants network and establish common-ground objectives. The employee-initiated groups meet in company-provided facilities and receive a stipend for educational and other developmental activities. Examples of funded activities include seminars for parents on how to talk to their children about racism, and a pilot program that provides $25,000 for each resource group to give to a community nonprofit organization with common interests.

3. *Holding managers accountable.* Managers at all levels are accountable for implementing diversity-related issues in their performance evaluations. On the flip side, employees complete a Management Assessment Form, rating their managers' effectiveness. Some managers are also required to develop business unit diversity goals with progress being reviewed on a regular basis. Managers are rewarded for achieving their goals.

BankBoston provides other programs that help employees balance work/family responsibilities. These include Lifeworks, a telephone consulting service that offers advice on childcare and eldercare; Extended Family Benefits, including domestic partners or adult dependents; and BKBFlex, a program of alternative work arrangements.

BankBoston's Workforce Effectiveness unit has also developed a Diversity Competence Continuum, enabling the bank to measure managerial effectiveness in this area. Evaluations may be at one of three levels. Quoting from the bank, they are as follows:[3]

1. *Role Model.* "Is familiar with and able to address diverse market opportunities and the needs of diverse internal and external customers; seeks out perspectives from those of different backgrounds; actively participates in creating an environment where various styles that contribute to the success of the business are welcomed, appreciated and sought-after; models language and behavior that is inclusive and respectful of all people and expects others to do the same; demonstrates self-awareness and initiates personal development related to diversity; effectively communicates the relationship between issues of diversity and the organization's success; recognizes the impact that decisions and actions have on individuals and groups."

2. *Moderately Effective.* "Does not discount, but does not solicit diverse perspectives in problem-solving; shows little creativity in identifying cross-cultural business opportunities; does not actively include people of varied backgrounds in his/her personal network; deals politely with diverse customers and colleagues, but does not assertively invest in building alliances; is willing to 'follow the lead' when diversity issues surface, but rarely takes a leadership role; believes that diversity impacts the bottom-line, but cannot effectively communicate how; does not demonstrate an understanding of the impact that decisions and actions have on individuals and groups."

3. *Not Effective.* "Ineffective in dealing with people of all different cultures and styles; shows disdain towards dealing with issues of diversity in the workplace; maintains a personal network that excludes people of different cultural backgrounds; takes little or no ownership for personal learning style related to dealing with issues of diversity; does not understand the impact of cultural biases on business relationships; contributes to creating an environment that discourages people of different styles and backgrounds from fully participating in the work environment."

BankBoston is considered one of the nation's leaders in diversity. Its report, "Investing in Diversity," was entered into the *Congressional Record* as an example of diversity excellence. Included among its measurable accomplishments, the bank has increased the proportion of minority employees in its total workforce and in management positions. The number of women in managerial positions has also increased significantly.

THE NEW LOYALTY

I recently heard a "dot.com" radio commercial for one of the many job search web sites that abound today. What distinguished this one, however, was the content of the lead-in. The voice of a well-known business leader authoritatively described the new workplace loyalty as being virtually nonexistent—tentative at best. He went on to say that on-the-job longevity was a thing of the past and that today's employers don't want to hire people who have gone stale working in one company for more than a couple of years. "Move around," he urged. "Look out for yourself and make a lot of money! Worried about loyalty? Don't be! Your boss isn't going to be loyal to you!"

As I pondered the implications of these sentiments, my phone rang. It was John, a sixty-something first-line supervisor from a company for which I occasionally did some consulting. He had some questions concerning a long-term employee who until recently was a reliable performer. Unfortunately, personal problems were interfering with his work, and John didn't know if he should take disciplinary action. Before answering, I asked John if he had discussed the matter with his manager. "What for?" he lamented. "She probably won't be around next week."

I understood what he was saying. During his thirty years with the company, he had reported to fourteen different managers; six of them had come and gone in the last decade. As an "old-timer," John was bothered by the lack of commitment demonstrated by the incumbents who seemed to view the position as little more than a career stepping-stone. John had confided on several occasions that he felt increasingly like a dinosaur. "Whatever happened to loyalty?" he moaned. "Am I the only one who believes in it anymore?"

John's concerns are valid. Workplace loyalty is increasingly scarce, whether it's employee loyalty to an employer or vice versa. Many young workers who have seen their parents laid off after years of loyal service are skeptical of any lasting commitment on the part of an employer. Consequently, today's typical young worker averages nearly nine jobs between the ages of 18 and 32, with more than half of the job changes occurring before age 23. Add to this a competitive job market, the pressure to pay off student loans, and parental prodding to find a suitable position, and it's not hard to develop an "I'm in it for myself" mentality.

Employers, too, have demonstrated a lack of loyalty to their workforce as a result of acquisitions, mergers, relocations, downsizing, restructuring, and outsourcing. During a time of robust economic growth and record earnings, thousands of jobs continue to be cut. According to a recent Loyalty Institute study, the percentage of workers who are concerned about being laid off continues to rise. One sixty-five-year-old worker summed the situation up this way: "Until the 1960s or 1970s, loyalty was not demanded—it was offered freely on both sides. However, when the companies started working more for the stock analyst, the employee seemed to become as dispensable as a blunt screwdriver. That is when loyalty went out the window. And that's a shame."

This sentiment is echoed by Bob Brudno, managing director of the executive search firm Savoy Partners, who states, "No matter how aggressively they were recruited, no matter how much discussion there was about long-term commitments, most executives today know that they can be surprised at any time by the sale of their company or the acquisition of another that will mean months of reorganization and uncertainty."

Such an atmosphere can foster unethical behavior. For example, a recent MBA graduate accepted a position with a New England electronics company. Just prior to starting, he was approached by a recruiter from the company's top competitor, who urged him to renege in favor of a better offer with a starting salary of $5,000 more. So the young graduate retracted his original commitment. One week before he was to begin at the second company, the offer was revoked for "budgetary reasons." In this instance, the student behaved unethically, as did the recruiter from the second company. The first company is likely to be wary of future student commitments. And unfortunately, in the future, the student (despite his own unethical actions) may justify inappropriate behavior because of what the second company did.

Rehiring Former Employees

Is workplace loyalty being replaced with self-serving behavior on the parts of both employers and employees? Certainly there are changes necessitated by a tight labor market in which we see the issue of loyalty taking a backseat. For example, employers are reversing how they view former employees who resigned. Employers previously adhering to strict "no rehire" policies are now aggressively recruiting former workers. Instead of treating resignations as rejections, employers are regarding them as second opportunities to build long-term relationships. By contacting alumni group members via letters and e-mail, placing notices in newsletters, and attending cocktail parties, employers are swallowing their collective pride and going after those who once left them. Their goal: to turn former hires into new hires.

At Deloitte & Touche, employees who resign are sent surveys three months later asking, on a confidential basis, if they'd consider returning. As a result, about nine hundred workers were hired back in a twelve-month period. At the Chubb Group of Insurance in Warren, New Jersey, managers hiring for specific positions work from lists naming former employees. And at Gensler, a San Francisco–based architectural firm, staffers who quit, then return, are treated to a special welcome-back package that includes a letter of appreciation and a plastic boomerang.

While hiring former employees may alleviate job vacancy problems, it also sends a negative message to a company's current workforce—that is, the best way to get ahead in an organization is to leave it. After all, many of these former employees are given more money and promotions upon returning.

Importance of Workplace Loyalty

How important is workplace loyalty? In his March 23, 1998, keynote speech at the Human Resources Planning Society's Annual Conference, James P. Kelly, chairman and CEO of United Parcel Service (UPS), referred to a recent study conducted by the Sloan School of Management. The study determined that loyalty's long-term impact on corporate performance cannot be dismissed or downplayed. The school surveyed hundreds of employees in *Fortune* 500 companies and found that "there are systemic links between employee loyalty and organizational performance."

Despite the corporate world's current poor showing when it comes to displaying loyalty to employees, a premium is placed on a worker's willingness to stay for at least four or five years. Troy Campbell, a senior HR staff member in the construction services division of the engineering firm Parsons Brinckerhoff, put it this way: "It's an investment for us to spend time with these people and nurture them along. Then to have them jump ship after a year because someone has flashed a nickel or dime more, or because they don't like their boss, it's hard on us."

Others agree. As Dan Kobick, southeast regional human resources director for the tax and legal services division of the accounting firm PricewaterhouseCoopers, said, "The return on our investment increases over time, and the amount of in-house training we invest in our people is enormous. In order for us to see a return on that investment and develop someone's skills set to its natural potential, loyalty is very important."[4]

But what strategies are organizations willing to explore to cultivate a greater sense of employee loyalty? The process must begin with companies demonstrating greater loyalty to their current workforce and communicating that loyalty to new hires. In other words, if a company wants its new hires to stick around, it must engender a reciprocal sense of loyalty in its existing workforce.

Until recently, the common perception has been that there are two kinds of employer-employee loyalty models. The original job-for-life model rewarded productive employees with guaranteed long-term employment or employment for life. This has been replaced with an employment relationship that seems governed by self-interest: Businesses look out for bottom-line profits, and workers move around to gain the most in pay, benefits, and perks. What the workplace needs is a middle-ground model that enables employers to rebuild a sense of loyalty. This may not translate into the long-term commitments of years past, but the length of time during which an employee remains with an employer can be defined, with both parties committing to that term a demonstration of mutual loyalty. Employees will outline how they can benefit the company at the outset, even identifying the approximate period of time they intend to stay. The employer will agree to provide training and resources as needed, as well as to inform the employee what the company expects before employment is terminated. There will be no hard feelings, and no resentment; rather, a mutually rewarding relationship can be developed.

The first step in forming this new work order is for companies to survey employees as to what they want, what the company is doing well, and what needs to be improved upon. These surveys can enable companies to address workplace relations issues and, at the very least, let the workforce know that senior management is committed to working at a sound, long-term relationship. At UPS, an Employee Relations Index surveys 80 percent of employees— that's roughly a quarter of a million people—twice a year. The results reveal a greater level of productivity in those regions where the Employee Relations Index is higher.

Motorola has a similar program. Its managers ask all employees a series of questions four times a year, including "What prevents you from doing your job 100 percent?" Managers review the responses and strive to remove whatever has been identified as an obstacle to total job satisfaction and career fulfillment.

Next, employees need to feel they're accomplishing something meaningful at work. In this regard, setting goals accomplishes more than establishing rules: Goals help employees focus on what they should be doing, while rules, on the other hand, tell them what they should avoid doing. Consider how focusing on objectives helped Continental Airlines. When Gordon Bethune became president, the airline engendered loyalty from neither its travelers, stockholders, nor employees. To turn the company around, Bethune keyed in on what was determined to be every airline passenger's primary goal: to arrive at his or her destination on time. This became the company's number one objective and rallying point. Airline staff was empowered to take whatever steps were necessary to make this happen on a consistent basis, regardless of cost. Employees rose to the challenge. Within one year, Continental went from last place among the top ten airlines to seventh. The following year it hit number one. Travelers were appreciative, and so was Bethune: He turned a demoralized workforce into a loyal group of employees.

Employers must also offer employees a greater stake in the business. Today, if a company does well financially, employees expect to share in the profits. New forms of pay can help rekindle loyalty, such as bonuses to lower-level employees and offering shares of company stock at discounted prices.

At Continental Airlines, each of the 40,000 employees receives a share of the money saved every month that the airline realizes its on-time goal. Since the employees have made the company successful, it stands to reason that they share in the financial rewards.

UPS also works hard at sharing its successes. As an employee-owned company, it expanded the offer of UPS stock ownership from the managers to all full- and part-time employees, implementing the concept that employees whose own financial successes are directly tied to the success of the company will care more about cost control, productivity, and customer service.

Both the Continental and UPS approaches are supported by a Towers Perrin survey of more than 3,000 private industry workers who agreed that, above all, employees want active involvement in their work and more control over their own futures.

In addition, employers can offer flexible career paths for long-term employees. Estimates are that today the average adult changes careers six to seven times in the course of a working life. One reason is that when work becomes routine, we tend to lose interest and look elsewhere for new challenges. With this in mind, think about transferring productive employees to other departments or divisions within the company instead of losing them to other organizations. Allow them to "experiment" through special assignments, training, and education, thereby broadening their experiences and expanding their knowledge base. The result could be a whole new career with a renewed commitment to the company on the part of the employee.

AT&T has developed a program based on this premise, whereby employees start out by having their skills and goals assessed. Next, they are matched up with like-minded colleagues. In this way they form one of AT&T's Knowledge Centers, available to work on a variety of company projects. As suitable assignments arise, these centers move from one unit to another, utilizing their core competencies and skills. The program keeps employees interested, stimulated, and loyal.

The Loyalty Institute conducted an employee study in 1997 to provide a workforce commitment norm for medium to large private-sector organizations. Companies can use the institute's Workforce Commitment Index (WCI) to measure the loyalty of their employees against a national baseline. The WCI is based on answers to several questions regarding employee attitudes toward their employers. Areas of inquiry include:

▲ Whether they would recommend their company's products or services
▲ Whether they would rate their company as a desirable place to work
▲ Whether they intend to stay with their company for two or more years
▲ Whether they would stay even if offered a similar job elsewhere at slightly higher pay

The survey also examines demographic factors that might affect loyalty. For example, it is not surprising to find that older workers are more loyal than younger workers. However, unlike previous studies, men revealed a higher level of commitment than women. Married people were more loyal than those who are single, and single women have the lowest scores. Levels of education were found to have no impact on loyalty. Job and industry factors that might impact loyalty were also examined. Scores tended to be highest for companies with more than one thousand employees and for companies with fewer than one hundred employees. Also, workers in hourly and customer service categories scored the lowest. Utility industry workers have the highest loyalty scores, while food, beverage, and tobacco industry workers have the lowest scores.

The study also examines six company-controlled factors that can affect loyalty:

1. The direction in which the organization is heading
2. Work satisfaction
3. Recognition and rewards
4. Opportunity for growth
5. Work environment
6. Work/life balance

According to the Institute, companies that showed the lowest levels of employee loyalty would be advised to focus on recognition and rewards, as well as opportunities for growth.

Of course, employees must also share certain responsibilities in developing and maintaining workplace loyalty. They need to remain employable, which means taking advantage of the training and educational opportunities offered by the employer designed to teach cutting-edge skills in addition to the latest knowledge that is essential to remain competitive in their respective fields.

Employee loyalty is not as much of an issue in today's high-technology fields. Especially in a tight labor market, employers are happy just to find skilled workers. Loyalty is considered a luxury.

WORKER OVERLOAD

Another characteristic of today's changing workforce is worker overload. Unquestionably, this is a time of prosperity for many Americans. Rising incomes and the lowest jobless rate in more than three decades have enabled many workers to convert dreams into realities in the form of new houses and cars, home renovations, vacations, and other material goods heretofore outside their reach. However, these same Americans are bemoaning, "We're earning more, but enjoying it less."

The reason typically cited is that there is too much work. We are in the midst of a combined growing economy and labor shortage, with no end in sight. This means existing workers are increasing regular work schedules by 50 percent or more, just to stay on top of their workloads. Also, many of today's jobs inherently require longer hours, e.g., management and professional jobs. What were once considered crisis-mode workloads are now commonplace. A study by the International Labor Organization found that the number of hours Americans work each year has climbed upward, putting the United States in first place among such countries as Japan, Canada, Great Britain, and Norway.[5] On average, Americans work the equivalent of nine weeks more each year than Europeans and have even surpassed the Japanese by about seventy-seven hours per year. The Department of Labor reports that about one in five Americans works more than forty-nine hours per week. The result is that a quarter to a third of U.S. workers have high job stress and are drained by the end of the workday.

This explosion in hours has helped keep the United States in the lead productivity-wise, enabling Americans to enjoy living standards that make workers in other countries envious. But the increase in sixty- and seventy-hour workweeks is taking its toll. Indeed, in one poll, more than 20 percent of Americans said they would gladly accept lower wages in exchange for fewer hours.

The problem is exacerbated by the fact that our world has become transformed so that we can work anywhere, anytime. Because of the Internet, laptop computers, fax machines, e-mail, voice-mail, pagers, and cellular phones, employers expect employees to work en route to and from the job as well as on days off, often at recreational and sports functions. Traits that once characterized workaholic professionals now describe increasing numbers of corporate employees. The Associated Press reported that in 1999 the average business manager received 190 messages a day, many of which demanded an immediate response. The result is that the line distinguishing work time and "leisure" time is often blurred, rendering difficult a calculation of exactly how many hours are actually worked.

What's more, the pace of today's business environment is speedier than ever, and immediacy and the demand for feedback is the norm. Franklin Delano Roosevelt's prophetic words, "Never before have we had so little time in which to do so much," might well be the motto seen hanging on the wall of many busy employees. There is an epidemic of "time famine," as workers struggle to get beyond a survival mode.

Worker overload is directly linked to information overload. More information has been produced in the last thirty years than in the previous 5,000. The World Wide Web contains an estimated

320 million pages of information, and the English language has grown by 70,000 words since the mid-1960s. Many managers wail, "By the time you check your e-mail, voice-mail, faxes, and database, it's already time to go home."

To cope, some full-time workers are "dropping out" and seeking part-time employment instead. But in many instances, this is not providing the sought-after relief because part-time work is often considered thirty-five or forty hours a week. Those who can afford to do so—e.g., are financially secure as a combined result of high earnings and stock market investment returns at the turn of century—are retiring earlier than originally planned.

There is also the emerging health issue connected to workplace stress. Tight deadlines, high expectations for productivity, and fewer people available to do the job are causing dangerously high levels of tension. Studies indicate that three-fourths of workers believe there is more on-the-job stress than a generation ago. A wide range of health effects are attributed to stress, including increased risk of cardiovascular disease, psychological disorders such as depression, gastrointestinal disorders, and workplace injuries.

Workers, especially white collar "knowledge" workers, are increasingly expected to put in long hours without being compensated with extra time off or pay. With little or no "down" time, some stressed-out employees are acting out in the workplace. Here are some instances of bizarre workplace behavior attributed to stress:

- ▲ An employee whose work was criticized turned on his supervisor and hit him over the head with a stack of files.
- ▲ An employee who was given an additional assignment at the close of business stood up on her desk and screamed, "I'm not going to take this any more!"
- ▲ A supervisor burst in on his department's celebration of an employee's birthday and declared, "What's the matter with all of you? There's a pile of work on every one of your desks and you're in here feeding your faces with cake!"
- ▲ A worker sat at her desk and stared ahead, even as coworkers tried to get her attention.
- ▲ Two managers started a food fight in the company cafeteria after realizing they had missed an important meeting.

Incidences such as these are occurring with greater frequency. The more serious acts, such as those involving workplace violence, capture our attention briefly, before we return to work. We tend to reason that these are individual problems or characteristic of particular work environments. However, it may be time to view such acts as a sign of workplace dysfunction. The International Labor Organization tells us that the U.S. economy loses approximately $200 billion annually because of stress-induced declines in productivity. A related report published by the National Institute on Drug Abuse showed there was $80.9 billion in lost productivity attributable to alcohol and drug abuse. And the U.S. Department of Justice says that those who are victimized at the workplace cost employees about 3.5 days of work per crime; that totals over $55 million in lost wages, not including days covered by sick and annual leave. The impact of stress strikes even closer to home when you factor in the following data provided by U.S. Substance Abuse and Mental Health Services Administration: One in every twelve full-time employees under 50 is an alcohol abuser, 6 percent of alcohol abusers and 15 percent of drug abusers admit to having been high or drunk on the job, and 40 percent admit that they work while impaired at least one day a week.

With ever-increasing numbers of workers succumbing to time-crunch problems, a new industry has emerged. Consultants are being hired to help employees squeeze more from their work day, seminars propose solutions to time/stress problems, and millions of people rely on planners and agendas, both online and in book form. As we cram more projects and activities into our schedules, we are too often forced to scan rather than digest information, seek immediate feedback, and make decisions quickly. As a result, the wrong conclusions are sometimes drawn. That often translates into redoing a task, which requires additional time.

Many experts, including Anthony Aveni, professor of anthropology and astronomy at Colgate University in Hamilton, New York, believe that there is a point beyond which we simply cannot process information any faster. This concept that workers must slow down has also been embraced by at least one author, Joey Reiman, whose book *Business at the Speed of Molasses* predicts that we are about to enter the "era of slow." "The deadlines, finish lines and fast-food lines are going to be removed, and we are going to see a new dawning inside the corporate culture, a dawning of wisdom, which is the ability to take knowledge and process it to make it something greater," he writes. His prediction is that a slow company will triumph because it will be more deliberate and purposeful. The solution, then, these authorities maintain, is to go slower, not faster, and literally set aside time to think. But many wonder just how plausible this advice is, given the pressures and pace of today's business environment.

The impact of sleep deprivation is also beginning to emerge as a serious workplace concern. Adequate sleep is necessary for alertness at work, and yet Americans average fewer hours of sleep than they need—roughly 20 percent less than their great-grandparents. Two out of five workers report that fatigue regularly interferes with their ability to function, according to the National Sleep Foundation in Washington, D.C. Estimates of the annual cost of sleep deprivation, including lost productivity, absenteeism, illness, and injury, are $18 billion. The problem is expected to worsen, as a result of round-the-clock use of the Internet, all-night television, and twenty-four-hour stock trading.

One of the latest innovations designed to address the problems of stress and sleep deprivation is the institution of on-the-job naps for employees. Advocates of workplace napping say it is the wave of the future. Many doctors say there is scientific support for naps, pointing to afternoon drowsiness as part of the body's natural rhythm, not just a response to a heavy meal. Studies have shown that sleepy workers make more mistakes and are more susceptible to heart attacks and gastrointestinal disorders. Ideally, naps should be scheduled for midday, since late afternoon naps can cause a shift in your internal clock, causing difficulty in getting adequate sleep at night that will allow you to get up feeling refreshed the next morning. A nap eight hours after you wake up is just about the right time. Even if you don't feel tired, experts such as Dr. James B. Maas, a Cornell psychologist, recommend taking a short rest rather than a coffee break.

Apparently, a number of employers agree, since a growing number of organizations have come to realize that a nap of twenty to forty-five minutes during the day actually increases morale and productivity and reduces accidents and errors. Many now provide nap rooms, complete with ceiling-to-floor shades, reclining chairs, blankets, lap robes, alarm clocks, eyeshades, and classical-music CDs to lull workers to sleep. Here are some of the companies that recognize the merits of napping on the job:

▲ Union Pacific Corporation, the nation's biggest railroad, and its main rival, Burlington Northern Santa Fe Railway Corporation, allow conductors and engineers to take sleep breaks of up to forty-five minutes, as long as the train is stopped and another crew member is awake. Burlington Northern also allows its 8,000 track workers to nap.

▲ British Airways allows pilots on transoceanic flights to take a brief nap prior to landing.

▲ The U.S. Army permits its officers to take naps whenever possible, encouraging them to "nap early and nap often."

▲ Wal-Mart, the country's largest employer, allows its 815,000 employees to visit company lounges for rests during scheduled breaks.

While not every organization is ready to promote sleep breaks, many employers have begun to promote other forms of good health practices in the workplace. In fact, 81 percent of workplaces have wellness programs including smoking cessation campaigns, weight-reduction classes, guidelines to healthful eating, and exercise plans. The most effective wellness programs are those consisting of three main components: (1) medical screenings to identify any serious health conditions; (2) health and wellness education programs offering tips on how employees can develop lifestyles that incorporate proper diet, exercise, and sleep habits; and (3) on-site exercise programs.

Chevron Corporation, located in San Francisco, and Sentara Health Care, of Norfolk, Virginia, are two examples of companies with successful wellness programs. Chevron's Health Quest Program includes an on-site fitness center and trained coaches who lead stretching exercises during breaks. Sentara's Health Edge Program is based on three principles: awareness, knowledge, and action. Employees participating in the program receive credits redeemable to defray the cost of any contribution to their benefits. Both companies won the 1998 C. Everett Koop National Health Award. Additional information concerning wellness programs in other companies appears in Chapter 3.

Promoting an atmosphere of good health can also head off worker burnout. Burnout occurs when employees experience increasing amounts of stress, often to the point of emotional, physical, and spiritual exhaustion. Often, a company's top performers are the ones to develop burnout since they usually spend the greatest amount of time at work and take work most seriously. CCH Inc., an Illinois human resources information business, recently conducted a survey of more than four hundred companies. It determined that "family issues" were cited as the primary cause of unexpected absences, and personal need, coupled with stress, accounted for 52 percent. In a similar study conducted by Aon Consulting, stress and personal causes were also the fastest-growing reasons for missed time.

Signs of burnout are often subtle and sometimes mistaken as representative of other issues. If you identify any of the following changes in your workers, consider the possibility of burnout as the cause:

▲ Overreaction to minor on-the-job problems
▲ Complaints of minor health ailments
▲ Excessive absenteeism
▲ No longer laughing or having fun at work
▲ Becoming increasingly irritable toward coworkers or customers
▲ Inability to complete or perform routine tasks
▲ Becoming easily distracted
▲ Questioning the value of work performed
▲ Feeling lethargic

Traditionally, it was believed that people burn out because of character, behavior, or productivity flaws. Recent research supports a different view, however: that burnout is the result of the social environment in which people work. Discord between management and employees, as well as failed relationships among teammates, can damage the work environment. When the workplace does not recognize the human side of work, then the risk of burnout grows.

Unfortunately, excessive stress and burnout are too often treated with the offer of counseling rather than by employers making changes in the workplace and in workloads. Employers think they are being helpful by instituting work/life programs or sending workers to an Employee Assistance Program (EAP), rather than by making actual changes in the work environment.

Consider how one corporation responded to employee complaints about overwork. Merck & Co., the giant pharmaceutical company based in Whitehouse Station, New Jersey, assigned employees to teams that were devoted to solving worker overload problems. Work was reorganized so that employees felt as if they had more control over their functions and schedules. For example, employees in the payroll department who were unhappy about the extensive overtime requirements received greater technological assistance so data could be input at home. This resulted in reduced turnover (down from 45 percent to 32 percent in a matter of three months), lower overtime costs, less absenteeism, and reduced commuting time. All of this translated into improved morale and reduced stress.

Worker burnout is best combated by altering the source of job stress. Here are some of the ways in which employers can help improve the work environment and thus reduce worker stress and burnout:

▲ Create job diversity, especially for employees performing repetitive tasks.
▲ "Dejob" the workplace, by blurring the lines between jobs and moving away from traditional job descriptions.
▲ Develop more flexible, cross-functional work teams.
▲ Increase the amount of control that employees have in their work.
▲ Focus on the interaction among people in the workplace.
▲ Ensure that employees take sufficient time off.
▲ Head off worker overload.
▲ Reward good work.
▲ Outsource certain tasks.
▲ Eliminate extraneous work.
▲ Redesign workspaces, e.g., have furniture more like what you'd find at home to invite an atmosphere of relaxation.
▲ Revitalize how existing technology is used, e.g., equipping remote workforces with laptop computers.
▲ Encourage regular "fitness breaks."
▲ Allow frequent and regular rest breaks.
▲ Avoid assigning tasks that have little meaning and do not use workers' skills.
▲ Allow participation by workers in decision making.
▲ Establish "friendly" policies.
▲ Encourage upward and lateral growth.
▲ Provide concierge services (Chapter 2).
▲ Provide "think time."
▲ Encourage employees to create a balance between work and their personal lives.

SUMMARY

Today's workforce reflects a change in the age mix, gender, ethnic composition, numbers of immigrants, and numbers of persons with disabilities. In addition, employers are turning increasingly to previously untapped resources, such as welfare recipients, and prison labor. We are also witnessing a greater emphasis on diversity-driven work environments—workplaces that embrace employees with multiple dimensions of similarities and differences. Diversity is increasingly being viewed as an ongoing strategic business imperative. Successful diversity programs treat all people with equal regard, incorporate different skills and interests to enhance an organization, and result in increased productivity and profits.

The profile of today's changing workforce also reveals a new dearth of loyalty. Whether it's employee loyalty to an employer or vice versa, workplace loyalty is growing scarce, being replaced by self-serving behavior. The link between workplace loyalty and organizational performance has been documented, resulting in many companies working at cultivating a greater sense of employee loyalty. The process must begin with the company demonstrating greater loyalty to its workforce. Indeed, a new form of workplace loyalty may be emerging, whereby employees will outline what they can do for the company, as well as identify the approximate period of time they plan to stay in the job; in return, the employer will agree to provide training and resources, in addition to telling the employees what the company expects from them before the anticipated job change.

Finally, the combination of a growing economy and labor shortage has resulted in a major worker overload dilemma. The average number of hours Americans work each year has increased dramatically, today's pace is speedier than ever before, and we are suffering from information overload. This has resulted in dangerously high levels of tension, bizarre workplace behavior attributed to stress, sleep deprivation, and employee burnout.

NOTES

1. Department of Labor, "Futurework: Trends and Challenges for Work in the 21st Century."
2. *Mosaics SHRM Focuses on Workplace Diversity,* January/February 2000.
3. *Staffing and Selection,* Watson Wyatt Worldwide People Management Resources, 1999.
4. *Washington Business Journal,* April 26, 1999.
5. *The New York Times,* September 5, 1999.

CHAPTER 2

Attracting and Retaining Top Performers

"It's never been this crazy before. The perks some companies are lavishing on employees sound less like innovation and more like desperation."

—Unknown

I recently sat in an upscale New York City hotel restaurant waiting for a colleague to arrive for a breakfast meeting. As I sipped my coffee, I became increasingly aware of the group of people seated at the table next to mine. There were four of them, and while the table was round, three members of the group were clustered so closely together that they actually appeared to be seated across from the fourth person, a young man around 25 years old. The collective body language on the part of the trio seemed adversarial. Dressed in dark-colored, conservative business suits, they sat tall in their seats, arms folded across their chests, chins pointed slightly upward, eyes focused intently on the young man across the table. While all three were smiling, their smiles seemed forced and strained.

I glanced at the recipient of this rather hostile display to see how he was reacting. I was surprised to observe that he was not only undisturbed but actually seemed to be enjoying himself. Wearing casual trousers and a short-sleeved shirt, he sat with his chair pushed back from the table, the ankle of his right leg crossed over his left knee, posture slightly slouched. He rocked gently in his chair as he lazily twiddled his thumbs. What really took me aback me was the look on his face: He was grinning! At that point it became clear that I was witnessing a job interview; more specifically, the kind of interview that has become increasingly common in to-day's labor market—one in which the applicant had the upper hand. The portion of the conversation that I overheard went something like this (I took notes):

Interviewer #1: "As you know, we've put together an extremely generous package of pay, health benefits, and perks. Everything we discussed at our last meeting is included."

Interviewer #2: "I've got to say, nobody ever offered me anything even close to this package when I started!"

Interviewer #3: "So, now that you've had a chance to look everything over, I'm sure you'll agree that everything we talked about—that is, everything you wanted—is included. All that's left is for you to say yes!"

An uncomfortably long period of silence followed. There was some nervous shifting in the seats on the part of the interviewers before the applicant finally spoke: "I can see that everything you said you would include is here. I just don't know if I'm ready to make a decision yet," he replied slowly.

Interviewer #2, leaning forward, hands clasped tightly, responded with, "Listen. I'm not going to beat around the bush. I've been authorized to sweeten the pot a bit more, just in case this happened. Say yes right now and we'll throw in a $5,000 signing bonus! Let's just close this deal and get on with it."

The applicant did not say a word. Instead, he pushed his seat back further and focused his gaze downward. As he did so, Interviewer #3 asked nervously, "We're giving you everything you asked for. What else do you want?" At this point, the applicant pulled his chair in close to the table, cupped his face in his hands, looked at each interviewer in turn, and said in a slow, deliberate tone: "I want you to offer me something no other employee has. Then maybe I'll come to work for you."

The three interviewers were visibly shaken. The first one murmured something about needing more coffee, and the other two glanced nervously at one another. The applicant returned to his food, seemingly nonplused. Finally, the first interviewer quietly said, "We believe we've offered you an exceedingly comprehensive package and the opportunity to work for a fine organization. We weren't prepared to go beyond that. However, if you could be more specific about what it is you want, perhaps we can work something out."

At this, the applicant smiled and responded: "I don't know. I guess I don't really want or need anything else. But I appreciate the fact that you'd consider offering me more. I think I've heard what I need to know. Let's say we have a deal."

This unnerving scene illustrates what many employers are experiencing today in trying to staff their companies with qualified workers. They are scrambling to understand what workers want and then translate this combination of tangibles and intangibles into specific incentives and perks to lure them aboard. Then they are forced to compete with equally desperate, and sometimes more generous, competitors. Sometimes it comes down to just how well they market and sell their image. And once they have succeeded in hiring top performers, employers are forced to become increasingly creative in order to hold on to these employees for an appreciable period of time.

WHAT WORKERS WANT

In a speech concerning trends and challenges for work in the 21st century, then Vice President Al Gore stated the following on January 12, 1999, about what workers need:

> "First, workers need lifelong economic security for themselves and their families. They need the opportunity to obtain skills that will guarantee them high wages. Workers should be able to use technology to their advantage, without fearing that it will make them 'jobsolete.' Workers should be skilled, not stuck, in the new economy. Second, workers need to balance work with caring for their families. Some workers can be helped by on-site childcare. A variable schedule enables others to care for children and aging parents. For still others, nontraditional working arrangements are the answer. But all workers need to know that they can achieve a balance between work and family without having to forego adequate earnings and health and pension benefits. Third, workers need workplaces that are safe and fair—protected from health hazards and free from discrimination and other unfair employment practices. In the last thirty-five years a great many of the barriers have fallen which prevented America's women, minority, and disabled workers from participating, let alone succeeding, in the workplace. The future workforce is destined to be even more diverse. Future employers will have the advan-

tage of multicultural, multilingual workforces that offer new opportunities to compete more effectively in the global market."

These observations on the part of Vice President Gore may have identified workers' needs in general, but do they fully reflect what workers want? To some extent, yes. But today's workers expect employers to provide more than economic security, a balance between work and family, and a safe and fair environment in which to do their jobs. In fact, these basic tenets of employer-employee relations are assumed to prevail by many, if not most, workers. What, then, do today's workers want? Employers may find some of the answers surprising.

Atmosphere and Impact

Numerous surveys reveal that what many employees really want these days is an enjoyable atmosphere and a feeling that they're making an impact in their jobs. Secure in the knowledge that they can easily find another job, many are also asking about the personalities of other workers and supervisors with whom they will interact, and what the company plans to do to make them want to remain employed there. Money is low on their list of primary concerns. Consider the junior executive at an online consulting firm who recently left to work for a rival. "I didn't feel like I was doing something that mattered," she said of her original employer. When she gave notice her boss was surprised and offered her more money to stay. "They just didn't get why I wanted to leave," she said sadly. Another example of the need to make an impact involves a middle manager at a major conglomerate who left to become executive vice president for marketing and sales at a small Internet access company. She left behind stock options, a generous vacation offering, and spontaneous bonuses for the novelty of working on a brand new project. The potential payoff was more appealing to her than a steady career path at a big company. "We're doing something that no one else is doing," she said. "How can you really beat that?"

Nonmonetary Factors

One study conducted by Gerald Graham, a management professor at Wichita State University, surveyed 1,500 employees concerning what they considered to be the top five workplace incentives. The responses, ranked by number of replies, were: (1) personal thanks from manager, (2) written thanks from manager, (3) promotion for performance, (4) public praise, and (5) morale-building meetings.[1]

Graham followed up on these results and found that 58 percent of employees reported that they seldom, if ever, received personal thanks, and 76 percent said that they seldom, if ever, received written praise.

Other studies support Graham's findings that nonmonetary factors attract people to one employer over others. Key factors include open communication between workers and management, management appreciation of work done, the opportunity to gain new skills, and company sympathy for personal problems. And a Saratoga Institute survey of more than one thousand U.S. workers asked employees to identify factors that attracted them to organizations. The top three responses were (1) performance evaluations based on a worker's ability to develop improved methods of doing things, (2) goals mutually developed by supervisors and the employee, and (3) job success based on the employee's responsibilities and accomplishments.

Yet another report identifying what today's workers are looking for revealed that control over their current and future lives ranked at the top of the list. Next came work that was fun, interesting, and exciting, followed by instant gratification. Fourth was working in an environment with leading-edge technology; then came having leverage, mobility, money, and finally self-fulfillment.

McKinsey & Co. surveyed executives in seventy-seven large U.S. companies to determine those factors that strongly influence business leaders in wanting to work for an organization. Overwhelmingly, "company values and culture" received top kudos, followed closely by "freedom and autonomy" and "a well-managed company." Other factors that ranked high in importance were (in descending order): the opportunity for career advancement and growth, challenges provided by the company, strong performance on the part of the organization, a good fit with their boss, differentiated compensation, high total compensation, working for an industry leader, the chance to work with many talented people, a desirable geographic location, working for a company that is good at developing its workforce, working for a company with an inspiring mission, respect on the part of the employer for employees' lifestyle, fun with colleagues, job security, and an acceptable pace at work.

This study clearly reveals that working for a great company and having a fulfilling job are more important to most executives than compensation.

Managers' Mistaken Perceptions

Ironically, other surveys reveal that many managers believe top lures to be high salaries, job security, and promotional opportunities. They also feel that one of the best ways to attract and retain people is to provide childcare facilities and services. While this may appeal to many working mothers and even an increasing number of men who assume more and more responsibilities for childcare, there are many young people who are not concerned with childcare at the present. With women putting off having children into their late thirties and forties childcare is not as much of a reason to join one company over another as employers may think.

Evidently, what managers perceive as being most important to employees contrasts with what employees themselves report as most important.

Moreover, employers must take care not to assume that everyone in a similar job classification places the same degree of emphasis on the same work factors. For example, in one study, it became evident that five perks stood out as being important to all information systems (IS) workers: high salaries, training, alternative schedules, telecommuting, and signing bonuses. Armed with this information, many employers pursued IS workers at varied levels, without considering that their levels of work could impact the workers' expectations. They reviewed the perks relevant to executive IS management-level workers and assumed that the same order of importance prevailed for all levels of IS staff. As it turned out, they were wrong. Executive IS management staff placed the highest emphasis on high salaries, followed by signing bonuses, training, alternative work schedules, and telecommuting. In contrast, IS nonmanagement staff with three or more years' experience deemed training to be the most important perk an employer could offer them. Next came alternative work schedules, high salaries, signing bonuses, and telecommuting. Entry-level nonmanagement IS workers who had less than three years' experience agreed that training was most important, followed by alternative work schedules and high salaries. But then they ranked telecommuting as being important, placing signing bonuses last on the list.

Similarly, a 1999 Society for Human Resource Management/ CHH "Recruiting Practices Survey" showed that executives, managers, and line workers all responded to many of the same incentives. A closer examination of the list of incentives, however, revealed some significant variations in their ranking. All three

groups ranked highest 401(k) matching plans. Executives next valued relocation assistance, while managers and line workers rated
educational assistance as number two in importance. Third in relevance to executive-level employees was year-end bonuses. For
managers it was relocation assistance, and for line workers it was
the ability to wear casual clothes to work. Executives ranked as
fourth educational assistance, while managers rated casual dress as
coming in fourth, and line workers ranked fourth a flexible work
schedule. In last place for importance to executives was casual
dress; for managers, as well as line workers, it was year-end bonuses.

Sometimes employers strive to come up with overly grand
packages to lure and retain top performers when, in fact, something
relatively small and cost-free is all it takes. Such was the case with
Sam, a twenty-nine-year-old engineer from San Francisco. When
he decided it was time for a job change, he received eleven invita-
tions for interviews within forty-eight hours. Soon there was a bid-
ding war for his talents, with the starting salary offer rising from
$70,000 to $100,000. In addition, there were generous offers for
stock options. Sam's head was spinning. While the money was important to him, so too was the culture where he would work. What
it came down to for him was attire. Sam wanted to work in an
environment where he could dress casually all the time, specifically jeans and T-shirts. He found what he wanted in a web design
company where the work was meaningful and the look casual:
Even the interviewers wore shorts and sandals. Sam accepted a position as a senior engineer, content that he could dress the way he
pleased.

The Concept of Moonlighting

Businesses that need employees must also adjust their thinking
when it comes to the old concept of being overqualified for certain
work. There was a time when an applicant's background and skill
bank nearly always aligned with the type of work he or she was
seeking. Candidates with college degrees and several years' experience in a particular field naturally sought work and pay commen-
surate with their experience and educational accomplishments.
Sure, on occasion someone would want to "cross over" into another industry and was therefore willing to take a temporary cut in
pay. Then, too, during times of high unemployment, workers were
willing to settle for work beneath their status and earning capacity,
only to bolt as soon as something more suitable opened up. And in

rare instances, notably during the 1970s and 1980s, there were people who had accomplished a great deal career-wise in a short period of time and yearned for a simpler life, deciding to "drop out" of the corporate rat race, content (albeit, temporarily) to sell hot dogs in Central Park. Anyone who worked two jobs did so as a financial necessity. Rarely did anyone leave one job to go to another in the same day for reasons other than need.

Now we're witnessing a variation on this theme—that is, an increasing number of successful business executives are moonlighting. Wall Street analysts, auditors, human resources administrators, engineers, and others are taking second, low-paying jobs (usually at less than ten dollars an hour) for—are you ready for this?—fun and relaxation. There are a number of specific reasons professionals with full-time jobs enjoy working second jobs, notably in retail. Some work in retailing to have interaction with people, to not have to think too much, to get a second wind, for lack of stress, and for the chance to unwind. Others enjoy wrapping merchandise because it gives them a chance to browse in the stockroom, be surrounded by pretty things, and shop vicariously.

When and how did work become therapeutic? Well, for many professionals who are fed up with stressful desk jobs and never-ending phone calls, the contrast of working a cash register, stocking shelves, or responding to customers' needs is exactly what's needed to reenergize them. Others are attracted to the change in pace and type of people they can interact with. Retail store customers have different needs and demands which, in comparison with corporate expectations, are refreshing.

The professionals who moonlight in part-time retail jobs generally target upscale stores that they typically frequent, like Williams-Sonoma and Restoration Hardware, as opposed to less notable shops or fast-food restaurants. They reason that friends or colleagues who see them behind the cash register or helping customers in prestigious locales will realize that they are doing so for fun and not out of necessity.

Psychologist Barbara Reinhold, director of the career development office at Smith College in Northampton, Massachusetts, isn't surprised by this influx of upwardly mobile professionals who are working as sales clerks or in comparable positions. "It's a sound career-management and life-management tool," says Dr. Reinhold. "For somebody who needs to move around, to spend forty hours a week in front of a computer, with no other outlets, is a invitation to depression, anxiety, lower back pain, or abandonment by their immune system."

Whatever the reasons and however long this trend may continue, retail store managers are thrilled to have the help. One store manager put it this way: "Because they [the workers] are having fun, there is a levity that makes the customers less cranky and more apt to be patient."

INCENTIVES AND PERKS FOR ATTRACTING AND RETAINING TOP PERFORMERS

Despite all the studies revealing what today's workers really want from their jobs and work environments, businesses continue tripping over themselves offering a wide range of tangible incentives and perks to applicants and employees. And, with all bravado aside, workers are lapping it up, taking home considerably more than a turkey with all the trimmings at Thanksgiving.

The offerings range from compensation and benefits (see Chapter 3) to previously unheard of and sometimes bizarre items. (See the checklist of many of the nonmonetary benefits, employment incentives, and perks being offered these days later in this chapter.) One example of a unique benefit may be seen at ERC Dataplus Inc., in Fairfield County, Connecticut. While bringing pets to work has become increasingly popular, it is rare to find an animal actually seated at the company conference table. Yet that is precisely what happens during staff meetings in this small consulting firm, located in a region where unemployment stands at 2 percent. Employees are joined by Ginger, the CEO's poodle, as a reminder that they too are permitted to bring their pets to work. As CEO Paul Rathblott says, "It's a sellers' market out there, and pay alone won't make disgruntled people stay. It just makes them better-paid unhappy employees." His reasoning is that if he doesn't offer such perks, someone else will. Since it is pretty much a free agent market, companies feel that they have no choice but to be exceedingly flexible in their offerings.

Perks related to pets have become a focal point for a number of businesses. In addition to allowing employees to bring animals to work, a small but growing number of companies are now offering some form of health insurance for their workers' pets as a defense against a tight labor market and booming economy. Among those that are offering this work incentive are Lenox Hill Hospital in New York and Mirage Resorts Inc. in Las Vegas. "Employers are looking for ways to attract and keep their favored employees," said Jerry

Hirsch of Pet Assure Inc. in Dover, New Jersey, which manages the Lenox Hill pet insurance program.

That kind of thinking is why John S. Herold Inc., an oil-and-gas research company in Stamford, Connecticut, allows one analyst to work from 4 A.M. until noon. "He just feels like it," reasons Executive Vice President Christine Juneau. Apparently, the employee is valuable enough to the company to get away with setting his own, unusual hours.

Companies that offer such unique perks are hoping that word will spread and top performers will want to work for them over their competitors. That's just what happened at Revenue Systems Inc., an Atlanta software developer. With more than five hundred software developers in the area, Revenue knew it had to come up with something unusual to attract employees. In 1999 the company was paying a headhunter $50,000 a month to find new hires. This became a costly deal, since the headhunter was producing only three workers a month when the company needed five. Chief Executive Bill Glover then came up with a winning idea: Give every full-time employee a brand-new BMW. Each employee is permitted to choose one of two models. The cost to the worker is nothing: The company pays for the lease, insurance, and taxes. Once news of the free Beemers hit the press, the company was flooded with resumes. The cost of leasing the cars is less overall than the headhunter fees, the workers feel special, and the company no longer has recruitment problems.

Michael Holland, who hails from an earlier generation at Salomon Smith Barney and now runs his own money-management firm, summarized a list of demands compiled by junior investment bankers this way: "It looks to me like, because of the supply-demand situation for talent, the inmates are trying to take over the asylum, and they're having some success." Among the list of thirty-six demands at his company were laptops with dial-up access, cell phones, and corporate credit cards "where the analyst never sees the bill" yet accumulates the reward points or cash back. They also wanted use of the company gym on weekends, business-class or better when visiting the West Coast, and concierge service to pick up their dry cleaning.

Concierge Services

No longer are concierge services associated exclusively with upscale hotels and expensive uptown high rises. Increasingly, companies are signing up with a growing number of concierges who can provide employees with a wide range of services. While some companies put concierges primarily at the disposal of upper management and professionals, others are making this relatively new corporate benefit available to all employees. This is a definite plus for time-pressed staff with ultra-busy work/personal lives.

According to the National Concierge Association in Chicago, about five hundred companies are currently offering concierge services in the United States. One example is The Pampered Professional in Hewlett, New York. It offers a variety of services, from gift giving to events planning, to about two thousand clients, including Merrill Lynch, Paine Webber, First America Title Insurance, and CMP Media. The service is often introduced to employees through e-mail and staff meetings. Generally, there is no additional cost to the company or employee; they simply pay whatever the fee is for the service being requested. The biggest request is for help with gift giving, followed by tickets for the theater and sporting events. Often, however, employers treat workers to free massages, manicures, and pedicures, as a reward for outstanding performance. Providers may perform these services at the office or go to an employee's home. Other popular concierge "gifts" from employers include time with a personal trainer, someone to walk their dog or baby-sit a pet, paying for maid service, and picking up and delivering an employee's laundry.

In competition with concierge services are a handful of entrepreneurs who are hiring themselves out as "professional servants." These enterprising individuals recognize that in today's booming economy, more people in two-income households feel pressed for time and, therefore, need someone else to prepare their meals and research the best value for a new car. Working in conjunction with businesses much the same way as formal concierge services, these "servants" do everything from buying pet food to going to people's homes to cut their children's hair. Their fees are generally paid by the individual employees, although increasingly employers are picking up some, if not all, of the bill.

Additional Perks

Here are additional examples of what some companies offer in order to attract and retain qualified workers:

▲ At Zero-Knowledge Systems, an Internet privacy company, employees can view new movies at private screenings while having their laundry picked up, washed, folded, pressed, and delivered.

▲ Onstott Group, an executive search firm in Wellesley, Massachusetts, grants $5,000 a year to workers with children in college to help pay for tuition. The only criterion: The student must maintain a B average.

▲ Kron Chocolatier, a small business with its headquarters in Aventura, Florida, gives workers all the chocolate they can eat, a free lunch each day, a cake and a $25 gift certificate on their birthday, and a honeymoon cruise when they get married. (Note: Turnover at the store is remarkably low, with some workers staying ten years or more.)

▲ At Born Information Services, employees receive a $250 clothing allowance.

▲ SAS Institute, Inc. offers its employees a potpourri of perks, including a preschool childcare facility for seven hundred children, the services of a full-time in-house eldercare counselor, meditation rooms, a putting green, a 36,000-square-foot gymnasium, a pianist in the cafeteria at lunchtime, and all the free juice and sodas employees can consume.

▲ In addition to bonuses and clothing discounts, Adams Haberdashery, a high-end clothing store in New Providence, New Jersey, offers employees Pet Assure, a discount club for pet owners. The cost to the company is $59 per year for each enrolled employee. Members get 25 percent off vet bills and up to 50 percent discounts on certain pet supplies.

▲ Sullivan Higdon & Sink, an advertising agency with Cessna Aircraft and Rockwell Collins among its main clients, offers its employees free flying lessons. The $4,000 perk is available to all ninety employees with preference given to those working on aviation projects. The program has been so well received that the company bought one Cessna and leased another. Now the staff's pilots can fly to client meetings or check out a plane for a weekend spin.

▲ Linnton Plywood Association in Portland, Oregon offers extended personal leaves without pay. Some workers have taken off several months a year.

▲ Levi Strauss & Company, with headquarters in San Francisco, provides employees with a Quiet Room where workers can take a solitary break to relax or read.

▲ PepsiCo, headquartered in Purchase, New York, provides a full-time concierge to help its eight hundred–plus employees with personal errands. These include making dinner reservations, purchasing theater tickets, arranging events for employees' children, and making appointments for household repairs. PepsiCo also provides a dry cleaning service, a mobile oil-change service in the company's parking lot, and a shoe repair service. In addition, employees can purchase take-home dinners in the cafeteria.

▲ Liebert Corporation of Columbus, Ohio, manufacturer of air-conditioning and power-supply systems, provides a limitless supply of popcorn to employees every day.

▲ Merle Norman Cosmetics in the San Fernando Valley sponsors an employee night every other Saturday, showing first-run movies. Employees are invited to bring up to six guests to watch the show and join in make-your-own ice-cream sundaes afterward. The company's employees also enjoy a seven-course lunch daily for twenty-five cents. In addition, refreshments are provided throughout the day, free of charge. In the morning, employees can choose among muffins, pastries, and croissants, and in the afternoon, they can have an assortment of pies, cakes, doughnuts, cookies, and ice cream.

▲ Hewlett-Packard employees may stay, at a modest cost, at any of the company's recreation areas, including Little Basin Park in the Santa Cruz Mountains, a resort in the Pocono Mountains of Pennsylvania, a beach villa in Malaysia, a lake resort in Scotland, and a ski chalet in the German Alps.

▲ Johnson Wax has nine resort facilities in different parts of the country for vacationing employees, including Lighthouse Resort in northern Wisconsin and resorts at Cape Cod and Lake Tahoe.

▲ 3M (Minnesota Mining and Manufacturing Company) offers employees the use of its Tartan Park Clubhouse, a country club in Lake Elmo, Minnesota, for the nominal cost of four dollars per year.

▲ At Quad/Graphics, Inc., located in Pewaukee, Wisconsin, printers are entitled to a free trip to New York City. The company pays for airfare for two and provides use of the company's midtown apartment.

▲ Steelcase, the manufacturer of office furniture, offers free camping to employees, their families, and guests at Camp Swampy, a 1,700-acre recreation area sixty miles north of Grand Rapids, Michigan.

▲ J.P. Morgan & Co., the financial services company located in New York City, provides its six thousand employees with free lunch daily, at a cost to the company of $8 million annually.

▲ Many companies give employees their own products at no cost: Anheuser-Busch Companies in St. Louis gives every employee two free cases of beer a month; Mirage Resorts provides free tickets to Las Vegas shows; Southwest Airlines hands out free standby airline tickets for employees and their families; Random House offers all employees ten free books a year; and Ben & Jerry's gives free pints of ice cream to every worker.

▲ Production workers at Worthington Industries, the steel processor and plastic products manufacturer in Columbus, Ohio, can fish for bass and bluegill during their off-hours at a stocked pond near the corporate headquarters.

While perks like these are rarely high on any applicant's list of "must haves" before they'll work for a company, it is, admittedly, nice to be offered warm fuzzies like all the chocolate you can eat, concierge services, and free theater tickets. Receiving a brand-new car doesn't hurt, either! But as attractive as some of these lures may be, companies sometimes go too far and irritate would-be employees.

Consider the twenty-one-year-old soon-to-be-graduate from a prestigious New England college who was being considered by several potential employers. With a degree in computer science, she'd probably have no trouble finding a job but didn't expect to be pursued.

"Last week I was taken out to dinner five nights in a row. At first it was kind of fun. You know, fancy restaurants with no limit to what I could order. Three of the companies even sent a car to pick me up! It was really cool knowing these big shots from a bunch of fancy companies wanted me to work for them. What's funny is that hardly anyone asked me any questions about what I actually knew or could do. They all just sort of assumed that if I had this degree I must be smart. Well, I am smart, but I thought I'd have to demonstrate it. Anyway, the first two or three nights were fun, but then it almost became like a chore. By the time Friday night rolled around, I was tired of eating all those shrimp cocktails and rich desserts. I also felt like I was taking advantage of these people—letting them spend all that money on me when I obviously couldn't work for all of them. I guess what I'm trying to say is that the novelty wore off pretty quickly. I ended up working for one of them, but not because they took me out to dinner. I liked what I knew about the work environment and felt I'd fit in there. I would have worked for them whether they took me out or not."

Another student received so many gifts from prospective employers that his roommate began to complain about how crowded their room had become. Gifts from General Mills alone included Bugles chips, a *Jurassic Park* water bottle, Wheaties cereal, Nature Valley granola bars, Stir 'n' Bake brownies, a Cheerios basketball, Sweet Rewards snack bars, Fruit by the Foot, and Golden Graham Treats. Johnson & Son sent a stash of cleaning supplies, including Windex, Draino, Shout, and Raid. And Pillsbury sent Progresso Soup and a mug with the inscription "Good luck with exams!" "It got to the point," said the student,"where I'd head back to my room each day and try to guess what kind of goodies I might find. It got kind of boring after awhile, and then it was annoying. Whomever I decide to work for doesn't have to buy me gifts; they just have to treat me well."

Guidelines to Giving Perks

No one can definitively state whether perks are the answer to the staffing woes plaguing companies today. While workers claim to want intangibles like a good fit with their boss, a chance to work with many talented people, and an acceptable pace, they are not exactly turning down the chance to bring their pets to the office, have a massage between meetings, and go home to a free computer. To help you determine how far to go in this quest to attract applicants, follow these guidelines:

1. *Offer the moon, but only if you have it to give.* If you are a small business, you can't expect to be able to compete with huge corporations. Large corporations, such as IBM or Microsoft, can probably offer an array of perks that you can only dream about. But as a small company, you may be able to offer greater flexibility and opportunities for growth. In addition, you may have products that are low-cost giveaways.

2. *Find out what your competitors are giving away.* If you can match or top these perks, fine. Just be careful not to get caught up in competitive strife to see who can "out-gift" whom.

3. *Balance perks with substance.* Giving away free club memberships and concierge services is great, but remember that you want to be able to keep these new hires after you've lured them

aboard. To avoid earning the reputation of being long on talk and short on substance, as well as incurring high turnover costs, put as much energy and thought into keeping employees motivated as you do your efforts to attract them.

4. *Be fair to applicants.* Dan, a recruiter from a well-known clothing manufacturer, was certain a bright MBA being actively pursued would accept what he considered to be a generous offer. The young woman, while impressed with Dan's company, was considering another offer from a competitor. She made the apparent mistake of telling this to Dan. He immediately became defensive and told her he refused to be blackmailed. She assured him that wasn't her intention; she just hadn't been able to make up her mind. He didn't believe her and thought she was holding out for more of an incentive. His reaction pushed her right into the offices of his competitor.

5. *Remain ethical.* One small information technology company wanted to hire a particular employee currently working for another organization. The tech company's lead recruiter called the employee and offered him a job, at considerably more money. When he turned it down, the company called his wife at home and told her about the offer and how he had responded. She was horrified that her husband would turn down such a hefty salary and pressured him into accepting the offer. Chagrined, he accepted the job. Six months later, he left to work elsewhere.

6. *Get personal.* A shotgun approach to perks may find a few targets, but you're likely to be more successful if your gifts suit the personal tastes of the recipients. This shows effort and interest on your part and is more likely to accomplish the desired results. While you certainly can't be expected to know what each individual likes, there are a few approaches to consider that will more closely appeal to individual tastes. One is to offer would-be employees catalogs from which they can choose gift items within certain price ranges. Another is to have generic categories, such as "membership," and allow recipients the option of perhaps joining a health club rather than a country club. You might also have a list of a dozen or so comparably valued perks and allow candidates to choose three that appeal to them.

7. *Be honest.* Don't offer perks and incentives you can't deliver or describe a work environment you only wish existed. One recruiter posed this question to a software developer candidate: "How would you like to have an aquarium filled with exotic fish in your office?" Not surprisingly, the response was positive. The

recruiter later sheepishly admitted that he wasn't actually offering the candidate the aquarium and that his approach was easily misconstrued as a commitment. Another recruiter told a candidate that the new company offices would be next to a luxurious golf course, bordering a lake. He failed to mention that the projected move, still in the planning stages, was at least a year away. When the candidate accepted the job offer and inquired further about his office location, the recruiter confessed that his description, while accurate, was for a future site. The candidate reneged on his acceptance of the offer. Several weeks later, after taking another job, the candidate sent the recruiter a simple note: "You lose."

Noncompensation and Nonbenefits Employment Incentives and Perks

The checklist in Exhibit 2–1 represents many of the noncompensation and nonbenefits incentives and perks currently extended to applicants and employees by companies throughout the United States. Review the list in the left-hand column and place a checkmark next to each item in the appropriate column: "Something Our Company Currently Offers," "Something Our Company Would Consider Offering," or "Something Our Company Would Never Consider Offering." After you have finished with the list, review how many perks you currently offer and how flexible you are with regard to increasing your offerings.

Exhibit 2–1. Checklist of noncompensation and nonbenefits incentives and perks.

Incentive or Perk	Something Our Company Currently Offers	Something Our Company Would Never Consider Offering	Something Our Company Would Consider Offering
Adoption assistance	☐	☐	☐
Airline tickets	☐	☐	☐
Air travel, free	☐	☐	☐
Alternative work schedules	☐	☐	☐
Bringing kids to work	☐	☐	☐
Bringing parents to work	☐	☐	☐
Car financing at below-market prices	☐	☐	☐
Car maintenance allowance	☐	☐	☐

Incentive or Perk	Something Our Company Currently Offers	Something Our Company Would Never Consider Offering	Something Our Company Would Consider Offering
Car service to and from work	☐	☐	☐
Car washed and waxed	☐	☐	☐
Casual attire	☐	☐	☐
Cell phones	☐	☐	☐
Childcare	☐	☐	☐
Cleaning services	☐	☐	☐
Clothing allowance	☐	☐	☐
Club memberships	☐	☐	☐
Company car	☐	☐	☐
Company-supported childcare center	☐	☐	☐
Company-supported eldercare center	☐	☐	☐
Concierge services	☐	☐	☐
Customized surroundings	☐	☐	☐
Dependent-care flex spending account	☐	☐	☐
Dry cleaning	☐	☐	☐
Eldercare	☐	☐	☐
Financial planning, free	☐	☐	☐
Flexible hours	☐	☐	☐
Flying lessons	☐	☐	☐
Food shopping services	☐	☐	☐
Gift certificates	☐	☐	☐
Guaranteed severance packages	☐	☐	☐
Home maintenance services	☐	☐	☐
Home security systems	☐	☐	☐
Housekeeping services, free	☐	☐	☐
Lactation program	☐	☐	☐
Laptop/home computers	☐	☐	☐
Makeovers, free	☐	☐	☐
Manicures, pedicures, and facials	☐	☐	☐
Mobile dental vans	☐	☐	☐
Nap time	☐	☐	☐
One-day vacations to wherever the employee wants to go	☐	☐	☐
On-site massages	☐	☐	☐

Incentive or Perk	Something Our Company Currently Offers	Something Our Company Would Never Consider Offering	Something Our Company Would Consider Offering
Personal loans at below-market lending rates	☐	☐	☐
Pet insurance	☐	☐	☐
Pets at work	☐	☐	☐
Prepaid legal services	☐	☐	☐
Professional development	☐	☐	☐
Recreation	☐	☐	☐
Recreation room	☐	☐	☐
Roadside assistance	☐	☐	☐
Self-defense training	☐	☐	☐
Tax services, free	☐	☐	☐
Tickets to sporting and cultural events, free	☐	☐	☐
Transportation reimbursement	☐	☐	☐
Tuition reimbursement (full or partial) for employees and for children of employees	☐	☐	☐
Tutoring of an employee's child	☐	☐	☐
Use of employees in commercials	☐	☐	☐

COMPETING FOR TOP PERFORMERS

"It's become a very predatory environment." That's how one recruiter describes what it's like trying to find employees in today's economy. The competition is as fierce as it's ever been, and recruiters are resorting to tactics never before considered, much less practiced. For example, when layoffs occur at a company involved in a merger or experiencing a downturn, recruiters are literally waiting in the parking lot to scoop up the ex-employees leaving after their last day of work. Some recruiters also try the relationship-building approach to gain an edge. They go into companies and make friends with the receptionist in order to gain access to staff phone numbers and e-mail addresses. Others prefer to go online at the crack of dawn to snatch up the latest talent that may have posted their resumes overnight on a growing number of Internet services, like Monster.com. Still others try to stand out by prominently positioning themselves at job fairs with banners that promise hard-to-resist perks such as every other Friday off.

Another technique that has become increasingly popular is attending college sporting events. During the 1998 University of Michigan football season, companies spent between $2,500 and $5,000 to sponsor tailgate parties. And Sprint recently spent over $5,000 to host 450 students at a breakfast tailgate party before a game against Ohio State. The company pitched a tent next to the football field and kept it warm with propane heaters. They had chefs prepare pancakes and quiche Lorraine while student bartenders mixed mimosas. Meanwhile, Sprint representatives handed out six hundred phone cards good for fifteen minutes of long-distance calls and gave away Polartec scarves with Sprint's logo.

Some companies are increasingly turning inward to their own staff for referrals. While employee referral programs are nothing new, some of the referral techniques used by some organizations deserve credit for being unique. Consider Thomson Financial Services, a Boston-based financial research and analysis firm. Thomson recently spent $33,000 to promote its employee recruitment program. More than half of that sum went toward a small zoo, complete with an elephant, llama, and other animals, that was brought to company headquarters. The menagerie heralded a prize trip to the San Diego Zoo for the employee who referred the greatest number of job candidates to HR. The company also pays referral bonuses, ranging from $1,500 to $5,000.

We even see states using home ties to attract former residents back. States like Iowa, Wisconsin, and Nebraska, which report some of the lowest unemployment rates in the United States, are considering forgiving entire student loans and offering 2 percent home loans in an attempt to lure workers back home to fill thousands of available jobs.

Developing school/business partnerships is the choice of yet others competing for future top talent. For example, Seaman's Furniture Co., based in Long Island, New York, is a member of the Half Hollow Hills School and Business Partnership Advisory Board. The board's mission is to expose students to the work environment. At the elementary school level, students see firsthand the value of work and the importance of an education by participating in the Students Go to Work Program, a six-lesson curriculum presented by their teacher, preparing them for a visit to the company. Middle school students participate in the Mentoring Program, which pairs them with people from the business community, meeting weekly before the workday begins. At the high school level, there are programs such as Internships, Job Shadowing, Guest Speakers, and Tours to Industry, all of which are designed to help the kids acquire the skills, knowledge, understanding, and behavior needed to compete as leaders in the global economy. Additional information about organizations partnering with educational institutions appears in Chapter 11.

Brand Images

Another lure companies can use is to enhance their overall brand image. A recruiter from a midsized manufacturer of electronic equipment attending a workshop on recruitment and retention recently asked: "If our company name isn't a household word, how are we supposed to compete in today's labor market?" Her concern was immediately echoed. "No one knows who we are," moaned one person. "And there isn't any time to become known, given the current competitive nature of recruiting," complained another. "How can we possibly go up against giants like Microsoft, Rubbermaid, Procter & Gamble, Whirlpool, and . . ." the list of brand names went on.

On the surface, this seems like a plausible, even insurmountable, concern. A company's brand is what differentiates its products or services from others. Recruiters from well-known companies need not describe to candidates what it is that they make or do. Think about the above names or others like General Motors, Sara Lee, Disney, Hewlett-Packard, and PepsiCo, and you immediately conjure up an image of their products. Some companies are so well-known that all you have to do is mention initials, like IBM, HP, 3M, AMF, or AT&T. Yet others are recognized simply by their logos, like Nike and McDonald's. With recognition comes a sense of identity, or what their brands stand for. For example, Rolex stands for quality, Burger King means fast food, and Starbucks represents trendy coffee. But while it's certainly true that lesser-known and unknown organizations must work hard at cultivating their brand image, even those giants that are household names work at brand redevelopment, especially in today's labor market. The bottom line is this: Every organization needs to hone its brand image.

Brands involve public perception. Use the simple, yet revealing, questionnaire in Exhibit 2–2 to start thinking about your organization's overall image and what you can do to enhance it.

Exhibit 2–2. What you can do to enhance your organization's overall image.

1. What does our organization stand for? _____

_____

2. What have our customers/clients come to expect from us? _____

_____

3. When our company's name is mentioned, what are people likely to envision? _____

_____

4. When our name is mentioned, what would we like people to envision? _____

_____

5. What must we do to get people to change how they envision us?

_____

_____

6. Which of the following words or terms are people likely to associate with our product or service? _____

_____

    ☐ Cleanliness
    ☐ Consistency
    ☐ Dependability
    ☐ Fun
    ☐ Good service
    ☐ Good value
    ☐ Innovativeness
    ☐ Integrity
    ☐ Quality
    ☐ Quick service
    ☐ Reliability
    ☐ Safety
    ☐ Other

7. Which of the following words or terms do we want people to associate with our product or service?

    ☐ Cleanliness
    ☐ Consistency

☐ Dependability
☐ Fun
☐ Good service
☐ Good value
☐ Innovativeness
☐ Integrity
☐ Quality
☐ Quick service
☐ Reliability
☐ Safety
☐ Other

8. What must we do if we want to be perceived as more _____?

_____

Companies can't let down their guard even after they have hired employees. Top performers have been known to accept a job offer and then back out or just not show up. According to one survey of 110 search firms, this is most prevalent among midlevel sales, finance, and information technology employees. Recommendations for avoiding this include shortening the amount of time between the job offer and starting date, negotiating the offer quickly, and offering signing bonuses, especially for hard-to-fill openings.

Keep Them Laughing

There are lots of companies that encourage laughter and fun on the job. Books and articles teem with examples of how companies celebrate specific achievements and results with humor. Here's a sampling:

▲ Wilson Learning Corporation, based in Minnesota, gives each employee a Mickey Mouse watch after three months of employment as a reminder always to have fun while working. On their tenth anniversary, employees are given a gold Mickey Mouse watch.

▲ Hewlett-Packard Co., in Palo Alto, California, marks special events with informal beer parties.

▲ At Dow Corning, in Midland, Michigan, managers make and serve sundaes to employees as a token of thanks for a job well done.

▲ Bank of America in San Francisco has a Laugh-a-Day Challenge for one month. Each employee tries to make coworkers laugh every day with cartoons and jokes. Winners receive T-shirts and books containing the best of those jokes and cartoons.

▲ Advanta Corporation, a financial services firm in Horsham, Pennsylvania, has the company's senior managers host a Grill Your Boss cookout at which they dress up as chefs to cook hamburgers and hot dogs for all employees.

▲ At Eastman Kodak in Rochester, New York, an executive formed a Humor Task Force to gather Monty Python videos, Woody Allen books, plastic chattering teeth, and other props for a "Humor Room."

▲ Children's Hospital/King's Daughters Corporation in Norfolk, Virginia hosts a stress-relief fair for employees with food and activities like dunk tanks, Velcro dartboards, and massage booths.

There are even companies that offer humor seminars and suggestions for ways companies can maintain a work environment that is fun. Tips include:

▲ Having theme dress days, such as Hawaiian Day
▲ Arranging for a surprise picnic in the company parking lot
▲ Thanking people by handing out chocolate kisses or balloons
▲ Providing employees with short "joybreaks" during which the workers can enjoy such activities as listening to a comedy tape or reading cartoons
▲ Holding contests, such as bubble blowing, or playing games, like charades

All of these innovations are sound if they serve to relieve workplace stress and monotony.

Best Practice: Southwest Airlines

With employers scrambling to attract and retain top performers, Southwest Airlines stands out as an enviable role model. After all, not many companies can proclaim that with approximately four thousand openings, it had the luxury of choosing from among 142,000 applicants. Furthermore, many of the candidates worked hard to capture the attention of the company through creative tactics such as submitting a shoe with the resume headed by, "I'd walk a mile," and standing outside the company's headquarters holding a sign that said, "I will work for peanuts." And at least one applicant had a resume mowed into a large field near the airport so landing pilots would see it.

Once selected, new hires gladly partake in extensive training at the company's University for People facility, a site described by many as a Disneyland environment. It features rain-forest decor and a graveyard mural showing what can happen to airlines—such as Braniff, Eastern, and Pan Am. The required homework and studying is frequently interrupted by musical chairs and other games.

How do they do it? Why do applicants flock to work at this quirky company, where the CEO publicly hugs and kisses his employees, telling them how much he loves and values them?

Part of Southwest Airlines' draw has to do with having fun. There's hardly a manager around who isn't familiar with its reputation for cultivating fun as part of the working atmosphere. This attracts would-be workers by the droves. A company much studied for its unique culture, Southwest has succeeded in cultivating an exceptional working atmosphere with great success in its industry. Much of the credit goes to Herb Kelleher, cofounder and CEO, for his creative ideas and warm personality. However, the workplace ideas that he spawned have caught on, so that experts believe his philosophy will prevail long after he retires.

Kelleher was once dubbed "The High Priest of Ha Ha" by *Fortune* magazine. Known as Herb to his workers, he has dressed up as Elvis, Roy Orbison, a medieval knight, a sheik, and General George Patton for company functions, and he has sung a rap solo on Southwest's recruiting video. Kelleher believes the basis for his company's success is fun: "If you feel real good about coming to work, if you feel real good about what you're doing, if you feel you are doing something for a meaningful cause and you're having fun while you're doing it, then you look forward to coming to work. You don't succumb to stress as easily and you cooperate with other people more quickly and more easily. If you have a sense of humor it tends to not allow you to make mountains out of molehills."

Some of the events that take place at Southwest include its "perfect attendance contest of the millennium" (featuring generous prizes like Ford Expeditions and two thousand shares of stock); contests for Halloween costumes, Thanksgiving poems, and best decorated Easter eggs and bonnets; design contests for the company newsletter; and an annual chili cook-off. In addition, there is the annual "Heroes of the Heart" celebration on Valentine's Day, the President's Award Banquet, aircraft dedications, and spirit parties. Kelleher also sends cards to all workers four times a year: for their birthday, December holiday, company anniversary, and Valentine's Day.

At Southwest Airlines, fun accomplishes more than just comic relief: It is part of a culture dedicated to high employee morale, motivation, and a positive attitude. In addition to having a sense of humor ("they don't have to be a comedian, but they have to appreciate that someone else is," says Libby Sartain, vice president for people), would-be employees are carefully screened for how well they will fit the airline's profile for caring, warm, compassionate, altruistic workers. Southwest looks for candidates to join its workforce of more than 27,000 employees who are strong team players with a solid work ethic, have a high tolerance for stress, exhibit good time management skills, demonstrate the ability to challenge traditional thinking, and show initiative. The latter is a significant trait since much of the important work at Southwest is unsupervised.

Of course, skills are important—just not enough. The company's motto is to "hire for attitude, train for skills." (This is not the case with pilots and maintenance personnel who are hired primarily for skills.)

In addition to creating a work environment that is creative and fun-filled, Southwest is highly employee-oriented, dedicated to open and ongoing communication. There is a true open-door policy between executives and staff, and the employee phone book contains fact sheets on all senior management employees, including what they do when they relax. There's even a culture committee charged with maintaining the Southwest spirit. That's because, according to the company, everything good that has happened to Southwest Airlines has come from capturing the hearts of its employees. This committee consists of representatives from the company's fifty-four locations who meet on their own time to focus on areas such as what the company is doing well, how to keep morale high, how to better handle employee suggestions, and how to improve the operations, as well as the overall company culture.

In addition, instead of policies, rules, and procedures, there are guidelines. Says Kelleher: "We don't adopt rules. We don't have somebody put out rule books saying this is over the line and you can't do this anymore. We just gently talk to the person involved and say we know your intentions were real good, but perhaps this went a little far and we can't do that any more."

The company also prides itself on providing employees with the ongoing opportunity to learn and grow (a number of employees have moved from entry level to upper management in less than five years), treating employees with the same level of respect the company expects them to give to passengers, generous profit-sharing (in 1998 this totaled more than $91 million, about 12 percent of salaries), and a flexible benefits program that allows for lifestyle choices. Training is also important at Southwest, and numerous courses are offered, such as "Customer-Care Training" and "Front-Line Leadership."

Surprisingly, there is little use of incentive pay. While the airline is the second most unionized organization in the country, 85 percent of Southwest's employees do not receive pay based on performance. Amazingly, the company's relationship with the pilots' union is so strong it has an unprecedented ten-year pact based on long-term stock incentives, as opposed to the traditional automatic pay raises. There is such a good rapport between management and the union that the pilots often help clean the interiors of the planes between passenger loadings and volunteer to help scrub down the planes' exteriors in their free time.

Not everyone is impressed by Southwest's approach. Some focus, instead, on selected tangible corporate issues. For example, there is the feeling that the airline's operating procedure of giving out numbered boarding passes instead of assigned seats, which allows the earliest passengers on board to choose their seats first, is a step backward. And not everyone feels announcements such as "There is no smoking on this aircraft, and if we see you smoking we will assume you're on fire," and "There may be fifty ways to leave your lover, but there are only six ways to leave this aircraft," are appropriate. In addition, Southwest employees themselves are the first to acknowledge that they probably could make more money elsewhere. Critics also feel that Kelleher's emphasis on fun and games detracts from the real issue at hand, which is success.

But Southwest has succeeded. The airline has posted seven consecutive years of record profits. In one year alone, 1998, its profit gain contrasted sharply with other major airlines that reported disappointing results. In addition, its unionized workforce has never seen a layoff. And for five consecutive years starting in 1992, the airline won the U.S. Department of Transportation's "Triple Crown" award for best on-time performance, fewest customer complaints, and fewest mishandled bags. What's more, Southwest has been praised by management experts such as Tom Peters and honored on *Fortune* magazine's best-companies-to-work-for lists.

Kelleher is generous with insight as to how and why Southwest, which began in 1971 with ten customers and a small group of employees, has become such a success story. The company even offers four Culture Days a year for outsiders during which employee motivation "secrets" are shared. These include information about the company's core values of profitability, low cost, family, fun, hard work, individuality, ownership, legendary service, egalitarianism, common sense, simplicity, and altruism. Beyond that, says Kelleher, there really are no secrets. "It's a fairly simple thing, I think. But it's like Einstein said, the simplest things are the hardest to understand. People get together and they talk about communicating as if it were some arcane art that had to be explored in a physicist's laboratory. Of course, while they're talking about it they're not doing it, number one. Number two, communication is a very simple and very informal thing in my estimation. You just start off by acknowledging people as people, 'Hi, how are you, glad to hear you had a baby and everything is going well.' "

Patrick Wright, chair of the human-resource studies department at Cornell University, believes that the foundation for Southwest's successful approach has to do with its beginnings: "It's a function of their unique history, fighting against the big guys, at the same time focusing on cooperation and having fun. They started off that way and have grown that way." But does that explain the atmosphere of devotion that prevails? Wright believes it does. "People want to believe in something and be part of something bigger than themselves. Southwest gives them that opportunity. It's cult-like in a good way."

Working at Southwest Airlines can probably be summed up best by employee Pamela Hartley, a customer-service agent: "It's the hardest I've ever worked, but the most fun I've ever had."

SUMMARY

Today's workers want more than a comprehensive compensation and benefits package. In fact, many studies indicate that nonmonetary factors attract applicants to one employer over others. Key factors such as the chance to make an impact, appreciation for work well done, open communication between themselves and management, the opportunity to gain new skills, and control over their current and future lives are of particular importance to applicants and employees alike. They also want work that is fun, interesting, and exciting. In addition, many of today's workers want to work in an environment with leading-edge technology. Executive candidates rank high in importance company values and culture, autonomy, and a well-managed company. Other areas relevant to executives include career advancement, challenge, and a good fit with their boss.

Employers should take note of these and other cost-effective factors before offering overly grand compensation and benefits packages to employees. In addition, they should not overlook candidates who, on the surface, appear to be overqualified for certain work. Increasingly, we are witnessing an influx of successful business executives who are taking second, low-paying jobs for fun and relaxation. Fed up with stressful, demanding professions, these executives are attracted to the contrast of working a cash register or stocking shelves.Work, it seems, has become therapeutic.

Despite all of the studies revealing what today's workers really want, businesses continue tripping over themselves offering an array of incentives and perks. And, with all bravado aside, workers are lapping it up. In addition to generous compensation and benefits packages, the offerings range from the unique to the bizarre, including such perks as pets at work, all the chocolate you can eat, private movie screenings, concierge services, on-site massages, and a free new car.

In determining how far to go in this quest to attract applicants, employers are urged to balance perks with substance, remain ethical, and get personal. This last point, of suiting your gifts to the personal tastes of the recipients, shows genuine effort as well as interest on your part and is more likely to accomplish the desired results.

No question about it, competition for top talent is fierce. Employers are attending sporting events, turning to employee referrals, and developing school/business partnerships. Companies are also working to enhance their overall brand image to gain an edge over the competition, and creating an atmosphere of fun and laughter. When word of a layoff leaks out, some recruiters are literally waiting in the parking lot to scoop up ex-employees on their last day of work.

With employers scrambling to attract top performers, Southwest Airlines stands out as an enviable role model.

NOTES

1. *HRfocus,* April 1999.

CHAPTER 3

Compensation and Benefits Packages

"Show me the money!"
—Cuba Gooding Jr.,
in the film Jerry McGuire

T ed came in to work Monday morning, clearly chagrined. Over coffee, he shared a weekend experience with his colleague, Pat. It seems Ted's twelve-year-old son, Mark, had his eye on a new bike. Ted, however, felt that the bike was too expensive and not worth the money. Mark persisted. It was the only bike he'd consider, and he said he'd do anything in order to get it. Ted began to see this as an opportunity to teach his son a lesson in working for what you want in life. So he offered Mark a proposition: Ted would pay up to a certain amount for the bike; anything over that amount, Mark would have to pay for himself. Mark was thrilled—that is, until he realized he'd have to work to earn the money. Undaunted, Ted suggested a number of chores Mark could perform after school and on weekends that would generate enough income to make up the difference in the cost of the bike in a matter of three or four weeks. He also suggested tasks, such as walking their neighbor's dog and watering plants while another neighbor was away on vacation, to generate additional income.

Ted was pleased with his suggestions and thought Mark would be too. After all, in less than a month he'd have his treasured bike and would have learned a valuable lesson as well. One look at Mark's face and Ted realized his enthusiasm was not shared. Mark glared at his father and proclaimed, "I am not giving up my life for a month! I'm not even sure what you're suggesting is legal!" Ted sighed. "What do you suggest?" he asked his son.

This next part, he told Pat, was what really threw him. His son took a deep breath and disappeared into his room. Several minutes later he returned with a pad, upon which he had identified what he considered to be a fair arrangement. After reading the contents, Ted turned to his son in disbelief. "This says you want benefits! You want benefits? You're going to work a few hours after school and on weekends at home and in the neighborhood, and you want benefits? You're twelve years old!" "Relax, Dad. I hear you talking about this stuff all the time. You're always saying how important it is to keep employees happy, and that money and benefits are two of the ways of doing that. Well, if I'm going to work for you, that makes me your employee. And if I'm your employee, then I should be receiving benefits in addition to my salary—which, by the way, is a little on the low side, but we'll let that go, seeing as I'm your son and all."

Pat was amused by what he was hearing. Ted hadn't realized that his son was well on his way to becoming a new millennium employee—one who is confident enough to tell a prospective employer what kind of a compensation and benefits package suits his needs. "Come on, Ted. Mark is just echoing what he hears from you: If you want people to work for you, you have to meet their expectations. Oh, and that reminds me. We have a meeting this morning to go over the compensation and benefits studies comparing what we're currently offering with what other companies give, and then we have to sit down and work at revamping our package. Come on, relax. Mark is just growing up. Are you coming?" "Yeah, I'm coming. And I guess you're right. Hey, at least he didn't ask for a signing bonus!"

ELEMENTS OF COMPENSATION AND BENEFITS

For the purposes of this book, *compensation* refers to money and money-related extras. Hence, in addition to a person's base pay, compensation could encompass signing bonuses, merit increases, variable pay, and long-term incentive compensation. *Benefits* refer to just about everything else, including healthcare, pension plans, stock options, and legal services. Alternative work arrangements, while certainly a benefit, are addressed separately in Chapter 10.

Since both compensation and benefits are comprehensive topics that could readily be the subject of entire books, only selected aspects of each are discussed in this chapter.

Compensation

An organization's compensation program sends a message to employees about its commitment to motivating, recognizing, and rewarding employee performance. While money should certainly never be the sole motivator, it is indisputably important. In an Aon Consulting survey of 1,800 U.S. employees, all things being equal, 25 percent said they would leave their current jobs for an increase of 10 percent or less, and more than 55 percent would leave for somewhat less than or equal to 20 percent. These numbers indicate that every organization should embrace a compensation philosophy that identifies its desired market position—that is, where it wants to position pay levels with respect to competitive market practice, e.g., at the median point. Once this philosophy is adopted, an organization can decide what elements of a total pay program are most appropriate in relation to its business objectives and corporate culture.

To be successful, a compensation program must align employee performance with business performance. Employees need to understand what the company expects of them, why the company expects it, and the potential rewards when performance expectations are met. Taking this approach to pay design provides an ownership context for employees—knowing they're important to the ongoing success of the organization, and that if they do their part, they'll share in the rewards generated by that success.

Base Pay

Base starting salaries—the fixed rate of compensation an employee receives for performing the standard duties and tasks of a job—are escalating at a rate that many companies consider alarming. Just take a look at some of the expected starting salaries for the year 2000 college graduates with bachelor's degrees for specific majors, as reported by Michigan State University:

Accounting:	$36,200
Business Administration:	$33,900
Civil Engineering:	$39,500
Chemical Engineering:	$49,200
Computer Engineering:	$48,000

Computer Science:	$46,800
Economics:	$36,500
Electrical Engineering:	$45,600
Engineering Technology:	$45,600
Finance:	$39,100
Information Sciences:	$47,200
Management Information Systems:	$44,100
Mathematics:	$43,700
Mechanical Engineering:	$43,900
Programming:	$46,900

Twenty years ago, the average college graduate earned 38 percent more than the average high-school graduate. Today, it is 71 percent more.

Savvy employers recognize that base-pay programs should be designed to reflect market practices within their identified competitor group. In order to accomplish this, organizations must first identify their competitive market. This can be done by considering various factors, including the nature of the industry, geographic location, total employment, and annual revenue. In addition, it's wise to consider all the organizations from which you win or lose talent, regardless of their size, industry, or location. Next, conduct an assessment of market pay practices for similar jobs within the identified competitor group. This assessment should include the duties, skills, and impact levels of each job analyzed—that is, each job of similar size and scope.

Then, develop a salary structure for managing competitive base-pay levels for all jobs throughout the organization. Salary structures typically consist of a series of pay ranges or bands that reflect competitive rates of pay for specific jobs, as well as allowing room for salary growth. Jobs of similar value from both a market and an internal perspective are grouped together. Then a competitive salary range is developed around the market rates for the specific jobs. Most structures consist of a minimum, a midpoint or control point, and a maximum. The minimum represents the lowest competitive rate for jobs within that range and is typically used as a starting point for entry-level employees. The maximum represents the highest competitive rate for jobs in the range. This is typically a premium market rate for top performers and those with extensive experience. Compensation experts discourage hiring at the maximum as this forces special consideration for out-of-range increases when it comes time for salary reviews. The midpoint represents the competitive market rate for fully performing employees in jobs assigned to that range. It provides a guideline for slotting various jobs and individuals into their appropriate salary ranges.

Signing Bonuses

These days, generous base-pay offerings are not always enough to convince applicants to work for your organization. Employers frequently try to entice potential hires by offering generous signing bonuses. In many cases, the dollars just aren't there to offer hefty salaries. However, most companies can afford a few thousand dollars for signing bonuses. And that few thousand may be the incentive it takes to recruit top talent. According to one survey, signing bonuses typically range from $1,000 to $15,000 but can go higher. When computed as a percentage of salary, the range is from 5 percent to 25 percent of a year's pay. Other surveys reflect bonuses running the gamut from as little as fifty dollars for rank-and-file positions all the way up to $25,000 for executives.

Not surprisingly, the highest figures are usually offered to information systems (IS) and information technology (IT) professionals, although signing bonuses are being used to secure positions from front-line workers to chief executive officers. While once reserved for the upper echelon of corporate management, the offer of a signing bonus to attract workers is increasingly utilized at every level. And while a signing bonus isn't likely to make or break a candidate's decision to work for a particular company, it may just be that little something extra that shifts the decision in your favor.

For employers, signing bonuses are an effective way to get noticed among a slew of competing companies without having to inflate salary levels. In addition, they save money down the road because base salaries are not affected. A onetime-only bonus is also less likely to cause tension between old and new employees.

In certain industries, such as construction, signing bonuses are necessary to attract employees at every level. In fact, these bonuses have become so commonplace that there's an expectation from the entry-level candidates to the highly skilled workers that they will be given a signing bonus.

Champion International Corp., a Hamilton, Ohio–based integrated paper and forestry products company, offers signing bonuses because it has a conservative pay scale. Bonuses run anywhere from $2,000 to $20,000. Canon USA uses signing bonuses selectively, generally reserving them for jobs that are particularly hard to fill, such as technical managers. Bonuses typically range between $3,000 and $10,000, though some occasionally go higher.

While there are no hard-and-fast rules as to how signing bonuses are paid, most companies, including Canon, tend to disburse them in one lump sum during the first pay period. Champion also pays the bonus in one lump sum but requires that an employee stay ninety days before collecting it. In certain circumstances, paying in installments is desirable. For example, during the anticipated Y2K crisis, an early departure was viewed as potentially catastrophic, so many companies stretched out signing bonuses to help ensure that the workers stayed on. Likewise, TD Industries, a mechanical contractor and service provider in Dallas, offers unskilled entry-level employees $100 up front and $400 after six months. And for the highly skilled, much-sought-after licensed plumber or electrician, the company pays surprisingly little—just $250 when hired and an additional $250 after six months, to keep workers from straying prematurely in what is a notoriously nomadic industry.

Whether paid in one lump sum or installments, most signing bonuses have some conditions attached. Employers often require employees to sign a statement promising to pay back the entire amount of the bonus if they depart prior to an agreed-upon time, typically twelve months. Since companies cannot legally withhold such a refund from the final paycheck of departing employees in most states, it's important to have a well-worded agreement to this effect.

At Canon, employees are asked to sign a statement promising to refund the signing bonus if they leave before a year is up. For bonuses in the $10,000 to $15,000 range, employees are asked to make a two-year commitment.

Many employers are also willing to absorb the withholding taxes that come with signing bonuses, making them all the more appealing to potential employees.

Merit Increases

Assuming a company can afford to hire employees at its base salaries and, in many instances, throw in signing bonuses, it then must be able to provide periodic increases. Commonly, companies implement this practice by granting merit salary increases once a year, following an annual performance evaluation. Merit pay is intended to provide a system of rewarding employees' performance through increases to their base pay. Generally, two factors impact the amount of merit increase awards: (1) the amount of money a company sets aside in its merit budget for performance-based increases, and (2) employee performance as determined through a formal performance evaluation system. Sometimes, too, "position in range" plays a role—that is, where an individual's pay falls with respect to the range midpoint. In companies that are interested in tightly managing salaries close to the midpoints of ranges, this can be good news for employees at the low end of the competitive range: They may be eligible to receive a higher percentage increase than their colleagues currently being paid above the midpoint.

In today's economy, merit increases are becoming increasingly ineffective in achieving the original intent of rewarding employee performance and contributions to the organization. Indeed, often perceived as an entitlement or merely a cost of living adjustment, merit increases rarely are sufficient to motivate and reward outstanding performance.

Variable Pay

Performance-based variable pay continues to gain momentum as a more effective way to recognize and reward employee performance. Once restricted to senior management levels, these incentive or bonus plans are being redesigned to reward the achievement of specific company and/or individual performance objectives regardless of level. In variable pay plans, the size of the award varies among individuals and from one performance period to another, based on levels of achievement measured, as well as against pre-established company and individual performance targets. Amounts are often calculated as a percentage of base pay depending on job category and position. Awards are commonly paid in cash on an annual, semiannual, or quarterly basis, depending on the plan design. Plan designs range from sales-commission types, to individual incentive or bonus plans, to team awards.

The latter is granted to reward project or work team members based on achievement of specific goals. Payouts may be issued at project milestones or the completion of specified performance periods. Team awards are generally the same for all team members and are paid out either as a flat dollar amount or as some percentage of pay.

In today's competitive labor market, variable pay programs are increasing in importance and value. As one manager put it, "Wages are always negotiable for these workers." Another said, "We adjust in response to each new crisis." According to the 1999 issue of *Compensation & Benefits Review*, a survey conducted by American Management Association to review compensation and benefits, of those respondents that adjust salaries more often than once a year, about half do so twice yearly. In many instances, top performers are receiving additional increases ranging from 10 to 15 percent, and in some cases surpassing the 20 percent mark.

Banding

The practice of banding includes *broadbanding* and *career-banding*. Broadbanding eliminates all but a few (generally three to ten) comprehensive salary and job classifications. For instance, Rockwell Automation, a manufacturer of automation products in Milwaukee, adopted a broadbanding approach to compensation by collapsing twenty-five pay grades into five bands, A through E. General Electric went from 291 pay grades to five bands.

Bands usually have minimum and maximum dollar amounts that overlap, and an average width of 130 percent of the minimum. Band I may cover technicians from $3,000 to $74,000, and Band II may cover a range of $60,000 to $140,000. Careerbanding is similar but more closely tied to career development. With careerbanding, there are no minimums or maximums; salaries are based on market surveys.

Both banding plans stress skill development and the newer, flatter organizational structure. They eliminate narrowly defined job titles and allow lateral in addition to downward movement, aside from the traditional upward movement. Lateral moves help employees gain broader experience and new skills that make them qualified for more positions; this, in turn, benefits the organization by creating a more resilient, cross-trained workforce. Downward movement, also known as realignment or downshifting, can be desirable for employees who need less time-consuming, less stressful work, either temporarily or permanently. For instance, an IS manager may find that he prefers programming computers to managing the programmers. Broadbanding and careerbanding, then, allow both the company and employees greater flexibility.

Skill- and Competency-Based Pay

Skill-based pay offers employees extra compensation when they master new skills specifically identified by the company as critical to achieve a competitive advantage, such as the ability to use a particular computer software program. Skill-based pay can be especially beneficial for employees who like their current jobs but seek new challenges. Competency-based pay is more comprehensive than skill-based pay because the criteria encompass not only measurable skills but also knowledge, performance behaviors, and personal attributes. It helps employees grow in place and gives them guidance for closing knowledge gaps needed for lateral moves.

While competency-based pay programs should clearly communicate to the employees what behaviors are valued by the organization, some intangibles, such as good customer relations and effective communications skills, are harder to gauge than measurable skills, such as computer software knowledge. It's also not always evident whether something is a skill or a competency. Accordingly, it's not always easy to determine when a skill or competency has been mastered.

According to a study by the then-named American Compensation Association (now called World at Work), 40 percent of companies surveyed use competency-based programs to determine salary increases.[1]

Long-Term Incentive Compensation

Long-term incentive compensation vehicles, such as stock-option plans and other deferred-compensation plans, while not frequently used to reward performance, are gaining desirability among employees. These plans reward employees based on company performance over the long term—typically three to five years. Stock-option plans are a prevalent form of long-term compensation at public organizations. At private companies, incentives that mirror stock plans, but are based on internal values or deferred compensation, are often used for key employees.

Long-term compensation plans can be valuable retention tools. At their most effective, they focus key employees on driving and improving the financial performance of the company over the longer term.

Best Practice: Holiday Inn Worldwide

Holiday Inn Worldwide takes a total value approach to its compensation plan. Its philosophy is to offer an appropriate mix of base and incentive pay to drive the accomplishments of the company's strategic objectives.

All positions are evaluated based on a common point factor program, with the recognition that differences may arise because of the competitive nature of certain positions (these positions have a separate salary structure). Holiday Inn also sets premiums on base pay based on geographical competitive pay differentials. As of this writing, the organization was contemplating the possibility of piloting broadbanding in its Information Technology group.

Each employee belongs to one of the company's incentive programs, all of which are based on the achievement of performance results. These plans include the annual incentive plan, whereby pay is tied to performance results; a specialized incentive plan, which targets certain groups, such as salespeople; and a tactical incentive plan, which identifies the extraordinary accomplishments of onetime projects. Incentive payouts are typically in cash.

Holiday Inn has a competency-based system measured by nine key competencies viewed as effective predictors of successful performance:

1. *Customer service orientation* assesses a person's ability and willingness to understand and satisfy the needs of others.
2. *Achievement orientation* evaluates a person's desire to experience success by achieving beneficial goals.
3. *Creative problem solving* measures an employee's ability to address problems with new and effective solutions.
4. *Initiative/proactivity* reflects how self-motivated and persistent employees are, as well as how effectively they are able to preempt problems and anticipate opportunities.
5. *Flexibility* addresses a person's ability to adapt to, and work effectively with, a variety of situations and people.
6. *Organizational influence and impact* measures a person's ability to positively impact organizational performance.
7. *Organizational/professional commitment* relates to an employee's capacity to align with the values and strategies of the organization.
8. *Developing others* reflects a person's demonstrated talent for effectively improving the skills of others.
9. *Enablement* pertains to an employee's ability to exercise self-management in a way that benefits the organization.

Everyone is measured against these same competencies; however, the benchmarks against which employees are rated differ. Standards are based on an individual's job category of executive, managerial/supervisory, professional/technical, or administrative support.

Holiday Inn communicates to employees its pay philosophy as well as the general guidelines that are used to manage salaries and incentive pay. The initial introduction to compensation occurs at orientation, during which employees are given information pertaining to company salary structures, administrative guidelines, and their particular incentive plans. The pay philosophy and structure are also communicated through focus groups.

Holiday Inn examined the performance results of twenty-three company-owned and managed hotels in the southern United States. The company found that those hotels providing the best performance management, while using the competency-based system, had higher customer satisfaction, lower annualized turnover, and higher operating profits than those hotels providing the least performance management. In addition, managers perceived as providing the best performance management had guest satisfaction scores at their hotels that were nearly 10 percent higher than managers who provided the least effective performance management. At those same top hotels, the annual turnover was 38 percent lower, or about forty fewer turnovers per year. At an estimated replacement cost per lost employee of $3,120, that's a savings of $124,800.

Benefits

Applicants and new hires reviewing their choices of benefits plans often feel confused and overwhelmed. The terminology can be difficult to discern for employers as well (see Appendix A of this book for a glossary of some common employee benefit terms). While the various plans are typically designed to address the health and welfare of the employee population, comprehending them can be a laborious task. Further complicating matters, to help offset the significant expenses associated with comprehensive benefits plans, costs in varying amounts are often shared with employees. Company benefits can encompass a wide range of offerings from standard medical insurance to more innovative perks like prepaid legal services, and applicants who are comparing job offers often narrow their choices down to those that offer the most generous benefits package.

To some employees, training means more than money. For example, according to one survey of HR executives conducted by the American Management Association, technical and employability training were rated significantly higher than pay-for-performance or bonuses. Companies typically respond to this interest by sending workers to outside conferences and seminars, reimbursing employees for tuition, offering managerial training, and supporting employees in degree programs.

One recent survey of salaried employee benefits provided by

one thousand major U.S. employers, released by Hewitt Associates in Lincolnshire, Ilinois, found that the major benefits were retirement, healthcare, and time off with pay. More specifically, the survey found that nearly all employers offer some type of defined contribution plan, such as 401(k) plans, while 77 percent provide a defined benefits pension plan. In addition, 93 percent of the companies offer a matched savings plan as part of the defined contribution plan. The maximum that companies will match is fifty cents per one dollar, up to 6 percent of salary. In the healthcare arena, most of the employers offer three or four plan choices, as well as healthcare spending accounts and programs that encourage healthy lifestyles. Spending accounts are offered by 82 percent of the businesses, while 93 percent offer preventative programs that include training and education, health risk assessments and screenings, smoke-free workplaces, and disease management programs. On average, employees get 10.5 vacation days and eleven paid holidays.

Another survey conducted by Hewitt Associates revealed that the "100 Best Companies to Work for in America" provide more health and well-being benefits than other companies. For example, the one hundred companies offer 80 percent more maternity leave, stress reduction programs, on-site fitness facilities, and prenatal and well-baby programs.

Here's a closer look at some specific benefits.

Healthcare

Industry projections concerning healthcare costs are scary: They are anticipated to more than double from $1 trillion in 1996 to $2.1 trillion in 2007. According to the Health Insurance Association of America (HIAA), the fastest-growing healthcare plans in the nation are those with flexibility. In today's era of cafeteria-style benefits plans, employees increasingly view individual benefits within plans as negotiable. In addition, employees with highly marketable skills often expect that everything they medically want or need will be covered.

Industry analysts pinpoint several factors that currently influence the healthcare market. One is the accelerating pace of new treatment development. New therapies are introduced into the marketplace on a regular basis, and employees are pressuring employers to cover a widening variety of treatments. Accordingly, experts suggest that organizations review their healthcare benefits annually to assess the full range of requested coverage in relation to their overall premium costs and healthcare utilization.

Another factor compels employers to focus on employees who take higher-than-average risks with their health. Experts see an increasing trend by employers to charge employees additional premiums for potentially hazardous activities or conditions, such as smoking, skydiving, obesity, drinking, motorcycle riding, or piloting private airplanes. Although most group coverage is offered to everyone in the group at the same rate, the practice of charging a premium appears to be legal as long as no individual is targeted. Higher premiums charged smokers, for example, must apply to all smokers.

Yet another factor affecting healthcare options is the access employees have to medical information on the Internet. According to *The Journal of the American Medical Association*, nearly 40 percent of people who use the Internet are seeking medical information. That means American consumers of healthcare can now readily learn about their options.

When faced with a difficult decision concerning what to cover, many companies follow the counsel of a third-party administrator. For example, if a company has numerous requests for a particular treatment, it would seek expert medical review of the pros and cons based on cost, as well as effectiveness.

Choosing the Right Healthcare Plan

Experts agree that the best method of choosing the right healthcare plan for your organization is to follow these six steps:

1. *Ask employees what they want.* You may be surprised at the number of employees who want coverage for services you never considered germane, such as chiropractic care, acupuncture, or homeopathy. Ask employees what treatments or options they want in their plans and what types of plans they prefer. Note that regional surveys might reflect local attitudes toward healthcare plan types. For example, according to research by Milliman & Robertson, a Seattle-based actuarial and business management consulting firm, health maintenance organizations are highly regarded on the West Coast but are not favored in the South. If your company has offices in several regions of the country, there may be different preferences based on geography.

2. *Offer a choice of plans.* Your survey is likely to reveal that you can't cover everyone's priorities under one healthcare plan. Employees today typically pay a higher portion of the healthcare premium, and the employer functions more as a broker by offering

a range of plans and subsidizing the cost of using one of them. Here are the primary characteristics of four different plans:

▲ *Health maintenance organizations (HMOs).* These plans offer a predetermined set of benefits for a fixed cost to the employer. They usually emphasize preventative care, and frequently there are minimal or no copayments and no deductibles. Because the HMO absorbs the costs of any treatment that exceeds the premium, some employees may associate HMOs with media stories about refusal to cover particularly costly treatments.

▲ *Managed care.* According to the Health Insurance Association of America, 70 percent of Americans who have health coverage through their employer are enrolled in managed care. The attraction for employers is that managed care allows them to control costs far more effectively than in plans where employees can see any doctor they wish. Each enrollee is typically assigned to a primary care physician who becomes the gatekeeper to all specialists in the plan. The employer contracts with selected providers for a comprehensive set of services to enrollees. Enrollees have financial incentives to use the providers covered by the plans.

▲ *Preferred provider organizations (PPOs).* PPOs are groups of hospitals that and health providers who form an organization and contract with employers to provide healthcare at a discounted fee. Employees incur that fee only when they obtain services from a PPO-member provider or hospital.

▲ *Point of service (POS) plans.* Employees who select POS plans want an unlimited choice of providers and hospitals. Usually the employee is responsible for a deductible and a copayment. POS plans are the most expensive healthcare options. Often, if a group of employees insists on a POS option among the plan choices, the premium is much higher than the premium for an HMO, managed care, or PPO option.

3. *Show employees the plans and costs.* Putting together an information sheet that lists the options you offer, their key characteristics, and the premium costs to employees helps workers understand the differences and similarities among the plans. It is even more helpful if you further break down the costs to employees by detailing premiums for the employee only, employee and spouse or partner, and family coverage.

4. *Clearly explain the benefits.* Before distributing an insurance company's summary benefits plan, reread it and ask yourself

if it's likely that the average employee will understand the contents. Are unique terms defined? Is the information easy to discern? Can employees readily distinguish one plan from another? Does the summary provide examples to help employees understand the contents of each plan? If not, you need to rewrite it.

5. *Give employees a confirmation statement.* Once each employee has selected a plan, confirm the selection in writing. Include the name of the plan, who's covered, basic covered services, deductibles, copayments, and annual cost. Also confirm the amount of the employee's regular payroll deduction. It is also advisable to send the employee two copies, asking that one be signed and returned to you for the payroll file, with the employee retaining the other.

6. *Review your plan usage annually.* You may decide to replace plans that have limited or decreased use, or to resurvey employees regarding what they want in the way of a healthcare plan.

Home Healthcare

As employers struggle to control skyrocketing healthcare costs, many are finding a key strategy in decreasing hospitalization with the use of home healthcare services, one of the fastest growing segments of the healthcare industry. Such services employ healthcare professionals and other trained personnel to work with patients and their families at home to help patients achieve a maximum level of health. Although home healthcare encompasses a broad range of services, from skilled nursing care to medical-equipment repair, its main advantage is bringing necessary hospital services to the home rather than allowing the patient to linger in the hospital.

According to one home healthcare provider, "Home healthcare is the most cost-effective component of healthcare today on a dollar-for-dollar basis when compared with hospital or skilled nursing-home healthcare. Ultimately that translates to the employer as a lower cost per insured employee per month."

The growth of home healthcare services is being influenced by a combination of demographic, technological, economic, and consumer trends:

▲ Demographic considerations include the aging of the U.S. population, the increase in opportunities for Americans with disabilities, and higher survival rates for premature and low birthweight infants.

▲ Advances in medical technology have reduced hospital

lengths of stay and have enabled physicians to perform more surgery in outpatient settings. Many products once found only in hospitals are now miniaturized, portable, and less expensive, allowing for equipment to be installed in the home.

▲ Home healthcare services are often more cost-effective than institutional care, while providing a high level of satisfaction among employee patients. One study, by Aetna Life & Casualty Co., found that home healthcare resulted in a savings of approximately $20,000 per patient per month for AIDS patients and approximately $40,000 per patient per month for infants with breathing problems, over the same care provided in a hospital. Another study, commissioned by the National Association of Medical Equipment Suppliers, compared home healthcare with hospital care for three conditions responsive to home medical care. The potential cost savings of home healthcare compared with institutional care for a hip fracture, for example, was $2,400 per incident. Multiplied by the 250,000 diagnoses of hip fractures in the United States each year, the annual potential savings amounts to $600 million.

▲ A study conducted by the American Association of Retired Persons (AARP) revealed that 72 percent of people prefer to recuperate from a serious accident or illness at home.

Home healthcare services generally are rolled into a company's overall health-insurance benefits package, but specific coverage can be negotiated. Before renewing your policy, you might want to ask these questions:

1. *How does the managed-care organization check accreditation of home healthcare providers?* The Joint Commission on Accreditation of Healthcare Organizations, based in Oakbrook Terrace, Illinois, accredits home healthcare providers, but accreditation is voluntary. Many managed-care organizations are now pressuring home healthcare providers to provide accreditation and other credentials.

2. *What home healthcare services are provided?* Many policies cover skilled nursing care. Find out if your policy also covers such services as physical, occupational, speech, and respiratory therapies, home-health aides, and such medical equipment as wheelchairs, adjustable beds, and traction devices.

3. *Are there limits to the amount of services a patient can receive?* Some policies have set limits per episode or per year.

4. *What are the grievance procedures?* Representatives of the organization should provide satisfactory responses to patients and patient advocates concerning coverage of home healthcare services.

Alternative Medicine

Increasingly, employees are requesting alternative medicine as the most desired means for addressing health concerns such as back problems and headaches. And more companies are responding favorably to these requests. According to Clement Bezold, president of Alexandria, Virginia–based Institute for Alternative Futures, by the year 2010, alternative medical treatments are expected to be widely recognized as appropriate for a wide range of conditions, and two-thirds of Americans will use some form of what we now think of as alternative medicine. As employers constantly look for ways to reduce their long-term health costs and improve benefits packages to attract and retain top talent, alternative medicine is appearing with increasing frequency in healthcare packages. For example, NYNEX, IBM, AT&T, Nike, HBO, and Apple currently offer on-site yoga classes as a regular employee benefit.

Alternative medicine covers a broad range of therapies falling into several categories. Alternative medical systems involve theories and practices that have been developed outside the Western biomedical approach. These include acupuncture, herbal formulas, massage and manipulation, homeopathy, radionics, and orthomolecular medicine. Mind-body medicine involves psychological, social, and spiritual approaches to health and includes practices such as yoga, internal qigong, tai chi, spiritual healing, and pastoral care. The category of lifestyle and disease prevention involves theories in addition to practices designed to prevent the development of illness, identify and treat risk factors, or support the healing process. This includes electrodermal diagnostics, medical intuition, enzyme measures, and panchakarma.

Biologically-based therapies include natural as well as biologically-based practices, interventions, and products, such as herbalism, special diet therapies, orthomolecular medicine, and pharmacological, biological, and instrumental interventions. Manipulative and body-based systems are based on manipulation or movement of the body. Typically included are chiropractic medicine, massage and body work, reflexology, applied kinesiology, acupressure, rolfing, colonics, and hydrotherapy. The category of biofield involves systems that use subtle energy fields in and around the body for medical purposes. This includes therapeutic touch, natural healing, huna, external qigong, and biorelax. Finally, there is bioelectromagnetics, which involves the use of electromagnetic fields for medical purposes. It usually encompasses magnetic or electromagnetic therapy.

Interestingly, 75 percent of U.S. medical schools currently offer instruction in alternative therapies, although not because the American Medical Association endorses it. On the contrary, patients are asking doctors to recommend or provide specific alternative treatments. This is a case, then, of consumers being more educated than the physicians themselves.

Major health groups, such as Oxford Health Plans, Aetna Life & Casualty, Blue Shield, and Harvard Pilgrim Health Care, are responding to employee and consumer interests. For example, Oxford's Alternative Medicine Program offers either a rider that employers can purchase by adding 3 percent to the cost of annual premiums per individual, or a contracted rate for all health plan members, which means a 15 to 25 percent lower charge for services. Such services include chiropractic care (the most common alternative choice), acupuncture, nutritional counseling, and, in some states, naturopathic (nondrug) treatment. Other health groups are reportedly adding acupressure and vitamin therapy to their list of offerings.

Managed care companies and hospitals increasingly offer alternative medical benefits as a way to differentiate themselves in the competitive healthcare market. At the same time, consumer pressure has generated state laws requiring coverage of services from alternative providers. For example, in January 1996, Washington State became the first in the nation to require all healthcare plans and insurers to include "every category of provider." The law includes chiropractors, physicians, acupuncturists, physician assistants, registered nurses, podiatrists, licensed massage therapists, midwives, and osteopaths. And in 1997, when the Washington, D.C.–based National Institutes of Health deemed acupuncture as an acceptable alternative to medication for the treatment of chronic pain, the alternative medicine movement received a credibility boost.

Behavioral Health (Mental Health)

Behavioral or mental healthcare covers conditions such as debilitating anxiety, clinical depression, emotional stress, substance abuse, and workplace violence. The U.S. Surgeon General states that 20 percent of all Americans will have incapacitating depression sometime in their lives, and statistics continually point out that workers are suffering emotional stress that translates into workplace difficulties. According to the Employee Assistance Program Association (EAPA), the return on investment for every dollar invested in behavioral health is five dollars to seven dollars. In other words, for every dollar spent, there's a huge return in improved productivity, lowered absenteeism, and reduced use of medical benefits.

In spite of this impressive return, however, the percentage of healthcare dollars spent on behavioral healthcare has declined 54.7 percent between 1988 and 1998. At that time, behavioral health as a percent of the total healthcare benefit costs was 6.1 percent; ten years later, it was 3.2 percent. This is due largely to the fact that the Mental Health Parity Act of 1996, while prohibiting healthcare plans from imposing more restrictive limits on mental health benefits than on medical or surgical benefits, doesn't require companies to offer behavioral health benefits. It also permits higher copayments and deductibles for mental health services.

Adolph Coors Co., based in Golden, Colorado, is one example of a company that approaches employee health from a holistic standpoint. According to Joe Vollmer, supervisor of Employee Family Counselor Services, "If you look at the costs of depression, anxiety, and other mental health–related illnesses, and the dollars of impact to businesses, it's foolish not to provide services. From a humanitarian perspective, we want to give our employees the benefits they need. If we contribute to their health, it's a dual benefit—for them and for the company." Accordingly, Coors's 5,800 employees can choose among several insurance plans that include inpatient or outpatient mental health and chemical dependency coverage.

Choosing a behavioral healthcare program can be complex and confusing. These guidelines can help:

1. Call current clients of several providers under consideration and ask what the experience is like for the employees. For example, when they try to get help, do they access the system right away, or are kept waiting for a long time?
2. Find out as much as you can about the types of services each potential provider provides.
3. Weigh, carefully, the advantages of buying a separate mental health plan or a "carve-out" plan that is part of the overall

healthcare package. Carve-out plans are generally tightly managed, and care must be preapproved.
4. Check on emergency care benefits and accessibility.

Best Practice: Merrill Lynch

A good healthcare medical plan has always been the cornerstone of any benefits package. Merrill Lynch has taken this concept and expanded upon it. In cooperation with the Hospital for Special Surgery in New York, the company's World Financial Center workforce of eight thousand has access to one of three physicians three days a week, right in the comfort of their own worksite. The doctors are in Merrill Lynch's medical plan network, which is a Blue Cross/Blue Shield preferred provider organization (PPO). Anyone who is in the PPO can visit these physicians. The doctors see between forty-five and fifty patients per week.

The program has proved so successful that Merrill Lynch may expand it to the entire workweek and add another doctor. In addition, Merrill Lynch workers from the office in Jersey City, New Jersey and other smaller company facilities are able to use the on-site physicians.

While the company has always offered a variety of emergency and diagnostic services to its workers, the new service allows workers convenient access to primary care physicians without ever leaving the office. The arrangement is beneficial to employer and employees alike. First, when Merrill Lynch surveyed about 250 employees and asked them how long a doctor's appointment took when it was scheduled off-site, the company found that it takes, on average, about two hours and forty minutes. On-site visits take about fifteen minutes. In addition, easy access to medical care leads to better care. The company pays less for medical costs due to illnesses that are preventable or that are caught sooner rather than later, and employees are more likely to take better care of themselves because of the convenience of seeing a doctor on the premises. The program also helps the company's corporate image.

Healthcare Resources

Healthcare coverage options can be tricky. Fortunately, there are plenty of resources to help employees understand their options and choose those that are most useful for themselves and their families. Here are a few that are available on the Internet:

▲ Employer Quality Partnership: www.eqp.org
▲ Health Insurance Association of America (HIAA): www.hiaa.org
▲ Joint Commission on the Accreditation of Health Care: www.jcaho.org
▲ National Business Coalition on Health: www.ncbh.org/nbch
▲ National Committee on Quality Assurance: www.ncqa.org
▲ President's Advisory Commission on Consumer Protection and Quality in the Health Care Industry: www.hcqualitycommission.gov
▲ "Trends & Resources" section of Workforce Online: www.workforceonline.com/trends/healthcare
▲ U.S. Department of Health and Human Services (DHHS): www.hhs.gov

Pensions

Retirement or pension plans are ranked by employees as second in importance only to medical coverage. However, many employers offer no pension coverage to their employees. Roughly half of the private-sector workforce is not covered by any employer-sponsored retirement plan, and only 20 percent of workers in small businesses have any retirement plan.

There are two primary types of pension plans: defined benefit (DB) and defined contribution (DC). In DB plans, the benefits are computed as a percent of the last few or the highest years of earnings multiplied by years of service. They are then paid in the form of life annuities. These plans are oriented toward those who expect to work for the same company throughout their career. Such workers tend to prefer a guaranteed monthly income, think more of the long term, and save more money than their younger, mobile counterparts. The DB plan, then, operates to protect and ensure a long-term relationship. Employees do not make contributions under this type of plan, and the employer is the only one who bears the risk for providing the guaranteed level of benefits. No individual accounts are maintained; instead, employers contribute to a trust fund the amounts that are necessary to provide the benefits specified. The proportion of covered workers enrolled in DB retirement plans declined from 87 percent to about 50 percent in the last quarter of the 20th century.

DC plans generally appeal to younger workers. This type of pension plan allows workers to save directly into some portfolio assets of their own choosing. The popularity of this plan is also part of the larger movement to empower workers to control their own retirement savings and investments. Moreover, DC plans tend to be easier to understand because the statements aren't projected based on life expectancy, interest rate, and salary projections, but are reported at their present value. For the roughly half of private-sector workers with pension coverage through their employment, coverage through DC plans has more than doubled in twenty-five years, rising from 33 percent in 1975 to about 80 percent by the end of the century.

Increasingly, employers have added 401(k) tax-deferred provisions to their existing DC plans or established new plans with 401(k) provisions. In fact, today, 401(k)s represent the largest pool of money invested in capital markets—more than $11 trillion by some estimates. Many employees invest only in 401(k)s. Depending on how the stock market is doing, this can be either an excellent investment or potentially devastating. Some employers help ease employee investment anxiety by offering up to a 50 percent match on the first 5 to 10 percent invested. For example, Maxsys Technologies Corporation in Santa Ana, California offers a 25 percent match on the first 6 percent invested. Others, like Coca-Cola and BankAmerica, include their own stock in employees' 401(k) plans. In fact, according to the Employee Benefit Research Institute in Washington, D.C., employees have an average of 20 percent of their 401(k) assets invested in company stock.

Companies cannot force employees to put more than 10 percent of their 401(k) plan funds in company stock or assets, according to the January 1999 provision of the Taxpayer Relief Act of 1977. The provision does not apply, however, to the employer's matching contributions or if plan participants have discretion as to how their assets are invested.

Experts urge employers to assist workers to recognize the types of risks that are inherent in all investments and to diversify their 401(k) investments. Compaq Computer Corp., working with mutual-fund giant Vanguard Group, developed a 401(k) intranet to make its retirement plan more accessible to employees. Other companies use videos and seminars to educate employees. Roughly 80 percent of the companies researched by the Spectrem Group, a San Francisco–based financial-services consultant, offer a daily valuation of 401(k) portfolios.

DB plans require more administrative effort than DC plans because of an annual actuarial evaluation. They also require tracking of breaks in service, compensation over long periods of time, and additional reporting requirements to the Pension Benefits Guarantee Corporation, which warrantees certain levels of pension in company plans. Organizations with fewer than five hundred employees are advised against offering DB plans, from a strictly administrative point of view.

Approximately one in five covered workers has both a defined contribution and a defined benefit plan. (Higher-paid executives reap the greatest benefits via a combination of DB and DC plans.) By offering two plans, employers are better able to recruit and retain workers with different retirement needs.

Cash balance and other hybrid plans that combine characteristics of DB and DC plans provide additional pension plan options. To participants, cash balance plans look like DC plans because they use an account balance to communicate the benefit amount. However, the employer credits contributions, usually on an annual basis, to each participant's personal account. Each account also is credited with investment earnings set at a predetermined rate of interest. The contribution credited each year may be a flat percent of pay, such as 5 percent, or may vary based on age or service. The interest credit may be a fixed rate but is more often tied to Treasury securities, such as the rate on thirty-year Treasury bonds at the beginning of the plan year plus 1 percent.

While the plans appear to participants as consisting of account balances similar to 401(k) plans, the accounts exist only on paper. The pension fund that exists to cover the accounts may be more or less than the total of the accounts. As with traditional DB plans, an actuary calculates the present value of the future benefit payments and recommends the employer's contribution to the plan. The contribution requirement may be larger or smaller than the sum of the contribution credits for all participants for the year, depending upon how well funded the plan is. If the pension fund investment earnings exceed the interest credits allocated to participants, the plan sponsor may benefit from the fund's strong performance by reducing future contributions.

Most cash balance plans specifically define the pay and interest credits. This means that if the trust fund does not perform well, the plan sponsor must make contributions to fund the shortfall, as is the case with any other DB plan.

Cash plan participants relate better to the account balance concept. Benefits are evenly distributed to different age groups, lump sum benefits are attractive to participants and easier to administer than annuities, the plan is attractive to younger recruits, funding is flexible, and the employers have investment control.

You can visit these web sites to find out more about pension planning:

▲ BenefitsLink: www.benefitslink.com
▲ International Society for Retirement Planning: www.isrplan.org
▲ International Foundation of Employee Benefits Plans: www.ifebp.org
▲ RetireNet: www.centerforretirement.com
▲ U.S. Department of Labor: www.dol.gov/dol/pwba

Stock Options

Stock options give employees a chance to buy stock in their company at a preset price during a limited time period. If the stock then rises beyond that price, the employee profits. In today's strong economy, employers have found it increasingly necessary to provide stock options to attract the most valued workers. For example, 50 percent of junior technical employees now have stock options, up from 35 percent in 1997. And 5 to 10 percent of U.S. companies offer stock option plans to all employees, typically granting from one hundred to two hundred option shares annually, or an amount based on a percentage of salary. Unquestionably, the 90s have seen a definite trend toward "employee ownership," wherein employers use company stock options to attract, reward, and retain key employees. The most recent figures reveal more than 14 million workers through 15,000 U.S. companies now participate in some sort of stock ownership plan.

Broad-based stock option plans—plans that allow all employees to participate regardless of their position—are frequently seen in high-tech, telecommunications, and pharmaceutical companies. Examples of high-tech companies that have instituted stock option plans include Apple Computer, Data General, Electronic Data Systems, Intel, Microsoft, Oracle Systems, Seagate Technology, Tandem Computers, Texas Instruments, Wang Laboratories, and WMX Technologies. Telecommunications companies include Air Touch Communications, AT&T, GTE, and U.S. West. Examples of pharmaceutical businesses include Bristol-Myers Squibb and Merck. Other types of organizations are offering stock options, such as Du Pont and PepsiCo. The latter has a "Power Plan" that provides options worth 10 percent of an employee's annual pay.

Generally, there are two types of options:

1. *Discounted stock options.* This type of plan allows an employee to buy the employer's stock at a price below the fair market value. The employee may exercise the option as soon as permitted, to realize an immediate profit, or wait in the hopes that a rising stock price will bring additional gains. Discounted stock options allow employees to defer current income taxes, use pretax dollars to invest in company stock, and choose when to receive the compensation, and, accordingly, when to pay the inevitable taxes.

2. *Index options.* Some companies have issued stock options with exercise prices tied to the Standard and Poor's 500 Index or other peer group stock index. With this approach, if the stock price outperforms the index (e.g., the stock appreciates 30 percent while the index appreciates only 10 percent), then the exercise price will be at less than the fair market value. If the index outperforms the market, the exercise price will be greater than fair market value.

The National Center for Employee Ownership, based in Oakland, California, found that over a ten-year period, companies with significant worker ownership grew 40 to 60 percent faster than they would have without such ownership. "When you combine a significant amount of employee ownership with quality ownership–culture management, you get a company that, according to research, will grow faster than other companies," says Corey Rosen, the center's executive director.

Unquestionably, stock options frequently translate into success. When the Fort Worth, Texas–based Union Pacific Resources Group departed from its parent company, Union Pacific Corp., it sought ways to encourage its employees to help the new company to succeed. The solution was to create an ownership culture among workers by rewarding 1,600 petrotech workers and all administrative staff with shares of stock. Union Pacific Resources Group grouped employees by salary and responsibility level, then assigned an appropriate number of shares—fifty to hourly and nonexempt employees, one hundred to midlevel staff, 150 to senior management. Dividends began immediately, although employees who left the company within a year couldn't take the stock with them. Karen Wresinski, director of compensation and staffing for Union Pacific Resources Group, summed the move up this way: "We felt that if employees had a share of the company, no matter how small, they would be more focused on the business results and in helping the business succeed."

Of course, not all stock options plans are created equal. Some high-tech entrepreneurial companies, including many of the Internet businesses that have popped up over the last few years, for example, rely heavily on stock options to provide compensation. Accordingly, many pay salaries far below market value. This may appeal to some workers, such as those in their twenties without a home or family to support, who are attracted to the opportunity of hitting the options jackpot.

Despite their enormous popularity and success, stock options can create problems. In some cases, companies have struggled to keep vested employees on the payroll once they've cashed in options to the tune of millions of dollars. Companies like Oracle and Microsoft have hundreds of employees who have joined the "millionaire" club as a result of stock options.

Many employers seek to condition the exercise of stock options on a noncompetition agreement. Under such an agreement, if an employee exercises the option to buy stock in the company and then leaves shortly thereafter to work for a competitor, that employee would be required to forfeit any profits earned as a result of the option. Some states, such as California, prohibit agreements that unreasonably restrict the ability of employees to engage in their occupations. Other states do not have such prohibitions.

Legal Services

Many people who need legal counsel don't have the money or resources to hire an attorney. Accordingly, employers are offering their workforce legal benefits plans whereby a lawyer represents employees in various matters such as divorce, wills and estate planning, and house closings, in addition to providing tax and financial planning assistance. Although many companies offer the plan as a voluntary employee benefit without absorbing any of the cost, others are increasingly picking up some portion of the cost. Regardless, costs to employees are usually very affordable. For example, LegalWise, a plan available for as little as three dollars per month, provides unlimited telephone access to attorneys, simple document review, a free will, unlimited third-party calls and letters, and discounted rates on other services. The top-of-the-line plan is available for under twenty dollars per month and covers both basic services as well as expanded offerings, including up to two hundred hours per year per family for in-person representation by a lawyer, unlimited tax advice, and financial counseling.

Employees find these services so useful that the average length of stay with the LegalWise plan, for example, is six years. The primary reason for leaving a plan is termination of employment. However, many providers offer portability, so employees leaving the company can retain the benefit.

Generally, there are two types of prepaid legal plans that employers offer: (1) comprehensive plans with fully covered benefits, and (2) access or discount plans. Comprehensive plans provide employees with complete service for matters such as wills, trusts, adoptions, divorces, civil litigation, real estate closings, consumer debt problems, and tax audits. The monthly payroll deductions for comprehensive plans typically range from thirteen dollars to twenty-three dollars. Access or discount plans provide members with access to an attorney for consultation, usually over the phone, at no charge. For more complex matters that require consultation or in-office services, members are referred to attorneys who provide services at a discount from their regular hourly fees. Access plans have the lowest premiums, ranging from five dollars to ten dollars a month.

If you are considering a legal benefits plan for your workforce, weigh certain variables:

▲ *Look for an A.M. Best rating of "A."* A.M. Best is an independent organization, based in Oldwick, New Jersey, that rates insurance companies on financial strength, operating performance, and their ability to meet obligations to policy holders. Ratings of "A" ensure that your legal insurance provider is financially sound.

▲ *Screen lawyer-members through the local and state bar associations.* Attorneys also should be required to maintain malpractice insurance coverage of at least $1 million per incident.

▲ *Identify the breadth of services that the premium provides.* For example, some plans do not offer coverage for domestic issues, especially postdivorce; yet this accounts for almost half of employee usage. A plan that covers only uncontested divorces does not add much value. Some insurers provide discounted rates for noncovered matters, which ensures that some level of benefit is available for all legal issues. Minimally, every legal services plan should include wills and estate planning, including living wills and trusts; real estate matters, such as closing fees; consumer matters, such as credit card debt and bankruptcy; family law, such as uncontested divorce and custody matters; and criminal defense, usually limited to juvenile matters and misdemeanors.

▲ *Look at the payout value.* LegalWise plans, for example, provide an average of $1.65 in legal service value for every one dollar of premium received.

▲ *Look for a plan that offers emergency service.* Twenty-four-hour emergency service is preferable, since legal problems don't always occur during the business day. Good plans provide for legal information online and quick emergency service at any hour.

▲ *Make certain that an out-of-network benefit is available.* Although these plans usually cost a bit more, they allow members to use an attorney of their choosing.

▲ *Look for some mechanism that monitors employees' satisfaction with the program.* Pre-Paid Legal Services in Ada, Oklahoma, for instance, sends monthly questionnaires to several hundred randomly selected members who recently received benefits. And Midwest Legal Services, located in Des Moines, Iowa, sends customer satisfaction questionnaires to all first-time claimants and a percentage of other claimants.

The checklist in Exhibit 3–1 represents many of the benefits that U.S. companies currently extend to their employees. Review the list in the left-hand column, and place a check mark next to each item in the appropriate column: "Something Our Company Currently Offers," "Something Our Company Would Consider Offering," or "Something Our Company Would Never Consider Offering." After you have finished with the list, review how many perks you currently offer and how flexible you are with regard to increasing your offerings.

Exhibit 3–1. What companies are offering.

Incentive or Perk	Something Our Company Currently Offers	Something Our Company Would Never Consider Offering	Something Our Company Would Consider Offering
Adoption assistance	☐	☐	☐
Basic medical	☐	☐	☐
accident	☐	☐	☐
insurance	☐	☐	☐
Business travel	☐	☐	☐
Cafeteria benefits	☐	☐	☐
Conversion privilege	☐	☐	☐
Defined-benefit pension plan	☐	☐	☐
Defined-contribution pension plan	☐	☐	☐
Dental insurance	☐	☐	☐
Employee Assistance Programs	☐	☐	☐

Incentive or Perk	Something Our Company Currently Offers	Something Our Company Would Never Consider Offering	Something Our Company Would Consider Offering
Employee Stock Ownership Plans	☐	☐	☐
Experimental drug coverage	☐	☐	☐
Final average pay pension	☐	☐	☐
Fitness center	☐	☐	☐
Flat benefit pension	☐	☐	☐
Guaranteed severance	☐	☐	☐
Legal services	☐	☐	☐
Life insurance	☐	☐	☐
Long-term disability	☐	☐	☐
Major medical	☐	☐	☐
Mortgage payment for one month each year	☐	☐	☐
Noncontributory benefits	☐	☐	☐
Paid personal days	☐	☐	☐
Paid sick leave	☐	☐	☐
Paid vacation	☐	☐	☐
Pension trust fund	☐	☐	☐
Prenatal programs	☐	☐	☐
Prescription plan	☐	☐	☐
Savings plan	☐	☐	☐
Smoking cessation program	☐	☐	☐
Stock purchase plan	☐	☐	☐
Stress reduction programs	☐	☐	☐
Term life insurance	☐	☐	☐
Training	☐	☐	☐
Transportation reimbursement	☐	☐	☐
Tuition reimbursement (employee and children)	☐	☐	☐
Vision plan	☐	☐	☐
Weight loss program	☐	☐	☐
Well-baby programs	☐	☐	☐

SAMPLE OFFERINGS

The following represents the variety of compensation and benefits perks offered by employers.

Monetary Awards

▲ Managers at the Veterans Administration Philadelphia Regional Office and Insurance Center spontaneously give twenty-five dollars to workers they believe are doing an exceptional job.

▲ Pitney Bowes, headquartered in Stamford, Connecticut, gives out twenty-five dollar savings bonds for the best questions submitted at the annual stockholders' meeting.

▲ Great Western Drilling Company in Midland, Texas, offers a twenty-five dollar savings bond to the employee who asks the most challenging question to the president at the company communication meetings.

▲ Celestial Seasonings in Boulder, Colorado, gives every employee a twenty-five dollar check on his or her birthday, fifty dollars at Thanksgiving, and one hundred dollars at Christmas.

▲ At Delta Business Systems in Orlando, Florida, secretaries and administrative assistants compete monthly for a fifty dollar award for "Most Valuable Associate," each dispatcher can earn up to forty dollars a month by scheduling preventive maintenance calls, and workers in the company's warehouses can divide up to four hundred dollars every two months if they function smoothly as a team.

▲ At the Internal Revenue Service, cash awards ranging from one hundred dollars to four thousand dollars are given for productive ideas.

▲ Temps & Company, based in Washington, D.C., gives out quarterly one hundred dollar rewards to employees who admit mistakes they have made on the job.

▲ Remington Products in Bridgeport, Connecticut, maintains a $25,000 discretionary fund to give instant cash recognition to workers who have been spotted by their supervisors doing an exceptional job.

▲ At Gunneson Group International, a total quality consulting firm in Landing, New Jersey, employees receive a cash award of 1 to 5 percent of the gross sale when they bring in new business to the company.

▲ Quad/Graphics, a printing company in Pewaukee, Wisconsin, pays employees two hundred dollars if they quit smoking for a year.

▲ Coupons worth thirty-five dollars, redeemable for gifts, are given to employees at Wells Fargo Bank in San Francisco for extra effort.

▲ Employees at the Naval Publications and Forms Center in Philadelphia have a chance to earn a top award of $35,000 for an outstanding suggestion.

▲ At Communication Briefings/Newstrack communications services in Blackwood, New Jersey, "Employee Recognition Coupons" are redeemable for gift certificates.

▲ Taylor Corporation, a printing company in North Mankato, Minnesota, uses catalog selections instead of year-end bonuses, allowing employees to choose items they want.

▲ The fibers department at E.I. duPont de Nemours & Co. in Wilmington, Delaware, has an Achievement Sharing program in which all employees put 6 percent of their salary at risk and are paid a sliding percentage of the amount based on how close their department comes to its annual goals. Less than 80 percent means no increase; 80 to 100 percent means a 3 to 6 percent increase; and 101 to 150 percent means an increase of 7 to 19 percent.

▲ Solar Press, a direct-mail and packaging business based in Naperville, Illinois, has an incentive system that generates bonuses based on production rates.

Health and Wellness

▲ In an effort to lower healthcare costs, Quill Corporation of Lincolnshire, Illinois, which distributes office supplies and equipment, estimates its healthcare costs for six months and places the money in a pool. If funds remain in the pool at the end of the six months, they are divided equally among participating employees. Healthcare costs for the company declined approximately 35 percent in each of the first two years of the program.

▲ Security Pacific employees receive up to a year's worth of counseling for personal problems.

▲ At Time Inc., employees get free physical exams after five years of service.

▲ Tenneco, Inc., the Houston-based pipeline operator and manufacturer of farm and construction equipment, provides a health and fitness facility complete with all the clothing employees need for a workout.

▲ IBM provides health classes and physical examinations.

▲ Employees at Johnson & Johnson have access to a large fitness center that includes a comprehensive program in which enrollees undergo a physical examination and then have professionals guide them in a physical fitness regimen.

▲ As an incentive for staying healthy, Johnson Wax deposits $300 in every employee's flexible health plan at the beginning of each year to be used to pay for healthcare charges not covered by the company's health plan. Unused money in the account at the end of the year is paid to the employee in cash.

▲ Mesa, the Dallas oil company, gives workers up to $700 a year in bonuses if they exercise three times a week, don't smoke, don't take sick days, and don't submit major medical claims. Since the program started, the company has cut healthcare costs to 25 percent below the industry average.

▲ Westinghouse in Pittsburgh gives $200 annual bonuses to workers who do ten minutes of aerobic exercise three times a week for at least nine months a year. The company estimates it saves close to $2,000 annually on every fit versus unfit employee.

▲ Reader's Digest reimburses up to 50 percent of the cost of health club memberships for its employees.

▲ Steelcase, Inc., based in Grand Rapids, Michigan, has a minihospital staffed by nurses and physicians. The company also employs a psychologist and social workers to counsel people for free, on company time or after hours.

▲ Southern California Edison has staff physicians and part-time specialists to provide for its employees.

Vacation

▲ Employees at Polaroid, based in Cambridge, Massachusetts, get to choose by vote one paid holiday a year in addition to the nine regular ones provided by the company.

▲ At Apple Computer in Cupertino, California, all employees were granted an extra week's paid vacation when the company had its first $100 million sales quarter.

▲ After seven years at Intel Corporation—a manufacturer of semiconductors, memories, computer systems, and software in Santa Clara, California—employees become eligible for eight weeks off, with full pay, on top of their regular three-week vacation.

▲ At Moog Automotive, a St. Louis manufacturer of electrohydraulic control products, employees can take a seven-week vacation on their tenth anniversary. If employees don't want to take the time off, they can take money instead.

▲ The H.B. Fuller Company, a St. Paul maker of glues, adhesives, and sealants, extends a special bonus vacation every five years starting on an employee's tenth anniversary. At the tenth, fifteenth, and twentieth year and every fifth year thereafter, a person gets an extra two weeks off with pay as well as $800 to spend on a vacation.

▲ Pitney Bowes gives employees with twenty-five years of service an extra month's vacation. The same benefit is then offered to that employee every fifth year thereafter.

Stock Ownership

▲ At D'Agostino's, the supermarket chain headquartered in New Rochelle, New York, every employee, including part-time workers, is eligible for the gain sharing program. Stores that exceed their budgeted profit goals for the quarter share most of the excess with their employees.

▲ All employees of Tandem Computers, based in Cupertino, California, are eligible for stock options. When stock was first publicly offered, employees were given the right to purchase three hundred shares at a future date. Every year since, all employees have been given one hundred share options.

▲ At Citibank's Diners Club subsidiary, outstanding customer service can earn an employee $400 worth of stock.

▲ All full-time workers who have spent at least a year at Publix Super Markets in Lakeland, Florida participate in an Employee Stock Ownership Plan.

(Among the largest ESOPs in the United States are Publix Super Markets, HealthTrust, Avis, Science Applications, EPIC Healthcare, Charter Medical, Parsons Corporation, Weirton Steel, Avondale Shipyards, and Dan River Company.)

▲ Marion Laboratories in Kansas City, Missouri, offers each employee stock options. After being with the company for one year, an employee can purchase up to one hundred shares of stock at any time during the next ten years at the price it sold for that first anniversary date.

Transportation

▲ Tenneco, Inc., has a large fleet of vans to pick up workers, covers most of the cost for monthly bus passes, and subsidizes parking expenses for car pools.

▲ Reader's Digest subsidizes employee van pools.

▲ Physio-Control Corporation subsidizes a bus service during off-hours for employees who are working odd shifts.

▲ Xerox Corporation in Stamford, Connecticut, gives workers discounts off monthly bus or train passes, subsidizes van pools, and provides preferential parking for car pools and van pools.

▲ More than a thousand companies in the New York metropolitan area give out transitCheks to their employees for buses, subways, ferries, and commuter railroads.

SUMMARY

A company's compensation program sends a message to employees about its commitment to motivating, recognizing, and rewarding employee performance. While money should certainly never be the only motivator for potential hires, it is indisputably important. Hence, every organization needs a compensation philosophy that identifies its desired market position—that is, where it wants to position pay levels with respect to competitive market practice. Once this philosophy is established, an organization can decide what elements of a total pay program are most appropriate given its business objectives and corporate culture. That said, in addition to establishing fair and competitive base pay scales, businesses should consider other monetary means to attract and retain top workers, including signing bonuses, merit increases, and variable pay.

There are many indications that benefits mean more to employees than pay. Company benefits can encompass a wide range of offerings from standard medical insurance to more innovative perks like prepaid legal services. Applicants who are comparing job offers often narrow their choices down to those that provide the most generous benefits package. Whether offering comprehensive medical benefits, a pension plan, stock options, or legal services, experts agree that employers would do best to remain flexible and competitive in their offerings.

NOTES

1. *HR Magazine,* April 1998.

Chapter 4

Recruitment Sources and Techniques

"Help wanted. Pulse needed."
—Want ad

T here was a time when applicants went looking for a job only to be told, "Sorry, we don't have any openings." That's certainly not the case these days. Employers are, of necessity, approaching recruitment more proactively as they compete to attract prime candidates to their organizations. They are carefully weighing the benefits and drawbacks of various recruitment resources and sometimes abandoning traditional sources, substituting more creative techniques. In addition, employers are turning increasingly to electronic recruiting to fill jobs. With regard to the latter, approximately 96 percent of all U.S. employers now are going online to recruit. (Chapter 5 discusses electronic recruitment at length.)

RECRUITMENT METHODOLOGY

Deciding which recruitment source to tap each time you have an opening can be challenging. Some organizations simply ignore the multitude of options and resort to using the same sources each time. This isn't a good idea. Aside from the possibility that market conditions and certain internal factors may have changed, thereby impacting the effectiveness of the resource, there is the possibility that this practice could lead to charges of systemic discrimination—that is, some element of your hiring process is inherently discriminatory. Even though inadvertent, the disparate effect produced by systemic discrimination may develop into a prime area of vulnerability for employers. Relying on the same recruitment source each time a particular position becomes available could have an adverse impact on members of certain protected groups lacking the same access as others to that source. This, in turn, could translate into the denial of equal employment opportunity.

As complex as the arena of recruitment sources and techniques may be, then, it's wise to explore your options each time there's an opening. The process becomes more manageable if you first consider four factors:

1. *How much money is available.* The amount of money allocated for recruitment can reduce your options considerably. For example, display ads and search firms can run into big bucks, with no guarantee that they will produce a substantial number of qualified candidates. On the other hand, some of the most effective recruitment sources cost very little or nothing at all.

2. *How quickly the opening must be filled.* No matter how well you anticipate staffing needs, an opening can occur suddenly and unexpectedly, especially in a tight labor market where employees sometimes leave without giving notice. When this happens, focus on recruitment sources most likely to yield immediate results. In such instances, advertising in professional journals, attending job fairs, or running an open house takes too long. On the other hand, going through your HR files of past applicants may prove effective, since these candidates have already been interviewed and assessed (although their resumes need to be updated). More important, they have already expressed an interest in working for your company.

3. *Whether a wide audience must be reached.* Some positions are highly specialized and more difficult to fill. To improve the chances of a job match, then, you want to reach as many candidates as possible. Also, if you are uncertain as to the type of individual being sought, interview as many applicants as possible. Employment agencies and search firms may be helpful in these instances; ads in newspapers and journals can also be effective.

4. *The exemption level of the available position.* Recruitment sources that produce qualified exempt or professional candidates do not always work as well for nonexempt applicants. Effective resources for exempt-level, professional positions include direct mail recruitment, search firms, campus recruiting, job fairs, research firms, and professional associations. Nonexempt applicants

are frequently found via employee referrals, high school guidance counselors, government agencies, advertisements in the classified section of newspapers, and employment agencies. In addition, most walk-in candidates are looking for nonexempt-level employment.

Of the factors indicated—cost, immediacy, audience, and level—each recruitment source may meet some of your criteria, but not others. Employers are advised to explore the ramifications of utilizing each resource in relation to these four factors, deciding which of the factors are most important for each job opening. Newspaper ads provide a prime example. They are expensive (failing criterion number one), but more likely to yield immediate results (meeting criterion number two). Assuming they appear in the most-likely-to-be-read section of an appropriate paper, on the right day of the week, at the right time of year, and contain the necessary text, newspaper ads will reach a wide audience consisting of the level you are trying to reach (meeting criteria numbers three and four).

After examining these four criteria, consider too how aggressive you need to be in order to fill a particular opening. If immediacy is a primary factor, search out proactive recruitment sources that will make a concerted effort to find employees. This is the reverse of reactive recruitment, where you wait for applicants to apply, hoping that the right person is among them.

Some recruitment sources are inherently reactive and by their very nature prohibit recruiters from aggressively pursuing candidates. The responsibility for finding applicants is placed elsewhere. Consider one of the most popular recruitment sources: employee referrals. HR provides current employees with the job description and a laundry list of requirements for an opening, then waits to see who is referred and applies. The onus for referring candidates is on the employees. This is fine and also cost-effective, if time is not a factor. Perhaps you have an employee who wants to retire but is willing to wait until a replacement is found. Or maybe one department is thinking about creating a new position with no pressure to fill it immediately. Whatever the scenario, time is not a key issue; hence, reactive recruitment can work under the right circumstances. More often than not, however, time is crucial. When an employee resigns, giving two week's notice if you're lucky, you must move fast. That means being proactive in your attempts to find a replacement.

Proactive recruiters start recruitment efforts as soon as they learn that there will be an opening. They expand their recruitment pool to encompass other than traditional recruiting sources and aggressively go after candidates, luring them with attractive employment packages.

Being proactive means more than avoiding a lengthy gap between the time an incumbent vacates a position and the time someone new is hired. It also provides a clearer shot at attracting prime candidates and making a hiring decision after interviewing a number of qualified applicants. That's because you are in control of those targeted as candidates. With direct mail recruiting, for example, employers contact specific candidates known to have certain skills and knowledge. While the response rate is usually low, around 2 percent, you know at least that those responding are viable candidates.

Another example of proactive recruitment is preemployment training that provides a supplemental workforce. These are employees recruited through conventional means over time, and then trained in job- and industry-specific areas. They are then placed in a standby pool. When there is an opening, employers can turn to their supplemental workforce and select a suitable candidate. Of course, there is no guarantee that the right person will remain in the pool, waiting to be offered a job.

Professional associations and inter-HR networking can also provide employers with the opportunity to recruit proactively. Direct contact with potential employees or communication with others in your field can often put you in touch with qualified applicants.

This is not to say that you should never use reactive recruitment sources. Rather, identify each recruitment source as being proactive or reactive so you can gauge how involved you are likely to be in the recruitment process.

TRADITIONAL RECRUITMENT SOURCES

Despite the fiercely competitive nature of recruiting, many employers still turn to traditional recruitment sources, at least initially. Some of these are reactive in nature. According to a joint survey conducted by the Society for Human Resource Management (SHRM) and Aon Consulting, the top ten sources of job applicants are as follows:

1. Employee referrals
2. Newspaper ads

3. Recruiting firms
4. College recruitment
5. Contingent firms
6. Job fairs
7. The Internet
8. Targeted minority recruiting
9. Walk-ins
10. Government employment services

Let's look at each of them.

Employee Referrals

Employee referrals have traditionally resulted in the hiring of prime employees and also serve to boost morale. This recruitment technique entails having employees spread the word among friends and acquaintances as soon as a position becomes available. To make this approach more effective, employers typically offer incentives of varying worth.

Such awards or bonuses are often in the form of cash, generally ranging from $25 for nonexempt referrals to several thousand dollars for executive positions. Other forms of incentive include savings bonds, gift certificates, and drawings for prizes such as televisions and trips. The value of the award usually ties in with the level of the position filled, with higher-level positions yielding greater awards.

Employee referral programs are more likely to succeed if employees have a clear understanding of the duties and responsibilities of the available position. In addition, employees must be clear as to how the referral program works, e.g., how long the referred employee must remain in the job and the minimum level evaluation the person must receive before the award is given. On the plus side, employees respond favorably to the incentives offered. These incentives usually cost the company considerably less than expenditures for other recruitment sources, such as advertising or search firms. Exercise caution, however, in overusing employee referrals. Because it has been shown that "like tends to refer like" (for example, white males tend to associate with and therefore refer mostly other white males), women and minorities may not receive equal employment opportunities if they are not proportionately recommended.

Newspaper Ads

Advertising in newspapers remains a popular and often effective means for attracting applicants. Four powerful ad placement strategies can help ensure the generation of a large response:

1. Capture the job hunter's attention through the location of the ad in the newspaper, appropriate job title, creative graphics, color, use of white space, clever job-related language, tasteful humor, and placement of a logo.
2. Keep the job hunter's attention by providing enough information to pique the reader's interest as well as allow him or her to establish compatibility between your needs and his or her skills. This may include information concerning key duties, key responsibilities, and the work environment.
3. Leave out some information, forcing those interested to establish contact in order to learn more.
4. Make your ad the last one the job hunter will want to read by using language that creates a strong, positive image of what working for your company would be like.

In addition, cross-reference your ads under at least one other appropriate title.

Recruiting Firms

There are two types of recruiting firms: search firms and employment agencies. Generally, search firms handle professional openings, while employment agencies recruit for nonexempt jobs. Organizations turn to employment agencies and search firms to access a large labor pool and to fill positions more quickly than is feasible on their own. But companies tend to shy away from recruiting firms because of the high cost. Before agreeing to register an opening with a recruiting firm, consider these guidelines:

1. Be certain the firm will evaluate applicants and refer only those who meet the standards stipulated.
2. Be definite about the job's requirements.
3. Ask for a written agreement detailing the fee arrangement.
4. Be selective in determining which firms receive your business.
5. Formally notify all firms with which you are working that you are an equal opportunity employer.

It's also a good idea to encourage agency representatives to learn as much as possible about both your company and the specific job opening. The more information an agency has, the better able it will be to meet your needs effectively and expeditiously.

The traditional compensation arrangements between recruiting firms and employers are changing. Increasingly, firms are being compensated, in part, with stock options or gain sharing. With stock options, as much as half of a recruiter's fee could be in equity. With gain sharing, no equity changes hands, but a recruiter's fees are boosted over time if the candidates placed excel and add value to the company. These arrangements can benefit both the recruiters and the companies: Recruiters stand to make a lot more money than through traditional fee arrangements, and companies gain by having recruiters take a vested interest in the long-term outlook for the company, rather than focusing on quick profits.

These practices, while more prevalent in the technology field, are catching on in other fields as well.

College Recruitment

College recruitment is on the rise. Among those industries that have increased their hiring of college graduates, according to a survey of employers by the National Association of Colleges and Employers, are the following: computer and business equipment manufacturers (66 percent increase), computer software development employers (36 percent increase), automotive and mechanical equipment manufacturers (32 percent increase), banks (29 percent increase), consulting organizations (17 percent increase), and merchandisers (15 percent increase).

In general, college students are attracted to companies that enjoy a good reputation, are successful, will look impressive on their resumes, have shown an interest in their school over a long period of time, and keep up with technological change. To gain students' attention, many employers are replacing traditional company recruitment brochures with technological tools. Often, this means distributing CD-ROM presentations that include more than the traditional recounting of company history, products, services, customers, work environment, and culture, and answers to typical questions. Students today are looking for more concrete information, such as what life is like in the company, how people treat each other, and any bad publicity the company has received recently. The CD-ROM offers students a comprehensive sense of what working for the company would be like. Some companies substitute CD-

ROM presentations for on-campus information sessions, cutting travel costs for recruiting in half. Increasingly, companies also set up home pages on the Internet to broaden their exposure and use videoconferencing to interview students "live."

Contingent Firms

Contingent workers carry their portable skills from job to job. Their work is literally contingent on an employer's needs. Traditionally thought of as clerical temps, today's contingent workers provide services in every field, at every level. Extensive information concerning contingent-help firms and contingent workers is provided in Chapter 7.

Job Fairs

Job fairs allow company representatives, usually over a period of two days, to interview numerous applicants, often from a specialized field or population. Companies can host their own fairs or participate in those run by others, paying a flat fee to interview and subsequently hire a possibly unlimited number of qualified candidates. To get the most for your money, conduct brief interviews during the job fair; this way, a maximum number of candidates can be screened, with potential employees set up for full interviews at a later date. Often, businesses are able to hire several people for what it would otherwise cost to hire one employee using a search firm. On the other hand, it's possible that you will walk away empty-handed, having found no suitable candidates.

The Internet

The primary advantages to recruiting online are cost, speed, a reduction in paperwork, and access to a greater number of candidates. Disadvantages include a lack of breadth of reach, attracting inappropriate or unqualified responses, and difficulty in tracking resumes. As previously indicated, electronic recruiting is discussed in greater detail in Chapter 5.

Targeted Minority Recruiting

The term *minority* encompasses a broad spectrum of ethnic groups including, but not limited to, African-Americans, Hispanics (e.g.,

Puerto Ricans, Cuban- and Mexican-Americans, and people originally from more than twenty additional Central and South American nations and Spain), Asian-Americans (e.g., Korean-, Japanese-, Chinese-, and Filipino-Americans), and Native Americans. Recruiters can develop and maintain an ongoing relationship with various minority professional associations as sources of job candidates. In addition, you can view your company's own minority employees as a minority recruitment source by training existing staff for higher-level jobs.

Walk-Ins

Interviewing walk-ins can be especially productive, because they might meet the requirements of hard-to-fill positions. These positions are generally nonexempt. Interviewing walk-ins is also cost-effective.

Government Employment Services

State or federal employment agencies, which screen and refer many applicants, usually for entry-level or nonspecialized positions, are cost free. Because they generally keep detailed EEO records, government agencies can be counted on to assist in furthering an organization's affirmative action goals. An additional advantage is that candidates referred by government agencies are currently unemployed and can usually begin working immediately. Unfortunately, government agencies frequently refer unqualified applicants despite the specified requirements. In addition, the agencies are more prone to challenge the reasons offered for rejecting a candidate.

ADDITIONAL RECRUITMENT SOURCES

Here are additional recruitment sources you may want to try.

Clients and Customers

Applicants referred by clients and customers come with personal recommendations. In addition, you can probably learn more about their work habits than through references from former employers.

Deciding against a candidate referred by a client or customer, however, can lead to strained business relations, as can hiring a referral only to end up disciplining or terminating that person.

Of course, you can also recruit customers and clients. You have probably already learned a great deal about their skills, abilities, and interests, facilitating a preliminary determination as to whether they would be assets to your company. Be careful, however, about stealing from the competition. It could damage future business relations as well as your reputation.

Direct Mail

Direct mail targets specific individuals for a job match. The first step in this process is defining the prospective applicants to be contacted. Since the customary response rate is between 0.5 and 2 percent, you need to work from several different mailing lists to generate any kind of a meaningful return. These lists can be obtained through professional associations, business directories, trade groups, and magazine subscription data. *Direct Mail List Rates and Data* (published by Standard Rate and Data Service, Inc., 5201 Old Orchard Road, Skokie, Illinois 60077), can offer additional assistance. You may also opt to hire the services of direct mail specialists or consultants to help plan and implement your mail campaign.

If you are embarking on an extensive mailing effort, it is advisable to hire a mailing house to fold, stuff, seal, and mail the solicitations. If, however, the mailing list is rather small, you can handle these tasks yourself. Obtain a copy of the "Mailer's Guide" from your local post office for guidance.

Direct mail campaigns often fail because recipients do not even open the envelope. This problem can be mitigated by putting an attention-getter on the outside. However, teasers—such as "We want to give you $75,000!"—may be viewed as unprofessional and therefore not advisable. On the other hand, it is acceptable to print "Personal" or "Confidential" on the outside. Not only is it more likely that the addressee will open the envelope but others, such as clerks or secretaries, are less likely to do so. The letter should contain a clear, brief, easy-to-read message. The first sentence should inform the reader of your purpose and interest. Include information about the requirements of the job, its duties, responsibilities, and benefits. Try to anticipate any relevant questions an applicant might ask, and provide appropriate answers. Enclose a response card or ask to be contacted by telephone. If possible, provide a brochure or CD-ROM promoting your company.

One final suggestion: Ask for a referral. Your initial prospect may not be interested in the position but may know of someone who is.

HR Files

It is quite possible that a job seeker applied for a similar position with your company not too long ago and although not hired was a viable candidate. Maybe there were several qualified applicants at that time. Or perhaps there were no suitable openings when this individual applied. It's also possible that the applicant's salary requirements exceeded the amount then being offered.

When scanning HR files for existing applications, carefully compare background and skills with the requirements of the newly available position. Also, review the notes of the previous interviewer and, if possible, talk to that person. The previous interviewer may recall the applicant well enough to provide you with valuable insights.

Job Posting

Job posting encourages current staff to apply for openings. Promoting or transferring employees from within offers several advantages: It usually creates an opening at a lower, easier-to-fill level; the company saves considerable time and money by transferring a worker already familiar with the organizational structure and methodology; employee morale is boosted; and hidden talent may be uncovered.

Some organizations have a policy of posting all openings; others post only nonexempt positions. Some steer clear of job posting altogether. Reasons for this include the following:

▲ Supervisors and managers may want to promote someone they have groomed for a particular position. Therefore, they are reluctant to consider other candidates.
▲ Some managers may resent employees who apply for jobs outside their department, taking a move personally.
▲ Losing an employee to job posting may mean a less qualified replacement in the employee's old position.
▲ Some companies prefer to bring in "new blood" rather than recycle existing employees.

The success of a job-posting system depends largely on how well it is designed and monitored.

Military Recruiting

Military personnel frequently have a great deal of hands-on experience in a variety of tasks. They tend to have a strong work ethic and understand organizational structure. Other advantages include a background of providing support, both up and down the chain of command, and prior training in teaming as well as managing. In addition, the physical fitness requirements of military service lead to veterans who tend to be healthy employees. This can translate into reduced costs for healthcare claims and fewer workdays lost to illness. Of particular significance in today's tight labor market is the fact that 45 percent of the 200,000 people coming out of the military each year are under age 25 and have up-to-date technical skills.

A growing number of employers are taking advantage of the military as a viable recruitment source. Here are some of them:

▲ Litton, a company located in West Conshohocken, Pennsylvania, that designs and develops information technology systems, saved more than $200,000 by hiring eighteen veterans over a two-year period.

▲ General Electric hires a reported two hundred junior military officers each year.

▲ Timeplex Group, a Clearwater, Florida–based computer network consulting firm, has hired dozens of personnel from the Defense Outplacement Referral System.

▲ Goodyear Tire & Rubber Co. received an award from the American Legion for its efforts in hiring veterans.

There are several programs that can facilitate your company's publication of job openings and recruitment from the ranks. Many of these are free: the Retired Officers Association (703-838-0537), the Army Career and Alumni Program (www.acap.army.mil), the Non-Commissioned Officers' Association (www.ncoausa.org), and Transition Assistance Online (www.taonline.com).

Open Houses

Organizations hosting an open house generally place newspaper ads stretching across numerous geographic locations. These ads announce a recruitment drive on specific dates. Unless the company is well-known, a lengthy description of the company's products and reputation is included, along with its benefits packages. All available jobs, with starting salaries or salary ranges, are listed as well. On the date advertised for the open house, company recruiters gather to greet and interview interested candidates. Either hiring decisions are made during the open house, or arrangements are made for more in-depth interviews later on company premises.

An open house is usually a risky proposition in terms of cost and time. It is difficult to predict whether there will be a large turnout of qualified candidates or if such candidates will ultimately be hired. Prescreening applicants by telephone or asking them to submit resumes in advance are two ways of safeguarding against a disappointing result.

Outplacement Firms

Outplacement firms are generally retained by companies to help higher-level managers and executives find new employment following termination. Lower-level management and nonexempt workers who have lost their jobs through plant closings or other major workforce reductions may be provided with partial or group outplacement services. While outplacement firms can be very effective for those seeking guidance in finding new employment, they can also be a valuable recruitment source. Most of these firms are staffed with generalists who do not specialize in placing people in particular occupations or fields. Therefore, they may know of a number of candidates meeting various job specifications. In addition, the immediate availability of candidates referred by outplacement firms can be a big plus.

One significant disadvantage of interviewing outplacement firm referrals is that these candidates may not provide a clear overview of their intangible qualities. The traumatic experience of losing a job and the stress of having to market oneself, added to the pressure of finding new employment, can greatly impact an applicant's self-image. This, in turn, affects how the applicant comes across and is perceived by the interviewer.

Professional Associations

Most employers agree that a primary benefit of joining a professional association is the opportunity to network with colleagues from other organizations. For HR specialists, this can mean exchanging information about the market in general and about specific job openings, accompanied by abbreviated job descriptions, in particular. If your colleagues' lists bring to mind some viable candidates you have either interviewed or whose resume/application you have reviewed, you can share this information assuming you have the applicants' permission to do so. Hopefully, your colleagues will do the same for you. In addition to the cost-effectiveness of these exchanges, you may benefit from receiving a professional impression from your peers of particular candidates.

A variation on this technique is to join professional associations in those fields related to your recruitment responsibilities. The associations' membership directories, mailing lists, placement services, and publications could provide the names of your company's future employees.

Radio and Television

There are two main advantages to using radio or television advertising to fill an opening. First, you can appeal to a large audience in a short period of time. Second, you can reach and tempt prospects not actually looking for a job. This can be a real plus when you have a hard-to-fill position.

In the past, employers have tended to shy away from radio and television advertising primarily because of the cost. But radio and television have become more accessible media. The growth of independent stations and cable television has created greater opportunities for employers with limited budgets.

Proponents of radio advertising emphasize that radio often reaches people when "their guard is down"—that is, when they are not necessarily thinking about job hunting. For example, they may have the radio on while getting ready for work in the morning or sitting in traffic, commuting to and from work. Companies looking for candidates in technical fields should determine which music stations candidates prefer in order to run ads on those stations. This is a valuable resource since many technical people are also musicians (music and technology are said to use the same side of the brain).

Television advertising receives high marks from supporters because aspects of the job can be demonstrated as well as described. Done well, this can encourage job seekers to respond.

Research Firms

Research firms can be described as abbreviated versions of full-service executive search firms, providing essentially one-half the services. Their primary function is to supply organizations with information about potential high-level employees; the interviews and evaluations are then up to the employers. Research firms generally charge by the hour, rather than on a percentage basis, although some offer flat-rate fees.

Research firms are most useful when a company is looking for a cost-effective way to recruit top-level professionals or when more hands-on involvement in the interviewing process is desired. The *Executive Search Research Directory* provides a list of research firms. It may be obtained by contacting the Recruiting and Search Report at 800-634-4548.

BEST PRACTICES

Let's look at how three companies successfully approach recruitment by using traditional sources.

Best Practice: Mirage Resorts Inc.

Mirage Resorts, headquartered in Las Vegas, Nevada, employs approximately 18,000 workers at four locations. Recently, the hotel chain opened two new casino-hotels—the Mirage Resort, and Treasure Island. Each site staffed more than four hundred types of jobs in a five-month period using advertising as its primary recruitment source. Ads were placed in the local newspapers several months before the hotels opened. The Mirage ad read: "We're looking for 5,000 people who wouldn't mind working in a tropical rain forest with live sharks and a volcano that erupts every 30 minutes." The Treasure Island ad read: "We're looking for ruffians, scalawags, and other people who don't mind a good fight while they're working." The clever wording of the Mirage ad generated 57,000 applications, and the equally intriguing Treasure Island ad resulted in 80,000 responses.

Every applicant was required to complete a questionnaire on company premises before being screened by company representatives. At the Mirage, 22,000 applicants were eliminated at this stage; at Treasure Island, 29,000 were cut. Those who passed the first screening were seen by the head of the department to which they applied. Asking competency-based questions, the interviewers explored each candidate's communications skills, prior work experience, job stability, and other job-specific skills. Background reference checks and drug tests were then conducted.

As a result of this process, the Mirage ultimately hired a total of 7,400 people, and Treasure Island hired 5,800. Each new hire received extensive department training and orientation, culminating in certification for each of the fifteen to twenty tasks specific to each job. To "try out" their new jobs before the hotel opened, new hires participated in role-playing exercises called Play Days. Half of the hotel personnel performed the jobs while the other half assumed the role of guests. The groups then switched. Play days utilized 60 to 140 HR personnel at each location during various points in the process.

Mirage Resorts believes its selective staffing process creates a competitive advantage. The company has the lowest turnover in the industry, averaging 12 percent a year for all jobs. Management turnover is 2.5 percent.

Best Practice: Hallmark Cards Inc.

Hallmark Cards, located in Kansas City, Missouri, employs approximately 19,600 full-time employees. Its staffing strategy is to recruit, develop, and promote a diverse mix of new college talent and seasoned professionals. Potential employees are drawn to Hallmark by its brand name, emphasis on diversity, and reputation for stability. Turnover at Hallmark is low and tenure is high. For these and other reasons, Hallmark is considered one of the one hundred best companies to work for in the United States.

Despite its fine reputation, the company still approaches recruitment aggressively. Hallmark's college recruitment strategy is to hire diverse, high-quality candidates in the most efficient and effective manner possible. The company recruits at twenty-five to thirty undergraduate and graduate schools, primarily in the Midwest. On average, Hallmark hires fifty to seventy-five students each year to work in the Kansas City headquarters as interns or entry-level staff in business marketing, business services, retail support, field sales, business research, purchasing, finance, manufacturing, distribution, engineering, human resources, and information technology.

In determining which schools to target, Hallmark considers its past success rate of hiring students from the school, the performance of those individuals hired, and the diversity of the school's student body.

Hallmark's recruiting efforts are year-round, with increased activity in the fall and the spring. The company frequently invites college representatives to visit the company to gain greater insight into its operations and the kind of work environment offered. The company has three recruiters, often joined by a team of line managers, to help make campus presentations. Hallmark recruiters go through training, and accountability is a factor in their performance reviews.

In addition to its internships, Hallmark has a career development program that rotates students through various project management roles. This is geared to those employees demonstrating managerial potential. The company also actively solicits qualified minority candidates by participating in career fairs and attending minority conventions such as the National Black MBA Conference and the National Society of Hispanic MBA Conference. Hallmark also advertises in *Black Enterprise*, *The Black Collegian*, *Hispanic* magazine, and *Winds of Change*. In regard to minority hiring, the company has received many honors, including recognition as one of "The 50 Best Places for Blacks to Work" (from *Black Enterprise* magazine), one of the top one hundred companies providing opportunities for Hispanics (*Hispanic* magazine), and one of the best companies for minorities (in the book *The Best Companies for Minorities*).

Hallmark uses a global measurement for evaluating the impact of its recruiting strategy: It looks at the success of the company. It also analyzes more direct measurements of individual performance, namely the promotion and retention rates of those individuals employed through college recruiting.

Best Practice: General Motors Corporation

This Detroit automotive giant—with more than 450,000 employees—faced a major recruiting challenge when constructing its information technology (IT) operations from the ground up. The evolving IT Division needed about three hundred leaders in technology, telecom, networking, business process engineering, systems engineering, and processes (including manufacturing, engineering, sales, finance, purchasing, human resources, communications, quality, and legal). Three staff members were selected to devote full energy to the challenging recruitment effort. In addition to lining up internal candidates, they functioned as liaisons to the recruiting firms with which GM elected to work, reviewing resumes of qualified candidates and arranging interviews.

GM identified specific criteria for selecting recruiting firms, including strong customer service, high quality of candidates, history of IT recruiting success, quick turnaround time, a reputation for being an ethical business partner, diversity of candidate pool, knowledge of GM, and the ability to present as well as sell information to candidates.

GM paid particular attention to out-of-town candidates, recognizing that, in addition to selling the job, recruiters had to sell the Detroit area to potential employees, many of whom were considering positions in more desirable U.S. cities. Accordingly, on-site vendors arranged tours of the city and arranged for realtors to show prospective hires various neighborhoods so they could evaluate the housing market. GM also provided information on schools, entertainment, sporting events, cultural activities, and weather patterns.

When it came time to extend offers, GM found that, given the specific requirements of the IT industry and difficulty in finding quality candidates, it had to be flexible with regard to its compensation structure and benefits packages, especially concerning such issues as vacation time and stock awards.

To evaluate the results of its IT staffing efforts, HR examined turnover. At the time of this writing, almost all of the three hundred IT executives hired have remained with GM. The company's focus on retention reflects its effort to remain competitive within the industry, provide challenges and interesting job opportunities for employees, as well as maintain a productive work environment.

CREATIVE STAFFING SOLUTIONS

When traditional recruitment sources don't yield the results you need in terms of quality candidates or timelines, consider more creative recruitment solutions.

Airplane Banners

Flown over sporting events and rock concerts, airplane banners can capture the attention of 40,000 to 50,000 would-be employees in a matter of hours. 1-800-Sky-Write, in Long Beach, California, is one of several companies that advertise in the sky. The company flies aerial banners for theme parks, fast-food companies, aerospace companies, and computer companies, among others, that are seeking employees. The cost for the service runs about $375 per hour, depending on the area. Banners are usually flown for two to three hours at a time.

Banners and Signs

You can use banners and signs as successful recruitment tools if your business occupies a separate building that is located on a main street. Drape a banner across the front of your building or post a sign inviting customers, clients, and passersby to stop in to inquire about employment opportunities. The banner or sign can simply state that there are jobs available, or it can list the openings, which requires that you prepare a new banner or sign each time a different job needs to be filled. Companies using this technique can also list their main benefits to lure potential employees. Also, unless the nature of your business is well-known or has name recognition, identify your product in a few words. Be sure to specify if interested candidates should walk-in to apply or call for an appointment.

Banners and signs are real "you never know" recruitment sources. The investment is minimal, but the payoff could be substantial.

Billboard Advertising

Billboard advertising is still a relatively new and virtually unexplored recruitment source. Since most people view billboards while driving, often at high speeds, they do not have much time to take in the details (unless, of course, they are stuck in traffic). Therefore, an effective billboard ad must catch one's eye immediately, offering a limited amount of information that the average driver can both understand and remember, since it's unlikely that pad and pen are handy. This usually limits a company to a statement about employment advantages, available jobs, an enlarged logo, company name, and phone number in an easy-to-recall format. Since so many drivers use car phones, encouraging calls at all hours can increase the number of applicants who respond.

Billboard ads seem to work most effectively for hotel/motel chains, restaurants, and airlines, and are generally targeted toward nonexempt-level workers.

Bumper Sticker Advertisements

Like billboard advertisements, bumper sticker ads are a relatively new and as yet unexplored recruitment source. Space is limited, and there is not much one can do to make the stickers outstanding visually. Also, unless someone is stuck in traffic directly behind a car sporting a bumper sticker advertisement, there is very little time to read what is written. For these reasons, companies that advertise on bumper stickers usually include little more than a generic statement about employment opportunities and note, in large characters, their easy-to-remember phone number.

If company employees are willing to place this inexpensive form of advertisement on their car bumpers, employers may get some viable nonexempt candidates. On the other hand, bumper sticker ads may be viewed as an act of desperation by job seekers and, as such, might not be taken seriously.

Company-Sponsored Social Affairs

If your organization goes in for huge social events to celebrate special occasions, such as a picnic on Independence Day, encourage employees to bring family and friends. Then set up a "job opportunities" table with brochures and a list of openings. This form of recruitment requires an investment of only additional food and one or two employees willing to answer questions from interested applicants. It is advantageous to have employees attending the affair say good things about you as an employer and pass their endorsement on to others.

Movie Ads

You get to the movies in plenty of time to grab a tub of popcorn and a drink. You find a seat and settle in, ready for the show to begin. If you are lucky, instead of listening to music, you see previews of coming attractions. Imagine, in addition to clips of upcoming shows, your company's name on the screen, advertising job opportunities! This technique is gaining in popularity. Businesses are beginning to target captive, unsuspecting audiences with recruiting ads during movie previews. The amount of information is kept to a minimum, usually just the company name, an easy-to-remember phone number (few moviegoers are prepared to write in a dark theater), and either a list of openings or just a statement about job opportunities. Some employers try to link their promotions to specific movies, anticipating attendance by a particular type of viewer; others go for the shotgun approach and simply run their ads, regardless of what's showing.

Newspaper Inserts

Newspaper inserts represent a relatively untapped recruitment source. Arguments against their use include the possibility that they could fall out of the paper or be overlooked as job hunters head straight for the classified or special employment sections. Others feel that inserts are not taken seriously.

Proponents, on the other hand, view newspaper inserts as a refreshing approach to advertising and consider a plus the fact that this is an infrequently used medium. In addition, unlike ads that must be cut or torn out, inserts can be slipped out of the paper easily. The higher quality of the paper customarily used for inserts as well as the absence of newsprint on one's clothing and hands might also appeal to job seekers. Moreover, because they are generally larger than standard newspaper ads, inserts are less likely to be misplaced. Finally, newspaper inserts can use several colors, making them more appealing visually.

On-Site Recruitment

On-site recruitment is limited to the types of businesses that attract large numbers of people to their locations each day. Still, it can be quite effective, especially for nonexempt-level positions. For example, railroad companies may place pamphlets that describe employment opportunities on car seats, airlines might do the same with seats on planes, department stores might attach fliers to packages at cashier stations, and fast-food chains or family restaurants might describe job openings on tray liners and table tents.

The brief message, which usually describes the benefits of working for the company, is often framed in bright, eye-catching colors and graphics. Pictured, too, may be people representing diverse traits. Interested candidates are invited to visit or call the employment manager to obtain an application form. In some instances, postage-paid applications are attached to the message so that those who wish to apply can complete the form later and submit it.

Preemployment Training

Preemployment training ensures the hiring of those candidates "guaranteed" to possess the basic knowledge and skills needed to perform a given job. This may be accomplished through the promotion of a program that offers, free of cost to participants, various skills training. Such prospects are not necessarily being trained for specific jobs, nor are they being offered employment. The emphasis is on preparation, so that when jobs do become available, the trained individuals are considered first. Employers benefit by having an available workforce of skilled individuals from which to choose, without wasting time screening a group of untested applicants. Once hired, program graduates need not devote the first several days, or in some cases weeks, to learning their jobs. Program participants benefit by acquiring marketable skills and being first in line for employment opportunities. Of course, there is no guarantee the acquired skills will not ultimately benefit another company.

In today's tight labor market, many businesses are extending preemployment training beyond primary job functions. By tapping into unconventional markets, such as the homeless and ex-convicts, prospective employers, of necessity, provide training in social skills and office etiquette. Since businesses seldom have the time, resources, or know-how to teach these "softer skills," they enter partnerships with nonprofit organizations that specialize in helping the disadvantaged. Together, the two prepare would-be employees for various situations likely to arise in the world of work.

Companies seeking nonprofit organizations that teach intangible job skills to homeless adults can contact Binding Together Inc. in New York. Among the prestigious organizations that have collaborated with Binding Together are Chase Manhattan Bank, Ernst & Young, Estee Lauder, Morgan Stanley Dean Witter, R.R. Donnelly, and Salomon Smith Barney. After one year of full-time work, 70 percent of those graduating from such programs have a track record of successful employment. For help in training ex-offenders, you can contact South Forth Corp., also in New York. It provides a wide range of vocational services to assist former offenders seeking employment.

Response Cards

Response cards can be viewed as a takeoff on direct mail recruitment in that cards are mailed to the homes of targeted candidates. The language on the card is designed to pique the interest of even those who are not looking for new employment. After a brief description of the job opportunities available, potential applicants are invited to complete a brief questionnaire that is easily detached from the informative portion of the card and mailed, postage-paid.

Response cards can also be attached to ads appearing in magazines. General information about the company and available jobs is provided; those interested are invited to complete the card and mail it in.

Companies report that they continue to receive responses up to a year after ads with detachable cards have run. While the return rate is not especially high (under 5 percent), many employers report a high ratio of hires as a result.

Employers can also add a twist to using response cards. Try sending out letters inviting people to return an accompanying coupon entitling them to a free poster or calendar. Ask them to provide basic information about their skills and knowledge. They get a free poster; you get names for your data bank.

Sporting Events

Sporting events provide prime recruitment opportunities these days. Booths set up at football games and tennis tournaments make information about the company available to thousands of fans at one time. National Semiconductor, a software developer based in Santa Clara, California, even worked out an arrangement whereby a company representative was able to throw out the first pitch at an Oakland A's game.

State Recruitment Campaigns

Increasingly, companies are linking up with their states' recruitment campaigns to attract new, would-be residents and workers, as well as former residents, by playing up the advantages of their state. Advertised advantages run the gamut, including low housing costs, ideal weather conditions, low crime rates, small communities, a slower pace, outdoor and recreational offerings, and low taxes. For example, when Nebraska determined that many of its former residents were leaving for warmer locales, such as Texas, Florida, Arizona, and California, it decided to launch a campaign that emphasized the advantages of living and working in Nebraska. True, it couldn't offer a warm climate, but it could boast of having "the best student-to-teacher ratio in the country," according to Patty Wood, workforce development supervisor for Nebraska. It also proudly described a lifestyle that included a low crime rate and less traffic.

Businesses can hitch a ride on their states' recruitment efforts by posting their job openings on state web sites. They can also benefit from the labor force data compiled by their state departments of labor to develop targeted recruitment strategies.

Try-a-Job

Some companies offer to pay potential hires to work with their staff for a day. The going rate is generally around $100. This process gives both parties a chance to make an informed decision and, if necessary, opt out before it's too late.

Additional Staffing Solutions

Look around you. Recruiters are searching for talent in child-care centers, recreational centers such as YMCAs and public pools, religious group centers, senior citizen centers, and social service agencies. Indeed, virtually any location or technique that produces results can be considered a recruitment source. This list of suggested additional creative staffing solutions is not, therefore, intended to be all inclusive:

▲ Audiotapes
▲ Flyers on car windshields in parking lots
▲ Job ads distributed in large apartment complexes
▲ Kiosk ads in malls and airports
▲ Messages slipped in with customer billings
▲ Mobile recruiting vans
▲ Posters and signs with tear-off application forms in banks, community centers, doctors' offices, grocery stores, laundromats, mass transit stations, and real estate offices
▲ Retiree job banks
▲ Skywriting
▲ Talent scout cards (distributed when you get good service)
▲ Telemarketing
▲ Twenty-four-hour telephone lines

EDS, a professional services firm based in Plano, Texas, that supplies consulting, business systems, and technology to clients worldwide, has been known to go to incredible lengths to recruit new hires. For example, while sponsoring the U.S. Sunrayce, an intercollegiate competition to build and race solar-power cars, EDS sought to recruit talented college students. One student, after graduating with a bachelor's degree in mechanical engineering, went on to become one of the company's systems engineers. Since the company recruits two thousand to three thousand new employees a year from colleges, promoting such events is just one way it attracts job candidates. EDS has targeted fifty colleges where HR develops a relationship with the placement office, business and engineering school deans, financial aid offices (EDS offers scholarships), and several multicultural business organizations. EDS representatives have gone so far as to work ski resorts and, while literally whooshing down mountain trails, distribute EDS flyers and T-shirts.

Companies such as EDS believe that it's more productive to tap creative resources than fight over the same resources with competitors. For instance, Inacom Corporation Inc., an Omaha, Nebraska–based company with approximately five thousand employees that designs, builds, and maintains large corporate computer networks, has established a Chinese Internship Program. The company brings in highly skilled workers from China with master's degrees or doctorates in computer science who have never worked in an American business. They are given a three- to six-month internship to learn about the company. During the internship, to ease the transition, Inacom offers English language skills at the University of Nebraska. Other companies focus on foreign markets as well, including the United Kingdom, Germany, India, Taiwan, Japan, and western Europe, looking in particular for high-tech and telecommunications employees.

ABC Guidelines for Successful Recruitment

Every time you have a job opening in your organization, apply as many of the twenty-six "ABC Guidelines for Successful Recruitment" as possible, regardless of the recruitment sources you use. This means being:

- ▲ *Attractive.* Promote your organization as the kind of place employees will want to call their place of work. Highlight your most generous and unique benefits, have employees promote your attributes among friends, and publicly pat yourselves on the back for accomplishments.
- ▲ *Believable.* If what you're offering sounds too good to be true, repackage your wares. Applicants today can't be bothered tracking down prospective employers to find out if they really do offer more vacation time than any of their competitors or will top any offer received in the past two months.
- ▲ *Centered.* Identify from three to six critical qualities you're

seeking in your employees. Clearly communicate and adhere to them in your recruitment efforts.

▲ *Diligent.* Effective recruiting requires a steady and energetic application of effort.

▲ *Empathetic.* Consider and attempt to understand an applicant's needs and interests in relation to organizational goals in order to strike a balance and find common denominators between the two.

▲ *Flexible.* If you've tried one recruitment source and it's not yielding the kind of results you need, move on to others.

▲ *Greedy.* Tell yourself that your company is as entitled as your competitors to be staffed by the best possible workforce. Seek out those candidates that maximally meet your needs.

▲ *Hip.* Stay informed when it comes to the latest developments in recruitment, as well as what sources and techniques your competitors are using.

▲ *Informative.* Anticipate what applicants want to know about the job and your company and be prepared to tell them, either verbally, in the form of some written material, in a CD-ROM, or online.

▲ *Judicious.* Exercise sound judgment when matching candidates with jobs. Avoid decisions ruled by emotion.

▲ *Knowledgeable.* Be thoroughly familiar with the parameters of the job and how it interfaces with other positions, the department, and the company. Also, be aware of how other organizations view this job in terms of responsibility, status, and compensation.

▲ *Linear.* Think in terms of a series of straight lines connecting the applicant, the job, and the company. This helps keep you on track and accomplish your goal of filling an opening as quickly as possible with the most suitable employee.

▲ *More.* Review your current recruitment efforts and think of whether you could be doing more. In fact, take each of the key words in these guidelines and ask yourself if you can be *more* attractive, *more* believable, *more* centered, *more* diligent, and so on.

▲ *Notorious.* Strive to become the organization everyone talks about. Your goal is to become the company applicants want to work for and other companies want to imitate.

▲ *Open-minded.* Whether you're recruiting IT specialists, engineers, or secretaries, view the job from the applicant's perspective. Ask employees in the classifications you're trying to fill to identify what's important to them so you can emphasize those significant aspects to applicants.

▲ *Persistent.* Continue exploring various recruitment sources until you find the right employee. Resist pressure to settle or compromise your standards if you are unable to fill an opening right away. Rather, reexamine the sources you've chosen, applying the methodology described earlier.

▲ *Quick.* The moment you discover you're going to have an opening, act on it. Spread the word among employees, run an ad, do whatever you can to spread the word that you have a job to fill.

▲ *Realistic.* It's one thing to seek out the best possible candidate for a job, yet quite another to hold out for the ideal employee who may exist only on paper or in your mind.

▲ *Sensible.* Carefully determine the best recruitment source based on a number of factors, including the nature of the job and the current job market.

▲ *Tireless.* If you relax your recruitment efforts, chances are another organization will grab the candidate you failed to pursue.

▲ *Unified.* Make certain everyone concerned with the recruitment effort is working toward the same goal—that is, that they are in agreement with regard to the qualities and skills being sought.

▲ *Vocal.* Openly and clearly express the qualities and skills needed in a candidate to agencies or firms assisting your company with a job search.

▲ *Watchful.* Look for signs that confirm that the recruitment sources you're using are producing the kinds of results wanted, and that the candidates coming forth possess needed qualities.

▲ *Xentigious.* I made this word up (the last two syllables rhyme with "litigious") to mean "keep it legal."

▲ *Youthful.* In order to compete for top performers, especially the scarce but vitally important group of younger workers, be youthful in your thinking and in spirit.

▲ *Zealous.* Applicants are more likely to be interested in becoming part of a company if the recruiters are enthusiastic and appear to genuinely enjoy working there.

Let's take a look at how these guidelines may be applied to an actual recruiting situation. We'll begin with Roger, a customer service representative, as he informs Anita, the director of human resources, of his intention to resign:

> *Roger:* Anita, there's something I need to tell you.
> *Anita:* Sounds serious. What's up?
> *Roger:* Well . . . this isn't easy to say, but I'm leaving.
> *Anita:* Leaving? For where? What do you mean?
> *Roger:* I mean I'm leaving the company. Resigning. Effective two weeks from today.
> *Anita:* I don't understand. And I must say, I'm also totally stunned.
> *Roger:* You shouldn't be. You knew I was disappointed when I offered suggestions for improving the customer service department, and you basically told me I was just a rep and should mind my own business. Our working relationship hasn't been the same ever since then.
> *Anita:* So you're leaving because I hurt your feelings?
> *Roger:* No, I never said that. And by the way, that's a perfect example of part of what's wrong. You don't hear what I say. Never mind. It doesn't matter any more. I'm leaving.
> *Anita:* To do what?
> *Roger:* I found another position in customer service where I'll be able to help shape policy. I'm really looking forward to it.
> *Anita:* Can I convince you to stay?
> *Roger:* I'm afraid we're past that point.
> *Anita:* I guess there's nothing more to say. Except that I'm disappointed. I had a lot of hope for your future here.
> *Roger:* So did I, Anita. It's just we saw my future differently.
> *Anita:* One more thing. What do you think your replacement will consider to be a significant aspect of the job *(open-minded)?*
> *Roger:* That's easy. The opportunity to make a real contribution and not just spend seven hours a day soothing customers' ruffled feathers.

As Roger left Anita's office, she got up, closed the door, and returned to her desk. She was annoyed with Roger but had to admit she knew he was growing discontented in his work as a customer service rep, and she hadn't done anything to keep him from leaving. Be that as it may, she now had a problem: There was no one else in the company who could do Roger's job. That meant she had to find a replacement from the outside and bring that person on board, ideally before Roger left. This was going to be a challenge, and she needed to begin her search immediately *(quick).*

She began by listing the primary qualities she needed in a customer service rep: excellent interpersonal skills, the ability to be empathetic, and good listening skills. She thought for a moment and then added "interested in improving departmental procedures" *(centered)*. Now, where should she go to find someone fast? At the last regional meeting of HR practitioners, Anita recalled a colleague from another company commenting that they had luck using a particular agency when replacing customer service reps *(hip) (sensible)*. Anita had successfully used the agency in the past and decided to get in touch with them now. She e-mailed the following message to Jim, her contact there:

> Call me ASAP re: immed. open. for a CS rep. $ is so-so, but benefits are super., incl. health club member., 4 wks. vacat., and on-site med. services *(attractive)*. In fact, I'm pretty sure we offer a better benefits package than anyone else in our business *(believable)*, but you probably shouldn't say that. Instead, I'll give app's a copy of our benefits video when they come in for interviews *(informative)*. Send app's to me since I know the job thoroughly *(knowledgeable)*. Jim, we need someone who has great interpersonal skills, listens well, and is empathetic. Also, someone who's interested in getting involved *(vocal)*. Ideally, I'd like to see candidates with experience in our industry *(greedy)*, but I'll consider folks with CS exper. elsewhere. The important thing is that we get someone who can do the job and will work well in this environment *(linear)*. As always, stress to anyone interested that we pride ourselves on being an EOE and won an award last year for our efforts in workplace diversity *(xentigious)*.

As soon as she finished e-mailing Jim, Anita called her employee relations manager, June. "Roger is leaving. Would you please post the opening? I don't think we've got anyone in-house for the job, but let's be sure. I also want to let our staff know so they have a chance to make referrals. Also, call Josh at the ad agency and see if we can make the deadline for the next issue of *All the News*. Come down to my office this afternoon and I'll give you the particulars" *(flexible)*.

Anita stuck her head out of her office and called out to one of her HR reps, Sandy. "Sandy, got a minute? I need your help." Sandy got up from her desk and approached Anita's door. "What's going on?" "Roger is leaving and we need to fill his job fast. I'm going to need you to stay on top of the details for me—you know, screening applicants on the phone, lining up interviews, that sort of thing. We've got to be organized and focused—he's only given us two weeks notice" *(diligent)*.

Anita sat back in her chair and reflected on what she had done thus far with regard to the customer service opening. She was satisfied that she had started the recruitment search appropriately and had everyone working toward the same goal *(unified)*.

The next morning, Anita received a call from Jim. "I've got two top-notch people for you to see, both with prior experience. One of them said he'd heard good things about your company and was hoping something would open up so he could apply" *(notorious)*. Anita scheduled appointments with both applicants for later that day. Meanwhile, she learned from Sandy that one of their employees had referred a friend of his for the job. Anita scheduled him for an interview as well.

Before meeting the three candidates, Anita went over a checklist of things to do: She reminded herself to try and understand the applicants' needs and interests in relation to company goals *(empathetic)*, to exercise sound judgment based on skills and abilities *(judicious)*, and to be practical in making a selection *(realistic)*. She also knew applicants were more likely to be interested in joining the company if she came across as enthusiastic *(zealous)*.

Anita interviewed the three candidates and came away unimpressed. She contacted Jim to ensure that he understood the qualities she was seeking. Then she talked to June to make certain employees understood the nature of the job before making referrals *(watchful)* and to confirm that an ad would run in the next edition of *All the News* *(persistent) (tireless)*. Anita left her office disappointed, but not disheartened. She knew she had followed the "ABC Guidelines for Successful Recruitment," thereby improving her chances of finding a good replacement for Roger.

SUMMARY

Knowing which recruitment source to tap each time you have an opening can be challenging. Begin by considering four factors: how much money is available, how quickly the opening must be filled, whether a wide audience must be reached, and the exemption level of the opening. Identifying each source as being proactive or reactive can also prove helpful.

Despite the fiercely competitive nature that prevails in today's recruitment arena, many employers still turn to traditional recruitment sources. The top ten sources of job applicants, according to one SHRM survey, are employee referrals, newspaper ads, recruiting firms, college recruitment, contingent-help firms, job fairs, the Internet, targeted minority recruiting, walk-ins, and government employment services. Other popular sources include clients and customers, direct mail, HR files, job posting, military recruiting, open houses, outplacement firms, professional associations, radio and television, and research firms.

When traditional recruitment sources don't yield adequate results, consider recruitment solutions that are more creative, such as airplane banners, banners and signs, billboard advertising, bumper sticker advertisements, company-sponsored social affairs, movie ads, newspaper inserts, on-site recruitment, preemployment training, response cards, sporting events, state recruitment campaigns, and try-a-job.

Finally, apply the "ABC Guidelines for Successful Recruitment" every time you have an opening to ensure the best possible results.

CHAPTER 5

Electronic Recruitment

"Technology is seductive; the more you have the more you want."

—Paul McKinnon,
senior vice president of human resources,
Dell Computer

Unquestionably, businesses today must use the Internet to remain competitive in the labor market. Approximately 96 percent of all U.S. employers are going online to recruit, either by linking up with job search services or developing web pages of their own. Companies are spending $48 million for electronic advertising per year, and that number is expected to increase to a whopping $460 million over the next several years. According to *Electronic Recruiting News*, one of the most popular sites, Monster.com, reportedly has an average growth rate of 14,000 hits per day. It is considered the best national career site by 56 percent of recruiters, says recruitersnetwork.com,[1] followed by Headhunter.net (16 percent), Hotjobs.com (13 percent), CareerPath.com (11 percent), and CareerMosaic.com (3 percent).

These numbers must not be taken literally or even too seriously, however. They change quickly and are, according to experts, easy to inflate. For example, less than three months after the statistics above were reported in *Human Resource Management News*, *HR News*, a publication of the Society for Human Resource Management, reported that Headhunter.net and CareerMosaic.com had decided to merge.[2] Headhunter.net said the merger would permit job seekers to find more jobs in more states than on any other site, and companies would be able to access twice the number of applicants as before. By the time this book reaches your hands, it's anyone's guess as to which ".com" sites still exist, have joined forces, or been replaced.

Many of the companies that turn to electronic recruitment are, as one might expect, large and influential, such as Microsoft, Unisys Corporation, and Sun Microsystems. These giants maintain that electronic recruitment sources produce the greatest number of applicants as well as some of their best new hires, ranking second only to employee referrals. But users also include organizations that, in the past, scorned online recruiting. An example of the latter is the Central Intelligence Agency (CIA). Gary Cluff, national staffing director for the CIA, said that the agency once viewed electronic recruitment with contempt. "I have little or no confidence in the self-proclaimed traffic reports touted by the sites themselves," he adds. Today, however, the CIA uses online recruiting to make "same-day offers," and electronic recruitment accounts for the hiring of 15 percent of its staff. And Alexa Finkler, HR supervisor for Intermet Corp., a manufacturer of cast metal automotive parts, said that she has used electronic recruitment to find 90 percent of the people she has hired for the company's Stevensville, Michigan plant, after traditional methods didn't work.

Significantly, employers are turning to electronic recruitment for a greater variety of jobs than ever before. While historically the Internet was associated with technical jobs and later expanded to encompass executive and professional positions, today recruiters can find qualified candidates for every type of position imaginable. As one corporate recruiter stated, "I never thought that we would ever recruit a receptionist online, but we recently hired an applicant we found by using the Internet."

In a survey conducted by Cambridge, Massachusetts–based Forrester Research, it was determined that recruiters who spent $105 million online in 1999 will spend $1.7 billion in 2003. Generally, online recruiting is less expensive and easier to manage than its in-print counterparts, averaging 5 percent of the price of placing a help wanted ad in a major newspaper for thirty days. It tends to generate faster responses from applicants, thereby shortening the hiring cycle. Also, databases can be searched with prescreening options that eliminate resumes that clearly don't fit a company's job profile. Given the current and projected state of low unemployment, the faster a company can engage an applicant via the Internet, the better its chances of hiring that person. The lower job search costs for both applicants and employers are also hard to ignore.

The Internet, then, is rapidly moving up in the ranks of recruitment resources, as greater numbers of applicants and employers communicate with one another, computer to computer. Internet recruiting offers so many advantages it even behooves those with limited Internet skills to explore its benefits. Among the many recruiting web site reference guides available are *WEDDLE's Guide to Employment Web Sites 2000* by Peter Weddle (AMACOM, 2000), *The Employer's Guide to Recruiting on the Internet* by Ray Schreyer and John McCarter (available by calling 703-361-7300), Tiburon Group's Internet Recruiting Workshops (773-907-8330), and *CareerXroads* by Gerry Crispin and Mark Mehler (Jist Works, 2000).

ELECTRONIC RECRUITMENT SOURCES

Typically, electronic recruitment sources post help wanted ads and/or collect resumes. Employers can choose from general or specialized job sites. The former invites postings and applicants for a wide range of positions; the latter appeals to specific fields, such as technology, human resources, sales, or healthcare. Employers can also visit sites that exclusively target specific populations, e.g., college students, or even particular geographic locations. If you are concerned that you won't find what you need on large, general job boards, look for those that group occupations into specialized "channels" or "communities."

Once you have settled on the job boards that best meet your needs, customize your postings so they are easy to locate and read through. Experts such as Margaret Dikel, a recruitment consultant and creator of *The Riley Guide*, an Internet recruitment directory, warn against making your postings too broad or too narrow. "If it's too broad, then your posting will be listed with a bunch of jobs with similar or even slightly similar qualifications and will just get lost in the shuffle. If the posting is too narrow, then the job applicants probably won't be able to find it."

There are more than 30,000 job boards worldwide.[3] It is also estimated that there are more than 2.5 million resumes online. There are services such as Junglee (www.junglee.com) that offer assistance with formatting job listings and content for various web sites.

Many organizations use inexpensive general sites, like E.Span (www.espan.com), and The Monster Board (www.monster.com) to complement traditional recruitment strategies. These general sites typically cost in the neighborhood of $100 to $200 per posting, but may range from costing nothing to as much as $400. Various packages are offered, such as ten postings per month plus access to the resume database for $500 per month. Length of time for postings may span a week to six months or longer. Sometimes job boards allow you to post jobs until they are filled. Some job boards require a minimum number of postings per month for a reduced per posting fee. Others offer unlimited postings and database access to businesses willing to pay as much as $100,000 a year. Some electronic recruitment sources also offer free trial subscriptions lasting several months. Taking advantage of these free offers enables you to assess the site's job-seeker traffic and decide if it's a viable source of candidates for your company.

Even at a hefty cost, online recruiting is usually more cost-effective than printed help wanted ads. Display ads can easily cost $2,000 or more to run in major metropolitan newspapers for one day. More and more newspapers realize that printed ads are losing their appeal; consequently, many now offer their own online job boards.

Specialized sites address the needs of particular segments of the market. For example, JOBTRAK (www.jobtrak.com) is an online job listing service for college students, offering some 40,000 listings, linked to approximately 750 campuses throughout the United States. Another leading college recruiting site, run by the National Association of Colleges and Employers, is JobWeb (www.jobweb. org). It has more than 1,600 member universities. JobEngine (www. jobengine.com) is a job posting and resume search site for computer industry professionals, and Net-Temps (www.nettemps.com) is a leading site for recruiting contingent workers, offering more than 75,000 listings.

Smart agents—sophisticated software programs that automatically search the web for high-quality resumes, sorting them into a database—are used by some companies to sift through the thousands of resumes appearing on a given web site. Some programs can extract e-mail addresses in order to send a potential employee news of a job opening.

Exhibit 5–1 provides detailed information about twelve broad-spectrum electronic recruitment sources. Exhibit 5–2 offers web sites for fifty additional specialized sources. All of these sources were selected at random to illustrate the wide variety of sources available.

At least one Internet recruiting source, DiscoverMe (www.dis coverme.com), bills itself as a personality-based placement service available to both job seekers and *Fortune* 1000 companies. The service is free to candidates who provide information such as location preference, skills, and work experience, and then go on to complete the personality assessment tool online. The result is a one-page personality summary. If the summary matches the profile of a job opening for a DiscoverMe client-employer, the applicant may be contacted for a job interview. DiscoverMe's allure for employers is that the profile provides greater insight into a candidate's personality before valuable interview time is scheduled. The cost is about the same as using a search firm or recruitment agency.

Whether personality profiling is performed via testing as part of the interview process or online, there are risks involved. You might be exposing your company to legal problems if you use a personality profiling tool that hasn't been validated. It is advisable, then, to use such instruments with caution and in conjunction with other evaluative tools that measure tangible areas.

To increase visibility, some companies purchase banner ads on computer job banks and recruiting sites. Banner ads are similar to printed display ads in that they promote a company's job openings. The difference is that they appear on your computer screen. When a job surfer enters a key term—e.g., human resources—your company's ad pops up. Depending on the site, banner ads can run from a few hundred dollars a month to several thousand. The steep price tag makes this approach more useful in creating long-term, brand-name recognition than as a way of filling a couple of job openings.

Web Site Selection Guidelines

Peter Weddle, author of the above mentioned *WEDDLE's Guide to Employment Web Sites 2000*, offers step-by-step guidelines for effective web site selection. Following is a modification of his steps:

1. Identify web sites that have a proven track record in the fields for which you are recruiting.

2. Isolate the most important factors for your selection of a web site. For example, you might determine that the length of time you can post an opening is of paramount importance. Or perhaps you need to know whether the site permits banner advertising.

3. Assess the attributes of each site identified in Step 1, such as information relating to job posting or resume sourcing.

4. Compare the factors isolated in Step 2 with the attributes of each site, and segregate those that match up.

5. Log on to those sites that match up with or come close to your idea of the ideal web site. *WEDDLE's Guide* "strongly recommends that you never place an ad on a site until you have 'test driven' it from a job seeker's perspective." This includes looking for a "candidate-friendly" Internet address, quick download time, clear identification of contents, and easy navigability.

6. Once you have decided which sites best suit your needs, plan on tracking the performance of each site. Measure success by the number of applicants generated, the cost-per-applicant, and, most important, the caliber of the applicants.

7. Periodically reassess your web site selections by repeating Steps 1–5 to ensure that these sites still meet your needs.

Sourcing Tips

Sourcing is a term used by online recruiters to mean finding any source of potential employees. This may include searching job boards where active applicants are likely to be found, or seeking out passive candidates—that is, individuals who aren't looking for a job but may be an ideal fit for your job opening. The latter can be found on association web sites (especially those with online conference information) or, more typically, by using a web search engine, such as AltaVista.com or surfenginewatch.com. These search engines explore the web for sites in response to user queries.

Sourcing can be time-consuming and complex. Consequently, many organizations turn the task over to specialists. Typically, in-house recruiters provide the search specialists, often called search or source strategists, with job descriptions. The strategists then go to work, tracking down suitable sources and potential employees, commonly using a technique called flipping, a method whereby links to other web sites are traced. Strategists also weed out all the online "junk" and provide recruiters with viable leads.

For organizations that do not want to hire sourcing strategists, the services of a consulting firm can be retained to provide varying services. For example, Advanced Internet Recruitment Strategies, located in Hanover, New Hampshire, trains recruiters to use sourcing strategies, while Netrecruiter in Bethesda, Maryland, conducts searches and provides recruiters with lists of potential candidates.

COMPANY WEB SITES

Companies that put up their own web page are recruiting proactively, increasing their chances of finding suitable employees.

Thirty-eight percent of all U.S. companies currently have web sites or web-based listings, and an estimated 75 percent of *Fortune* 500 companies have their own sites.

For companies that already have web pages, adding a job opportunity section is relatively simple and inexpensive. If your human resources staff is unfamiliar with Internet recruiting, information systems (IS) experts may have to work with them initially. Postings may need to be updated through IS, but ultimately your HR staff should be able to accomplish this themselves. In some organizations, managers independently post job openings on the Internet without going through human resources. At the very least, HR should be notified of what jobs have been posted since most resumes (paper and electronic) go through HR for an initial job-match assessment.

Starting a Web Page

The first step in designing a web page from scratch is to determine what you want to accomplish. It's tempting to answer "to lure applicants," but that is not really specific enough for any recruiter who has ever used a recruitment source that did not target applicants with the required credentials or skills. It's discouraging to run an ad and get only a handful of responses; it is worse, however, to be inundated with responses from unqualified candidates. Every recruitment source must be properly directed; cyberspace postings are no different. Think, then, about what you want the postings to accomplish: You want them to attract qualified candidates whose backgrounds and interests are compatible with the environment of your organization. Make a statement identifies your company as unique and immediately sets it apart; hence, your web page should stand out as unlike any other.

Now you can focus on what viewers want from a web page. Consult with competitors, and try to determine who accesses their web pages and the kind of feedback they are receiving. For example, are they like the company that was the recipient of numerous e-mail messages chastising it for not changing its job postings for several months? Consult with your IS staff, other employees, and even external candidates about what they expect to find on a web page. Also, talk with recruiters from similar work environments. Information from these sources can supplement advice from outside web experts. Better yet, surf around your competitors' web sites on your own. Are they easy to navigate? Does it take a long time for images to appear? Can you readily access the information you need? Some experts suggest strictly abiding by the "two-click rule"—that is, taking only two clicks of the mouse to get where you want to go. Be demanding and impatient as you move around each web site. After all, most applicants aren't going to hang around if they can't get what they want quickly and easily.

Experts also recommend having a section on your web site devoted to describing life as an employee. Applicants today want to know what it would be like working for your company before they bother submitting a resume. Describe and illustrate the environment, culture, benefits, opportunities, and any unique qualities.

Now determine how your web page should best be organized. It may be set up by job function, geographic location, or business unit. Perhaps you want to offer generic information about the work environment, company missions, and benefits before listing actual job postings. Consider, too, providing the format for an instant electronic resume. A table of contents will allow those browsing the site to readily locate topics of interest. Experiment, asking for feedback from staff and consultants as to which format is likely to draw the greatest number of qualified candidates. Also, do not overlook the impact of visual design. Too much text is a turnoff; so, too, are huge graphics that slow things down to a crawl and make viewers impatient. Few users are willing to wait more than thirty to sixty seconds for a page to load (some experts say this advice pertains to home pages only; second- and third-level pages can take longer to load since the person obviously wants to see the materials). Strike a balance between smaller graphics that load quickly and meaningful text, to capture and retain the interest of job hunters.

You may elect to use an outside web site consultant in putting up your site. Before making a commitment to outside consultants, verify their effectiveness by talking with companies that have used them. Preferably, consult with those businesses that are similar to yours. This process is not unlike conducting references checks on prospective employees. Here are some of questions to ask previous clients of potential consultants:

- ▲ Do they have both technical expertise and design experience?
- ▲ How helpful were they in a set-up situation?
- ▲ How patient were they in explaining terms and processes to nontechnical HR people?
- ▲ Did they bother to find out what your company was all about, in terms of products, markets, and direction?
- ▲ Did they acknowledge that you know your business best and

therefore should either write the text for the page or at least contribute to it?

▲ Did they make suggestions as to the best format and design of your page?

▲ Did they advise you as to the appropriate equipment for high-speed access to the Internet?

▲ Did they try to start you off with more than you needed?

▲ Did they continue to offer support services after building your web page?

▲ Did they recommend upgrades to your page after a probationary test run?

It may not be particularly helpful to ascertain how long a web page consultant has been in business since this is still a relatively new field. Prior business experience, however, with much of it being computer-related, is relevant.

If you decide to forgo the help of a consultant and create a web page on your own, try one of the many web authoring programs, such as Microsoft Front Page, Assistant Pro, and Internet Design Shop. Many of these programs assist with content and visibility but not design.

Companies generally start with a web "presence." This is a bare-bones home page that provides the company name, geographic locations, phone and fax numbers, basic information about the company (such as a brief history and its primary product areas), and whom to contact. These pages can be upgraded later on, depending on requests received over the Internet for more information, as well as the company's own observations and advice from consultants. On average, start-up pages are upgraded two to three times in the first twelve to eighteen months.

Web Site Upkeep

Once established, an up-to-date web site is the key to successful recruiting on the Internet. Experts recommend that job listings rarely should remain for more than thirty days before scrolling off, since sorting through old listings and dated information is irritating to web browsers. Add new postings every week, and review electronically submitted resumes daily. Also, keep current with regard to new web capabilities, such as colors, backgrounds, and effects. And to keep from becoming complacent, give the site a facelift every few months, even if you have nothing significantly new to add.

The issue of exposure is also critical. Any web site is rendered ineffective if not seen or accessed. "It's all about driving traffic and bringing people to what you have done," says one recruiter. While employers need to display their Internet address, or Uniform Resource Locator (URL), on all printed marketing materials, such as business cards, letterhead, brochures, and advertisements, that alone may not ensure sufficient web site exposure. Many companies also purchase hypertext links or hotlinks—buttons that lead directly into its server from other Internet services such as Online Career Center, one of the more popular employment service sites. Hypertext links allow web surfers to jump from one site to another, ensuring easier access and greater exposure. Think, too, of running banner ads on other web sites, such as newsgroups, to attract potential employees to the career portion of your web site. Establishing portals that feed into your company's web site is another way to increase exposure. For example, college students can view their school's career section and be able to click onto current job opportunities at your company.

Tracking results is critical to the future success of your web site. The number of hits is not really an accurate measure of success, although it can offer insights into how the web site should be redesigned and what features should be revised, included, or eliminated down the road. More important is the number of "unique visitors"—that is, the number of people who visit a site in a given period, with each individual counted only once. Also significant is the number of pages viewed. Checking the ratio of pages viewed to the number of visitors allows you to see if viewers are using the site extensively or just checking it out briefly. The more pages viewed, the more extensively the site is being used. Look, too, at which pages are the most popular and how long they are being viewed, on average.

GE Power Systems, a leader of power generation solutions, measures the results of its web site against its corporate goals on a weekly basis. Steven Labate, the company's manager of recruiting and staffing, states, "The e-business scorecard shows how many people visited our site during the preceding week and is reviewed by senior management. In addition, we calculate the average page views per visitor to monitor how deeply into the site the typical visitor goes."

Web Site Guidelines for Recruitment

Recruiting online is a popular way of increasing the visibility of job openings at a reasonable cost. Assuming you have decided to establish a corporate web site, here are guidelines for making your effort a success:

1. *Make searching for job openings easy.* A user-friendly web site means making an "employment" button available in a prominent place on your home page, and offering a resume builder service or form that routes the data into your e-mail or database.

2. *Make the site navigable.* Broad appeal is an important ingredient to web site success. For people who know exactly what they want, speed and easy access are crucial. Browsers, on the other hand, want to explore, interacting with stimulating graphics and interesting text.

3. *Be prepared to respond quickly to applicants.* In describing the recruitment capabilities of the Internet, a frequent user accurately noted that it "offers incredible new opportunities to disappoint." Since applying for a position takes only a few minutes, candidates expect a quick response. If they do not get it, chances are they will lose interest and move on. At the very least, e-mail an acknowledgment message as soon as resumes are received.

4. *Maintain an up-to-date employment opportunity database.* The importance of keeping a web site current cannot be overemphasized. If you cannot manage this internally, hire the services of an outside company.

5. *Screen out unqualified candidates.* This sounds unrealistic, yet there is a technique that Texas Instruments Inc. has been using for years with success: a candidate profiler (www.ti.com/recruit/dosc/fitcheck.htm). Here's how it works. Before applicants apply for a job opening, they take a "FitCheck." This involves answering a series of questions designed to determine their qualifications and compatibility with Texas Instruments' corporate culture. After reviewing the results of the FitCheck, the company can decide whether to proceed with an application. The result: a prescreened, interested, and qualified applicant pool.

6. *Balance content with design.* Suggesting that appearances matter to job seekers may seem superficial, but the reality is that they do. As with newspaper display ads, visual appeal draws candidates to your page, and stimulating content piques and holds their interest.

7. *Keep it organized.* Job seekers want to focus on the relevant data right away. While some may want to browse the entire site, taking everything in, most zero in on what you have to offer, decide if they are interested, and apply for a specific job. If this cannot be done with ease, chances are they will move on to another site.

8. *Take advantage of all the information that is available about your web site's visitors.* You will not hire every applicant expressing an

interest in your company, but you can collect data about them that may prove useful to recruitment strategies later on. One of the great aspects of electronic recruitment is that everything is measurable. So decide what you want to know; there is bound to be an Internet service that can provide the information you seek. For example, it may be useful to find out which schools or organizations visited your web site. Or perhaps you are interested in what other pages were viewed. This kind of information can prove valuable as you continually reevaluate your approach to online recruiting.

9. *Make your address easy to remember.* People have been personalizing license plates for years, so it's no surprise that companies are custom-designing their web site addresses. For a small additional sum of $100 or so, you can register a unique, easy-to-remember URL.

10. *Invite visitors to provide their e-mail addresses so you can inform them of future openings.* This allows you to line up candidates for jobs as soon as they become available, saving valuable time and resources.

11. *Consider outsourcing aspects of the design, development, or upgrading of your web site.* While this costs more than doing everything in-house, the result is usually a more professional, efficient site. If outsourcing is not an option, be sure to get input from the right people in-house. This includes IT staff, HR professionals, and marketing representatives.

12. *Don't say too much.* This last tip can be a tough one to follow. Many companies believe more is better. But a web site is not a laundry list of data or meant to read like a book. Be selective about the information you provide and the form in which it is offered.

CYBERSPACE RESUMES

The number of resumes transmitted electronically continues to rise. Accordingly, more employers are screening resumes electronically using a database that "reads" electronic or cyberspace resumes for specific criteria.

Reviewing a cyberspace resume is somewhat different from reading a paper resume. While the focus remains the same—searching for information that reflects a person's ability to perform a job—the process differs.

An automated system provides a method of transferring information from resumes into an applicant database, then organizing the data into a format that recruiters can search. The process scans resumes using optical character recognition technology for key words and phrases that describe the skills required for each job. Action words, indicating the nature and level of work accomplished, are less important than industry-specific language. The scanning process benefits applicants with the most measurable, tangible skills; applicants who exclude relevant terms and familiar industry acronyms are likely to be bypassed. The process can also search for years of experience, education, and other desired specifications. Employers can even assign weighted values to the various criteria.

Employers advertising on the Internet are learning to accept "cookie-cutter" resumes—that is, electronic resume formats. Increasingly, applicants are taking advantage of the many sites on the web that offer electronic resume writing forms. Resumix Creating Your Resume (http://www.resumix.com/resume/resumeindex. html) and Intellimatch Power Resume Builder (http://www. intellimatch.com/watson/owa/w3.html) are among the numerous electronic resume preparation services available. Some services offer a "one-size-fits-all" resume format, while others walk the job hunter through a series of categories to develop a detailed, more personalized resume. Most do not, however, assist the applicant in organizing the resume, e.g., chronologically or by function. That kind of guidance is offered by other services, such as the Job Smart Resume Guide (http://jobsmart.org/tools/resume/index.htm). Tips on design are offered by yet another category of Internet resume writing experts, such as *The Riley Guide* (http://www.jobtrak.com/ jobguide/index.html).

Since paper resumes, neatly set on one to two pages of high-quality ecru paper, are rapidly being replaced by the Internet version—dull plain text that may never be printed out—it is the norm to offer practical advice on coping with the computer, rather than actual design tips.

Cyberspace resume-writing guides recommend inclusion of a cover letter. Recruiters are accustomed to reading a summary of the applicant's objectives and personal characteristics, so the contents of a cover page, electronic or paper, have remained much the same.

APPLICANT TRACKING AND HIRING MANAGEMENT SYSTEMS

Electronic tools such as job boards, the Internet, and e-mail bring to mind the old adage "Be careful what you wish for." You wanted applicants? Well, you've got them! Thousands of them! But what do you do with all of them? How do you know who's qualified? Many recruiters today complain about not being able to sort, track, and process the seemingly endless stream of both cyberspace and paper resumes that come in daily. Fortunately, help is available in the form of two similar types of systems: (1) applicant tracking systems and (2) hiring management systems, both or which provide needed support for overworked HR employees.

Applicant tracking systems have been around for some time. They typically collect information about job candidates, e.g., skills and education, and also track various steps in the hiring process, such as the interview. There are numerous applicant tracking systems to choose from. The HR Demo-ROM/Applicant Tracking 2000 Edition, compiled by Dick Frantzreb, identifies more than fifty systems. Sample systems include !Trak-It Solutions, askSam Systems, Recruitsoft.com, and MyHRIS. To use applicant tracking, open the module, identify the type of search you want (such as education), and click to match applicants with available positions. The process allows employers to identify and respond to "hot" talent quickly. Many of these systems also allow you to prepare reports. For example, MyHRIS produces an "applicant interview summary report," iVantage provides reports on "cost of recruitment per hire," and Abra prepares an "EEO applicant summary" as well as a report on "applicants by reject reason." Abra also automatically sends e-mails to applicants in response to resumes received online.

Hiring management systems, a more recent development, focus on quickly matching applicants with positions. One major advantage is that these systems allow companies to integrate their corporate web sites with job boards. Examples of hiring management systems include Personic, Softshoe, Webhire, Hire.com, POWERHiring.com, and BrassRing Systems. These systems allow companies to create postings for either internal or job board use or to select the right job board for them. In addition, some of these systems write ads, process resumes as they are received, and place relevant information into a proprietary database. Companies can then perform searches against the information. Some hiring management systems also compile information on the number of resumes received, phone interviews, first and second interviews, offers extended, offers accepted, and offers declined. Others conduct background screening, negotiate offers, and even track performance and measure hiring success once candidates are hired. Some hiring management systems allow for "relationship building" with applicants by staying in touch with future prospects.

Employers have the option of a client/server–based system, whereby they purchase the software and install it on their own network, or on an application service provider, whereby the application remains on the provider's network and employers, via a rental option, access it through the Internet. Most hiring management systems exclusively offer the latter, while traditional applicant tracking systems still provide the option to buy. While the rental option allows HR to be up and running quickly, there are security issues to weigh; specifically, data does not reside safely within a company's own "firewall."

Trying to decide which applicant tracking or hiring management system to use can be confusing. Asking yourself the following questions may help:

▲ What do we need help with?
▲ What are our objectives?
▲ Will we be able to import and export data from a new system into an existing system?
▲ How much will integration of data cost?
▲ Should we buy or rent?
▲ What are the long-term costs?

COMPUTER-ASSISTED SCREENING

Increasingly, interactive voice response (IVR) is being used with other database technologies to capture competency-related information about potential employees. One major clothing manufacturer used computer-assisted screening to conduct the first round of interviews as a means of eliminating unqualified applicants. This resulted in a savings of $2.4 million during a three-year period, by reducing turnover from 87 to 51 percent. Another company, one of the nation's top six accounting and consulting firms, uses computer-assisted screening online to hire qualified candidates fresh out of college. The system is a big time and money saver in that partners and managers no longer find it necessary to spend time on the initial applicant screening.

Let's look at how computer-assisted screening works, using Nike as an example. A couple of years ago, Nike used computer-assisted screening to staff a store in Las Vegas. With 250 openings and 6,000 applicants, IVR technology enabled Nike to make the first cut. Applicants responded to eight questions over the phone;

3,500 applicants were screened out because they weren't available when needed or didn't have the requisite retail experience. The computer identified those candidates who had been in customer service environments, had a passion for sports, and would make effective Nike customer service representatives. Screenings were done in batches. The computer screening included a video show, given every forty-five minutes to a group of job candidates, of three customer service scenarios that asked the applicants to choose the best one. As applicants answered the questions, a printer in another room recorded their responses. Areas that needed to be probed further were flagged, as were areas that indicated particular strengths.

The computer screened for applicants prone to lose their temper in work situations and those demonstrating other undesirable behaviors. In addition, it helped the interviewers determine what to ask to reconcile inconsistencies or to probe applicant strengths in desired areas. While the applicant completed an application form online, the interviewer used the printout to prepare for the applicant's face-to-face interview. Nike then used competency-based interviewing, requiring applicants to document their answers at this stage of the process with specific examples.

Nike maintains that computer-assisted screening helped the company staff up fast and reduce turnover in the retail division by 21 percent over two years.

The accounting firm Coopers & Lybrand was one of the first companies to put its computer-assisted screening system on the Internet, using a web site called Springboard. Interested job seekers can complete an employment application and four screening modules at their convenience by accessing the web site (www.clspring board.com).

Indeed, today, dozens of companies, including Target, Hollywood Video, Home Depot, and Macy's, are replacing paper applications and in-person interviews with computer kiosks as their initial screening tool for applicants. The computer programs query prospective employees on job history and work habits, then delve into psychological tests that the companies claim can match job skills and personalities with the available positions.

Many of these companies rely on third-party companies, like Decision Point Systems Inc. of Beaverton, Oregon, to process the applications and summarize the answers to screening questions. The number and scope of questions range widely. There may be as few as four questions or as many as ninety, and inquiries may be heavily weighted toward the applicant's view of drugs and alcohol in the workplace, or how the applicant might respond to stressful situations. When the application is complete, the data is sent online to Decision Point, which culls the information within ten minutes and sends a three-page synopsis back to the employer, including a summary with one of three ratings: green (good candidate), yellow (employer needs to probe further), and red (warning).

Sometimes the synopsis also includes suggested interview questions. Based on the synopsis and summary, the employer decides if the candidate is worth pursuing. Decision Point has a database of 2 to 3 million applications that have been processed in a period of three years. While the company "co-owns" the data with its clients, contract provisions currently prohibit the sale or dissemination of information about individual candidates.

Needless to say, computer-assisted screening is controversial. Proponents maintain that applicants tend to respond more honestly with a computer than in a face-to-face interview. They maintain, too, that the system is fairer to everybody. In addition, it streamlines the hiring process, helps the interviewer choose the right applicant for the face-to-face interview, and allows the company to capture data that can be used in subsequent hiring waves or down the road in employee development and succession planning. Some proponents envision a day when individuals will be able to apply for jobs from home over the Internet and even foresee putting prospective employees into virtual video environments to gauge how they might react to work-related situations.

On the other hand, there is concern that electronic profiling could exclude those who don't fall within the desired response range, even though such applicants might possess skills the company values. (For example, there is speculation that Bill Gates would never have been hired for computer work if profiling had been used.) How can a computer program accurately judge a person on the sole basis of an initial screening? The face-to-face interview, opponents continue, can pick up on things that the computer cannot. By factoring in information the computer can't anticipate, interviewers would be in a position to make better decisions. In addition, computer-assisted screening selects people who have similar personality traits. This could adversely impact a company's diversity efforts. Also, depending on how a third-party agency words its contract with clients, current laws in most states could allow the sale or dissemination of the database without prior notice.

Most experts agree that a computer should never substitute for a face-to-face interview. As one Georgetown University graduate discovered after exploring numerous employment opportunities online, sometimes the best way is the old-fashioned way. She landed her dream job as an IT analyst for Chase Manhattan Bank by meeting with company representatives face-to-face at a campus interview, paper resume in hand.

INTERNATIONAL INTERNET RECRUITMENT

Web sites offer a global presence as an increasing number of companies are posting their job openings online in more than one hundred countries. Not surprisingly, most of these sites are produced in English. Since English is the most widely spoken language in the world, this may seem advantageous. However, for most people, English is a second language. They may be familiar with the basic structure of the language and able to converse in or read it. This does not mean, however, that they are aware of the nuances we so often use without regard to whether they constitute "proper English."

Since it is impractical, costly, and excessively time-consuming to prepare variations of each web page in several different languages, it behooves you to develop one site in a language that most people are able to understand. This requires a focus on how the English language is spoken and read.

Guidelines for Web Pages.

▲ *Avoid jargon.* Jargon refers to made-up words and the specialized language of a particular field or profession. Examples of jargon include "dumbsizing," "HRese," and "DPer." These made-up words can interfere with a clear, precise message. Readers may be confused by inferred meanings that slow them down. Industry-unique buzzwords or acronyms may be appropriate, but only if you are certain that at least 90 percent of your readers understand their precise meaning. With terms that are ambiguous, provide a definition the first time the word or term appears in the text. It is also a good idea to review the document from the perspective of someone outside the culture of a U.S. organization. If you have the least suspicion that readers will not share the meaning that is intended, either spell it out or make a clearer choice.

▲ *Select proper word usage.* The English language is full of words that are confused with one another. For example, do you know the difference between *assure, ensure,* and *insure; affect* and *effect; adapt* and *adopt*; *advise* and *inform*; or *accept* and *except*? We all probably learned the meanings to these words at some point in our education, but when the time comes to use these words in a sentence, we often play a guessing game as to which one is correct. To people for whom English is a second language, correct word usage is very important. They probably know the difference between *continual* and *continuous* and would find disturbing text that confuses the two.

▲ *Use proper grammar, punctuation, and spelling.* Web writing is unique, in that spaces between many words are eliminated and periods appear in the middle of sentences. In spite of this, the actual text of your job offerings should have proper grammar, punctuation, and spelling. Again, people for whom English is a second language are more likely to be aware of rules of grammar and to pick out errors. These errors could be viewed as a carelessness that is representative of your organization, influencing a candidate's decision to submit an application.

▲ *Do not avoid clichés.* In the context of business writing, I would say the opposite; however, in writing Internet text for a population consisting largely of people for whom English is a second language, clichés can actually be helpful. Certain overused, stock phrases, such as *ballpark figure*, *bottom line*, and *take the ball and run with it*, are probably familiar and more likely to convey your meaning.

▲ *Be careful about how you use numbers.* Something as simple as noting a resume filing date can be incorrectly interpreted by someone from another country. For example, in Europe, the numbers are reversed; hence, a filing date of 9/11/01 would be interpreted as meaning November 9, 2001.

▲ *Be careful about the colors you select for your graphics.* In many countries, colors have very distinct, important, and sometimes religious meanings. Hence, misusing a color on the web site can result in lost applicants. For example, in some cultures, purple is the color of royalty, while in Brazil it is associated with death.

You may choose to have your current web site translated, graphics included, into another language. Many translation companies do this for a nominal sum depending on the content and number and complexity of graphics involved. Such companies include Webtrans (Webtrans.com), Weblations (weblations.com), and International Communications (intl.com).

There is an additional problem that comes with translation. The alphabets of other languages may have characters not found in English. Therefore, you may need a product like Alis Technologies (alis.com) or Accent Software (accentsoft.com) that can create web sites in multiple languages. Likewise, if you decide to browse foreign-language web sites, such services as Globalink (globalink.com) can translate those pages into English for a nominal fee.

ELECTRONIC RECRUITMENT DRAWBACKS

We're bombarded with the advantages of using the Internet every day. Among the many indisputable pluses are speed, saving time and money, and greater access to applicants. Electronic recruitment is not without its drawbacks, however. Manny Avramidis, director of human resources New York City operations for the American Management Association, speaks for representatives from many different types of organizations when he describes his frustration with several aspects of the process. For example, says Avramidis:

> "The one empty promise most of these software firms makes is full integration with little effort. They also promise a satisfactory ROI, but they will not commit to a number. And they almost never complete their rollouts in the promised time frame. The other thing is making your other internal systems talk to your HRIS. I'm actually carrying extra staff because of our lack of systems integration. When you run an ad on Monster and receive two hundred hits over the weekend, what do you do with them? Will the resumes be captured or linked to your HRIS? Systems are supposed to simplify our lives, not make them more difficult. If they aren't integrated, what do you do with the hundreds of hits? If you maintain a separate system for recruitment, how do you run comprehensive reports from your HRIS? Another issue is that most of these tracking companies have very little history. In some cases, they are trying to sell you a product that's still in its beta version. Then, after you purchase it, they often pull the plug on the initiative. Believe me, it has happened to us."

There are ethical and legal concerns as well. One of the greatest concerns emerging from increased use of Internet recruiting is resume sharing. There is a sense that confidentiality and trust may be breached when a company shares a resume without the applicant's permission. Usually, a person sending a resume to a company is only interested in a particular job within that company, not a variety of jobs at other companies with whom the recipient may do business. Corporations have implicit agreements with applicants who apply to them directly that the resumes submitted are for that corporation's use only. On the other hand, if candidates submit resumes to an Internet resume bank, then it is presumed that they want the resume to be reviewed by as many potential employers as possible.

Other legal and ethical issues include the question of who owns the rights to retain, and possibly sell, resumes that are posted on web sites, and the impact on diversity efforts if women and minorities do not have equal access to Internet resources. Quality versus quantity is another concern. Many resume sites go for volume without considering how current their listings may be.

Also of concern is the conducting and interpreting of psychological tests online. This is especially problematic when third-party agencies are involved. The problem is that the profiles and grading are not always scientifically validated. Privacy advocates anticipate that their use in automated form and their storage in databases could become major ethical issues.

Some people cannot even get to the point of considering electronic recruitment because of their views of technology in general. There remains a fairly large population of people who are either skeptical or flat-out resistant to what they consider to be an electronic takeover of their lives. Indeed, even those who embrace technology may approach the latest set of electronic tools with some trepidation.

Research indicates that people who resist or fear an electronic approach to work cite diminished face-to-face contact as one of the primary reasons. Coupled with this is the inherent monotonous and repetitive nature of technology. Together, these factors contribute to feelings of solitude and impact worker effectiveness.

In a recent "Special Report on HR Technology," *HR Focus* identified several specific problems associated with workplace technology:[4]

1. Feeling inept, hopeless, unintelligent, intimidated, ashamed, and overwhelmed at not being able to keep up with technological changes
2. Decline in the actual quality of work and an increase in the number of work hours, until being able to learn the technology needed to accomplish tasks
3. Feelings of being enslaved or used by technology

4. Loss of privacy
5. Loss of clear-cut job responsibilities
6. Physiological changes, including mood swings, depression, exhaustion, and attention deficits, resulting from constant left brain–right brain shifting and hormone shifts (in levels of the hormones oxytocin and vasopressin, thought to be responsible for creating feelings of trust and bonding. They are found at suppressed levels when people are physically isolated from one another.)

Despite issues and drawbacks, businesses can't ignore the fact that more than a third of unemployed professional, managerial, and technical workers use electronic means for their job search. Even candidates for nonexempt jobs, such as clerical, are going online. Employers that lack access to or resist the use of electronic recruitment are likely to find themselves with openings long after their competition has filled theirs.

There are many companies on the cutting edge of electronic recruitment that use it wisely and well. One such company is Cisco Systems.

Best Practice: Cisco Systems

Cisco Systems, the San Jose, California–based technology leader, has enjoyed unparalleled growth, going from 250 employees in 1990 to more than 14,500 in fifty-five countries seven years later. Many of these employees were hired as a result of electronic recruitment (the company receives 81 percent of its resumes electronically). The company's pattern of growth continues, bringing in as many as 1,400 new hires in one quarter. These employees are additions to staff, not replacements: Cisco's turnover rate is estimated at 8 percent, far below the industry standard of 12 to 16 percent.

Cisco's objective is to hire the top echelon of engineering and business talent. This is accomplished largely through its recruitment web site. Other recruitment sources, e.g., newspaper ads and information tables at social gatherings, are used to direct applicants to the Cisco web site. Once there, applicants encounter recruiting pages—written in English, Cantonese, Mandarin, and Russian—that are informative, user-friendly, and entertaining.

The company's web site is carefully designed to target the most qualified candidates. Focus groups reveal the work practices, interests, and lifestyles of the most successful engineers and managers at the company. Cisco then identifies the most popular and influential web sites on which to post recruitment ads, as well as other web sites that applicants are likely to visit, such as Dilbert Zone.

Applicants can search jobs easily by title, job description, key words, field of interest, and location throughout the United States and the world. There is even a special "HotJobs@Cisco" page with unique positions that Cisco is especially eager to fill.

What distinguishes Cisco's site is that it goes beyond listing job openings. It gives potential recruits a glimpse into what it's like to work for the company. A page entitled "MakeFriends@Cisco" links applicants with Cisco employees, making it easier for them to talk about life at Cisco, potential job opportunities, and common interests. Cisco employees volunteer for the program, which matches them with recruits who share similar backgrounds and skills.

Currently, Cisco receives around 35,000 resumes each quarter, about 80 percent of which arrive electronically. As of this writing, Cisco was building a database that is predictive of the qualities and characteristics that make a top-notch Cisco employee. Applicants provide personal information online, such as education, professional skills, experience, and personal interests. The more information the applicant enters, the more the system asks relevant questions. The outcome is a resume that Cisco recruiters can match to job openings. Cisco views this as a system by which applicants are essentially recruiting themselves.

SUMMARY

There's no denying the revolutionary impact that the Internet has had on the job market. While it has not replaced traditional and other creative recruitment methods, online recruiting is being used by 96 percent of all U.S. employers for a greater variety of jobs than ever before. It is projected that recruiters will spend more than $1.7 billion on electronic recruitment in 2003—an increase from $105 million just four years earlier.

Electronic recruitment sources allow employers to post openings and/or collect resumes from general or specialized job sites. For a sample of electronic recruitment sources see Exhibits 5-1 and 5-2. When selecting a site, compare its attributes with your specific needs, e.g., the length of time you can post an opening. Also "test drive" it from an applicant's point of view before making a commitment. Consider, too, turning to sourcing strategists for help.

More than a third of all U.S. companies currently have their own web sites or web-based listings. For companies that already have web pages, adding a job opportunities section is relatively simple and inexpensive. Starting a web page from scratch may require the help of a consultant who can provide expertise on content, design, organization, upkeep, and exposure.

Since paper resumes are rapidly being replaced by the duller Internet version, recruiters unaccustomed to reading electronic or cyberspace resumes need to adjust to the automated method of transferring information into an applicant database and then learn to search for measurable, tangible skills and specifications.

With so many resumes being generated electronically, employers need help from applicant tracking or hiring management systems. The former collects information about job candidates and tracks various steps in the process, while the latter focuses on quickly matching applicants with positions. Employers have the choice of purchasing a client/server–based system or renting an application service provider.

Increasingly, interactive voice response is being used with other database technologies to capture competency-related information about potential employees. Despite the fact that the process can help companies staff up fast and reduce turnover, there is concern that electronic profiling could unfairly exclude those who don't fall within the desired response range, even though they possess valuable skills. Most experts agree that a computer should never substitute for a face-to-face interview.

With more and more companies expanding to include a global presence, web sites are currently posting jobs in more than one hundred countries. Since English is the most widely spoken language in the world, most sites are produced in English. However, since English is a second language for most people, care must be taken to develop sites that can be clearly understood in terms of word usage, jargon, and clichés.

Finally, despite the numerous advantages of using the Internet, such as speed and saving time and money, there are drawbacks. Systems that create additional work, ethical and legal issues surrounding matters such as resume sharing and interpreting psychological tests conducted online, and resistance to an electronic invasion are among the concerns voiced.

NOTES

1. *Human Resource Management News*, June 15, 2000.
2. *HR News*, September 2000.
3. *The New York Times*, July 20, 2000.
4. "Special Report on HR Technology," *HR Focus*, April 1999.

Exhibit 5–1. Broad-spectrum electronic recruitment sources.

The following electronic recruitment source listing represents a randomly selected cross-section of the thousands available. Provided for each of these twelve broad-spectrum sites is a self-description, the estimated number of potential candidates that companies can expect to visit the site each month, and information concerning job postings, i.e., the most prevalent types of job posted, the site's geographic distribution, fee to post one job, posting period, and whether postings can be linked to a company's own web site. In addition, information is provided concerning resume sourcing: how resumes are acquired, how many resumes are in the site's database, restrictions on posting resumes, and the fee to view resumes. Banner advertising availability is provided as well, and contact information is given. All of the information provided in this exhibit represents excerpts from *WEDDLE's Guide to Employment Web Sites 2000* by Peter Weddle (AMACOM, 2000).

1. Monster.com

Self-description:	The leading global online network for careers, connecting the most progressive companies with the most qualified career-minded individuals.
Number of visitors per month:	3.6 million
Most prevalent types of jobs posted:	Arts, entertainment/media, information systems & technology, finance & accounting
Geographic distribution of jobs posted:	National
Job posting fee:	$251–$300
Job posting period:	90 days
Job postings linked to company web sites:	No
How resumes are acquired:	Directly from candidates
Number of resumes in the database:	2.9 million

Restrictions on posting resumes:	No
Fee to view resumes:	$5,000 for 3 months; $10,000 for 1 year
Banner advertising:	Yes
Contact information:	Web site: http://www.monster.com E-mail: Sales@monster.com Phone: 1-800-MONSTER

2. TechJobBank.com

Self-description:	Focuses on listing high-tech job openings and resumes in the electronics, computer, and manufacturing industries.
Number of visitors per month:	350,000
Most prevalent types of jobs posted:	Information systems & technology, computer-related, electronics
Geographic distribution of jobs posted:	National
Job posting fee:	$101–$150
Job posting period:	60 days
Job postings linked to company web sites:	Yes
How resumes are acquired:	Directly from candidates
Number of resumes in the database:	40,000
Restrictions on posting resumes:	No
Fee to view resumes:	$600 for 6 months; $1,000 for 1 year
Banner advertising:	Yes
Contact information:	Web site: http://www.techjobbank.com E-mail: Deepka@techjobbank.com Phone: 510-226-8378

3. Minorities' Job Bank

Self-description:	Dedicated to providing career and self-development information to all minority job

	seekers, particularity to those of African/Asian/Hispanic/Native American ethnicity.
Number of visitors per month:	95,000
Most prevalent types of jobs posted:	Information systems & technology, sales & marketing, management
Geographic distribution of jobs posted:	National
Job posting fee:	$101–$150
Job posting period:	60 days
Job postings linked to company web sites:	No
How resumes are acquired:	Directly from candidates
Number of resumes in the database:	15,000
Restrictions on posting resumes:	No
Fee to view resumes:	$5,500 on average for 1 year
Banner advertising:	Yes
Contact information:	Web site: http://www.minorities-jb.com E-mail: Penny @minorities-jb.co Phone: 504-523-4616

4. 6FigureJobs.com

Self-description:	Premier site for experienced professionals to seek and be sought for high-paying (over $100,000) executive job positions.
Number of visitors per month:	Not reported
Most prevalent types of jobs posted:	Finance executives, consultants, CIOs
Geographic distribution of jobs posted:	International, U.S., Canada, U.K.
Job posting fee:	None
Job posting period:	30 days
Job postings linked to company web sites:	Yes

How resumes are acquired:	Directly from candidates
Number of resumes in the database:	5,000
Restrictions on posting resumes:	Must make over $100,000 a year
Fee to view resumes:	None
Banner advertising:	No
Contact information:	Web site: http://www.6figurejobs.com E-mail: mattm@6FigureJobs.com Phone: 203-966-3969

5. Campuscareercenter.com

Self-description:	The world's largest campus job fair. Through our network, students can begin the career exploration process with companies throughout the world.
Number of visitors per month:	50,000
Most prevalent types of jobs posted:	Engineering, computer-related, sales & marketing
Geographic distribution of jobs posted:	International
Job posting fee:	$101–$150
Job posting period:	90 days
Job postings linked to company web sites:	Yes
How resumes are acquired:	Directly from candidates
Number of resumes in the database:	9,500
Restrictions on posting resumes:	Must be a student
Fee to view resumes:	$6,000 per year
Banner advertising:	Yes
Contact information:	Web site: http://www.campuscareercenter.com E-mail: pram@campuscareercenter.com Phone: 617-621-4070

6. Telecommuting Jobs

Self-description:	Major U.S. link between job seekers interested in commuting to work via electronic means and employers who benefit by employing telecommuters.
Number of visitors per month:	76,000
Most prevalent types of jobs posted:	Information systems & technology, programming, data processing, administrative, design/graphics
Geographic distribution of jobs posted:	National
Job posting fee:	None
Job posting period:	60 days
Job postings linked to company web sites:	Yes
How resumes are acquired:	Directly from candidates
Number of resumes in the database:	18,000
Restrictions on posting resumes:	No
Fee to view resumes:	None
Banner advertising:	Yes
Contact information:	Web site: http://www.tjobs.com E-mail: slevine@tjobs.com Phone: 847-835-2180

7. CareerPath.com

Self-description:	Offers the most current database of newspaper classifieds and Internet-only job listings, and the most precise resume search engine.
Number of visitors per month:	1,004,000
Most prevalent types of jobs posted:	Information systems & technology, programming, data processing, administrative, design/graphics
Geographic distribution of jobs posted:	National

Job posting fee:	$151–$200
Job posting period:	Direct postings—30 days; others—14 days
Job postings linked to company web sites:	Yes
How resumes are acquired:	Directly from candidates
Number of resumes in the database:	745,000
Restrictions on posting resumes:	Registered on-site
Fee to view resumes:	$500 for 1 month; $5,000 for 1 year
Banner advertising:	Yes
Contact information:	Web site: http://www.careerpath.com E-mail: carola.conte@careerpath.com Phone: 310-234-1413

8. Diversitycareersonline.com

Self-description:	Will connect those companies and individuals which are seeking a balanced and diverse place of employment.
Number of visitors per month:	Not reported
Most prevalent types of jobs posted:	Information systems & technology, finance & accounting, pharmaceutical
Geographic distribution of jobs posted:	National
Job posting fee:	From less than $100 to $300+
Job posting period:	90 days
Job postings linked to company web sites:	Yes
How resumes are acquired:	N/A
Number of resumes in the database:	N/A
Restrictions on posting resumes:	N/A
Fee to view resumes:	N/A
Banner advertising:	Yes

Contact information:	Web site: http://www.diversitycareersonline.com E-mail: info@diversitycareersonline.com Phone: 888-262-8058

9. Hotjobs.com

Self-description:	Provides the most direct connection between employers and experienced professionals, free of distractions from third-party intermediaries such as headhunters.
Number of visitors per month:	2.5 million
Most prevalent types of jobs posted:	Information systems & technology, sales & marketing, finance & accounting
Geographic distribution of jobs posted:	National
Job posting fee:	$101–$150
Job posting period:	30 days
Job postings linked to company web sites:	Yes
How resumes are acquired:	Directly from candidates
Number of resumes in the database:	685,000
Restrictions on posting resumes:	No
Fee to view resumes:	Yes—included in membership fee
Banner advertising:	Yes
Contact information:	Web site: http://www.hotjobs.com E-mail: simon@hotjobs.com Phone: 212-302-0060

10. JobShark.com

Self-description:	A resource that uses sophisticated software to match job seeker and employer, sending full job descriptions to job seekers that match the skills the company is looking for.

Number of visitors per month:	200,000
Most prevalent types of jobs posted:	Administrative, sales & marketing, information systems & technology
Geographic distribution of jobs posted:	International, Canada, Ireland, U.K.
Job posting fee:	Over $300
Job posting period:	60 days
Job postings linked to company web sites:	Yes
How resumes are acquired:	Directly from candidates
Number of resumes in the database:	147,000
Restrictions on posting resumes:	No
Fee to view resumes:	N/A
Banner advertising:	Yes
Contact information:	Web site: http:/ www.jobshark.com E-mail: cmolson@jobshark.com Phone: 416-944-2444

11. Careers.wsj.com

Self-description:	The Internet's premier site for middle- to senior-level executives, featuring more than 2,000 articles on all aspects of job hunting and career management and a wide range of helpful tools.
Number of visitors per month:	350,000
Most prevalent types of jobs posted:	Finance & accounting, management, consulting
Geographic distribution of jobs posted:	National
Job posting fee:	$100 or less (average)
Job posting period:	Until updated by company
Job postings linked to company web sites:	Yes
How resumes are acquired:	Directly from candidates

Number of resumes in the database:	350,000
Restrictions on posting resumes:	No
Fee to view resumes:	Specific to each client
Banner advertising:	Yes
Contact information:	Web site: http://careers.wsj.com E-mail: tlee@wsj.dowjones.com Phone: 609-520-4305

12. USA Job Auction

Self-description:	In an auction-style format, USAJobauction allows employers, recruiters, and employees to bid on prospective jobs or job candidates. With over 1 million links to job opportunities.
Number of visitors per month:	Not reported
Most prevalent types of jobs posted:	Sales & marketing, management, healthcare
Geographic distribution of jobs posted:	International
Job posting fee:	$100 or less
Job posting period:	90 days
Job postings linked to company web sites:	No
How resumes are acquired:	Directly from candidates
Number of resumes in the database:	Under 100
Restrictions on posting resumes:	No
Fee to view resumes:	Yes—included in membership fee
Banner advertising:	Yes
Contact information:	Web site: http://www.usajobauction.com E-mail: info@usajobauction.com Phone: 877-600-4830

Exhibit 5–2. Specialized electronic recruitment sources.

The following electronic recruitment sources are identified by the most prevalent, specialized types of jobs they post. All of the information provided in this exhibit represents excerpts from *WED-DLE's Guide to Employment Web Sites 2000* by Peter Weddle (AMA-COM, 2000).

1. AAEA On-Line (http://www.aaea.org)
   Agricultural economics, agribusiness
2. Academic Physician & Scientist (http://www.acphysci.com)
   Anesthesiology, neurology
3. Accountantjobs.com (http://www.accountantjobs.com)
   Accounting
4. American Marketing Association (http://www.ama.org)
   Directors/managers of marketing, product managers
5. American Society of Limnology and Oceanography (http://www.aslo.org)
   Marine technicians, postdoctoral researchers
6. Asia-Net.com (http://www.asia-net.com)
   Information systems & technology, finance & accounting, sales & marketing in Asia-Pacific
7. Auto Careers (http://www.autocareers.com)
   Technicians, general sales/service managers
8. Bakery-Net (http://www.bakery-net.com)
   Bakers, bakery managers
9. Bankjobs.com (http://www.bankjobs.com)
   Banking, financial services
10. BenefitsLink.com (http://www.benefitslink.com)
    Pension administrative/sales & marketing, benefits managers
11. The BioCareer Center (http://www.biocareer.com)
    Research scientists, quality control
12. Casino Careers Online (http://www.casinocareers.com)
    Casino gaming/hotel operations
13. ChefJobsNetwork.com (http://chefjobsnetwork.com)
    Executive chefs
14. The Chronicle of Higher Education (http://chronicle.com)
    College faculty, administrators/executives
15. Construction Job Store (http://www.constructionjobstore.com)
    Construction-related
16. Cool Works—Jobs in Great Places (http://www.coolworks.com)
    Hospitality, outdoor recreation
17. CPAjobs.com (http://www.cpajobs.com)
    Controllers, financial analysts, auditors

18. Creative Freelancers On-Line (http://www.freelancers.com)
    Commercial artists, writers, tech support
19. Developers.Net (http://www.developers.net)
    Software development
20. Discovery Place Petroleum Directory (http://www.discoveryplace.com)
    Petroleum engineers, geologists
21. Drilling Research Institute (http://www.drillers.com)
    Oil field drilling, drilling operations
22. Earthworks (http://www.earthworks-jobs.com)
    Geoscientists, petroleum/geotech engineers
23. EAttorney (http://www.eattorney.com)
    Attorneys
24. Editor & Publisher Interactive (http://www.mediainfo.com)
    News media, publishing
24. EE-Link (http://eelink.net)
    Environmental education
26. EHarvest.com Agricultural Careers Site (http://careers.eharvest.com)
    Agricultural sales/research/management
27. The Employment Guide's HealthCareerWeb (http://www.healthcareerweb.com)
    Healthcare
28. ERP-People.com (http://www.erp-people.com)
    Enterprise resource planning, supply chain management
29. The Fiber Optic Marketplace (http://www.fiberoptic.com)
    Fiber-optic technicians, field engineers/managers
30. Finishing.com (http://www.finishing.com)
    Metal finishing
31. Hospitality Net (http://www.hospitalitynet.org)
    Hotel/restaurant management, sales & marketing
32. hrjobs.com (http://www.hrjobs.com)
    Human resources
33. I-Advertising (http://www.internetadvertising.org)
    Online advertising, sales & marketing
34. Idealist (http://www.idealist.com)
    All positions in nonprofit organizations
35. IEEE-USA Employment Services (http://www.ieeeusa.org/jobs)
    Electrical engineers, electronic, computer
36. Infoworks USA Computer Job Center (http://www.it123.com)
    Information services, high-tech
37. Insurance Career Center (http://www.insjobs.com)
    All insurance-related

38. K-12 Jobs (http://www.k12jobs.com)
    Math/bilingual/special education teachers
39. LotusNotes.Jobs.com (http://www.lotusnotesjobs.com)
    Power builder/visual basic/web programming
40. MedBulletin (http://www.medbulletin.com)
    Primary care, emergency medicine
41. National Federation of Paralegal Associations, Inc. (http://www.paralegals.org)
    Paralegals
42. Online Sports Career Center (http://www.onlinesports.com/pages/CareerCenter.html)
    Sales & marketing, coaches, event coordination
43. Real Estate Job Store (www.realestatejobstore.com)
    Real estate, mortgage, construction
44. SalesSeek (http://www.salesseek.com)
    Sales representatives/managers, inside sales
45. Skiing the Net (http://www.skiingthenet.com)
    Snow sports marketing, ski instructors
46. Summerjobs.com (http://www.summerjobs.com)
    Internships, summer/resort jobs
47. TELEPLAZA (http://www.teleplaza.com)
    Call center customer service, telemarketing
48. Truckdriver.com (http://www.truckdriver.com)
    Trucking
49. Unix Guru Universe (http://www.ugu.com)
    Unix-related
50. The Write Jobs (http://www.writerswrite.com/jobs)
    Writers, editors, journalists

Chapter 6

Competency-Based Recruiting and Interviewing

"If the nature of the work is properly appreciated and applied, it will stand in the same relation to the higher faculties as food is to the physical body."

—J.C. Kumarappa, philosopher and economist

Joel was apprehensive. As the senior recruiter for his company, he had the responsibility of filling a key vice president's position. The resignation by Marlene, the incumbent, seemed inevitable after she had spent just six months on the job. Despite her outstanding credentials and excellent track record, Marlene and the company just hadn't meshed. Her style of approaching tasks clashed with the company culture, so much so that fourteen months from the time she joined the company, she had become a "disconnect." Joel, who had participated in hiring Marlene, still couldn't figure out what had gone wrong. Her employment and termination, complete with generous severance package, had cost the company plenty, and Joel didn't know how to prevent the same kind of mistake from happening again. He had thoroughly familiarized himself with the parameters of the job before recruiting, and yet the "perfect candidate" had turned into a disaster. What had happened? How could someone who seemed so right for the job fail?

Joel was also concerned about where he would find a suitable replacement. He was acutely aware of shifts in employment and some of the new "hot" jobs. He was worried that his company couldn't attract the kind of candidate it needed.

The essence of the problem in this scenario and many others like it boils down to a combination of two key factors: (1) failure to properly identify job competencies, and (2) acquiring the right fit.

Competencies are skills, traits, qualities, or characteristics that contribute to a person's ability to perform effectively the duties and responsibilities of a job. They are, effectively, the gauges for job success. Too often, employers think they know what traits are being sought in a candidate, but they don't take the time to identify the specific competencies needed to perform a specific job successfully. Indeed, most jobs require as many as forty to fifty competencies.

Employers that establish a solid prerecruitment foundation, use a competency-based approach to recruiting, ask competency-based questions during the interview, and then look for the right fit between the candidate and the corporate culture stand the greatest chance of succeeding in properly matching a particular candidate with a specific job.

PRERECRUITMENT FOUNDATION

Before exploring various recruitment sources or interviewing candidates, employers are urged to establish a solid prerecruitment foundation. This means evaluating the specifications of a job every time it becomes available by reviewing the position's responsibilities, requirements, reporting relationships, environmental factors, exemption and union status, salary, benefits, and growth opportunities. This important familiarization process provides necessary answers to four key questions:

1. Am I thoroughly familiar with the qualities being sought in an applicant?
2. Are these qualities both job-related and realistic?
3. Can I clearly communicate the duties and responsibilities of this position to applicants?
4. Am I prepared to provide additional relevant information about the job and the company to applicants?

Duties and Responsibilities

If you are an HR specialist, make it a point to spend time in the department where an opening exists. Observe and converse with incumbents as they perform various aspects of the job. Talk to supervisors in charge for their perspective of the scope of work involved. If possible, seek out people who have previously held the position to see how the job may have evolved. Try to visit on more than one occasion so that you are able to observe a typical day.

If a personal visit is not possible, have lengthy telephone conversations with several departmental representatives. Also, request a job description and review its contents for a detailed description of the level and degree of responsibility. Well-written job descriptions can be an interviewer's most valuable tool.

In reviewing the duties and responsibilities of an opening, determine if they are realistic in relation to other factors, such as previous experience and education. Determine, too, if they are germane to the overall job function or overlap with the responsibilities of other jobs.

It is important to review the duties and responsibilities of a job opening each time a position becomes available. Even if an opening was filled six months ago and is now vacant again, assess the responsibilities of the job to make certain no major changes have occurred in the interim. This ensures up-to-date job information and accuracy when discussing the position with potential employees.

Education and Prior Experience

Generally, the department head in charge of the area where a specific opening exists describes the qualifications needed for the job. HR specialists then comment on their appropriateness. Together, they agree upon and establish any educational and experience prerequisites.

This process is most effective when managers and HR representatives ask these key questions:

- ▲ What skills and knowledge are needed to perform successfully the primary duties and responsibilities of this job?
- ▲ Why are these skills and knowledge necessary?
- ▲ Why couldn't someone without these skills and knowledge perform the primary duties of this job?
- ▲ Are the requirements consistent with the job duties and responsibilities?
- ▲ Are we being influenced by the background of the present or last incumbent?
- ▲ Are we subjectively considering our own personal expectations of the job?

▲ Are we compromising because we are in a hurry to fill the job?

▲ Are we unrealistically searching for the ideal candidate?

▲ Are we succumbing to pressure from senior management as to what are appropriate job requirements?

▲ Are the requirements in accordance with all applicable equal employment opportunity laws and regulations?

Arbitrarily setting high minimum standards with the hope of filling a position with the most qualified person can backfire. For example, suppose you are trying to fill a first-line supervisor's spot and you decide you need someone who not only has a great deal of hands-on experience but is also well-rounded. To you, this translates into someone with at least five years of supervisory experience and a four-year college degree. If asked some of the questions suggested above, you would probably conclude that these requirements are too high for a first-line supervisory position. Also, for reasons of equal employment opportunity, you would need to modify them. But even if there were no applicable employment laws, there is a good reason for setting more flexible standards: If you come across applicants falling short of this experience and educational profile, but who meet other intangible requirements and come highly recommended, you would not be able to hire them. It would be difficult to justify hiring someone not meeting the minimum requirements of the job, especially if you also rejected candidates who exceeded them.

In addition to asking yourself these basic questions regarding experience and education, there is a way of setting requirements that does not paint you into a corner but still allows you to be highly selective. By using carefully worded terminology in the job description, you can choose the candidate who best combines both concrete and intangible requirements. These phrases include the following:

▲ Demonstrated ability to _____ required.

▲ In-depth knowledge of _____ required.

▲ Extensive experience in _____ required.

▲ Knowledge of _____ would be an advantage.

▲ Proven ability to _____ required.

▲ We are looking for an effective _____.

▲ Proven track record of _____ needed.

▲ Substantial experience in _____ essential.

▲ Familiarity with _____ would be ideal.

▲ Degree relevant to _____ preferred.
▲ Degree in _____ preferred.
▲ Advanced degree a plus.
▲ College degree in _____ highly desirable.
▲ An equivalent combination of education and experience . . .

These sample phrases provide the necessary latitude to select someone who, for example, may be lacking in one area, such as education, but compensates with a great deal of experience. The use of such terms does not mean that hiring standards are compromised; rather, it means that care is being taken to avoid setting requirements that cannot be justified by the specific duties of the job, while at the same time offering the widest range of choice from among the most qualified applicants.

Intangible Requirements

Intangible criteria can help balance the lack of specific educational or experiential requirements. These might include:

▲ Ability to get along with coworkers, management, employees, clients, and customers
▲ Appearance
▲ Assertiveness
▲ Attitude
▲ Creativity and imagination
▲ Initiative
▲ Management style
▲ Maturity
▲ Personality
▲ Responsiveness
▲ Self-confidence
▲ Temperament

These factors can be significant, but only when examined in relation to the requirements of the job opening. That is, in addition to determining any relevant educational and experiential prerequisites as well as examining the scope and degree of responsibilities, you should explore the question of what type of individual would be most compatible with the position. This may be determined by learning as much as possible about such factors as the amount of stress involved, the amount of independent work as opposed to closely supervised work, and the overall management style of the department. The combined information should translate into a profile of the ideal employee.

Keeping this profile in mind as candidates are considered can be productive, particularly if two or more applicants meet the concrete requirements of the job. You can then compare intangible job-related criteria to assist with the final decision. Intangibles can also prove helpful in evaluating candidates for entry-level jobs for which there are few, if any, tangible educational and experiential prerequisites.

However, caution is advised when making comparisons based on intangibles, since the meaning of certain terms is highly subjective. For example, some of the more popular applicant evaluation phrases—like saying that an applicant has a bad attitude, a winning personality, a nice appearance, or a mature approach to work—may not always translate the same way for everyone. Furthermore, such descriptions really do not tell us anything substantive about what the person can contribute to a given job. Hence, be careful not to weigh intangible elements too heavily or select someone solely on the basis of any of these factors. If considered at all, such factors should be job-related, not based on personal bias.

Reporting Relationships

Another facet of the familiarization process has to do with reporting relationships. In this regard, ask yourself the following questions:

▲ What position does this job report to, both directly and indirectly?
▲ Where does this job appear on the department's organizational chart?
▲ What positions, if any, report directly and/or indirectly to this job?
▲ What is the relationship between this job and other jobs in the department, in terms of level and scope of responsibility?
▲ What is the relationship between this job and other jobs in the organization?

It is important to note that these questions pertain to positions, as opposed to specific individuals. This precludes the possibility of the answers being influenced by the personality or skill of a particular employee.

Work Environment

A job's work environment consists of four distinct areas. You need to familiarize yourself with:

1. *Physical working conditions.* This encompasses such factors as sitting or standing for long periods of time, working in areas that may not be well ventilated, being exposed to chemicals or toxic fumes, working in cramped quarters, working in a very noisy location, and working with video display terminals for long periods of time. If the working conditions are ideal, few interviewers hesitate to inform prospective employees of this. After all, this helps sell the company and the job, perhaps even compensating for aspects that are less ideal (perhaps the starting salary is not up to par with that of a competitor or the benefits package is not as comprehensive). However, if the working conditions leave something to be desired, the tendency is to omit reference to them when discussing the job in the hope that once employees begin work and discover the flaw in the work environment, they will adjust rather than leave. Unfortunately, what frequently occurs is that new employees resent the deception and either quit or develop poor work habits.

2. *Geographic location of the job.* If at all possible, show potential employees where they would be working. If recruiting from a central office for positions in satellite branches, be specific in the description of the job site, and offer videos, CD-ROMs, or brochures illustrating the location where an opening exists. Sometimes a position calls for rotation from one location to another. If this is the case, be prepared to describe the working conditions of each location and how long each assignment is likely to last. Be sure to elicit a reaction to the idea of job rotation. Many employees prefer to settle into a work routine where they are familiar with the environment, the commute, and the other workers. On the other hand, some people like the variety offered by a rotational position.

3. *Travel.* Be sure to discuss the geographic span and the expected frequency of job-related travel. Tell applicants, too, how much advance notice they can anticipate. In the case of local travel, applicants want to know whether they are expected to provide their own transportation. They also want to know how reimbursement for job-related travel expenses is handled.

4. *Specific schedule.* This is especially important for clerical and entry-level positions. Employees need to be told what days of

the week they are expected to work, when to report to work each day, and when they may leave. If alternative work arrangements are available, as discussed in Chapter 10, applicants need to know their options. Also, be sure you know how much time is allotted for meals, as well as other scheduled breaks throughout the day. Conveying this information to applicants can avoid disciplinary problems after they become employees.

Exemption Status

The Fair Labor Standards Act (FLSA) defines the term *exempt* literally to mean exempt from overtime compensation; that is, an employer is not required to pay exempt employees for time worked beyond their regularly scheduled workweek. Although this generally pertains to executives, managers, professionals, and some supervisors, the FLSA does not prohibit companies from paying managerial staff for overtime. However, with the exception of strikes and other work-related emergencies, this is rarely done. The term *nonexempt* literally means not exempt from overtime compensation. Nonexempt employees, such as clerical workers, must be paid for any time worked beyond their regularly scheduled workweek.

Familiarity with a position's exemption status is important so applicants know if they can expect paid or unpaid overtime work.

Union Status

The National Labor Relations Act of 1935 (also called the Wagner Act) clearly states, "Employees shall have the right to self-organization, to form, join, or assist labor organizations, to bargain collectively, through representatives of their own choosing, and to engage in other concerted activities, for the purpose of collective bargaining or other mutual aid or protection."

While union membership has been in a steady decline since the early 1980s, union organizing activities are on the upswing. Organizing efforts target primarily small, public-sector establishments with large numbers of women and younger employees, as well as private-sector companies with fewer than one hundred employees. Industries experiencing the greatest amount of organizing are nursing homes and other care facilities and computer manufacturers. Most organizing activity is taking place in the Northeast and Midwest, where traditionally labor unions have had a strong presence.

That being said, interviewers should be prepared to tell applicants whether they are required to join a union, and if so, which union it is, information relative to initiation fees or required dues, and, essentially, what being a union member entails. Exercise caution when discussing this subject: Do not express your personal opinions regarding unions or try to bias applicants, either for or against unions. Also, avoid inquiries regarding applicants' views toward unions or about their past union involvement. Your job is to be informative and descriptive only.

Salary Ranges

Whether this information is disclosed to an applicant at the initial interview is a matter of company policy, but interviewers should certainly know what a job pays so they can determine if a candidate warrants further consideration. If, for example, there is an opening for an administrative assistant paying an annual salary of from $35,000 to $47,500, and an applicant is currently earning $37,750, there is no problem. If, on the other hand, a managerial position becomes available paying a salary of from $50,000 to $68,000, and an applicant is currently making $67,000, there are some areas of concern. What is your company's policy regarding starting a new employee at the maximum of the salary range? If you offer the maximum, will this person accept an increase of just $1,000? What about subsequent salary increases? Does your company "red circle" employees at the ceiling of the range so that they remain frozen there until either the salary structure is reevaluated or the position is reclassified?

Other salary-related issues may arise. Applicants may currently be earning considerably less than your minimum salary for what may be considered comparable work. It could be that they are currently underpaid or not being altogether forthright about the actual duties and responsibilities they perform. This, then, calls for a more thorough line of questioning during the interview regarding the level and scope of tasks currently being performed.

Applicants sometimes indicate that they are currently earning considerably more than the maximum for an available position. Do not automatically assume that this translates into overqualification or that the person will not remain on the job. There are a number of explanations as to why a potential employee would be willing to take a reduction in pay, including the opportunity to work for a specific company, the desire to learn new skills or enter a new field, or an inability to find suitable work in one's own profession.

Note that the necessity for acquiring a job candidate's salary history is increasingly being challenged as concerns about pay inequities for men and women prevail.

Benefits

Describing your company's benefits package can be an excellent selling point, especially for hard-to-fill positions. It's advisable to prepare a brief, comprehensive summary identifying company benefits, such as medical and disability insurance, dental coverage, life insurance, profit-sharing plans, stock bonus programs, vacation days, personal days, leaves of absence, holidays, and tuition reimbursement.

Be careful not to give the impression that a discussion of your company's benefits means that you are seriously considering the particular applicant for the job. Make it clear that providing such information is merely part of the interview process, not an implied job offer, and that whoever is selected will receive more comprehensive benefits information at the time of hire.

Growth Opportunities

Generally, applicants are interested in whether they will be able to move up in an organization. It is therefore helpful to know about the frequency of performance appraisals, salary reviews, and salary increases; policies regarding promotions; the relationship of a position's level and scope of responsibilities to that of others within a job family; policies governing internal job posting; the likelihood of advancement; tuition reimbursement plans; and training.

It is advantageous to provide an accurate account of growth opportunities to preclude the possibility of morale problems developing later on. For example, if an applicant is applying for a position that is one step removed from the top position in a given job family, and that position has been occupied by the same person for the past ten years, the opportunity for growth by way of promotion is unlikely. There are, however, other ways to grow, such as an expansion of responsibilities that could, in turn, lead to the creation of a new job classification.

COMPETENCY-BASED RECRUITMENT

Key Competency Categories

Identifying job-specific competencies prior to recruitment enables you to determine gauges for success. A competency is a skill, trait, quality, or characteristic that contributes to a person's ability to perform the duties and responsibilities of a job effectively. While every job requires different competencies, there are four primary categories: (1) measurable, tangible, or technical skills; (2) knowledge; (3) behavior; and (4) interpersonal skills. Most jobs emphasize the need for one category over the others, but every employee should be able to demonstrate competencies, to some extent, in all four categories.

For many jobs today, measurable, tangible, or technical skills are critical to success. Such competencies demonstrate what people have done in past jobs. Technical competencies that are critical to success for many jobs today include having overall technical know-how, tailoring technical information to different audiences, applying technical expertise to solve business problems, staying technologically current, understanding the technologies of the organization, optimizing technology, balancing multiple projects, and communicating project status. While these technical competencies are indisputably necessary, the other three categories need to be examined as well. The reason for this is simple: Workers bring much more than technical skill to a job. Complex beings that we all are, we also carry an array of knowledge, behaviors, and interpersonal skills, all of which contribute to our success or failure on the job. This is true regardless of the job or grade level.

Consider this situation: There are two openings for the same type of job and two people are hired, both of whom are technically proficient. One of them, Paul, has slightly more experience than Justine, but both possess outstanding technical know-how. After one year, Justine's performance review reveals that she is doing above-average work, while Paul's indicates borderline, barely adequate performance. Why? Paul has trouble focusing on the key elements of a project and does not interact well with customers. In addition, while Justine responds well to feedback, Paul views suggestions as criticism. His poor performance evaluation derives from a number of nontechnical issues. What went wrong?

Looking back, the interviewer in this scenario focused all of his questions on the candidates' technical capabilities, erroneously assuming that inquiries relating to the other competencies were ir-relevant for a technical job. Had he questioned Paul about his inter-action with customers in past jobs, or asked for examples of how Paul handled past projects, he might not have extended a job offer, in spite of Paul's technical expertise.

The second competency, knowledge, concerns what candi-dates know and how they think. Included in this category are proj-ect-management skills, problem-solving abilities, decision-making skills, the ability to focus on key elements of a project, time man-agement, and the ability to use resources effectively. These are considered intangible qualities—more difficult to measure and quantify than concrete skills, but no less important. Every job, re-gardless of level, requires a certain degree of knowledge. Even an entry-level position demands some degree of decision making or problem solving. Interviewers should ask knowledge-related ques-tions appropriate to the level and nature of a job to determine not only what candidates know but how they think. This is especially important when jobs do not require previous measurable experi-ence, thereby precluding your ability to draw from past job-related experiences.

The third competency concerns a candidate's key behaviors, or how the applicant acts under certain conditions. For example, suppose the position calls for qualities that generate a high level of client satisfaction. In past client-oriented jobs, was this applicant committed to developing lasting partnerships with clients? Were clients kept informed of key developments? Was there follow-up to ensure client satisfaction? If part of a team, or the team leader, did the candidate help team members focus on client requirements? Were client views incorporated in decision making? There are numerous questions you can ask candidates with regard to job-specific behaviors that reveal whether they will function effectively in your company's environment, meeting client needs.

The fourth and final competency category involves interper-sonal skills—that is, how an applicant interacts with others. Find out if the job candidate actively listens, exercises self-control when upset, motivates and works effectively with a wide range of people, respects the views and ideas of others, remains receptive to feed-back, and manages conflict effectively. Every job requires some de-gree of interaction with others. Regardless of how competent they are, what they know, and how they behave, if job candidates are unable to interact effectively with managers, coworkers, employ-ees, or clients, then their work and the work of others will suffer. Interviewers must focus, therefore, on how the applicants interacted in past situations similar to those that are likely to occur in your organization.

Failure to identify job-related competencies can result in production, morale, and motivational problems. And of course, hiring mismatched candidates can be costly. Properly identifying job-related competencies prior to recruitment, on the other hand, allows you to identify how effective applicants have been in the past and, therefore, how effective they are likely to be at their new jobs.

Job-Specific Competencies

While each job thus requires competencies in the four categories of technical skills, knowledge, behavior, and interpersonal skills, each also necessitates a distinct set of job-specific competencies, depending on the particular responsibilities involved.

Several sources determine which competencies are relevant for a specific opening. Information about the job is generated primarily by the position description. Additional information can be gleaned from a job requisition and postings. Also, talk with department heads, managers, and supervisors having an in-depth understanding of the position. They are most helpful with the technical and knowledge competencies. Incumbents can prove helpful, too, as they can provide insight into the behaviors and interpersonal skills needed for the job.

Once you have gathered information about the job, isolate job-specific competencies. This two-step procedure consists of (1) making a list of all the required competencies, and (2) identifying each competency according to its category. For example, consider a programmer analyst. Here is a partial list of competencies needed to perform this job successfully, as determined after examining an HR-generated job description and posting, as well as having conversations with a manager and two incumbents. Note that the list consists of both responsibilities and requirements:

- ▲ Designs applications, significant subsystems, and/or complete individual programs
- ▲ Identifies alternative implementations or strategies, and weighs the impact of each
- ▲ Estimates time requirements for a set of modules with internal and external dependencies
- ▲ Experienced in real-time, multiprocessing systems within an event-driven architecture

▲ Experienced in C+ +/Unix
▲ Must be able to work as a member of a team
▲ Capable of learning new ideas quickly
▲ Able to develop software of the highest quality in a high-pressure environment with other team members
▲ Able to meet deadlines
▲ Experienced with complex modules/systems

Now you are ready to identify each competency according to its category. Review what each of the competencies represents: *Technical* reflects what candidates can do, *knowledge* refers to what they know and how they think, *behaviors* reveal how they act, and *interpersonal skills* indicate how they interact. Return to your list and mark each item with a "T" for technical (or tangible), "K" for knowledge, "B" for behaviors, and "I" for interpersonal skills. Note that a competency can reflect more than one category:

▲ T/K: Designs applications, significant subsystems, and/or complete individual programs
▲ T/K: Identifies alternative implementations or strategies, and weighs the impact of each
▲ T/K: Estimates time requirements for a set of modules with internal and external dependencies
▲ T/K: Experienced in real-time, multiprocessing systems within an event-driven architecture
▲ T/K: Experienced in C+ +/Unix
▲ B/I: Must be able to work as a member of a team
▲ K: Capable of learning new ideas quickly
▲ T/I: Able to develop software of the highest quality in a high-pressure environment with other team members
▲ B: Able to meet deadlines
▲ T: Experienced with complex modules/systems

Now go back over your list to ensure that all four categories are represented. You will no doubt see a greater emphasis of some competencies over others (in the case of a programmer/analyst, the emphasis is technical). Also, where competencies are paired, technical and knowledge generally fall together, as do behaviors and interpersonal skills. That's fine, as long as all four areas are represented. If they are not, go back and seek out additional information. This is a critical prerecruitment step that interviewers should perform to ensure that they probe all relevant areas during the interview.

Matching the Applicant to the Job

Having isolated job-specific competencies, you are ready to correlate what the job requires with what the applicant has to offer. Information about the applicant can come from several sources. Two of the most comprehensive are the completed employment application form and the resume. Do not assume the two are interchangeable, however. The application requires candidates to answer specific questions. The categories on the form direct them, seeking specific information. It is evident if candidates leave some categories blank or give vague or partial answers. The information provided on resumes, on the other hand, is entirely up to the applicants. They decide what is provided or concealed, and it is up to a savvy interviewer to zero in on missing, incomplete, or inaccurate information. The verbiage on a resume, generally more narrative than any answer to a question on an application, can also dazzle or misguide an interviewer easily influenced by important-sounding titles and fancy phrases. Note that reading cyberspace resumes requires some adjustment (Chapter 5). While the focus remains the same as with paper resumes, the organization of information and the style differs. Information on cyberspace resumes does not always appear chronologically or by function, and they are rarely as visually appealing. Also, highlighting key accomplishments with asterisks and capital letters is encouraged in cyberspace resumes; this rarely occurs on paper resumes. As one recruiter put it, "What pleases a computer is likely to bore a person."

It is a good idea, then, to require an application from all potential candidates submitting a resume. It should be completed on company premises to preclude the possibility of outside assistance, and applicants should be instructed to answer all the questions, precluding the use of "see resume" in response to some questions.

Applicant-related information can also be gleaned from referrals. If candidates come to you as a result of staff word-of-mouth recruiting, the referring employee can provide helpful job-related information. Perhaps they worked together as programmer analysts in the past. That could yield information about an applicant's technical, knowledge, and behavior competencies. Maybe your employee supervised the referral in a past job. Important information about interpersonal skills could be discerned from that relationship.

When considering data from a referral, do not be influenced by irrelevant factors. For example, if the referral comes from a colleague for whom you have a high regard, do not assume that the candidate will elicit the same response. Likewise, if you hold little regard for the person making the recommendation, you could be biased against the applicant before any meeting takes place. Avoid this trap by adhering to job-related competencies, derived from the four primary competency categories.

While sometimes difficult to obtain because former employers may fear charges of defamation of character or invasion of privacy brought by former employees, references can also provide valuable information about a candidate. Try to contact at least three former employers to establish a pattern. If one former manager indicates that the candidate was trouble from the outset and he was glad when she resigned, but two others say she was outstanding, it's probable that there are others issues affecting the first reference. Additional probing is needed to get a clearer, more consistent picture.

Once you have identified the job-specific competencies and have information about the candidate, you are ready to proceed with conducting the competency-based interview.

COMPETENCY-BASED INTERVIEWING

Some time ago, I arrived at a conference center in New Jersey to conduct a seminar on interviewing skills. I needed help transferring the training materials from my car to the center and enlisted the help of one of the center's employees. He was interested in learning why I was there, and when I told him he became very excited. "My father is an interviewer!" he exclaimed. "He's taught me a lot about interviewing." "Oh? Like what?" I asked. He stopped walking, faced me, and looked me over from head to toe. When he reached my feet, he looked up and smiled. "You're very good at what you do. I can tell." I was completely puzzled. "How do you know that?" I asked, a little apprehensive of his answer. "Because of your shoes. My father taught me that all you have to do to tell if people are good at what they do is to check out their shoes. If they take care of their shoes, then you can count on them being reliable. You have nice shoes. So I know you're good at what you do."

This encounter has since been placed in my ever-expanding file, alongside other, equally nonsensical reasons for hiring or not hiring someone. Here are a few samples:

▲ "The minute he walked in the room, I could tell he was right for the job. He just looked like a (manager)."

▲ "You can tell from the way a person shakes hands if she's right for the job."

▲ "If the person doesn't look you in the eye, you know he's lying."

▲ "If a person smiles too much, it means she's covering up something."

▲ "I know a good (accountant) when I see one."

▲ "I go by gut feeling."

▲ "I can just tell."

▲ "I would never hire someone who's taller than I am."

The list goes on. Competency-based interviewing precludes such notions and focuses on job-related criteria. By doing so, such interviews are more effective at evaluating the potential for job success than interviews based on gut feelings or shoes. Indeed, some experts maintain that competency-based interviewing can more than triple the likelihood of accurately predicting on-the-job performance.

Characteristics of Competency-Based Questions

Competency-based questions draw from applicants' past experiences and behaviors, relating them to specific requirements, responsibilities, or parameters of a given job-related situation. Such questions are based on information relevant to specific job-related skills, abilities, and traits; the answers reveal the probability of similar performance in the future. The process works because past behavior is an indicator of future behavior. Be careful not to translate this last statement as reading "past behavior predicts future behavior" or "future behavior is the same as past behavior." Past behavior is an indicator only: No one can predict, with absolute certainty, how someone will behave in a job. There are too many variables that can affect a person's performance, among them a significant change in the work environment; the approach, attitude, or personality of a supervisor or manager; difficulties in an employee's personal life; a long-term or degenerative illness or disability; the introduction of a new organizational philosophy; what is perceived as being an unfair performance appraisal or salary increase; or being bypassed for a promotion. Any of these alone can alter how an employee approaches work, and even the most conscientious, dedicated workers can be adversely affected.

Since interviewers cannot anticipate these influences when first meeting a candidate, they must develop a line of questioning that projects, as accurately as possible, how an employee is likely to behave if hired. This is best accomplished by asking the applicant to draw from past job experiences.

For example, suppose you have an opening that is known for its emergency projects and unreasonable deadlines. You can find out if a person is up to the challenge by asking about similar experiences in the past. This is how you might phrase the question: "Tell me about a time in your last job when you were given an emergency project with what you believed to be an unrealistic deadline. What did you do?" Suppose the applicant's response indicates a firm grasp of how to handle this type of situation. You still need to determine if the applicant was required to interrupt the normal workload frequently to attend to emergencies, or only once in a while. In addition, you want to know if other work suffered while the emergency project was being tended to. Some follow-up competency-based questions, then, would be:

▲ "Tell me about the last three emergency projects you had to take care of and how closely together they occurred."
▲ "Describe the steps you took to deal effectively with these emergencies and the impact it had on the rest of your work."
▲ "Who else was involved in meeting these deadlines, and what were the respective responsibilities?"
▲ "Has there ever been a time when you felt the deadline could not be met? If so, what did you do?"

Competency-based questions, then, seek specific examples. These examples will allow you to project how a candidate is likely to perform in your organization. If the environment, conditions, and circumstances are essentially the same in the candidate's current or previous company as in yours, then your task has been made simple. Of course, this is rarely the case. That's why you need to extract information about all four competency categories. You need to know not only if the candidate knew what to do and how to think but also how to act and interact. Answers to your follow-up questions reveal how effective the candidate is likely to be in all four categories when confronted with demanding emergency projects.

Competency-based interviews thus allow you to make decisions based on facts. They are structured, job-specific, and focused on relevant concrete and intangible competencies. In addition, they are legally defensible. For these reasons, competency-based questions should represent about 70 percent of any interview, supplemented by open-ended, hypothetical, probing, and closed-ended questions. This improves the interview in several ways, enabling you to:

▲ Identify the skills and characteristics needed to succeed in a specific work environment
▲ Isolate the competencies required for a given job
▲ Earmark relevant experiences necessary to have acquired these competencies
▲ Clarify what candidates have learned from their experiences
▲ Determine whether candidates can apply what they have learned to a given job and work environment

Competency-Based Lead-Ins

When preparing competency-based questions, remember two things: (1) they are designed to elicit specific examples concerning what the applicant has done in the past, and (2) they should tie in directly with job-specific competencies. That said, competency-based questions are among the easiest to formulate. Each one is introduced by a lead-in phrase that alerts the applicant to an important fact: You want specific information. Here is a sampling of competency-based lead-ins. Note that it is not always necessary to ask questions in the interrogative form. Statements can often be just as effective:

▲ "Describe a time when you . . ."
▲ "Give an example of a time in which you . . ."
▲ "Tell me about a time when you . . ."
▲ "Tell me about a specific job experience in which you . . ."
▲ "Give me an example of a specific occasion when you . . ."
▲ "Describe a situation in which you were called upon to . . ."
▲ "Describe the most significant . . ."
▲ "What did you do in your last job in order to . . . ?"
▲ "How often in the last year were you called upon to . . . ?"
▲ "Tell me about a time when you didn't want to _____. What happened?"
▲ "Describe a situation in which you felt _____. What was the result?"

By the time you have asked the third or fourth competency-based question, interviewees will realize that they must respond specifically whenever you begin with a lead-in phrase.

Suppose you were interviewing a candidate for a training specialist's position. Two of the primary skills required are the ability to line up outside consultants to conduct training workshops and designing course contents. Here are some of the competency-based questions you might ask:

- ▲ "Tell me about a time when you were responsible for lining up outside consultants to conduct in-house training workshops. What did the task require?"
- ▲ "Describe the steps you took to accomplish your goal."
- ▲ "How did you perform aspects of this part of your job that you didn't enjoy? Give me a specific example."
- ▲ "What aspect of hiring consultants do you find the most rewarding? The least rewarding? Why?"
- ▲ "Describe the contents of a course you've designed. Who else was involved?"
- ▲ "Tell me about the best course you've ever designed. What made it your best course? What about your least favorite course?"
- ▲ "Describe a time in which you were called upon to complete the development of a course that someone else had started. What was the end result?"
- ▲ "Give me an example of a specific occasion when you felt an existing course should be left unaltered. What happened?"
- ▲ "Has there ever been a time when you wanted to deviate from the standard formula for course development? What was the end result?"
- ▲ "Tell me about a time when you designed a program and were told to rework it. How did that make you feel, and what did you do?"
- ▲ "Has there ever been a time when you wanted to conduct a course that you developed? What happened?"

Developing Competency-Based Questions

The information you gathered regarding job-specific competencies can yield a great deal of data about a potential job match—if you know how to phrase your questions properly. Since about 70 percent of an interview should involve asking for specific examples related to past job performance, employers must convert relevant topics into competency-based questions.

Competency-based questions can also help you obtain contrary information. This entails exploring negative as well as positive aspects of a person's work experiences. The primary purpose of exploring contrary information is to identify those areas in which the person might have difficulties. For example, if the job requires contract negotiations with a union, you would naturally ask questions relative to past experiences in dealing with unions. However, unless you were aware of the concept of contrary information, you probably wouldn't ask the following: "Tell me about a time when you and a union representative locked horns and neither one of you was willing to budge. What ultimately happened?" and "Was there ever a time when you said or did something during contract negotiations that you regretted? What was it, and what were the ramifications?" These questions could yield valuable information about the applicant's temperament and ability to handle stress.

In addition, exploring contrary information precludes you from forming a one-sided picture of a candidate. For example, you might say, "I've gotten a really good sense of what you excel in, but I'm sure you'll agree that we all have areas that need improvement. Tell me about one of the areas you need to work on and how you would go about it."

Here are six competencies and accompanying competency-based questions that you might ask of candidates for an HR director's job. Note that each of these competencies reflects a specific, required skill. Note, too, that each question begins with a competency lead-in:

Competency #1: Ability to Recruit and Interview Applicants

- ▲ "Describe a time when you had a position open for an unusually long period of time. How did you eventually fill it?"
- ▲ "Give an example of a time in which you referred an applicant whom you believed should have been hired to a department manager, but the referral was rejected. How did you resolve your differences with that manager?"
- ▲ "Tell me about a time when you had more applicants than you could handle. What did you do?"
- ▲ "Tell me about a specific job experience in which you hired someone who later didn't work out."
- ▲ "Give me an example of a specific occasion when you and a

department head didn't agree on the requirements for a non-exempt opening."

▲ "Describe a situation in which you were called upon to fill several openings in one department at one time."

▲ "Describe the most rewarding recruiting experience you have had to date. Now tell me about the least rewarding."

▲ "What did you do in your last job in order to convince a department head to hire someone?"

▲ "How often in the last year were you called upon to recruit for especially hard-to-fill openings? Tell me about some of the openings."

▲ "Tell me about a time when you didn't want to continue using a longtime recruiting source. What happened?"

▲ "Describe a situation in which you felt uneasy with the answers given by a particular applicant. What did you do?"

Competency #2: Ability to Perform Reference Checks on Potential Employees

▲ "Describe your process for conducting references. How did you follow up with former employers who failed to respond to your phone calls or letters?"

▲ "Describe a time when you received negative references on a candidate whom the department manager wanted to hire anyway. What happened?"

▲ "Have you ever gone back to a candidate with a negative reference and asked if he could explain why he felt the former employer had given the poor reference? What happened?"

▲ "Tell me about a reference that sounded too good to be true and later turned out to be just that."

▲ "Tell me how you go about obtaining references from former employers who will only verify dates of employment."

▲ "Tell me some of the questions you ask former employers to determine job suitability."

▲ "Describe a situation in which you received conflicting references from two of an applicant's former employers. What did you do?"

▲ "Tell me about a time when you called the former manager of an applicant your company was interested in hiring, and she referred you to the HR department."

▲ "How have you handled verification of school records? Please be specific."

▲ "Tell me about a time when an applicant apparently falsified educational credentials. What did you do?"

▲ "Tell me about a time when you received negative references on an applicant after she had already started work. What happened?"

Competency #3: Ability to Plan and Conduct Regularly Scheduled Organizational Orientation Programs

▲ "Describe your role in your organization's orientation program."
▲ "What percentage of your time is taken up with preparing for and conducting your company's orientation program?"
▲ "What is your favorite part of the orientation process? Why? What about your least favorite part?"
▲ "Tell me about a time when you were asked questions to which you did not have answers."
▲ "Have you ever had a situation when speakers you had lined up as part of orientation did not show up, printed materials were not ready, or something went wrong with the audio-visual equipment? What did you do?"
▲ "Tell me some of the things you did in preparation for your first orientation that you no longer do."
▲ "Describe the relationship between you and the other orientation developers and participants."
▲ "How do you follow up with orientation attendees who are required to complete and return forms they received during the session?"
▲ "Tell me about some ideas you might have for making the orientation experience more meaningful and more helpful to new hires."

Competency #4: Ability to Prepare and Explain HR Policies and Procedures

▲ "Tell me about your role in preparing and explaining HR policies and procedures to employees."
▲ "How often do employees call you regarding policies and procedures? Give me some examples of the nature of these calls."
▲ "Describe a situation in which an employee required an explanation of an HR policy and became upset with the explanation. What did you do?"
▲ "Has there ever been a time when an employee challenged the interpretation of a policy or procedure? What happened?"
▲ "Give me an example of a specific occasion when a longtime policy was revised."

▲ "Describe a company policy or procedure that generates the most questions or concerns. Why do you think that is?"

Competency #5: Ability to Develop and Maintain Up-to-date Job Descriptions

▲ "Describe your responsibilities when it comes to developing job descriptions."

▲ "Tell me about some of the job categories for which you are responsible."

▲ "Describe how you gather information for the job descriptions."

▲ "Tell me about a time when you had difficulty developing a job description. Why do you think that was?"

▲ "Have you ever been in a situation where the incumbents and their managers described a job differently? What was the outcome?"

▲ "How do you ensure that the job descriptions remain up-to-date?"

▲ "Give me an example of a specific occasion when a job's responsibilities and the corresponding grade and salary range did not seem to coincide. What happened?"

▲ "What did you do in order to be more proficient in developing and maintaining accurate job descriptions?"

Competency #6: Ability to Administer a Compensation Program and Monitor Salary Increase Recommendations to Ensure Compliance with Merit Increase Guidelines

▲ "Describe your responsibilities in relation to your organization's compensation program."

▲ "Tell me how performance appraisals relate to salary increases."

▲ "Tell me about a time when you received a salary increase recommendation from a department head for an employee whose performance was below average."

▲ "Describe the most challenging aspect of your compensation responsibilities."

▲ "Give me a specific example of a time when an employee objected to the amount of his recommended increase. What was your role in resolving the dispute?"

▲ "Describe a time when an employee was already at the top of her range, but whose performance warranted a raise. What happened?"

These six ability-related competencies alone resulted in more than fifty questions that will yield a great deal of job-related information, reflecting all four competency categories.

Here are additional generic questions that reveal traits or characteristics germane to many jobs:

▲ "Describe your decision-making style. Tell me about a specific time in which you applied this style. What was the outcome?"
▲ "Tell me how you communicate unpleasant tasks to employees. Give me a specific example."
▲ "Tell me about a time when you wanted to approach a task differently than members of your team. What happened?"
▲ "What did you do in your last job in order to improve morale? Please be specific."
▲ "Describe the most significant contribution you made at your last job."
▲ "Give me an example of when you delegated a task, and the person didn't do what was required. What happened?"
▲ "Describe a situation involving an employee who violated company policy. What was your role, and what happened?"
▲ "What have you done about a disgruntled employee who felt she was passed over for a promotion?"

The process of asking competency-based questions is painless and highly productive, ultimately enabling you to make an effective hiring decision.

Cultural Fit

We read about them all the time in the papers: top executives with major corporations, ousted after a few months on the job. The term often linked to this happening isn't pretty, but it is accurate: organ rejections. *Organ* refers to the new outside hire, who never gains acceptance by the corporate body and is removed. Here are some familiar examples:

▲ John Walter, former CEO of publisher R.R. Donnelley & Sons, stepped down as AT&T president and COO after only nine months.
▲ Hollywood agent Michael Ovitz lasted a mere two tumultuous years as president of Disney.

▲ Gil Amelio became CEO of Apple Computer and lasted approximately sixteen months.

These individuals and many others like them are top-level executives. They probably possessed many of the necessary competencies for the jobs they were hired to perform. What they lacked, however, was the right fit. And it appears that they're not alone. According to Manchester Inc., an HR consulting firm based in Jacksonville, Florida, 40 percent of executives promoted or recruited into high-level positions fail within eighteen months. Ray Harrison, executive vice president of Manchester, believes that the disconnect rate for senior executives hired from the outside is notably high because of a lack of familiarity, and resulting clash, with the culture of the organization.

These mismatches are costing American business plenty. For example, when Michael Ovitz left Disney, his severance package was estimated to be worth $100 million. While not all departures are as expensive as Ovitz's, on average, the one-year replacement costs for managers and executives are said to be around $750,000. This, according to Development Dimensions International, an HR consulting firm in Bridgeville, Pennsylvania, includes the cost of severance pay, finding a replacement, training the new hire, and getting the new hire up to speed. In addition, mismatches of notoriety—that is, involving well-known people—can damage a company's reputation and standing in its field.

The most frequent reason for corporate mismatches is distinct management styles. When employees of an organization are accustomed to a leadership style that directly involves them in the decision-making process, has open lines of communication, and offers guidelines instead of rules, there is bound to be a clash if the new executive operates from an organizational chart that flows in one direction: from top to bottom. Unfortunately, employers don't always see this in time. They note a heavy hitter's accomplishments, see similarities in the issues arising from the executive's current environment, and extend an offer. Problems also accrue if an executive from a large company joins a start-up situation. It's tempting to hire someone with a track record; after all, he or she has a great deal of experience to contribute. Unfortunately, the environment in a start-up is inherently different from that of a big conglomerate, and often executives are frustrated, lacking the resources available to accomplish their objectives.

To prevent these costly mismatches, employers are urged to look for cultural compatibility. *Secrets From the Search Firm Files:*

What It Really Takes to Get Ahead in the Corporate Jungle by John Rau (McGraw-Hill, 1997) provides some guidance:

▲ *Look for a match between the energy level of the candidate and the pace required by the organization.* For example, hiring an academician accustomed to a rigid work schedule and lots of time off would be incompatible with a fast-paced operation.

▲ *Evaluate the candidate's views of risk taking.* A business that operates in a "fly by the seat of your pants" mode needs someone who is prone to taking risks, acting independently, and moving quickly. If you have a candidate who comes from a highly regulated industry and is accustomed to working within a rigid set of boundaries, you may very well have a cultural mismatch.

▲ *Consider the candidate's decision-making style.* Some companies utilize a consensual management style that typically requires a great deal of fact finding among executives before joint decisions are made. New blood accustomed to operating independently and making decisions quickly could lock horns with management colleagues.

▲ *Compare values.* While intangibles such as values cannot be measured, they can be compared with those of your company. A mesh in this area is important. Consider Patagonia Inc., for example, a Ventura, California manufacturer of outdoor apparel. Patagonia seeks employees who are active outdoor people, supportive of the company's environmental activism role.

▲ *Realize that appearances count.* Hiring someone from an environment that is conservative in terms of function and attire can create a clash with one that encourages a casual style of dress, reflecting a more laid-back work environment.

Employers should not assume that a candidate with a management style or approach to decision making that conflicts with their own cannot work out. The key to success is making candidates aware of cultural differences and determining whether the necessary adjustments can be made on their part as well as by the organization. For example, a high-tech manufacturer hired an executive to "shake things up." Unfortunately, his aggressive style shook things up too much. He irritated everyone and was on the brink of being terminated. This disaster could have been averted if, prior to hire, the employer had discussed with the candidate what approach would likely work, while emphasizing what tactics would tend to alienate the rest of the staff. That way, the candidate could have gauged his own willingness to adjust as needed. It's a matter of being proactive as opposed to reactive.

All of this seems contrary to the concept of diversity (Chapter 1). Instead of embracing different styles and approaches to, say, problem solving and leadership, some corporations seemingly want to go the "cookie-cutter" route and duplicate existing methodologies, at least at the executive level. This seems somewhat unrealistic in a tight labor market when companies are scrambling to find talent anywhere they can, at virtually any price. It is, unfortunately, the reality. Sometimes a new hire doesn't get the needed support and help from the rest of the staff, particularly if the previous executive was considered "better." Even if a company is willing to accept differences in style and approach, often the executive is not. Frequently, the result is a standoff, ultimately resulting in the dismissal or resignation of the person after a short period of time.

SUMMARY

Before exploring various recruitment sources or interviewing candidates, employers are urged to establish a solid prerecruitment foundation. This process includes reviewing the position's responsibilities, requirements, reporting relationships, environmental factors, exemption and union status, salary, benefits, and growth opportunities. This should be done every time a job becomes available.

Employers should also take time to identify job-specific competencies prior to recruitment in order to determine those factors necessary for success. A competency is a skill, trait, quality, or characteristic that contributes to a person's ability to perform the duties and responsibilities of a job effectively. While every job requires different competencies, there are four primary categories: (1) measurable, tangible, or technical skills; (2) knowledge; (3) behavior; and (4) interpersonal skills. Most jobs emphasize the need for one category over the others, but every employee should be able to demonstrate competencies, to some extent, in all four categories. Identifying job-specific competencies enables you to ask competency-based questions of job candidates. These are questions that draw from past experiences and behavior, correlating them to the specific parameters of a given job. Competency-based questions seek to elicit specific examples that allow you to project how a candidate is likely to perform in your organization.

Sometimes, despite conducting competency-based interviews, candidates don't work out. This is often the result of an improper fit of the candidate's management style with the prevailing corporate culture. To reduce the chances for cultural incompatibility, look for a match between the energy level of the candidate and the required pace of the organization, evaluate the candidate's views of risk taking, consider the candidate's decision-making style, and compare values. This is not to say that candidates with a different style won't work out. The key to success is making the candidate aware of any differences and determining whether appropriate adjustments can be made, on his or her part as well as by the organization.

CHAPTER 7

Contingent Workers

"One's Self I sing, a simple separate person,
Yet utter the word Democratic, the word En-Masse."
—*Walt Whitman*

When I was in high school, I had a friend named Barbara. She excelled in every course she took and graduated at the top of the class. We lost track of one another, but through a mutual friend, Pat, I learned that Barbara went on to college and graduate school, each time finishing at the top of the class. That came as no surprise to me. Nor did it surprise me to learn that within a few years of graduating, she became vice president of a prestigious investment firm on Wall Street, and soon thereafter became an executive vice president. As Pat put it, "Barbara could write her own ticket in any company." Once again, I was not surprised.

Then, about five years ago, I ran into Pat. What he told me about Barbara came as a complete shock: She had dropped out of the corporate life and was working as a temp. At first, I thought he was kidding. Barbara—temping? It wasn't possible. She could run an entire corporation. Why would she work as a temp? "What kind of a temp?" I asked Pat, thinking, at the very least, that she was now an independent consultant, charging clients big bucks for her knowledge and expertise. When Pat told me the types of jobs she had been working at, I sat down in disbelief. Over the past three years, Barbara had worked for about a dozen different companies in various capacities. Her favorite job, according to Pat, has been as a receptionist for a recording company. "She loves meeting the recording artists," said Pat.

"But why does she do this?" I asked. "She could have done anything she wanted!" Pat smiled and replied, "She did do everything she wanted. Then she turned around to see what else was left. She realized that she was tired of working eighteen-hour days in one industry and could afford to take some time off. She didn't want to stop working altogether, so she decided to experiment a little bit. She went to an agency and told them about only her computer and clerical skills. She knew that if she revealed her entire history, she'd be laughed out of the office. Before long, she received her first assignment. The longest she's been at any one company is four months. Sometimes her assignments are for just a couple of weeks. The point is, Barbara is enjoying herself. She probably won't do this much longer, but for now, she's having a ball."

When the initial shock of what Pat told me about Barbara wore off, I started to think about what she had done. I realized that she was part of a growing group of American workers who choose to work in some capacity other than a traditional full-time arrangement. This group, now commonly referred to as contingent workers, as opposed to temps, consists of people in a variety of job classifications. With today's employers looking everywhere for workers and often coming up empty-handed, the contingent workforce offers a viable solution to employment woes. In fact, a growing number of companies are managing a mixed workforce of core and contingent workers.

WHO ARE CONTINGENT WORKERS?

Contingent workers are defined as those individuals who perceive themselves as having neither an explicit nor implicit contract for ongoing employment. They carry portable skills with them, working in jobs that are structured to last only a limited period of time. Their work is literally contingent or dependent on an employer's need for them. Contingent workers usually have little or no job security, often work irregular hours, usually do not have access to benefits, and have no ties to any of the companies where they work. They may or may not be on a company's payroll.

Almost any work arrangement that differs from the commonly perceived norm of a full- or part-time, salaried, regularly scheduled job is considered to be contingent in nature. Most contingent workers hold from one to two assignments within a six-month period, although assignments can last as long as five years. Lengthy assignments are not advisable for the employer, since the longer contingent workers stay, the more they are perceived to be regular employees.

The American Staffing Association estimates that 90 percent of companies currently use contingent workers to supplement their regular workforce, spending approximately $72 billion per year on temporary staffing services. According to the Bureau of Labor Statistics (BLS), employment of contingent workers is expected to increase 53 percent between 1996 and 2006—that is, by nearly 1.4 million jobs by 2006—making the contingent staffing industry one of the fastest growing in the economy. Indeed, during peak project periods, contingent workers can represent up to 50 percent of the total workforce.

Characteristics of Contingent Workers

There was a time when contingent work was considered strictly clerical. Temp agencies would send over fill-ins on short notice when a secretary was out sick, on maternity leave, or on vacation. Today, contingent work is that and much more. Now, contingent assignments are available in virtually every field and profession. Attorneys, business executives, human resources professionals, software engineers, editors, accountants, clerical workers, hotel workers, industrial laborers, nurses and other medical personnel, restaurant workers, and technical support staff are examples of contingent workers. And in the project-oriented world of high-tech employment, contingent workers are all the rage, giving companies new levels of flexibility and efficiency while creating a class of high-tech nomads.

The most recent study prepared by the BLS, in conjunction with the *Current Population Survey* of more than 60,000 households, defines the characteristics of contingent workers based on four primary categories: (1) independent contractors, (2) on-call workers and day laborers, (3) workers who are paid by temporary help agencies, and (4) workers provided by contract firms. The CPS defines these terms as the following:

1. *Independent contractors.* Independent contractors include consultants, freelancers, rehired retirees, or downsized employees who are self-employed and work for a defined period or do a defined project. Workers who can answer affirmatively to the following question are considered independent contractors: "Last week, were you working as an independent contractor, an independent consultant, or a freelance worker? That is, someone who provided a product or services to customers, on your own?"

2. *On-call workers or day laborers.* These are individuals who may be defined as people ". . . in a pool of workers who are only called to work as needed, although they can be scheduled to work for several days or weeks in a row, for example, substitute teachers and construction workers supplied by a union hiring hall."

3. *Workers who are paid by temporary help agencies.* These are people who can answer affirmatively to the questions: "Do you receive your work assignments through a third-party temporary help agency?" "Are you contacted to work for different companies by a temporary help agency?" "Do you receive payment for your services by a temporary help agency?"

4. *Workers provided by contract firms.* These are people who can answer affirmatively to the question: "Some companies provide employees or their services to others under contract. A few examples of services that can be contracted out include security, landscaping, or computer programming. Did you work for a company that contracted out either you or your services last week?" These individuals would also answer negatively to the question: "Are you usually assigned to more than one customer?"

Here are other characteristics associated with the BLS's four categories of contingent workers:

▲ Contingent workers are more than twice as likely as noncontingent workers to be young, that is, sixteen to twenty-four years of age. Among sixteen- to twenty-four-year-olds, contingent workers are more likely to be enrolled in school. Among those in this age category not enrolled in school, a larger proportion of contingent than noncontingent workers had less than a high school diploma. This pattern is also true for persons ages 25 to 64.

▲ Contingent workers are slightly more likely than noncontingent workers to be women and black. About half of all contingent workers are women, and the proportion of contingent workers who are black is about 14 percent.

▲ The services industry accounts for more than half of the contingent total. The construction industry also accounts for a relatively large share of contingent workers. Large numbers of contingent workers are also found in administrative and support positions.

▲ Independent contractors are considerably more likely than workers in traditional arrangements to be men, white, and at least twenty-five years old. They also are more likely to be out of school and have at least a bachelor's degree. They are somewhat more likely than traditional workers to work part-time and to hold managerial, professional, sales, or precision production jobs. In terms of industries, independent contractors are more likely to work in construction, agriculture, and services and less likely to work in manufacturing or the wholesale and retail trades.

▲ The demographics of on-call workers, including day laborers, are similar to those of workers in traditional arrangements, but on-call workers are slightly younger. In terms of job characteristics, they are more than three times as likely to be in the construction industry and also more likely to be in the services industry. On-call workers are more likely than traditional workers to work part-time and to be in professional, services, fabricator, and laborer occupations.

▲ Workers paid by temporary help agencies are more likely than workers in traditional arrangements to be women, young, and black, and they are slightly more likely to be employed part-time. They are heavily concentrated in administrative support and operator, fabricator, and laborer occupations.

▲ Workers provided by contract firms are disproportionately male. The largest proportion of contract workers are employed in the services industry, although substantial proportions work in manufacturing, transportation, and public utilities.

While there are four official categories recognized by the BLS, there are numerous staffing classifications that fall under the heading of contingent worker. Examples include:

▲ Leased workers from an employee leasing company, typically including groups of workers who remain at a company for longer time periods than temporary workers

▲ Temporary workers who are direct hires and thus employees of the company

▲ Part-time employees who are on the payroll, often paid by the hour, as distinguished from part-time employees in the regular core workforce, whose work schedules are not subject to short-notice fluctuation

Why People Work in Contingent Jobs

A husband and wife, Shaun and Samantha, live in Philadelphia and are specialists in Windows NT and Novell NetWare networking. Over an eighteen-month period, they have worked as contingents at two different jobs in the chemical and airline industries. Says Shaun, "The pay is very good, and the flexibility is definitely welcome. We avoid the politics of working inside a company, and we get exposed to a lot of different technologies." For this couple, and many others like them, contingent work is the most desirable work arrangement.

People work at contingent jobs for a variety of reasons. While those cited by Shaun and Samantha are typical, there are many other reasons. Teachers, for example, often seek additional income during summer and other school vacations. Retirees who no longer want to work full-time, women with childcare or eldercare responsibilities, and college students also seek out contingent assignments for additional income.

Some take contingent assignments because they can actually make more money than by working for one employer. Such is the case with Gina, a programmer who splits her time between a consulting firm and a computer services business. Top companies, such as Symbol Technologies Inc. and Northrop Grumman, pay her well for her skills—more than she earned from a permanent job where, as she puts it, "The bonus was a pat on the back." Gina says, "I get offered full-time jobs all the time. I have to tell them I just can't do it. I would never, ever, ever go back to a full-time job." Many "free agents" agree with Gina, as contingent workers rarely earn less than ten dollars an hour and frequently earn upward of $100 an hour, even without a college degree. Project rates can run into the tens of thousands of dollars and beyond.

Others look to contingent work as a path to full-time employment. A study by the National Association of Temporary and Staffing Services reported that nearly three-quarters of all temporary jobs lead to full-time positions. Unfortunately, this has not happened to Claudia, a free agent who has worked for five years as a temp in the Chase Manhattan information systems department, hoping it would lead to a full-time job. A hiring freeze has kept that from happening.

Some take temporary assignments to improve skills or gain exposure to different work environments. Many enjoy the flexible work schedules that can accompany contingent assignments, despite the fact that there are often long, isolated hours of work on many new projects. Still others accept contingent work as a stopgap between full-time jobs. Many, however, treasure their independence, enjoying the ability to leave a job if they don't like the work or when a project is finished.

And then there are those who accept a contingent assignment but expect full-time status and benefits. This occurred at Microsoft, resulting in what's been viewed by many as a landmark 1999 ruling. The case stemmed from an IRS decision that said Microsoft had to withhold income and Social Security taxes for a number of freelancers—even though they had signed independent contracts. The workers then sued, arguing that they should be considered employees in other aspects as well. Specifically, they sought to cash in on the company's stock option plan, a benefit covered by ERISA (the Employee Retirement Income Security Act) and reserved for permanent employees. The technology giant was ordered to offer thousands of its long-term contingent workers some of the same employee stock discounts granted to permanent workers.

In the high-tech industry, contingent workers can often dictate when and how they want to work, as well as setting their own fee. Of course, there is an onus on them to keep current on the latest technology. As one company representative stated, "You're only as good as the latest software application."

People with Disabilities and Contingent Work

Contingent work can help workers with disabilities ultimately land regular jobs. According to a recent study by Manpower Inc., using a temporary or contingent staffing agency as a transition into full-time employment for people with disabilities is an effective way to gauge if such a match would work. The contingent agency has tested the employee's skills, making the selection skills-based; the disability is secondary, if it's a consideration at all. The emphasis, then, is on what people can do rather than what they can't do.

Temporary agencies like Manpower, Kelly, or Olsten are aware of employers' concerns with the potential costs of accommodating worker disabilities. In truth, these costs are minimal, with most averaging $45, and many others costing less than $500. In fact, the cost of accommodating qualified workers with disabilities is forty times less than training and replacing workers, says Peter Blanck, a professor of law and medicine at the University of Iowa.

Many employers have come to realize that hiring people with disabilities is an excellent way to compensate for long-vacant positions in a tight labor market. And while unemployment rates across the United States in virtually every category are the lowest they've been in more than thirty years, hovering around 4 percent on average, the rate for people with disabilities has remained about the same, at 60 percent, meaning that many candidates with disabilities are available to fill contingent positions.

Choosing a Contingent-Help Agency

Before contacting a contingent-help agency, ask yourself if you want to deal with just one agency or have a few to call on. Many experts recommend limiting the number of providers of temporary workers so that together you can develop a strategic partnership. First Bank System, for instance, works primarily with one vendor that does training, drug testing, and background checks for all the temps it provides. Other companies, however, have started moving away from the single vendor approach, focusing instead on finding the most effective service in their location for each specialty area. When companies use a high volume of temporary workers, they might elect to coordinate with a primary supplier that, in turn, establishes strategic partnerships with other specialty services.

In some cases, the primary vendor is situated on-site at the client location. This arrangement is typically referred to as a vendor-on-premise program, resident management program, or on-site management program, and is usually implemented for high-volume accounts of fifty or more temporary workers. This on-site presence removes the client from the day-to-day management of contingent workers, freeing up HR and supervisors to perform other functions. In addition, potential legal issues of coemployment are minimized.

Consider, too, whether you need an agency that specializes in certain industries or would prefer an agency that can provide workers for all departments in your company. If you select a multispecialty agency, determine if there are staff members who specialize in a particular field, such as technical, legal, secretarial, or administrative. Ask representatives to visit your facility so you can meet personally to better familiarize them with your particular needs. Also, explore the agency's reputation in the community, and determine if any complaints have been filed with the Better Business Bureau or any state agencies, such as the state Department of Labor.

Many temporary-staffing companies provide skills training to temporary workers without cost to the client. Such expenditures for skills training cost more than $720 million per year nationwide. More than 50 percent of temporary workers report that they have acquired new skills as a result.

One company that offers a training program to prepare workers for various jobs is Manpower Inc., whose headquarters are located in Milwaukee. Among its offerings are the Skillware program, Putting Quality to Work, and TechTrack. The Skillware program offers training in approximately three hundred different software packages. The program is self-paced and so well received that many of Manpower's customers have approached the company about training their regular staff using Skillware. According to a company representative, more than 2 million people have participated in the training program. Manpower's Putting Quality to Work training program focuses on "soft skills." The program evolved out of the company's research into what its customers want in a temporary employee. The answers included employees (regular and contingent) who ask questions when uncertain about how to accomplish a task, are problem solvers, go that extra mile, and get along well with customers and coworkers. The program is primarily video-tape-based and takes place in a classroom; instructor-led discussions are included. For technical individuals seeking new career opportunities, there is the TechTrack program, offering more than three hundred information technology courses. All of these courses are free.

Here are additional guidelines to ensure a productive relationship with agencies hired to help with your contingent worker needs:

▲ Clearly communicate your requirements for contingent help, in terms of skills and responsibilities, and estimate the length of time that the person will be needed.

▲ Clarify the agency's rates, including markups (the amount the agency charges above the amount it pays the contingent employees). Markups can range from 25 percent to as much as 100 percent over base wage, depending on employment costs and the availability of skilled workers. A 50 percent markup is average.

▲ Evaluate the agency's assessment process, including completion of an application, a personal interview, testing, validation of skills, and reference checks.

▲ Determine if the agency uses personality profiling or tests employees for proficiency with common computer software programs, such as word processing and spreadsheets, as well as for basic math and spelling aptitude and production skills, if relevant. Also, find out what kind of training, if any, the contingent workers receive.

▲ Assess the agency's job-matching process that links candidate skills and interests with what is available in the workplace.

▲ Find out about any restrictions on hiring an employee from the contingent agency for your staff. Most companies permit it but require the employer to wait a specified period of time. Depending on the availability of workers with the required skill level, this waiting period can range from eight to twenty-four weeks.

How and Why Companies Use Contingent Workers

Cost

Ask employers why they hire contingent workers, and one of the first responses is that it helps keep labor costs down. This is accomplished through lower wages. According to the Department of Labor, the median wage earned by full-time contingent workers is 82 percent of that earned by full-time regular employees. Sometimes, this figure is considerably lower. Consider the lighting specialist whose job was being eliminated. He was, however, permitted to continue as an independent contractor, earning approximately one-half of his salary but with a loss of overtime pay.

How much is actually paid contingent workers depends on the requirements of the employers that use them. In the case of agency temps, the fees charged by the agency must also be factored into the cost equation. While most businesses are guided by prevailing labor market rates, they strive to hire competent contingent workers for less than good core employees. However, in a tight labor market, most employers are willing to pay what's necessary to get good workers. At Avon, for example, contingent workers, called "reserves," get exactly the same rate of pay as regular employees performing the same job and are also eligible for wage increases on the same basis. However, since few reserves work on a consistent basis, it typically takes longer than the standard calendar year to earn a pay increase. Savings come into play when Avon hires part-time contingent workers, since they earn less than full-time employees. The greatest savings occur, however, when part-time employees are hired full-time, since this eliminates the hefty agency fees associated with hiring from temp agencies.

Contingent workers are also less likely to have employer-provided health or life insurance coverage, be eligible for employer-sponsored pension plans, or receive paid leave. Employers are not required to withhold employment taxes, contribute toward Social Security, pay unemployment insurance, pay disability insurance, or withhold for Medicare contributions. Neither are they responsible for retirement benefits or obliged to pay unemployment taxes. The federal laws that ban job discrimination, provide health and safety protection, and allow for family and medical leave don't extend to contingent workers. They are not eligible for unemployment insurance or overtime pay, nor are they covered by collective bargaining laws.

Some companies do offer benefits to contingent workers. At Avon's East Coast facility, for instance, "reserves" earn benefits according to the number of hours worked. The first benefits accrue after five hundred hours are worked in one year, and additional benefits are paid after one thousand hours. These benefits include health insurance, to which part-time reserves must contribute a portion of the premium, and retirement accounts, paid vacation days, and holidays. Reserves, however, are not eligible for sick leave or dental insurance.

Organizations like Working Today, a national company based in New York City, are trying to resolve the benefits plight of many contingent workers. While certain temporary agencies pay selected benefits, as well as the legally required employment taxes, to some of their people, these usually accrue after a specified number of hours worked and can prove rather costly. The goal of Working Today and similar organizations, then, is to allow these workers to purchase insurance that moves with them from job to job. For a nominal annual membership fee, these organizations provide access to group rates for comprehensive health benefits, dental care, vision coverage, life insurance, and prepaid legal services.

Additional cost savings related to the hiring of contingent workers can result from keeping payroll expenses under control and streamlining recruiting, administration, and HR expenditures.

Flexibility

Companies also use contingent workers because they provide flexibility in how much labor is hired and when. As demand for a company's products or services fluctuates, its need for labor also varies. Contingent labor allows an organization to maintain a match between the amount of hours it pays for and the amount of work to be done. For example, many commercial banks use contingent workers to meet changing labor demands. Often, contingent workers are hired for their backroom operations to enter the data from checks and other paper documents into computer files for processing. Some banks use contingent workers supplied by agencies, while others hire part-time employees onto their payrolls. Since the volume of data to be entered fluctuates enormously from day to day and week to week, banks often add or subtract labor hours on a daily basis to match the amount of work to be performed.

Here's a look at various ways contingent workers have been utilized at four different organizations:

▲ Hewlett-Packard has employed contingent workers to assemble electronic components, to protect core workers by reducing labor costs when work units are closed, to staff new product start-ups, and to match staffing with volatile or seasonal businesses.

▲ Avon has used contingent workers to assemble, pack, and ship products in order to match labor input to seasonal fluctuations in the workload.

▲ AT&T has hired contingent clerical support to achieve staffing flexibility and to avoid increasing the regular workforce.

▲ Ernst & Young has brought in contingent business support services to concentrate on core business issues and reduce costs.

Companies also gain greater flexibility in determining how core employees utilize their time. Increasingly, staff members, especially managers, must devote substantial portions of their day to recruit, hire, train, and retain regular employees. With contingent workers, none of this is required. In addition, performance reviews are unnecessary, as are salary reviews and career planning.

Protection against Job Loss

Employers also hire contingent workers to protect regular employees from job loss. The concept of hiring contingent workers to buffer core employees against layoffs gained popularity after the severe recession of 1981–1982 and was reinforced by the downturn of 1985–1986 in the previously high-growth computer industry. The ill will and lost talent caused by these events left their mark on many organizations. Now these companies consciously keep their core workforce at a minimum level and add a buffer of contingent workers to absorb the shocks of business downturns. Temp agencies like Olsten Staffing Services have these concerns in mind when they run ads such as the following:

> Upturns, downturns, recessions, depressions, sudden recoveries, and slumps . . . It's the nature of business. When the economy goes, so do people. But layoffs cost money. And morale. Not the best way to adapt to a changing business environment. Olsten has the solution: flexibility. With the Olsten Flexible Workforce, the ability to respond effectively to economic trends is built into the structure of your company. During slower periods, maintain a core staff of full-time workers. Then when production increases and needs change, Olsten supplies you with appropriately skilled temporary workers.

Contingent Staffing Options

Companies seeking to hire contingent workers for these or other reasons must first decide what type of contingent worker they require. In order to do this, they should consider five factors:

1. *The nature of the work that has to be performed.* For work requiring job-specific training or in-depth knowledge, you might want to consider rehiring retirees as part-time contingent workers. They not only understand the parameters of the work to be done but are also familiar with how the company operates. If the job is one that requires a high level of expertise and initiative, then an independent contractor is probably your best choice. With work that is short-term and project-based, on-call temporary workers obtained through an agency or contract firm will probably suffice. These workers also prove helpful when there are fluctuations in workload, requiring adjustments in labor input on a weekly, monthly, or quarterly basis.

2. *The characteristics of the local labor market.* Examine your local labor market in terms of the quality, skill levels, and numbers of contingent workers currently available. If conditions are favorable, you might prefer to have a direct hand in selecting contingent workers by contacting independent contractors. Consider, too, how

well agencies or contract firms can meet your needs in terms of training employees, satisfying specialized needs, fee structures, and services offered. Note that market conditions can and do change; therefore, check the factors that drive the local labor market periodically.

3. *Existing company policies and procedures.* It's not unusual to have a policy that prohibits adding permanent employees to your existing staff while permitting temporary additions. If this is the case, then you must avoid converting part-time employees or direct-hire temporaries who are on your payroll to full-time status. Consider, instead, going to agencies for temps. If your system counts staff in terms of full-time equivalents, it will behoove you to contract for two part-time employees to be counted as one full-time worker.

4. *The organization's culture.* If your company is committed to cultivating home-grown talent and promoting from within, you may want contingent workers who are on your payroll. Even though the arrangement is temporary, if spanning a number of years, these contingent workers become more a part of the company than if "lent" to you from an agency or contract firm.

5. *Legal issues surrounding the use of contingent workers.* This factor is discussed in detail later in this chapter.

MANAGING A MIXED WORKFORCE OF CORE AND CONTINGENT WORKERS

Many businesses now operate with a core group of regular employees whose skills are critical to the business, and then contract for contingent workers as needed. To do this effectively, evaluate your company's staffing needs and determine, in advance, which employees should form the core workforce and what positions can be more flexible. Analyze the nature of the work that needs to be done, the volume of the workload, the timing required to complete a given project, and the cyclical nature of the business to determine whether to hire core employees or contingent workers for particular functions. Examine your company's business plan, on both a short- and long-term basis. Is it to save money? Increase profitability? Expand operations? The kinds of workers you hire—core or contingent—depend on your industry and the answers to these questions.

Regardless of how skilled your core employees and contingent workers may be, productivity is likely to suffer if the two groups do not work harmoniously. Sometimes staff members are uncomfortable working side-by-side with contingent workers. Employees may feel threatened, fearing their jobs will be eliminated or that they'll be replaced by contingents with more up-to-date skills. After witnessing the degree of freedom and flexibility enjoyed by independent contractors, the morale of regular employees may decline, affecting their productivity and sense of commitment to the company.

To preclude this from happening, try the following approaches:

▲ Establish and communicate an internal job application policy that clearly outlines the company's position on internal posting and promotional decisions. Be sure it describes the process for both regular and temporary workers.

▲ Clearly identify the core competencies required for each position. Be sure to select from the four competency categories described in Chapter 6: technical or tangible skills, knowledge, behavior, and interpersonal skills. This makes hiring decisions easier to accomplish and to explain to those not selected.

▲ Give core staff members direction on how to prepare themselves for higher-level positions. This may include availing themselves of tuition reimbursement programs, internal and external training opportunities, mentoring programs, and the chance to work on special projects.

Deciding whether contingent workers should do the same jobs as core employees is an important process. Most experts advise against having a two-tier labor force in which regular staff receive the plum assignments while contingent workers are left to perform the undesirable tasks or high-risk work. This is not to say, however, that core employees and contingent workers should work side-by-side on identical assignments. There are legal reasons for not doing so (discussed below), as well as practical ones. If you accept the basic premise that contingent workers do not command the same status and privileges as regular employees, it stands to reason that their work assignments should be differentiated. The most logical way to accomplish this is to distinguish assignments by time or purpose. This makes sense since most contingent workers are hired for a specified period of time or to work on a particular project. If, however, both core employees and contingent workers are laboring in a unit that is being phased out or on a project that has a targeted completion date, then working together becomes less of an issue.

Here's an example of what can happen if contingent and core workers do the same jobs in the same environment. After successfully completing a merger, the CEO of a company gave all permanent employees one day off and a bonus as a reward. He did not extend the same courtesy to contingent workers who had worked side-by-side with the core employees and contributed equally to the successful merger. Several of the temps complained, maintaining that they had worked just as hard and were just as responsible for the success of the merger. The CEO refused to acknowledge them equally, suggesting, instead, that the temp agencies pay them bonuses.

In this instance, core employees received favorable treatment. Sometimes, however, the opposite occurs, and contingent workers come out on top. That was the case when contingent workers performed the design and development phases of an assignment, while core employees were given the maintenance chores. Clearly, the tasks assigned to the contingent workers were more desirable, and the core employees were furious. The result: a decline in morale and productivity.

The latter occurs more frequently when an independent contractor is brought in to spearhead a project, presumably because of his or her specialized skills and background, which are often superior to that of the core staff. Having an outsider come in and take charge, albeit for a limited period of time, can have major ramifications if the stage isn't set in advance. The situation can worsen if the consultant is offered a permanent job. To reduce or eliminate any resentment and ensure a productive working relationship, advise staff well in advance as to the nature of the project, why a consultant is being brought in, and what the respective roles will be. Also estimate the period of time the project is expected to last. In addition, have someone available—a manager in the department where the work is being performed, or a representative from HR—to act as a sounding board for core employee complaints. Seemingly small matters can quickly mushroom into full-blown grievances if conflicts are not aired and resolved quickly.

Contingent workers are more likely than core employees to complain of unfair treatment. Collectively, they emphasize eight key concerns in their relationships with employers and core employees:[1]

1. *They are treated impersonally.* Management and core employees frequently refer to them as "temps," rather than by name. John recalls one six-month assignment where he repeatedly overheard core employees say, "Just give that to the temp," or "The temp has what you're looking for." Professional contingent workers are also irritated over not receiving business cards, even after having been with a company for several years.

2. *They receive inaccurate or incomplete information about job assignments.* Many reportedly feel left out of conversations and meetings pertaining to the work they are doing, and they often find core employees talking about matters affecting their work, right in front of them, without requesting their input.

3. *They are given little information about the nature of the company's products or services.* It's hard to come into a work setting and perform an assignment in a vacuum. Yet, reportedly, that's what contingent workers are expected to do. Unless they come via an agency that provides them with information, they are left to their own initiative to gather company-related information. Many report being excluded from new hire orientations.

4. *Their performance is evaluated according to different standards.* While core employees receive formal performance appraisals during which goals and objectives are discussed, areas requiring improvement are assessed, and areas of excellence are praised, contingent workers are rarely told how they're doing.

5. *They are overlooked when there are permanent job openings.* Some companies have policies that preclude contingent workers from even being considered. Other contingents, who come from staffing agencies, can't opt for regular openings because of contract restrictions. But in some instances, like at Avon, regular employees have the first shot at job postings, and then reserve employees can apply before the job is offered to external candidates.

6. *They are excluded from company social events.* The list of events contingent workers complain about being excluded from include holiday parties, summer picnics, team sporting events, and celebrations over meeting deadlines. Some commented that they even felt unwelcome during celebrations of a core employee's birthday or when going out after work for a drink.

7. *They lack a sense of job security.* While core employees don't have a keen sense of job security these days, at least they enjoy the status of being employees. Contingent workers know their status is temporary from the outset, even though, in some instances, assignments can be several years in duration.

8. *They do not receive benefits.* This is a huge area of discontent. While employees around them are receiving health, dental, life, and disability insurance, paid holidays, vacation, sick leave, personal time, stock options, and numerous other benefits, contingent workers often receive nothing. This is just one more reminder that they are not employees—rather, they are temporaries.

In addition, contingent workers reported feeling underemployed, bored, and unchallenged.

Employers can improve relations between themselves and contingent workers by being forthright about the nature and length of an assignment, encouraging employees to treat contingent workers with respect, avoiding dumping undesirable or menial tasks on them, and providing them with orientation.

LEGAL CONCERNS

Increasingly, the courts are examining the relationship between companies and their contingent workers, requiring employers to act more responsibly. Employers are urged to consult with legal counsel before entering into any contractual agreements with staffing firms, or when hiring contingent workers under any circumstances.

One tool that is helpful to employers in this regard is a document prepared by the Equal Employment Opportunity Commission (EEOC) titled *Enforcement Guidance: Application of EEO Laws to Contingent Workers Placed by Temporary Employment Agencies and Other Staffing Firms.* Issued in December 1997, the *Guidance* addresses the application of the federal employment discrimination statutes to individuals placed in job assignments by staffing firms. The *Guidance* identifies contingent workers as those who are outside an employer's core workforce, such as those whose jobs are structured to last only a limited period of time, are sporadic, or differ in any way from the norm of full-time, long-term employment.

In general, contingent workers placed in job assignments by staffing firms are covered under all applicable antidiscrimination statutes and may not be discriminated against on the basis of race, color, religion, sex, national origin, age, or disability. That's because while not technically employees, contingent workers are effectively considered as such by the EEOC, which views the staffing firms, the clients to whom the workers are assigned, or both, as their employers. Accordingly, staffing firms must place and employers must treat contingent workers in a nondiscriminatory way. In addition, staffing firms and employers must ensure that contingent workers are paid wages on a nondiscriminatory basis. The *Guidance* identifies remedies should the EEOC find that a staffing firm and its client have engaged in unlawful discrimination.

The primary antidiscrimination laws that the *Guidance* addresses are Title VII of the Civil Rights Act of 1964 (Title VII), the Age Discrimination in Employment Act of 1967 (ADEA), the Americans with Disabilities Act of 1990 (ADA), and the Equal Pay Act of 1963 (EPA). These federal employment statutes, as well as other federal and state laws, were designed to protect only employees, not independent contractors. However, be advised that subsequent to the EEOC's release of its *Guidance* document, the courts have been applying, on a case-by-case basis, the "common-law" concept, as defined by the Internal Revenue Service (IRS) to determine if a person is an employee. This may encompass independent contractors.

Staffing Service Work Arrangements

The EEOC's *Guidance* identifies three categories of staffing firms:

1. *Temporary employment agencies.* These agencies recruit, screen, hire, and sometimes train their employees. They set and pay the wages when the worker is placed in a job assignment, withhold taxes and Social Security, and provide workers compensation coverage. The agencies bill the client for the services performed. The client is responsible for the individual's working conditions, supervises the individual, and determines the length of the assignment.

2. *Contract firms.* These firms contract with a client to perform a certain service on a long-term basis and place their own employees at the client's worksite to carry out the service. Examples of contract firm services include security, landscaping, janitorial, data processing, and cafeteria services. Like temporary employment agencies, contract firms typically recruit, screen, hire, and sometimes train their workers. They set and pay the wages when the workers are placed in a job assignment, withhold taxes and Social Security, and provide workers compensation coverage. Unlike temporary agencies, however, contract firms take on full operational responsibility for performing an ongoing service and supervise their workers at the client's worksite.

3. *Other types of staffing firms.* There are numerous variations on the staffing firm/client relationship. For example, "facilities staffing" is an arrangement by which a staffing firm provides one or more workers to staff a particular client operation on an ongoing basis, but does not manage the operation. Then there are staffing firms that place workers on the company's payroll, then lease the workers back to the client. The purpose of this arrangement is to transfer responsibility for administering payroll and benefits from the client to the staffing firm. A staffing firm that offers this service does not recruit, screen, or train its workers.

Throughout the *Guidance* document, the term *staffing firm* is used to describe, generically, all these types of firms.

Criteria for Determining Employee Status

Staffing firm workers are considered employees within the meaning of the federal employment discrimination laws if the right to control the means and manner of their work performance rests with the firm and/or its client rather than with the workers themselves. Some of the factors indicating that workers are covered employees include:

▲ The firm or the client has the right to control when, where, and how the worker performs the job.
▲ The firm or the client rather than the worker furnishes the tools, materials, and equipment.
▲ The work is performed on the premises of the firm or the client.
▲ There is a continuing relationship between the worker and the firm or the client.
▲ The firm or the client has the right to assign additional projects to the worker and to set the hours of work and duration of the job.
▲ The worker is not engaged in his or her own distinct occupation or business; that is, he or she is not hired as an independent contractor.
▲ The worker is considered an employee of the firm or the client for tax purposes, i.e., with regard to withholding federal, state, and Social Security taxes.

Here's an example that incorporates some of these factors. A temporary employment agency hires a computer programmer for one of the agency's clients. The agency pays the worker a salary based on the number of hours worked as reported by the client. The agency withholds Social Security and taxes and provides workers compensation coverage. The client establishes the hours of work and oversees the individual's work performance. The individual uses the client's equipment and supplies, working on the client's premises. The agency reviews the individual's work based on reports by the client. The agency can terminate the worker if his or her services are unacceptable to the client; the worker can terminate the relationship as well. Under these circumstances, the worker would be considered an employee.

Whose Employee Is the Contingent Worker?

Once it has been determined that a contingent worker is, indeed, an employee, then the question is: whose employee—the staffing firm's or the client's? The relationship between a staffing firm and its workers generally qualifies as an employer-employee relationship when the firm typically hires the worker, determines when and where the worker should report to work, pays the wages, is itself a business, withholds taxes and Social Security, provides workers compensation coverage, and has the right to discharge the worker. If, however, the workers are leased—that is, a client places its employees on the staffing firm's payroll solely to transfer the responsibility of administering wages and insurance benefits—then the staffing firm would not be considered an employer.

The client of a staffing firm typically qualifies as the employer of the contingent worker during the job assignment, along with the agency. This is because the client usually exercises supervisory control over the worker. In the example of the computer programmer given above, the agency and its client would qualify as joint employers of the worker because both have the right to exercise control over the worker's employment.

When determining whether a staffing firm or its client is covered under Title VII, the ADEA, or the ADA, the staffing firm and the client must each count every worker with whom they have an employment relationship. Although a worker assigned by a staffing firm to a client may not appear on the client's payroll, he or she must be counted as an employee of both entities if they qualify as joint employers.

Even if a business does not qualify as the worker's employer, it can still be liable for unlawful discrimination. The antidiscrimination statutes not only prohibit an employer from discriminating against its own employees but also prohibit an employer from interfering with an individual's employment opportunities with another employer.

Discriminatory Practices

A staffing firm is obligated to make job assignments in a nondiscriminatory manner. The fact that a staffing firm's discriminatory assignment practice is based on its client's requirement is no defense. Thus, a staffing firm is liable if it honors a client's discriminatory assignment request. A client that rejects workers for discriminatory reasons or discriminates against them while on the job is liable either as a joint employer or third-party interferer if it has the requisite number of employees to be covered under the applicable antidiscrimination statute. Here's an example where the client is liable but the staffing firm is not:

A staffing firm provides computer services to a company that has more than fifteen employees. The staffing firm assigns a qualified individual to work on-site for the client. When the client learns that the worker has AIDS, it tells the staffing firm to replace him. The staffing firm advises the client that doing so would constitute a violation of the ADA. The client continues to insist that the firm remove the worker from the work assignment and replace him with someone else. The firm reluctantly agrees. However, it refuses to replace him with another worker to complete the assignment because doing so would constitute acquiescence in the discrimination. Furthermore, the firm offers the worker a different job assignment at the same rate of pay.

Discriminatory wage practices are also prohibited by the EEOC's *Guidance.* Both staffing firms and clients are prohibited from discriminating in the payment of wages on the basis of race, color, religion, sex, national origin, age, or disability. However, wage differences that are based on bona fide distinctions between temporary and regular workers can be justified under the EPA as based on a "factor other than sex."

Remedies to Discrimination

If the EEOC finds sufficient evidence that both a staffing firm and its client have engaged in unlawful discrimination, both parties are jointly liable for back pay, front pay, and compensatory damages. Even if the client does not qualify as the claimant's employer, it is still covered under the applicable antidiscrimination statute if it interfered on a discriminatory basis with employment opportunities offered by the staffing firm and has the requisite number of employees. Under these circumstances, the complainant can obtain the full amount of back pay, front pay, and compensatory damages from either one of the respondents alone or from both respondents combined. In addition, punitive damages under Title VII and the ADA, and liquidated damages under the ADEA, are individually assessed against, and borne by, each respondent in accordance with its respective degree of malicious or reckless misconduct.

Independent Contractors

As stated earlier, federal and state employment laws were designed to protect employees, not independent contractors. However, an independent contractor agreement involving a potential consultant does not conclusively establish an independent contractor relationship. Look at what happened at Microsoft when the Ninth Circuit Court of Appeals overturned a lower court's ruling, stating that all of Microsoft's "common-law employees" were entitled to participate in the computer company's lucrative stock-purchase plan. Employers should not assume, just because they have written independent-contractor agreements with individuals, that those individuals will not ultimately be deemed employees. The Internal Revenue Service's reclassification of independent contractors to employee status at Microsoft, based on its "common-law" test, could impact any organization.

It makes sense, then, to exercise caution and review the IRS's "twenty-factor test" derived from the common law to determine whether sufficient control exists to establish an employer-employee relationship. Overall, the IRS is interested in how much control you have over the workers' behavior and work results, how much control you have over finances, and the relationship of the parties involved. More specifically, the IRS stipulates that workers should be considered employees if, customarily, they are expected to do the following:

1. Comply with instructions about when, where, and how work is done
2. Receive on-the-job training or formal instruction
3. Perform services that are integrated into business operations
4. Render services personally
5. Rely on the employer to hire, supervise, and pay assistants

6. Maintain a continuing relationship with the business where services are performed
7. Comply with set hours of work
8. Devote full time to the business
9. Work on the employer's premises or in locations sanctioned or required by the employer
10. Perform services in a set order or sequence
11. Submit oral or written reports
12. Receive payment by salary or time, not by job or commission
13. Receive reimbursement for business and/or traveling expenses
14. Look to the employer to furnish tools, materials, and equipment
15. Lack significant investment in the business
16. Realize no profit or loss from work performed
17. Work for one company at a time
18. Not make services available to the general public
19. Be subject to discharge at will by the employer
20. Have the right to terminate the employment relationship at any time

In this regard, the courts typically pose five questions to determine whether workers are common-law employees:

1. Who recruited the workers?
2. Who trains them?
3. What's the duration of employment?
4. Do you have the right to assign extra work?
5. Do you have control over such things as firing, discipline, and rewards?

If you recruit and train the workers, you face a greater risk for having them reclassified as common-law employees. The longer workers are with you, the more you're at risk. And if you assign extra work and exercise control over firings, discipline, and rewards, the risk increases.

If you discover contingent workers who meet these guidelines, take immediate action. Consider implementing what the Roy, Utah–based Iomega Corp., a manufacturer of portable zip drives, does. Of the company's 4,500 employees, about six hundred are independent contractors. HR representatives meet with each new manager and explain the difference between independent contractors and employees, including why they are managed differently. Or consider the procedure National Semiconductor has instituted. The Santa Clara, California–based company did not have a formal process for determining independent contractor status at the time of the Microsoft ruling, but then decided to create one. It also diligently trains managers in the distinction between independent contractors and employees, right down to matters of office socializing. "Some of the stuff may be hard to swallow, like not inviting them for the department birthday cake or picnic, and you're working right next to these people, but you have to do it," says Terry Gray, National Semiconductor's senior purchasing manager.

You can further lessen the likelihood of employer responsibility by using a temp agency that offers workers benefits and training. The more the agency controls the day-to-day routine, the less you are involved. Use contingent workers on a by-project basis, and don't keep them for months working on other assignments after they finish the project for which they were hired. In this regard, experts suggest making one year the absolute cutoff.

People running their own businesses and acting as their own bosses are legitimate independent contractors. When an individual is determined to be engaged in providing substantive consulting or creative services, it is important to enter into an independent contractor agreement. Companies benefit from such agreements, which define the terms of compensation, set out the rights of termination, protect against the disclosure of proprietary information, set forth any limitations on working for competitors, and define whether the contractor or the company will own any intellectual property created during the engagement. These contracts should be drafted on an individual basis specific to each independent contractor, as opposed to preparing generic contracts en masse. Such agreements should be designed to define the rights and responsibilities of the parties in addition to protecting the business from unwelcome surprises if a relationship deteriorates or terminates.

In addition to entering into individual contracts with independent contractors, establish and abide by a formal policy of qualifying independent contractors and evaluating the proposed relationships under the IRS guidelines. Don't bring a person in until you're sure she is qualified to do business as an independent contractor. At National Semiconductor, any manager intending to hire an independent contractor for a project must complete an online questionnaire. Together with the contractor, the manager answers about two dozen questions designed to determine the legitimacy of the independent contractor's status.

Also, gather documentation to verify the contractor's independent status. This might include her business license, liability insurance coverage, company letterhead, and business cards.

National Semiconductor goes a step further and runs background checks on any contractor who will be on-site for more than twenty-four hours.

Despite all precautions taken at the hiring stage of a relationship with an independent contractor, the circumstances can change, and the contractor may fall into a common-law employee status. Therefore, reevaluate the contractor's work assignments if the relationship continues for more than six months. When this happens at National Semiconductor, the person must join the payroll of a temp agency before being used again.

Benefits Exemptions

You can exclude a group of workers from a benefits plan if you properly word the exemption. Steer clear of reference to the length of time or relationship in which they're working for you. For example, if you don't want to include common-law employees in your 401(k) and stock plans, then state that any workers who are paid by a third-party firm are not covered. Also, add certain protective statements, such as those authorizing the plan administrator to interpret the terms of the plan, including eligibility criteria, as well as statements providing that benefits plans aren't open to workers the company reasonably determines to be independent contractors. Waivers can also afford protection. Include a statement in the contingent agreement providing that the worker acknowledges he or she has no right to any employee benefits programs.

Tax Issues

Federal tax law prohibits discrimination in favor of highly paid employees. Therefore, failure to provide benefits to staffing firm workers considered to be the company's common-law employees could lead to discrimination problems, depending on the number of covered, highly paid employees relative to the number of covered, lower-paid employees. Even if assigned workers aren't common-law employees, discrimination problems could arise under the so-called "leased employee" rules, if workers perform services for the company totaling more than 1,500 hours in a year.

Tax issues are of particular concern in the case of employee stock option plans qualified under Section 423 of the Internal Revenue Code (not all stock option plans are qualified under this provision). Unlike the discrimination rules applicable to retirement plans, the rules for governed stock option plans require, with limited exceptions, that all employees, not just a specified percentage, be included in order for the plan to receive favorable tax treatment.

A safe-harbor provision, Section 530 of the Revenue Act of 1978, provides protection to companies classifying their workers as independent contractors. In order to fall within this safe-harbor protection, a company must demonstrate that the workers were not treated as employees in the past, that it has filed federal tax returns consistent with nonemployee status, that a reasonable basis exists for treating the workers as independent contractors, and that other individuals, holding substantially similar positions, are not treated as employees for purposes of employment taxes. See Appendix B for additional information on legal issues.

SUMMARY

Contingent workers are defined as those individuals who do not perceive themselves as having an explicit or implicit contract for ongoing full- or part-time employment. They carry portable skills with them and work in jobs that are structured to last only a limited period of time. Their work is literally contingent on an employer's need for them. Approximately 90 percent of companies in the United States currently use contingent workers to complement their full-time regular workforce.

Contingent assignments are available in virtually every field and profession, including business executives, software engineers, accountants, clerical workers, industrial laborers, and technical support staff.

The Bureau of Labor Statistics identifies four primary categories of contingent workers: (1) independent contractors, (2) on-call workers and day laborers, (3) workers who are paid by temporary help agencies, and (4) workers provided by contract firms. In addition to these four official categories, there are other staffing classifications that fall under the heading of contingent worker. Examples include workers from an employee leasing company and part-time workers who are direct hires on a company's payroll.

People work in contingent jobs for a variety of reasons, such as flexibility, exposure to different work environments, additional income, as a gateway to full-time employment, and as an opportunity to improve skills. In the high-tech industry, contingent workers can often dictate when and how they want to work, as well as setting their own fees. And for people with disabilities, contingent work often leads to regular jobs.

Employers who opt to hire contingent workers through an agency should decide if they want to develop a strategic partnership with one or more agencies or retain a multispecialty agency, and they should investigate the agency's reputation before making a commitment. Determining the full scope of the agency's services is also critical.

Companies hire contingent workers for a number of reasons, among them to keep labor costs down, to provide flexibility in how much labor to hire and when, and as a buffer against job loss for regular employees. Companies intending to hire contingent workers for these or other reasons should first decide what type of contingent worker they require. This is best accomplished by considering five factors: (1) the nature of the work to be performed, (2) the characteristics of the local market, (3) existing company policies, (4) the organization's culture, and (5) legal issues.

Many businesses now operate with a core group of regular employees whose skills are critical to the business, and then contract for contingent workers as needed. Regardless of how skilled your core employees and contingent workers may be, productivity is likely to suffer if the two groups do not work harmoniously.

Increasingly, the courts are examining the relationship between organizations and their contingent workers. Employers are urged to consult with legal counsel before entering into any contractual agreements with staffing firms or hiring contingent workers under any circumstances.

NOTE

1. Arthur, Diane. *Recruiting, Interviewing, Selecting & Orienting New Employees*, Third Ed., (New York: AMACOM, 1998).

CHAPTER 8

Why Employees Leave

"Deal with things before they emerge; Put them in order before there is disorder."

—The Tao of Power

Jake was employed as a graphic designer in the San Francisco Bay area. At age 29, he was already on his third career. He enjoyed the work he was currently doing but wasn't sure it was what he wanted for the rest of his work life. He didn't feel particularly connected to his job and also lacked a sense of compatibility with his current employer. Jake had felt the same about his previous jobs and employers. He'd only been with this company for seven months but was already beginning to feel restless. The work lacked challenge, the environment wasn't motivating, and he was increasingly bored.

He looked around his office and noted, with a smile, tangible evidence of the many perks he'd been given to come aboard: the aquarium filled with exotic fish, a Yamaha keyboard in the corner that he played "for inspiration," and the breathtaking view from his window. As he bent down to pet his dog—being allowed to bring Harry to work every day was another perk—he thought about the company's generous salary and comprehensive benefits plan. And if he stayed a year, he'd be entitled to a car, loaded with extras.

But something was missing. Getting up to stretch, Jake glanced over at the clock. It was 1 P.M. Time seemed to passing especially slowly that day. He had been working for three and a half hours—minus an hour or so for lunch—but it seemed much longer. He returned to the project he was working on. What seemed like a long time later, he looked at the time again. It was only 2:45. He sighed and said aloud, "This isn't working out. Time is going altogether too slowly, and I'm not having enough fun to make up for it. I'm outta here!" He picked up his laptop, called to his dog, and started down the hall.

A colleague passed him and asked, "Hey, Jake, what's up? Where are you going?" "Looks like I just quit!" was Jake's reply. "What are you talking about? You can't just walk out in the middle of the day! Besides, you just started a few months ago. What happened? Why are you quitting?" asked his bewildered coworker. "And what should I tell Anne—you know—Anne, your boss?" "Tell her I got bored," replied Jake. "Tell her I ought to be able to work for more than a couple of hours without checking the clock. Besides," he added, "I'll have another job by the end of the week. I guarantee it!"

When Anne learned that Jake had quit, she was bewildered. After all, he was making lots of money, had access to a spa membership, got free lunch, and, well, the list just went on and on. What went wrong?

What Anne didn't realize was that all the perks dangled in front of Jake to convince him to join the company were not keeping him motivated enough to stay. Even the promise of a new car wasn't sufficient. She was especially disturbed because Jake was the third graphic designer the company had lost in less than eighteen months. The company's turnover rates were escalating, and no one seemed to know what to do about it. She decided to increase the perks being offered.

Anne was making a classic mistake. The solution to the company's turnover problems was not to offer more lures but to determine why people were leaving. And the only meaningful way to find out why people were leaving was to ask them. One of the most effective means for accomplishing this is through an exit interview. Only then, armed with specific reasons, could the company provide the components of a retention environment.

CAUSES OF HIGH TURNOVER

Most of us have been taught that quitting is undesirable, that bailing out too soon could mean missed opportunities or, at the very least, negate the chance to prove to ourselves that we can persevere and overcome adversity. On the other hand, the pleasure that comes from separating ourselves from an arduous task, moving on to more enjoyable endeavors, or simply moving on is undeniable.

When people like Jeff Bezos, Michael Dell, and Bill Gates quit their jobs or formal education to launch billion-dollar enterprises, who can argue with their formulas for success? During this prosperous economy, where money and jobs are plentiful, quitting has become more acceptable—indeed, nearly condoned. Never mind that quitting often leaves behind unfinished work for replacements to wade through; it is better to abandon tasks that aren't worth the trouble.

A case in point is the tale of Silicon Valley investment banker Frank Quattrone. In 1996 he accepted tens of millions of dollars to quit Morgan Stanley for a comparable job at Deutsche Bank, taking with him more than a dozen of his employees. Two years later, the team quit Deutsche Bank en masse and, for a package worth $250 million, joined Credit Suisse First Boston. Their "quits" were applauded by many as shrewd acts worthy of emulation.

Some employees are leaving longtime employers simply because they can. It's a seller's market, and even satisfied employees are actively looking because they just might land a job that pays more, provides better benefits, or offers some of the perks described in Chapter 2. As one article summarized the sentiment among dissatisfied employees: "Revenge is sweet, you know. That's right, all you downsizers and 'reengineer-ers,' all you executives who talked about the pain of laying off workers on the way to the golf course. All you employers who stretched and stretched the workweeks, who put careers on the back burner, and brushed families to the side. All you companies who treated employees poorly—just because you knew they had nowhere else to go. You had it good for most of the '90s. No more. It's payback time—and you know what they say about paybacks."[1]

Echoing this sentiment, one middle manager stated, "This upswing in the economy is a blessing. I'm getting out." With regard to his own imminent resignation, another middle manager said, "It's just desserts for a company that did a really poor job of reengineering. There was no communication. The executives didn't share their grand plan with anyone below the director level. . . . I feel like, hey, it's my turn to make you guys sweat it. I'm holding the cards, and it feels really good." Yet another said that money was not an issue for him. He'd even been willing to take a pay cut for the right position: "Right now I just want control over my life. Sane hours and a company that respects me." These middle managers' views are shared by many other employees. Turnover figures are the highest they've ever been in many industries: According to *The Wall Street Journal*, the national "quit rate"—that is, the percentage of people who voluntarily left their last jobs—is 14.5 percent. That's the highest it's been since the late 1980s.

Costs of High Turnover

The Saratoga Institute, in conjunction with Kepner-Tregoe Inc., provides a formula for estimating the cost of turnover in your company. Select a department or job function that experiences high turnover. Use an actual number, or estimate the number of people who left the job or department in the past twelve months. Write the number below on Line 4. The average cost of turnover is 25 percent of an employee's annual salary (Line 1), plus the cost of benefits (Line 2). Typically, benefits come to approximately 30 percent of wages (total cost of a complete benefits package on top of payroll). The total cost per employee (Line 3) is the total of Lines 1 and 2.

1. Annual wage: _____ $\times$ .25 = _____
2. Annual wage: _____ $\times$ .30 = _____ $\times$ .25 = _____
3. Total turnover cost per employee (add Lines 1 and 2): _____
4. Total number of employees who left: _____
5. Total cost of turnover (multiply Lines 3 and 4): _____

Here's a sample:

1. Annual wage: $35,000 $\times$ .25 = $8,750
2. Annual wage: $35,000 $\times$ .30 = $10,500 $\times$ .25 = $2,625
3. Total turnover cost per employee: $8,750 + $2,625 = $11,375
4. Total number of employees who left: 10
5. Total cost of turnover: $11,375 $\times$ 10 = $113,750

Simply stated, high turnover represents financial loss. According to a representative from Deloitte & Touche in charge of the human capital program in Michigan, it costs approximately $12,000 in recruitment and training expenses to replace the average nonprofessional worker and $35,000 to find a new professional employee. At the Families and Work Institute, experts advise companies that it costs about 75 percent of a nonmanagerial worker's annual salary to find a replacement and 150 percent of a manager's annual salary. As high as these numbers may seem, they can escalate during a tight labor market, especially if the lost employee vacated a hard-to-fill opening.

In addition to the high cost, the loss of top performers means lost knowledge and experience, making it more difficult for the organization, as a whole, to attain its goals. Those remaining feel the loss.

There are a number of tangible reasons people leave one company for another. Generally speaking, employees want to believe their company really cares about them. Concern can be demonstrated in a number of ways, but it generally boils down to career development, adult treatment, being taken seriously, and being appreciated for a job well done. In a word, workers want respect.

Consider what happened to Paul. He was recruited right out of college by a large financial institution to work as a compensation analyst in the human resources department. While he didn't have a clear sense of commitment to working in compensation, Paul was pleased with the way the job had been described to him by Bill and was anxious to begin. Not only would he be directly involved with revamping the company's existing compensation program, he would be reporting to a senior vice president, be able to interact with members of top management, and have the opportunity to learn, firsthand, about the workings of the organization.

When Paul reported to work on the first day, he was greeted warmly by his boss, Bill, an SVP. After talking for twenty minutes about the company in general, Bill commented that Paul was just what the company needed to resolve some of the compensation issues it had been wrestling with. Then Bill suggested that Paul meet everyone in the department. He personally escorted Paul throughout the HR department, introducing everyone by name and function. By then it was time for lunch. Bill informed Paul that he had made reservations for them to eat in the executive dining room. Paul was thrilled. He assumed he'd be eating in the cafeteria, yet here he was, two weeks out of college and three hours into his first job, eating with senior management. It got better! Once in the dining room, Bill took Paul from table to table, introducing him to the executives as "the young man who was going to get compensation back on track." That afternoon, Paul reviewed files and manuals, with Bill periodically asking him how he was doing. At around 4:30, Bill invited Paul into his office to discuss Paul's first day. By the time Paul left an hour later, he felt good about his decision to join the company and believed he had a future there.

But that all began to change as early as Paul's second day of work. Bill's grandstanding from the previous day never reoccurred. Paul was never invited to eat in the executive dining room again; in fact, he rarely saw Bill for more than a few minutes, and that was in passing. A vice president named Larry informed Paul that he was to come to him with any questions and that he would be giving Paul all of his assignments. When Paul said that Bill was his boss, Larry laughed and said, "I hope you got a real good look at him the first day of work, because that's just about the last you'll see of him. And forget about what he said about revising the compensation program. That's something we're taking care of at the VP level. You report to me. Adjust."

But Paul didn't adjust. Over the next three months, he became increasingly despondent. The projects he was given to work on seemed menial and not of the caliber Bill had described. Consequently, the quality of Paul's work deteriorated. He also started coming in late. Soon he began looking for, and found, another job. When Larry chastised him soon after for poor performance and attendance, Paul sighed and said, "This is all wrong. I don't know why Bill set this job up to be something it's not. I was going to tell you this at the end of the week, but I might as well just do it now. I have another job. I'm resigning. Tell Bill for me if you see him, OK?"

Unfortunately, what happened to Paul occurs all too frequently in companies today. That is, an employee's expectations, realistic or otherwise, don't match up with the realities of the job. Bill created an unrealistic picture of a compensation analyst's duties and responsibilities. And taking Paul to the executive dining room that first day gave him the impression that he would be going there regularly, when if fact, that would never happen again. Paul never found out why Bill behaved the way he did, but the impact was damaging.

Sometimes an improper match occurs because a job is not adequately explained during the interview. It may be that the recruiter, anxious to fill the job, inadvertently overlooks certain details that the applicant, once on the job, finds objectionable. Sometimes, too, employees are placed in jobs that underutilize their skills, or in other instances, are placed in jobs that are beyond the scope of their abilities or interests. Whatever the scenario, improper matches between an employee's skills and interests versus the actual job are almost certain to lead quickly to termination. Exhibit 8–1 shows some examples of reasons for high turnover.

Exhibit 8–1. Reasons for High Turnover

There are other reasons cited by employees for high turnover. Among the most frequent are:

- ▲ *Incompatible corporate culture.* Employees need to feel that their interests, goals, work styles, and experiences are valued and supported by the organization for which they work. Employees who find that their differences are just tolerated rather than embraced are likely to leave.

▲ *Feelings of not being appreciated or valued.* Most employees genuinely want to do a good job. It follows, then, that they want to know that their work is appreciated. Some employees require almost constant feedback on how they're doing, while others are content with an occasional "good job, keep it up!" Even the most experienced employee needs to feel appreciated and recognized. How you show appreciation, then, should fit an individual's work style and personality. (See Chapter 9 for tips on recognition.)

▲ *Not feeling part of the company.* Employees need to sense that what they do fits in with the company overall. While new employees, in particular, are anxious to understand the impact of their work on achieving organizational goals, the same is true of workers at all levels.

▲ *Not knowing how they're doing.* During a tight labor market, when employees know they can leave tomorrow and land another job in a week, few workers are willing to wait a year for their performance review to find out how they're doing. Day-to-day coaching is needed to acknowledge accomplishments and point out areas requiring improvement. With regard to the regularly scheduled performance reviews, many employees complain that these rarely take place on time. One worker complained, "I waited eight months for my last [review]. It's not just bad business, it's rude and thoughtless. I don't care if you're busy—to me it signals you don't give a damn."

▲ *Inadequate supervision.* While not every worker requires close supervision, all employees need a sense of direction and guidance. They also need to know that the person they report to is available and responsive to their questions or concerns.

▲ *Lack of opportunity for growth.* If you know that a position isn't part of a job family and there's no room for progression upward or laterally, let applicants know during the employment interview. Finding out that they've been hired into a dead-end job can make employees feel duped; that alone can make a person walk out the door. If, however, you are hiring for a position that allows for growth, be prepared to offer training opportunities and career planning.

▲ *Lack of training.* People want to strengthen their knowledge, skills, and abilities to maintain a high level of marketability in an ever changing employment market. While it's true that you may be training employees who will take what they've gained and leave to work for someone else, it's just as true that you may be able to cultivate a relationship with employees you train and then benefit from what they've learned.

▲ *Unequal salaries and benefits*. Employees talk to one another, and you can bet that if some of your workers are earning more in the way of pay or benefits, others earning less for comparable work are going to find out about it and be irked. Their reaction could include resignation and possibly legal action. Giving workers more choices about how their individual benefits dollars are spent can also discourage employees from leaving.

▲ *Lack of flexible work schedules*. There are still many companies that adhere to a strict 9 to 5, Monday to Friday work mentality. With so many alternative work arrangements available (see Chapter 10), employees with other-than-work interests and commitments are likely to leave an inflexible environment for a company that acknowledges life outside of work.

▲ *Unsatisfactory relationships at work*. Employees today expect a more collaborative work environment among themselves, coworkers, and supervisors. They're more discriminating about whom they spend time with during on-the-job hours, and they are likely to leave if they don't have a high comfort level.

▲ *Too much work, not enough staff*. This situation occurs with frequency during a tight labor market when employers cannot find enough workers, and existing employees are expected to take up the slack. Unless they are compensated in some way, monetary or otherwise, these workers are likely to leave.

▲ *Inadequate or substandard equipment, tools, or facilities*. Employees may not be willing to put up with poor working conditions, a workplace that lacks important facilities such as proper lighting and furniture, or outdated computers and other equipment. The environment in which a person works directly impacts his or her level of productivity, and in some instances, may be all that's needed to cause valuable employees to quit.

Even if you're unaware of any of these situations, there are certain signs of employee discontent that may tip you off to impending resignations. Employees who start to form cliques and avoid interaction with managers, for example, could be sharing tales of woe with one another, drawing strength from each other's bad experiences and preparing to exit, en masse. Often there's a decline in participation at meetings, a lack of initiative, and an increase in the number of errors made. Employees who are unhappy also seldom smile or laugh and rush out the door at closing time. These behaviors are clues to problems that could result in a high turnover rate.

Best Practice: Ernst & Young

One company that takes turnover issues very seriously is Ernst & Young, a leading professional services firm. It has created an Office of Retention (OFR) with a director, who reports directly to the firm's chairman and CEO, and seven other employees (the OFR started out with three employees). The company believes that it will be able to retain talent by attacking, head-on, the issues that cause employees to leave. This commitment and development of the OFR stemmed from a 1997 survey of more than 17,000 Ernst & Young employees, which revealed that the workforce needed more of a personal life/work balance, and that women, more than men, left the firm because they felt excluded from mentoring and networking opportunities.

The OFR's first task was to develop some key programs. One is Women's Access, designed to develop future leaders by linking women across the firm's practice areas, with an emphasis on mentoring and networking. The program was opened up to men as well as women and has been successful in providing employees greater access to senior management. Another program developed by the OFR is the Women's Partners Network, designed to offer senior-level women the chance to network with other women in the organization.

The OFR also focused on improving Ernst & Young's Life Balance operation. Recognizing the importance of encouraging employees to devote themselves to work without sacrificing their personal lives, the OFR implemented a Flexible Work Arrangements (FWA) plan. The company's 29,000 employees can access the FWA's database by job level, type of work, or type of flex arrangement, then read descriptions of these arrangements provided by other employees to tailor their own work schedules.

Ernst & Young's Flexible Work Arrangements plan can boast of impressive results:

▲ The FWA database received over seven thousand entries in the first month of operation.
▲ In two years, use of the FWA nearly doubled.
▲ Sixty-five percent of all FWA participants who were surveyed revealed that they would have left the firm if there had not been flexible work options.
▲ Twenty-nine people have been promoted to senior manager, one level below partner.
▲ Five part-timers have been promoted to partner.

The company also reaches out to its workers with regard to vacation time. The firm feels that it is very important for people to take a vacation without work-related distractions. Therefore, employees are encouraged to inform clients and coworkers that they will be on vacation during a certain period of time. In addition, they are strongly discouraged from checking their voice- and e-mail while on vacation.

Overall, Ernst & Young's efforts have saved the firm in excess of $21 million over a two-year period. In the words of the OFR's national director, "It's good for the employees. It's good for the clients. It's good for the firm."

Exit Interviews

Exit interviews are designed to yield information about how a terminating employee viewed various aspects of employment with the company, such as the working conditions, employer-employee relations, compensation, policies, and practices. It's also an opportunity to learn what suggestions employees might offer for improving the company overall, as well as the department in which they worked. This information can be especially relevant to hiring practices in the future, revising policies and procedures, and correcting morale or productivity problems in a particular department. In addition, such information can aid employers in the development of a strategy for the retention of key contributors. Sometimes, employers can gain insight into a competitor's practices and work environment.

All terminating employees should be given an exit interview.

While frequently conducted on an employee's last day of work, this is probably the worst time. There are last-minute details to take care of and often a celebratory send-off. In addition, the departing employee may harbor negative feelings about the company that would cloud an interview, as would anxiety about the future (even if that future is a new and desirable job). Accordingly, an increasing number of employers are conducting exit interviews after employees have left the company. Before employees leave, explain that you will be contacting them in about a week to schedule an exit interview as part of the company's efforts to improve employer-employee relations and overall working conditions. Tell them their input is valuable toward this end. Offer to call them at home if they have another job, since they may not feel comfortable discussing your organization while at their new place of employment. Waiting a week before calling gives employees time to think about what led to their departure and calm down if hard feelings persist. It also provides an opportunity for them to settle into a new environment, which is certain to lead to comparisons with their previous environment.

Proponents in favor of waiting seven to ten days before conducting an exit interview maintain that ex-employees are more likely to talk candidly and objectively. Waiting longer than seven to ten days, however, tends to have the opposite effect. By then, employees are likely to have separated themselves from their former employer and want to move on without looking back.

Here's an example of how waiting a week to conduct exit interviews proved beneficial to a major employer. At one point, a number of employees left the company at about the same time. Their resignations were accompanied by generalized comments suggesting feelings of hostility, anger, and resentment. The company was bewildered. What was going on? Were the employees being pirated by a competitor? These people were all from different departments, so a particular problem area could not be pinpointed. In each instance, the HR department waited approximately one week before contacting the former employees. By then, enough time had elapsed so that the anger and resentment had been replaced by objectivity and a willingness to be candid. Through a series of exit interviews, the company learned what the problem was: Even though the employees worked in different areas, they all had to deal with a particular person in management. Such dealings were so unpleasant that key people opted to leave rather than continue to contend with him. The company could now focus on correcting the problem and head off the additional resignations of other valued employees.

One major drawback to conducting exit interviews after employees have departed is that the exchange is generally conducted by phone. This means you can't assess the body language that accompanies a person's verbal responses, such as facial expressions, posture, and gestures. It also means the former employee can't sign a statement indicating that you have accurately recorded his or her responses.

Outsourcing Exit Interviews

There is some controversy over who should conduct the interview. Some experts maintain that there should be two exit interviews, one conducted by the employee's manager and another conducted by an HR representative. Others maintain that only HR specialists should be involved. Still others maintain that a neutral third party should conduct the interview. The rationale is that strong emotions are less likely to disrupt the process and employees are more likely to speak honestly if they can talk to someone "from the outside." In addition, the results of exit interviews conducted by an outside specialist may carry more weight with top management. Outsourcing also allows you to concentrate on running your business instead of spending time with departing employees.

Outsourcing groups usually provide objective and timely evaluations to help employers understand as well as address their turnover issues. The interviews should be conducted and reported with confidentiality. Outsourcing groups may cover generic categories such as overall job satisfaction, job content, quality of supervision, and reasons for leaving, or they can follow a plan individually developed with the client. They generally conduct interviews after hours, by phone, when people feel free to talk candidly about their experiences.

Most third-party outsourcing firms offer an hourly fee structure, which appropriately aligns cost with the selected level of service.

Interviewing Skills

Exit interviews require many of the same skills as employment interviews, including encouraging people to talk, actively listening when they answer questions, and understanding as well as interpreting their body language. The following suggestions presume a face-to-face meeting but may be modified for exit interviews conducted by phone.

Encouraging Exiting Employees to Talk

Repetition

One way of encouraging former employees to speak freely is through repetition. Repetition encourages the person to continue talking and also helps to clarify certain points. Repeating the last few words of the employee's statement and letting your voice trail off as a question mark should encourage the person to elaborate. For example, if an employee said, "I just felt that it was time for me to move on," the interviewer could follow up by saying, "It was time for you to move on . . . ?" The employee might then reply, "You know how it is—I'd been an analyst for a year, so it's time. I mean, that's the way it's supposed to work, right? You can't stay in one place very long in this industry or people will think you've gotten soft." The interviewer might then repeat: "So, you're concerned that people will think you've gotten soft . . . ?" This might illicit, "Yes, that's correct, although that's not the only reason I want to leave. I'm looking for more money too."

This dialogue elicited a more accurate picture of the employee's reasons for wanting to leave than did his original statement. Use of repetition encouraged him to provide more valuable information.

Summarization

Another technique for encouraging employees to talk is summarization. As with repetition, this allows the former employee to clarify points made up to that point in the interview, and to elaborate, if necessary. It further ensures an accurate understanding on your part. Summarization may be used at specific time intervals in the interview, e.g., every ten minutes or after a new topic has been discussed. For instance, a departing employee may have just devoted approximately ten minutes to describing how she sought but was rejected for a promotion. At that point, the interviewer might say, "Let me make certain that I understand what you have said thus far. For more than six months you expanded your scope of work to include some of the responsibilities that the compensation manager performed. In fact, in the manager's absence, you took over her job on a number of occasions without difficulty. When her job became available, you assumed you would get it. When you didn't, you decided to leave. Is all of this correct?"

The employee can now confirm all or part of what the interviewer just summarized. She can also correct or add information, as needed. Be careful not to include more than four or five statements in your summary. This way, it is not difficult to isolate any part that is inaccurate or requires clarification.

Key Phrases

Using key phrases or expressions such as "I see," "How interesting," "Is that right?" "Really?" and "I didn't know that" can also encourage an employee to continue talking. None of these phrases expresses an opinion or shows agreement or disagreement; they merely show interest and understanding. Suppose an exiting employee said that her reason for leaving was that her boss didn't appreciate what a great worker she was. If the interviewer replied, "Is that right?" chances are she would have continued: "Yes. Of course, I'm not perfect! There's always room for improvement, I guess." The interviewer could then have followed up with, "Like what?" The dialogue could ultimately have revealed the difficulty she had taking directions, leading her to resign in order to start her own consulting firm.

Silence

Most people find silence to be awkward and uncomfortable. Consequently, interviewers often feel compelled to talk whenever the employee stops. However, unless you are prepared to ask another question, talking when you need additional information from the employee is counterproductive. When the employee stops talking and you want him to continue, try silently and slowly counting to five before speaking. This pause often compels a person to go on. Of course, you must be careful not to carry silence too far. The interview can easily become a stressful situation if you simply continue to stare at a person who has nothing more to say or needs your encouragement to continue. However, if you combine silence with positive body language, the employee should continue talking within a few seconds. Silence very clearly conveys the message that more information is wanted.

Suppose an employee said she was resigning because her manager didn't listen to her ideas, then she stopped talking. Moving on to another topic would have been a mistake: The interviewer needs to learn more, such as what ideas she was referring to, why she felt her boss didn't listen, and what, if anything, she had tried to do about it. The interviewer could have asked a direct question such as

"Tell me about a time when you feel your boss did not listen to your ideas." This, however, might have made the employee feel defensive, causing her to shut down further. Instead, the interviewer could have employed silence, leaning in and nodding, encouraging the employee to continue. She might then have added, "I mean, take this thing with the salary survey we conducted. We got the survey results in last month, and he knows I disagree with how he presented them to senior management. But he just wouldn't listen to my ideas. I thought we could create a system similar to the one Jackson, Inc., has. They don't have the turnover problems we've got, and I believe it's because of their compensation program. But he just turned a deaf ear to my idea and went ahead and recommended his own plan, which I personally don't think will work as well."

That additional information gave the interviewer a much clearer picture of what the employee meant when she said her boss didn't listen to her ideas.

Active Listening

Active listening is distinguished from two other types of listening: casual and selective. Casual listening is essentially detached and unfocused. For example, listening to what a candidate says in response to icebreaker questions at the beginning of an employment interview does not require concentration or any real attention. In fact, how people respond to queries such as "Did you have any trouble getting here?" requires only that you hear what they are saying; focusing on their actual response is not necessary. This differs from selective listening, which can occur during business meetings where, say, a number of different topics are being discussed. Selective listening allows you to listen in spurts, tuning in and out as necessary. When not selectively listening, you may be making judgments, forming rebuttals, or thinking about unrelated matters. Active listening, on the other hand, requires the greatest degree of concentration. It involves being aware of and present in the moment and remaining keenly focused on the person who is talking. Active listening during exit interviews enables you to glean valuable information from terminating employees.

Exhibit 8–2. Talking Versus Active Listening.

Most people really don't know if they talk too much during interviews. Try taking this Talk/Listen Quiz, rating each statement with a 1, 3, or 5: 1 signifies "almost never," 3 means "most of the time," and 5 represents "almost always."

1. I enjoy hearing what other people have to say.
   ☐ 1 ☐ 3 ☐ 5
2. I wait until someone else finishes talking before I talk.
   ☐ 1 ☐ 3 ☐ 5
3. I listen to what a person has to say, even when I don't find what the person is saying to be interesting.   ☐ 1 ☐ 3 ☐ 5
4. I try to interrupt the other person only when he/she goes off on a tangent, just to get him/her back on track.
   ☐ 1 ☐ 3 ☐ 5
5. I give each interviewee my undivided attention.
   ☐ 1 ☐ 3 ☐ 5
6. I recognize that the interview is not about or for me, so I try to keep my share of talking to a minimum.   ☐ 1 ☐ 3 ☐ 5
7. I respect the other person's views and avoid disagreeing with him/her during the interview.   ☐ 1 ☐ 3 ☐ 5
8. I listen to the interviewee's questions and supplement with additional information at the end of an interview.
   ☐ 1 ☐ 3 ☐ 5
9. I think it's important to let the interviewee do most of the talking during an interview.   ☐ 1 ☐ 3 ☐ 5
10. I listen for points about which I can ask questions after the interviewee finishes making his or her point.
    ☐ 1 ☐ 3 ☐ 5

A perfect score is 50. If you achieved that score, you're an excellent listener and understand that you gain more from an interview by listening to what the other person has to say. If you scored between 30 and 48, you're a fair listener but probably miss out on a lot of valuable information during the interview because you're talking instead of listening. And if you scored below a 30, you talk too much!

The most effective talking/active listening ratio for any interview situation is 30/70: that is, only 30 percent of an interviewer's time should be devoted to talking. During an exit interview, your 30 percent should be spent asking questions about how a terminating employee viewed his or her employment and answering questions. The remaining 70 percent should be spent actively listening to the employee.

Many interviewers talk entirely too much, going so far as to reverse this ratio. This typically occurs when the interviewee is uninteresting to listen to, talks too slowly, goes off on a tangent, or has trouble organizing thoughts. The result of this reversal is that the interviewer fails to acquire the information needed.

Listening for Key Information

Many interviewers confuse active listening with focusing on every word a person says. That's not realistic, since many people muddy their statements with irrelevant thoughts and sentences. If you try to zero in on every word, you can easily get lost in a sea of verbiage, losing track of the main point. Instead, concentrate on key information.

Suppose an employee says he's leaving because of excessive criticism by his manager. The interviewer might then query, "Can you give me an example of a time you were unfairly criticized?" The employee may respond:

> "Well, I suppose it all depends on who you ask. I mean, my boss would probably tell you that I don't always follow up with department heads who are delinquent in submitting performance reviews for their employees. But I doubt if he would add that it's not my fault. I call them, I leave them e-mail reminders, I tell them face-to-face when I see them in the cafeteria. I even ran into one department head over the weekend at my daughter's soccer game—his kid was on the other team—and reminded him then! Although I'm not sure he heard me since his team lost 5-0 and he was kind of upset—it was their fifth loss in a row. Where was I? Oh, yes. I mean, what else can I do? I can't stand over them and make them write the evaluations, can I? He should try doing this and see if he gets better results!"

Wow! In this instance, the interviewer got more than she needed or wanted to hear. Still, it was wise to let the employee talk without interruption. He went off on a bit of a tangent when he mentioned his daughter's soccer game, but the rest of the information was helpful in conveying his frame of mind. Trying to focus on every word, however, would have made the interviewer's head spin. The relevant information that came out of the employee's monologue was that his boss believes he needs to work on following up with department heads regarding delinquent reviews, and the employee believes he has done all that he can in this regard.

Filtering Out Distractions

Distractions can include people coming into your office, the phone ringing, and having your thoughts focused elsewhere. The latter can easily occur when employees are not interesting to listen to. When this occurs, you may find yourself thinking about that last vacation in Mexico and how you would prefer to be there right now. If you find this happening, remind yourself of the objective for your interview and that by not listening actively, you are likely to miss important information.

A former colleague of mine once posted the following notice on his office door: "I'm interviewing. Unless there's a bomb threat in the building, go away and come back when I'm done!" His message was a bit dramatic, but it had the desired effect. No one bothered him when they saw that sign.

Let's look at some less startling but equally effective techniques for dealing with common distractions.

- ▲ Post a sign on your office door whenever you are conducting an interview. It might say "Interview in progress. Come back later."
- ▲ Put Post-it Notes on your door and ask that people write you a message.
- ▲ Ask someone to intercept any visitors when you are interviewing and take a message.
- ▲ Set your phone on silent voice-mail.
- ▲ Ask someone to take and hold your calls.
- ▲ If you typically conduct interviews during a set time each day, make it known throughout the office that you are not to be disturbed during those hours.
- ▲ Discipline yourself to focus on the person in the room by telling yourself that you would want the interviewer to pay attention to you if the roles were reversed.

Of course, there are always exceptions, and certain interruptions do occur. However, you can create an atmosphere more conducive to active listening by cutting down on the number of distractions.

Using Thought Speed

This is a wonderful tool available to everyone. Most people think at a rate of approximately four hundred words per minute, but they speak at a rate of approximately 125 words per minute. Obviously, this means that we think faster than we speak. However, there is much more to thought speed than this. While the other person is talking, you can use thought speed to accomplish the following:

▲ Prepare your next question.
▲ Analyze what the interviewee is saying.
▲ Piece together what the other person is saying now in relation to something said earlier in the interview.
▲ Glance down at your paperwork to verify information.
▲ Observe body language.
▲ Take notes.

Thought speed can also work to your detriment. For example, there can be repercussions if you anticipate how employees are going to complete their responses before they finish speaking. This can happen if you typically ask each exiting employee the same questions, and you typically receive the same or similar responses. Suppose one of your favorite questions is "Why are you resigning?" Let's say you've asked that question of the last fifteen employees, and every one of them has replied, "There's no room for growth." It's not hard to understand why you would assume that employee number sixteen is going to answer the question the same way. But everyone is different, and there is no way of predicting with certainty how someone is going to respond. If you go ahead and assume this last employee is going to answer, "There's no room for growth," you could prevent yourself from hearing his actual answer, which might be, "I found out that a coworker, with less education and less experience, is earning a lot more money than I am." This answer could lead to an investigation of the company's pay practices and possibly even head off discrimination charges.

Thought speed can also work to your detriment if you jump to conclusions too soon, get too involved in note taking, or just tune out the interviewee.

Effective Body Language

When asked by her interviewer, Michelle, why she was leaving her current job, Sandra, a seasoned operations manager, replied without hesitation, "Growth opportunities are limited." Not satisfied with that response, Michelle continued to probe until Sandra finally acknowledged that a disagreement with the operations vice president over departmental procedures had led to her resignation. After the interview, Sandra wondered what she had said that prompted the interviewer to pursue the issue. Sandra did not realize that her verbal response was not responsible. Rather, her body language indicated she was being less than forthright. Until that point in the interview, Sandra had been sitting with her right leg crossed over her left leg, hands resting in her lap, eyes focused directly at her interviewer's face. When Michelle posed the question about leaving her current employer, Sandra unconsciously shifted slightly in her seat, crossed her left leg over her right, leaned forward slightly, and placed her hands on the desk before her. The specific gestures were of no particular significance; however, the change in her body language was enough to suggest to her savvy interviewer that Sandra was not being completely honest.

Nonverbal communication, commonly referred to as body language, is a vital aspect of any interview. While not a "science" and subject to misinterpretation, interviewers can often learn as much about interviewees through their nonverbal messages as can be learned from verbal ones. In fact, experts have determined that people respond to body language 55 percent of the time, tone of voice 38 percent of the time, and actual words a mere 7 percent of the time. When a contradiction exists between what is stated verbally and what is being expressed nonverbally—as in Sandra's case—the silent message often is the one that "speaks" the loudest.

Recognizing that Translations Differ

Analyzing body language is complicated by the fact that no single aspect of nonverbal communication can be universally translated. That is, a gesture expressed by one person may mean something entirely different when expressed by someone else. For example, just because you have a tendency to avoid making eye contact when you are hiding something does not mean that an employee is avoiding your eyes for the same reason. It may very well be a sign that she is deep in thought. Each person develops a particular pattern of nonverbal messages and tends to react to a specific situation in the same nonverbal way each time that it occurs. Therefore, although there are no universal interpretations of body language cues, each of us has our own nonverbal pattern that may be consistently translated if observed over a period of time.

Different cultures also tend to translate body language differently. In the United States, for example, nodding the head generally indicates an affirmative answer or understanding. In the Middle East, however, a single nod means no. Such differences in interpretation occur not only among cultures but as a result of individual socialization processes. Our patterns of nonverbal expression, then, are attributable to a combination of cultural and environmental factors.

Be careful not to draw conclusions too early in the interview process, based on an interviewee's nonverbal messages. Allow time for the individual's patterns to emerge, and then relate these patterns to the other factors involved in making a selection.

Interpreting Body Language

To say that nonverbal communication cannot be universally translated is not to say, however, that specific gestures or expressions do not typically convey a particular meaning. For example, biting one's lip is commonly interpreted to mean the person is nervous, fearful, or anxious; flaring nostrils indicate anger or frustration; and tapping feet suggest nervousness or impatience.

Rather than focusing on how specific movements and gestures tend to carry a certain message, interviewers should be aware of any sudden changes in nonverbal communication. For example, if an employee has been sitting quite comfortably for twenty minutes or so, and then suddenly shifts in his seat when you try to confirm his reason for leaving, this is a clue that something is amiss. Even if the person offers an acceptable response without hesitation, the sudden change in body language should tell you that something is wrong. Additional probing is necessary. Do not ignore the conflict between the verbal and the nonverbal.

Questioning Techniques

Chapter 6 described how to formulate competency-based questions by asking for specific examples that relate past work experiences to anticipated job performance. While competency-based questions should constitute the majority of employment interviewing questions, they should not receive the same degree of emphasis during exit interviews. While they are useful, competency-based questions should be balanced with open-ended, probing, and closed-ended questions.

Open-Ended Questions

Open-ended questions require full, multiple-word responses. The answers generally lend themselves to discussion and result in information upon which the interviewer can build additional inquiries. Open-ended questions encourage employees to talk, thereby allowing the interviewer an opportunity to actively listen to responses as well as observe the person's pattern of nonverbal communication. They also allow the interviewer time to plan subsequent questions. Open-ended questions are especially helpful in encouraging shy or withdrawn employees to talk without the pressure that can accompany a competency-based question requiring the recollection of specific examples.

Here are some suggestions of open-ended questions to ask during an exit interview:

▲ "Why did you accept a position with this company?"
▲ "What is your reason for leaving?"
▲ "What has it been like working for this organization?"
▲ "How would you rate the compensation and benefits?"
▲ "How would you describe our on-the-job training program?"
▲ "How would you describe the environment in which you worked? Include interrelations with managers, coworkers, and subordinates."
▲ "What was the relationship between your department and the rest of the company?"
▲ "What could the company have done to prevent you from leaving?"
▲ "What did you like most and least about working for this company?"
▲ "What were the most rewarding and most frustrating situations you encountered while in this job?"
▲ "What occurred at this job that you would like to see repeated at your next job? What would you like to avoid in your next job?"
▲ "Identify specific things you would change about this organization that would make it a better place to work."
▲ "Is there anything else you would like us to know concerning your employment with this company?"
▲ "What are your future plans?"

Probing Questions

These are questions that enable the interviewer to delve more deeply for information. Best thought of as follow-up questions, they are usually short and simply worded.

There are three types of probing questions:

1. *Rational probes* request reasons, using short questions such as: "Why?" "How?" "When?" "How often?" and "Who?"
2. *Clarifier probes* are used to qualify or expand upon informa-

tion provided in a previous response, using questions such as: "What caused that to happen?" "Who else was involved in that decision?" "What happened next?" and "What were the circumstances that resulted in that happening?"

3. *Verifier probes* check out the honesty of a statement, for example: "You said that your boss chewed you out in front of your coworkers. Can you provide me with the names of three of these coworkers?"

Employees who have trouble providing full answers usually appreciate the extra help that comes from a probing question. These also show that you are interested in what they are saying and want to learn more.

Closed-Ended Questions

These are questions that may be answered with a single word—generally yes or no. Closed-ended questions can be helpful in a number of ways: They give the interviewer greater control, put certain interviewees at ease, are useful when seeking clarification, are helpful when you need to verify information, and usually result in concise responses.

Here are examples of functional closed-ended questions. Note that in almost all instances they are followed up with open-ended questions:

- ▲ "Were you given adequate equipment and facilities with which to do your work? If not, what was lacking?"
- ▲ "Were you able to utilize your skills and reach your potential here? If not, why not?"
- ▲ "Was your job accurately represented and described at the time of hire? If not, describe any discrepancies."
- ▲ "Was your style of working compatible with that of your supervisor's? If not, describe some of the differences."
- ▲ "Were you treated fairly? If not, please describe your experiences of being treated unfairly."
- ▲ "Did you ever take advantage of our job posting program? If so, what where the results?"
- ▲ "Based on what you've said so far, can I assume that your primary reason for leaving us is that you don't feel your work has been appreciated?"
- ▲ "Would you refer someone to work for this company? Why or why not?"

▲ "Would you ever consider returning to work for this company? Why or why not?"

Other Questioning Formats

For variation, try posing questions in a "scale" format. For instance, "On a scale of 1 to 5, with 5 representing the highest point value, how challenging did you find your job to be? Please explain your answer."

Another variation is to ask employees to rate certain aspects of their work by using "excellent," "above average," "average," "below average," and "poor." You could also use "excellent," "good," "fair," and "poor." For example:

How would you rate the following?

	Excellent	Above Average	Average	Below Average	Poor
▲ Benefits	☐	☐	☐	☐	☐
▲ Communications practices	☐	☐	☐	☐	☐
▲ Compensation	☐	☐	☐	☐	☐
▲ Computer hardware/software	☐	☐	☐	☐	☐
▲ Employee morale	☐	☐	☐	☐	☐
▲ Equipment provided	☐	☐	☐	☐	☐
▲ Growth opportunities	☐	☐	☐	☐	☐
▲ Personal leave policy	☐	☐	☐	☐	☐
▲ Physical working conditions	☐	☐	☐	☐	☐
▲ Resolution of grievances	☐	☐	☐	☐	☐
▲ Training and development	☐	☐	☐	☐	☐
▲ Tuition reimbursement program	☐	☐	☐	☐	☐
▲ Vacation policy	☐	☐	☐	☐	☐

You can also try offering the terms "always," "usually," "sometimes," and "never" as choices.

You should supplement all of these general inquiries with specific questions that relate to your industry, organization, region, and the job in question. And, of course, different responses, logically lead to other follow-up questions.

Don't be surprised if employees hesitate to answer many of your questions. They may fear reprisals as a result of their honesty or may not want to "burn their bridges," in case they ever decide to return. You, however, have nothing to lose by asking. And you may be surprised: People often want to express their feelings openly, especially if they think it will result in positive changes.

Here's a sample exit interview, illustrating the use of some of these and other questions. The scenario takes place between Janet, an HR representative, and Frank, a customer service representative who posted for an opening as an HR specialist. While Frank thoroughly enjoyed his work in customer service, he wanted to apply his people skills to another area of the organization. He felt he was a "natural" for human resources since he did so well with customer service. Besides, the HR job represented a promotion. Unfortunately, the director of human resources did not feel Frank's skills were strong enough and hired an outsider with HR experience. Frank was disappointed and concerned—disappointed because he had lost out on a job he really wanted, and concerned because he felt there would now be hard feelings between him and his current manager. A few days after being notified of his rejection, Frank learned of an HR opening in a competitor's company. He applied and was hired. Within two days of submitting his resignation, he received a call from Janet in HR. She explained that it was the company's policy to conduct exit interviews with all terminating employees, either before leaving or after. The choice was his. Frank opted to see Janet that afternoon. Here are highlights of that meeting:

Janet: Thanks for coming in today for your exit interview. We're interested in learning how you viewed various aspects of your employment with us. Let's begin with why you're leaving.

Frank: Well, Janet, as you know, I'm very interested in human resources. And as you also know, I was very disappointed when I didn't get the HR job I posted for. When I came upon this HR opportunity in another company, I didn't feel I could pass it up.

Janet: So it's safe for me to assume that your reason for leaving has nothing to do with your job being inaccurately represented and described at the time of hire?

Frank: The customer service job I was hired for was accurately represented and described. There was no problem in that regard.

Janet: Are you suggesting that you were unable to utilize your skills and reach your potential here?

Frank: That's a good way of putting it.

Janet: Tell me, Frank, what did you enjoy most about working for this organization?

Frank: That's easy: the interaction I had with people.

Janet: What would you have changed about your employment if you could have?

Frank: That's also easy—I would have moved from customer service to HR.

Janet: Let's switch gears for a moment: On a scale of 1 to 5, with 5 representing the highest point value, how would you rate the benefits you received while employed with us?

Frank: Hmmm, I'd have to say a 4. The benefits here are pretty generous.

Janet: How about your salary. Do you feel that you were fairly compensated for the work you did?

Frank: Yes.

Janet: Frank, what about the environment in which you worked? How would you describe it? And please include interrelations with managers, coworkers, and subordinates.

Frank: That was a large part of the problem. As much as I like my manager as a person, she was not very good as a manager.

Janet: What do you mean?

Frank: She really wasn't tuned in to what I wanted, career-wise. She made up her mind that I was great at customer relations, and that's where I should stay.

Janet: So are you saying that your manager adversely affected your work environment?

Frank: Yes, I would.

Janet: How would you describe the working conditions?

Frank: They were fine.

Janet: What, if anything, could have been done to dissuade you from terminating your employment with this organization?

Frank: I hate to sound like a broken record, but it's very simple: My manager just didn't listen to my interest in HR. Getting rejected for the job I applied for just pushed me over the edge and out the door.

Janet: Is there anything more you'd like to add?

Frank: Just that I'm sorry to be leaving. I'd hoped for a career here—just not one in customer relations.

Janet: Thanks for your openness, Frank. Your comments are helpful to us. We're sorry to see you go.

Janet: Me too, Janet. Thanks, and so long.

COMPONENTS OF A RETENTION ENVIRONMENT

Many companies pay well and offer competitive benefits and state-of-the-art technology. But in today's tight labor market, more is needed to keep top performers from leaving.

Communication

Without a doubt, the key ingredient to a retention environment is communication. Following are some common-sense suggestions for improving lines of communication:

▲ *Hold open forums.* Set up monthly open sessions during which employees can talk with decision-makers about issues of importance to them. At first, all that may come out is a stream of complaints. Soon, however, as employees begin to trust that their concerns will be heard and acted upon, complaints will turn into legitimate observations about issues that can be addressed.

▲ *Improve credibility.* The best way of accomplishing this is to follow through on what you promise. For example, survey your company's workforce and ask them to identify three aspects of working in the company that are in most dire need of overhauling. If they overwhelmingly select three things—say, the benefits plan, technology equipment, and the employee handbook—thank them for their feedback and advise them how and when they can expect to see follow-up action. You could then transmit weekly updates via the intranet, post notices on the bulletin board, make announcements at staff meetings, or run articles in the company newsletter on the steps you take. Whatever medium you select, keep it constant and current. Your employees may not end up getting everything they asked for, but at least they'll know you're trying.

▲ *Communicate regularly and often.* Let employees know what's going on throughout the organization, especially if there are rumors floating around concerning acquisitions, mergers, or downsizing. Welcome new hires, publicly congratulate employees on internal promotions, post policy changes, publicize additions to benefits, and announce social functions.

▲ *Eliminate fear of reprisal.* Don't tell employees to express their views and then chastise them for doing so. To eliminate any chance of this occurring, set up suggestion boxes into which they can place their observations and criticisms anonymously.

Communication is only effective if it is two-way. Take this Communication Quiz to see how you fare with regard to promoting two-way communication. Give yourself a 5 each time you answer "always," a 4 for each "almost always," a 3 for each "sometimes," a 2 for each "rarely," and a 1 for each "never."

1. When employees come in to talk with me, with or without an appointment, I put aside what I'm working on and give them undivided attention. ☐ 1 ☐ 2 ☐ 3 ☐ 4 ☐ 5

2. I talk with employees in private so they are more inclined to express themselves openly. ☐1 ☐2 ☐3 ☐4 ☐5

3. If the phone rings while an employee is talking to me, I answer but tell the person I'll have to call back.
☐1 ☐2 ☐3 ☐4 ☐5

4. I don't complete people's sentences for them, no matter how long it takes them to complete a thought.
☐1 ☐2 ☐3 ☐4 ☐5

5. I convey positive body language to employees when they talk, e.g., smile, lean forward, and nod in understanding.
☐1 ☐2 ☐3 ☐4 ☐5

6. I ask questions if I'm not clear as to what the person is saying or asking. ☐1 ☐2 ☐3 ☐4 ☐5

7. I take notes to help me remember what the employee is asking. ☐1 ☐2 ☐3 ☐4 ☐5

8. I periodically paraphrase or summarize what the employee has been saying to ensure understanding.
☐1 ☐2 ☐3 ☐4 ☐5

9. If a crisis requiring immediate attention arises while I'm talking with an employee, I apologize and reschedule our meeting. ☐1 ☐2 ☐3 ☐4 ☐5

10. Anytime a new policy or procedure is issued, rather than just distribute it, I go over it with my staff to ensure understanding. ☐1 ☐2 ☐3 ☐4 ☐5

11. I give as much attention to lackluster employees as I do to star performers. ☐1 ☐2 ☐3 ☐4 ☐5

12. I openly acknowledge hard work and extra effort.
☐1 ☐2 ☐3 ☐4 ☐5

13. I make myself available to employees after issuing assignments. ☐1 ☐2 ☐3 ☐4 ☐5

14. I make sure my employees understand how the work they're performing fits in with the company's overall goals.
☐1 ☐2 ☐3 ☐4 ☐5

15. I make sure employees have adequate resources for the work they've been assigned. ☐1 ☐2 ☐3 ☐4 ☐5

16. I respond to all phone calls and e-mails from my employees within twenty-four hours. ☐1 ☐2 ☐3 ☐4 ☐5

17. I drop by to see my employees just to say "hello."
☐ 1 ☐ 2 ☐ 3 ☐ 4 ☐ 5

18. I make myself available at company-sponsored social and sporting events, since some employees feel more comfortable talking when they're out of the office.
☐ 1 ☐ 2 ☐ 3 ☐ 4 ☐ 5

19. I don't tell employees I'm definitely going to do something, such as get them the raise they deserve, unless I know for certain that I can. ☐ 1 ☐ 2 ☐ 3 ☐ 4 ☐ 5

20. I communicate with employees the way I would want my boss to communicate with me.
☐ 1 ☐ 2 ☐ 3 ☐ 4 ☐ 5

Don't worry if you didn't end up with a perfect score of 100; that's nearly impossible. Anything above an 80 means you're tuned in to the importance of open, two-way communication between yourself and your employees. A score between 60 and 80 indicates you're receptive to the importance of communication but need to hone your skills. If you scored below 60, ask yourself if you'd want to work for someone like you!

Motivation

These days there seem to be two distinct categories of worksites: (1) those that are struggling to lure warm bodies and retain them for longer than six months, and (2) those that are able to attract and keep employees.

An example of the latter is Jamestown Advanced Products, a manufacturer of fabricated metal products in Jamestown, New York, with approximately eighty employees. Its ability to create a retention environment generates comments from its employees such as, "I work harder here than I have anywhere else I've worked, but I enjoy it more." Workers at Jamestown are encouraged by a motivating work environment that enables them to work hard and strive to achieve specific goals. There are distinct differences between what management does and the work performed by employees, but not in the traditional way. Management essentially coordinates with customers, provides the shop with information, orders materials, and pays the bills. Employees, on the other hand, are essentially in control. They run day-to-day operations and participate in designing manufacturing processes for greater efficiency. As one employee put it, "Gone was the old method I've encountered, in other places, of supervisors treating you as though you were stupid, or stealing your ideas and later passing them off as their own. Here everything is out in the open, so everyone knows who came up with a specific idea."

Employees work closely as members of a team, bouncing ideas off one another and solving problems. In the words of one employee, "We make group decisions. We lead ourselves." Leaders and followers evolve naturally according to individual strengths. When there is disagreement, the entire group gets together and works it out. If there is a serious disagreement, they go to management, but that doesn't happen very often.

Jamestown's approach is successful. The company's sales have tripled in seven years, and employees are motivated by an atmosphere of autonomy, management's confidence in their abilities, and a cooperative environment.

Motivational theories that have been around since the 1950s still form the cornerstone that successful companies are built on. These include *management by objectives* (MBO), which links compensation and incentives to individuals' performance; David McClelland's *need to achieve* theory; and Abraham Maslow's *hierarchy of needs*. In addition, Frederick Herzberg's book *Motivation to Work*, which was published in 1959 and promoted support of people's self-esteem and cooperative management, is still popular today. These practices don't always succeed, however, when companies interpret them to further a reliance on external inducements and rewards. Indeed, external incentives can actually backfire when employees view these tangible rewards as manipulative attempts by management to "buy" or exercise control.

For these and other motivational theories to work, the focus must be on intrinsic values. How people view and approach a project or assignment, how they feel available tools can best be utilized, and which resources they feel will assist them in achieving their goal are all components of individual intrinsic values. Studies by Teresa Amabile of Harvard University, as described in *A Better Place to Work* by Adolf Haasen and Gordon Shea (AMA Membership Publications, 1997), have shown that creativity is highest when there is strong intrinsic motivation; extrinsic approaches, on the other hand, constrain and undermine people's innovative efforts. And studies conducted by Mihaly Csikszentmihalyi of the University of Chicago reveal how "flow"—the term used to describe intrinsically motivated behavior—arises from the challenge and the sense of control an activity provides. Intrinsic motivation, then, is self-generated.

People are motivated when they are able to match their skills and abilities to a particular task. To do this, they need to work in an environment that values diversity and individuality—one that encourages more than a single way of doing things.

Work Isn't Everything

Companies valuing retention environments recognize that employees have commitments, obligations, and pressures outside the office. Accordingly, these companies work to alleviate some of the stress by providing such benefits as flexible work schedules (see Chapter 10), on-site daycare, and concierge services. In addition, they allow employees to express their individuality on the job through casual dress and personalized office decor, also allowing them to play while at work.

The notion of having fun at work is growing in popularity. In addition to the examples provided in Chapter 2, there are many others. At OddzOn Products, for instance, fun is part of an employee's daily schedule. The toy manufacturer, based in Campbell, California, has been known to close the office and take all one hundred employees to a movie in the middle of a workday.

Matt Weinstein of PlayFair, a Berkeley, California, company that offers humor seminars, suggests injecting fun into the workplace by wearing campaign buttons made out of employees' baby pictures and putting rubber fish in the water cooler. Humor seminars help relax employees at Digital Equipment's Colorado customer support center. When employees feel uptight after talking with a difficult customer, they juggle beanbags, which helps break the tension. Digital has also instituted a Grouch Patrol, consisting of employees who are authorized to tell grouchy people to take a break. Such breaks result in improved productivity.

At Remedy Corp., a software company based in Mountain View, California, fun is practically an art form. Managers have been known to put on hula skirts and sumo wrestling suits, sponsor pinball games and foam-ball shootouts, and show appreciation to workers by washing their cars. Employees even get to dunk executives in cold water tanks at company picnics.

Anyone who questions the merits of such behavior need only refer to some of the bottom-line results. Remedy, for example, has doubled its size, revenue, and customer base for five consecutive years. Not only that, retention averages forty-two months, while the industry's average is twenty months. That's impressive, considering the highly competitive nature of business in the notorious Silicon Valley.

Here are additional components of a retention environment:

▲ *A sense of purpose.* Employees favor companies in which they feel connected to the product, the corporate mission, or the overall vision of the industry. In environments such as these, employees feel they're making a contribution and have a sense of purpose. Take a look at the extreme to which employees go at Harley-Davidson Inc., the motorcycle manufacturer based in Milwaukee. Employees are so caught up with their company's product that many of them have tattooed the company's name on their bodies. And at Merck & Co., the giant drug manufacturer based in Whitehouse Station, New Jersey, the workforce is dedicated to the company's commitment of placing patients before profits, as exemplified by the fact that Merck gives away medicine in developing countries to prevent a disease known as river blindness.

▲ *Diversity.* As described in Chapter 1, diverse work environments are places where employees feel their differences are nurtured and appreciated, not just tolerated. Employees are encouraged to perform, not conform, and individuality is cherished. One such company is Nissan Design International Inc. in San Diego. The company has received high marks for its commitment to diversity in that the company hires people specifically for their unique work styles.

▲ *Participatory management.* Companies that encourage participatory management recognize that employees often have the best ideas for accomplishing a task, so it's counterproductive to tell them what to do. One such company is Nantucket Nectars, a juice company based in Cambridge, Massachusetts. The style of management is so participatory that there's no established hierarchy and no secretaries.

▲ *Learning environment.* Companies that promote lifelong learning encourage their employees to leave work at the end of each day knowing more than they did at the start. On- and off-site training workshops and continuing education are promoted by companies such as Motorola, based in Schaumberg, Illinois, and Trident Precision Manufacturing Inc., in Webster, New York.

SUMMARY

Many of today's employers are experiencing a double whammy: Not only are they having trouble finding qualified workers, they also have difficulty holding on to them. High turnover is often attributable to an improper match between an employee's expectations and the realities of the job, or incompatibility with the corporate culture. Or it may be that the employee doesn't feel appreciated or valued. Sometimes, too, high turnover can be traced to inadequate supervision, lack of growth opportunities, lack of training, or unequal salaries and benefits. It can also be a result of unsatisfactory relationships at work or inadequate equipment, tools, and facilities.

Exit interviews can reveal information about how a terminating employee viewed various aspects of his or her employment with the company, such as working conditions, compensation, and employer-employee relations. It's also an opportunity to learn what suggestions employees might have for improving the company. This information can be useful when hiring in the future and revising policies and procedures, in addition to analyzing morale or productivity problems. Whether conducted in-house or outsourced to a third party, exit interviews should encompass techniques such as encouraging employees to talk, actively listening when they answer questions, and understanding as well as interpreting their body language. In addition, interviewers should employ four different questioning techniques: competency-based, open-ended, probing, and closed-ended. Questions posed in a scale format can also be effective.

Keeping top performers from leaving derives from developing a retention environment. Such an environment encompasses two-way communication, intrinsic motivation, a chance to have fun while at work, a sense of purpose, participatory management, and lifelong learning opportunities.

NOTES

1. *Workforce*, June 1998.

CHAPTER 9

Rewards, Recognition, and Opportunities

"Adults need meaningful work in the same way that children need interesting play, in order to fulfill themselves as persons."

—Al Gini, philosopher

I recently spoke with a young woman about her job and intentions to continue working for her current employer. Laura started working for her company three years ago, after graduating from college, and she confided that she'd intended to stay for no more than a year. "Why only a year?" I asked. "Because I wanted to fast-track my career," she explained. "One year here, another year somewhere else—you know. I thought I should keep moving onward and upward until I got where I wanted to be." "Where is that?" I wondered. "Well, I used to know. I mean, I always assumed to be successful meant making tons of money and having lots of stuff. I didn't think about being happy. I didn't think you could afford to think about being happy if you wanted to succeed in a career."

"It sounds as if you've changed your mind," I commented. Laura smiled and relaxed back in her chair. "I certainly have. I'm content here. I like what I do, and there are opportunities to grow if I want to. If I have an idea about doing something differently, management listens. They not only listen, they reward me for my ideas! Creativity and innovative thinking are really encouraged here, at all levels. If I want to take a class or attend a workshop, they're right behind me. I mean, any course in any subject. I guess they figure the more I know, the more I can contribute to the company. I can also learn through our mentoring program." "That's quite an endorsement," I said. "Oh, that's not all! Management shows us a thousand different ways how much they appreciate our work." "Do you mean through salary and benefits?" I asked. "Sure, that too. But I'm talking about all the little things they do on a daily basis—the loads of small rewards that make us feel wanted and needed. Some of these things are material, sure, but others are intangibles that make us want to do our best."

"So is it safe to say that you plan on staying for a while?" I queried. Laura laughed. "That's very safe to say. You see, there's one more thing that's different from the direction I thought my life would take when I graduated college. I recently got married and found out last month that I'm going to have a baby. With the company's generous leave policy and lactation program, I wouldn't dream of leaving!"

This dialogue zeros in on many aspects of what it takes for a company to retain its workers. Of course, not everyone is as responsive as Laura. But employees are more likely to continue working for an organization that shows its appreciation for their efforts with rewards, recognition, and opportunities.

TALENT RETENTION

Increasingly, organizations realize that they must focus on retention as one of their most critical business objectives in order to remain competitive. When the Saratoga Institute surveyed forty-five *Fortune* 1000 organizations across the United States, over 89 percent indicated that their organizations viewed employee retention as a strategic business issue. Participants included Bank of America, Dell Computer Corporation, GTE Directories Corp., Honda of America Manufacturing, Inc., Union Carbide Corporation, and United Parcel Service. The companies that did not support this view were predominantly in nongrowth industries.[1]

Fifteen common elements were found in corporate retention programs:

1. Innovative compensation and benefits packages
2. Effective rewards and recognition
3. Performance management, aligning employee goals with business goals
4. Strategies for increasing employee satisfaction
5. Measures of employee satisfaction

6. Career planning
7. Work/life strategy
8. Building new-hire commitment
9. Competency-based strategies
10. Employee needs
11. Mentoring programs
12. Defined role of corporate culture
13. Use of coaching for career development
14. An employee strategy to support growth and loyalty
15. Merger and acquisition retention strategy

Each of these factors can be broken down further. For example, compensation and benefits packages could include stock options, work/life strategy can encompass work-at-home options and other flexible work arrangements, and career planning can extend to training and educational opportunities. Of course, all of these elements need not be implemented for a retention program to be successful. Other factors may influence the effectiveness of specific components, including the company's mission statement and objectives, the nature of the industry, the size of the organization, and the types of jobs. Measures of success include reduced turnover rates, reduced absenteeism, more positive feedback during exit interviews, improved employee morale, fewer counseling activities, improved customer and client relations, and increased productivity.

Retention costs reported by participants in the Saratoga Institute report give us an idea of what an organization must spend to retain top talent. For companies with approximately ten thousand employees, the average retention cost is $6.5 million. This figure includes direct costs, lost business opportunity costs resulting from learning curves, incentive pay, special pay, and base pay increases.

Ways to Retain Talent

Open Work Environments

Retention programs work especially well in environments where employees understand and work toward business as well as financial objectives, not just operational goals. Employees are encouraged to participate in discussions of strategic goals with the understanding that everyone has a financial stake in their success.

These are open work environments, where exempt/nonexempt lines are blurred, and titles have little meaning.

In open work environments, employees are hired more for attitude than aptitude. As previously mentioned, a prime example can be found at Patagonia, the Ventura, California–based outdoor clothing and gear company, where employees are hired specifically for their cultural compatibility with the company. Management seeks workers who are highly motivated and love outdoor activities like hiking and biking. In fact, with company headquarters located less than two miles from the beach, employees frequently go surfing while "at work."

Open work environments also favor peer reviews. For example, at TriNet Employer Group, located in San Leandro, California, employees are asked to rate team members on twenty different behaviors such as "Work product is complete and accurate" and "Radiates a positive attitude toward change and challenge." At other open work environments, such as McMurry Publishing, managers are expected to spend a minimum of four hours preparing an annual review for each employee.

Training plays a pivotal role in open work environments. Extending beyond traditional training workshop topics, employees are often schooled in basic business literacy. Seminars such as The Accounting Game, produced by Educational Discoveries, and board games such as Profit & Cash, developed by Capital Connections, enable employees to better appreciate the intricacies of making money. Some companies develop their own training games based on TV shows like *Family Feud* and *Jeopardy!* that encourage teamwork, in addition to learning.

Compensation in open work environments is linked with clearly defined performance goals that are identified in the company's annual plan. Bonuses are part of the compensation plan, but only after employees have a precise understanding of the criteria for payout. The progress made toward achieving bonuses is frequently tracked on scoreboards on a weekly or monthly basis. At TriNet Employer Group, for example, the benchmarks for determining the bonus appear on the company's monthly scoreboard. Employees earn their bonuses in the form of "Reality Checks."

Companies interested in open work environments should start out by making small changes, such as establishing a three-month improvement goal, and then set up a scoreboard to track progress and promise a bonus if that goal is reached. Simultaneously, they could introduce employees to some aspect of the company's financial picture to help them understand how it functions. In this connection, business-literacy training can be reinforced by scoreboards, and the importance of numbers on the scoreboards reinforced by a bonus system. The system becomes one that is mutually reinforcing.

Innovative Work Environments

If you consider yourself to be a traditional kind of employer with conservative ideas about what a work environment should look like and how it should function, you may be tempted to skip over this segment. Don't! In today's tight labor market, flexibility is critical for success. Indeed, in some instances, it's needed for survival. Some of today's most valued workers are what may be described as unique or nontraditional, needing an innovative work environment in order to thrive. In the past, employers called the shots, and creative people often remained stifled and uninspired. Today, however, many employees do not even consider working for an employer who does not allow them to challenge the status quo.

Several years ago, I was called in to consult for a publishing company in Pennsylvania. The company was having some employee relations problems and wanted me to sit down with members of management to "hammer things out." To eliminate distractions and the temptation for managers to return to their offices to work during breaks, the location for our meeting was at a local conference center. Upon arrival, I was ushered into the meeting room. It was a windowless room with six chairs lining each of two sides. Flip charts were standing in the two corners at the front, presumably waiting for me, poised with marker in hand, to record the group's collective pearls of wisdom.

Within minutes, twelve executives filed in and silently took their seats. We exchanged a few pleasantries and then I began talking. About ninety rather unproductive minutes later, I suggested a break. No one left the room. They just sort of milled around, drinking coffee. I left the room to get some air. I wandered outside and noticed there was a pool, as yet unopened since it was only April. There were, however, tables and chairs set up. I also noticed a swing set off to one side. The air was crisp and clear, the birds were singing, and gardeners were busy planting bushes and flowers. I liked what I saw.

When I returned to the conference room, I announced that we were having a change in venue. "Take your pads and pens, let's grab the flip charts, and let's go outside!" I said. They glanced nervously at one another but responded. We filed outside and I set up the flip charts so that they could be viewed from several vantage points around the pool, as well as from the swings. I picked up from where we had left off before the break.

At first, the tone and content were the same as when we were inside. But then wonderful things started to happen! These twelve somber executives started walking around and loosening their ties. Several of them went over to the swings and got on them. Two others found a ball in the shrubbery and started playing catch. And while all of this was going on, I was asking questions and they were coming up with ideas—fresh, exciting ideas! I wrote on the flip charts while they played and talked. By the end of the day, they returned to work with lots of interesting changes to recommend.

Today, what I did with this group of executives would not be considered all that radical. Many companies have accepted the notion that creativity flourishes in unconventional settings that support open ideas. 3M Corporation, for instance, established its Innovation and Learning Center to provide employees and teams with tools to help them think creatively. And IDEO Product Development, a design firm in Palo Alto, California, has brainstorming rooms placed throughout the organization. There, employees can draw, watch television or videotapes, or just think. Other companies implement "mindfulness breaks," whereby all employees, including the CEO, stop whatever they're doing at a designated time for five minutes to sit back and relax or get up to take a walk.

Innovative work environments are designed to inspire creative thoughts and activities. This includes unplanned communication among group members and the ability of those members to reconfigure their physical surroundings to suit changing needs. In this regard, the furnishings and layout of the office may be adjustable and fit a given function, project, or activity. Consider, by example, the floor plan at Offcon, the Danish hearing aid company. When CEO Lars Kolind took over the company, he eliminated all the individual offices and replaced them with a movable office arrangement. Each employee was given a two-drawer file cabinet on wheels in which to store personal files. Whenever employees work on a particular project or assignment together, they simply roll their files to any one of the available computer workstations situated throughout the building and set up a temporary office. Since the database of each computer contains all the information needed, it really doesn't matter where individuals work.

Another case in point is Sun Microsystems in Menlo Park, California. Since many of the employees spent a good deal of time in one of several kitchen areas conversing, the office space was redesigned to embrace an open area to encourage informal gatherings and brainstorming. In addition, the company created "Sun rooms" with exterior views, Ping-Pong tables, and stereo equipment. These are for employees taking a relaxation break, although some use the whiteboards in each room for work, if so motivated. Sun also made outdoor changes, setting up benches, tables, and chairs for employees to work outside, should they so choose.

Of course, settings such as these are no guarantee that employees' creative juices will flow and brilliant ideas will spring forth. They do, however, provide flexible settings that offer options. And choice is empowering. Contrast the two examples above with the more typical, traditional conference room setting: Which environment do you think your employees would find more enticing?

Employee Suggestions

One of the most productive methods for retaining top talent is to ask employees for their suggestions. Successful suggestion programs encourage ideas from employees at every level and provide quick feedback to everyone who submits an idea. In turn, the more ideas that you are able to implement, the more motivated the workforce will become. And the more the company will benefit. American Axle & Manufacturing Inc. in Three Rivers, Michigan, for example, saved close to $370,000 in just six months as a result of employee suggestions. And the Abex NWL division of Parker Hannifin Corp., in Kalamazoo, Michigan, saved more than $8.5 million in its five years of running the company's suggestion program. While most employers pay workers whose ideas are used, the amount expended is usually just a fraction of the resulting savings: American Axle paid out about $70,000 during the aforementioned six-month period, and Abex NWL paid out about $300,000 in rewards. Most important is the positive effect on employee morale and reduced turnover.

The particulars of how employee suggestion programs operate vary. Some organizations encourage any and all suggestions. Others want only those suggestions that will improve safety, quality of work, operational efficiency, or customer service. Also encouraged are suggestions for saving jobs, attracting more business, and remaining competitive. Suggestions that will save or make money for the company are almost always encouraged. Some companies require a certain number of suggestions from every employee; most leave it up to the employees to submit ideas, if and when they choose.

Almost all suggestion programs announce the names of those

employees whose ideas have been accepted. The details of the suggestion are also announced, as well as the anticipated benefits. Rewards are generally in the form of cash or gift certificates. Some companies put the decision of how much to give in the hands of an employee committee. Factors used to determine the amount include innovation, ingenuity, and cost savings. For instance, a seven-member team of employees working for a furniture manufacturer came up with an idea to change the material in the arm of a chair. The suggestion resulted in a savings of $1.5 million annually. Each member of the team received $500.

RETAINING YOUNGER WORKERS

The group that generates the greatest challenge when it comes to retention is younger workers. Scarce in numbers to begin with, this thirty-five-and-under group expects to balance fulfilling careers with familial responsibilities, as well as actively pursue personal interests. Their work must be challenging and reflect leading-edge technology. Not wedded to one job or even one field, young workers are open to alternatives and look for exciting or entertaining opportunities that will expand their skills, knowledge, and interests.

That's a tall order to fill in a competitive, shrinking labor market. And yet, even knowing the needs of these 45 million "baby busters," few companies can boast of special retention efforts to prevent younger employees—especially much-needed information technology specialists—from leaving.

Bruce Tulgan, author of *Winning the Talent Wars* (Boston: Harvard Business School Press, 2001), remarks that retaining young workers doesn't have to be difficult if employers just get on board with their attitude toward work. Specifically, many younger workers are more interested in quick success and its rewards, rather than in paying dues by climbing the ladder rung by rung over a period of several years. That said, employers should focus on trying to generate the most productive work out of valued employees on a consistent basis, and not fixate on longevity. This may mean sidestepping some of the old rules. For example, it may prove more productive to focus on how to get a certain job done rather than filling specific job openings. This means managing performance and results instead of time. When it comes to vacation days, tradition may dictate an allocation of a specific number of days based on a combination of rank and how much time an employee has put in. Today's younger workers may simply say, however, "I'm not going to be here on Wednesday," and expect that to be acceptable. If policies and rules reign supreme, there's likely to be a brief battle after which the employee will simply leave.

According to Tulgan, ideally, when a young employee comes to work, management should think about how to keep him or her interested. Ask, "Where would you like to work, and when would you like to do it?" Since it's harder to find younger workers who are qualified and motivated to stay in one job for any period of time, the question is especially appropriate for them.

The youngest of workers—those born after 1977—are starting to make a distinct mark on U.S. businesses. In terms of numbers alone, this Net or Echo-Boom Generation promises to be different: 80 million compared with a little more than half that number of Generation Xers. To put this in a clearer context, the number of Netters surpasses the 77 million baby boomers who have been redefining business practices since the mid-1960s.

What really sets this group of workers apart is the huge edge they enjoy when it comes to information technology. They've grown up with it, are comfortable with it, and expect it to prevail in the workplace. Mark Alch, an instructor in the business and management program at the University of California, identifies additional characteristics of this vital group of workers that is just starting to infiltrate the labor market:

▲ Many work at part-time jobs while in high school and college. Therefore, they are not averse to working.
▲ They have grown up understanding the need for global interconnecting and are comfortable doing it via the Internet.
▲ Their views concerning a "normal" household extend to encompassing numerous family configurations.
▲ Having seen their parents fall victim to downsizing, mergers, takeovers, and closings, their sense of loyalty is to themselves.
▲ They are accustomed to functioning in a state of change and can make adjustments readily.
▲ As advocates of lifelong learning, they take courses on topics of interest or even obtain a formal degree or certification from the Internet.
▲ They expect to go through numerous job changes and perhaps six to seven different careers in their lifetimes. Accordingly, they view themselves as contract workers, lending

their expertise to any one employer for a limited period of time.

Consequently, Netters work best in an innovative, self-directed, team-based environment in which they can participate in decision making and collaborate on several projects simultaneously. They expect to be rewarded for their efforts, but not with standard tools such as promotions, bonuses, and merit increases. Growth is important, but not in the traditional sense of moving up the ranks of the corporate hierarchy. They respect people who demonstrate expertise and knowledge, having little use for titles or rank.

Companies would do well to begin gearing up for this huge group of workers who are just beginning to infiltrate the workplace. Two important steps in this direction are ensuring that they are technologically current as well as upgrading the skills of their current workforce. Equally important is keeping an open mind in reaction to how these new workers think and what they expect from their employers.

TRAINING AND EDUCATIONAL OPPORTUNITIES

In a survey taken of senior human resources executives at the American Management Association's 1999 annual HR conference and exposition, companies with retention programs indicated overwhelmingly that training was perceived as more effective than increased salary or benefits. According to Eric Greenberg, AMA's director of management studies, "Programs that improve work skills and future career development are seen as particularly effective." Among the types of training programs used most often are attendance at conferences and seminars, tuition reimbursement, and managerial training. Other popular training incentives include technical training and interpersonal skills training. In another survey, done by the Society for Human Resource Management, 94 percent of U.S. companies offer professional development, and 85 percent offer educational assistance as benefits. In addition, 98 percent of companies with five thousand or more employees offer professional development, and 93 percent offer educational assistance. And according to Thomas Mahan, vice president and senior consultant with Saratoga Institute, 41 percent of American workers will leave their employers if they don't get the desired training. For a company of one thousand employees, that means turnover will cost about $14.5 million a year.

Not everyone is enthusiastic about training, however, or willing to add to the $55 billion per year that companies spend upgrading the skills of their employees. For example, one of my clients called a few months ago to advise me that it was slashing its training budget in half and that some of my workshops were among the casualties. I asked why they were taking such drastic measures. The reply was disturbing, but not surprising: "We're in the midst of a tight labor market. We're losing top talent and can't find replacements. Training is the last thing on our minds right now."

Typically, when companies experience budgetary problems, training is one of the first areas to be cut. The reasons offered include:

▲ "Why bother training them? They'll just take what we teach them and leave. Why should some other company benefit from our training programs?"
▲ "There's no immediate way to measure the return on our investment."
▲ "Our employees are stretched thin as it is, covering the work from vacant positions. They simply don't have the time to attend training workshops or take classes."
▲ "The money is better spent on other things, like recruiting to fill all those openings!"

These statements are not without merit: Some workers do leave right after having been trained, measuring the impact of training takes time, more employees are working overtime these days, and there's a limited amount of money in the budget. But the fact that businesses are experiencing recruitment and retention problems is exactly why training is needed. As Tom Peters has said, "When times are good, double your training budget. When times are bad, quadruple your training budget."

Traditional Training

"I had no idea what to expect at a company job, so I picked a company that had extensive training." So said a young woman about to graduate with a master's degree in computer science. Her statement echoes the sentiments of many of today's workers in the enviable position of comparing offers from several potential employers. Competitive salaries and benefits packages aren't always helpful in distinguishing one offer from all the others, and after a while, many of the perks seem redundant. What often stands out, however, is a company's training and educational program.

Not surprisingly, technology workers are especially interested in keeping their skills sharp and up-to-date. Since technology changes so rapidly, employees worry that they are falling behind even as they are learning something new. One company even offered technical training as an incentive to convince full-time workers to switch over to temp work. And Tech Central, a Minnesota temporary services firm specializing in technical workers, used the lure of free training to convince people to quit other jobs to work for them.

Today's workers aren't attracted only to technical training. They recognize the need for training in interpersonal skills, teamwork, leadership skills, decision making, conflict resolution, business ethics, time management, and numerous other areas in order to compete in today's market. One recent graduate with a bachelor's degree in electrical engineering from MIT described the basis for narrowing his selection of future employers to two large companies: "It'll be great. I can keep going to school forever. If I decide to be a project manager, I won't have to worry about how to do it because there's a course. Even more important to me, if the company ever has to lay me off, I know that my skills will be current."

And companies are responding, even though they may be training a competitor's future employees. The reason is simple: In order to remain competitive, businesses are required to maximize the talent on their payroll. Here's a sampling of the kinds of training companies are offering:

▲ The goal of Lucent Technologies, with headquarters in Murray Hill, New Jersey, is to provide employees with fifteen days of training each year. In addition, workers design their own "personal development plan."

▲ At Motorola University, with U.S. regional offices in Arizona, Florida, Illinois, Massachusetts, and Texas, employees can take a number of technical classes and can also choose training in interpersonal communications, parenting, and weight management.

▲ The SAS Institute, a software developer in Carey, North Carolina, offers programs on business ethics, time management, and leadership skills in addition to technical training. Its turnover rate is just 4 percent, compared with the industry average of 22 percent.

The company reports savings in the amount of between $50 million and $60 million a year. It is convinced that this is the result largely of its commitment to training.

▲ At Tech Central, the temporary services firm specializing in technical workers mentioned above, employees can take training in customer service, conflict resolution, interpersonal relations, and teamwork.

Some companies even train applicants. At Envirocon, an architectural glass supplier located in Statesboro, Georgia, candidates attend sixteen hours of training, receiving instruction in the areas of general plant safety and the metric system. This enables the company to evaluate employees in more than an interview situation and allows the applicants to see what working for the company would be like. While applicants can take the skills and knowledge acquired in those sixteen hours and apply them at another company, Evirocon feels it's worth taking that chance.

As the previously mentioned young woman who picked a company offering extensive training added, "Just that the company is willing to invest in me motivates me to give back. I feel that a lot of people want a company to really value them. Training and development are one way a company shows that." If you have a workforce of employees who feel as she does, you're less likely to suffer from high turnover, poor morale, and low productivity.

Interim Services of Fort Lauderdale, Florida offers advice on how to approach training:

▲ Evaluate your company's future needs, and provide training opportunities to prepare employees to meet those needs.
▲ Base training and growth opportunities on an employee's contributions, not on his or her tenure.
▲ Encourage managers to identify future leaders. Then give those individuals the tools to develop career goals and identify how the company can help them attain those goals.
▲ Offer a variety of training on a combination of hard skills, like computer training, and so-called soft skills, such as communication.
▲ Ask employees to evaluate the training workshops and their usefulness.
▲ Give employees slightly more responsibility than they ask for. This helps create an environment where employees are challenged and never stagnant.

"Training is another word for living." That's the opinion of a recent graduate from Boise State University, who summed up its value this way: "I think that every day you're in training because you're learning something. My dad is a business executive, and he's always going to seminars, so I figure that's what I'll be doing too. You can always learn something from somebody."

Strategic Training

If you have reservations about committing dollars and hours to traditional training, perhaps it's time to tweak your training objectives. Instead of training employees to perform a specific task or learn a new skill, think in terms of giving them the skills and knowledge needed to become more invested in your business. This strategic approach is consistent with the concept of an open work environment, discussed earlier in this chapter. Employees learn how the business operates, enabling them to perform various tasks if and when the company shifts direction or starts stockpiling openings. The approach tells employees that you are committed to their ongoing education and that you view them as valuable components of the organization.

This proactive, energizing approach to training benefits everyone: The company has the human resources needed to meet corporate goals, and employees are less likely to become restless only to leave for another job. Companies that participate in this relatively new form of strategic training maintain that they are more likely to increase worker productivity, report improvements in quality, increase operating profits, and enhance the value of their stock. Among those businesses that have approached training strategically are New York–based J.P. Morgan & Co. (considered a pioneer in this regard) and U.S. Steel's Monongahela Valley plant in Dravosburg, Pennsylvania, which conducted a two-month program in which all 2,400 of the plant's employees were trained in every aspect of U.S. Steel's operations.

Computer-Based Training

Some forms of computer-based training (CBT), or e-learning, enable employees to "attend" sessions whenever they want. The courses can be viewed repeatedly in their entirety, or specific modules can be selected. Since many modules are approximately twenty or thirty minutes in duration, employees can take frequent "CBT learning breaks." Live E-learning, on the other hand, refers to online courses that are conducted by instructors at specific dates and times. Students basically have every feature of a classroom learning available to them, including the ability to interact with instructors and fellow students.

Although computer-based training may stand on its own, CBT is often used to enhance traditional classroom training. CBT trainees are often tested on their knowledge and certified upon satisfactory completion of the course. Since the process is geared toward self-study, often at each user's pace, CBT is particularly effective in situations where the workforce is diverse, multiple skills are required to do a job, and job-skill requirements continually change.

Many companies purchase off-the-shelf CBT packages, while some link up with E-learning course offerings from colleges and universities, thereby allowing for "distance learning." Still others prefer to author their own computer courses. If you choose to author your own CBT program, strive for standardization for maximum effectiveness. If there are several courses in a training curriculum, each course should meet certain guidelines for organization, screen composition, text placement, and feedback to users:

▲ *Organization.* Each course should provide directions on how to use the CBT system, identify course objectives, describe the contents of the course, provide a summary, and list references to supporting materials, such as the user's guide.

▲ *Screen composition.* Each course should contain one main idea per screen, bulleted lists of ideas, paragraphs of no more than six to eight lines, boxes containing instructional information of the same size and in a consistent location on the screen, and typing directions in the boxes.

▲ *Text placement.* When placing words on the screen, focus attention on one idea at a time, keep sentence length short, use one- and two-syllable words, use the second person *(you),* and be consistent in the use of command syntax.

▲ *Feedback to users.* When designing CBT program feedback for users as they make choices, utilize nonjudgmental words; make the feedback format consistent in location, punctuation, and so forth; explain why an answer is incorrect and provide the correct answer; and reinforce correct answers by restatement in slightly different terms.

By some estimates, CBT is now a $1.5 billion industry. Benefits over the physical classroom include media-rich resource materials available over the Internet. On the other hand, critics observe that the dropout rate for e-classes is high, with rates exceeding 40 percent in some instances. This may be because online courses often require more preparation work and, if live E-learning is involved, greater student interaction.

Tuition Reimbursement

Many employers have traditionally offered some sort of tuition aid to employees who want to further their formal education. This includes part or all of the cost of tuition, books, and supplies. In some companies, the policy is quite restrictive and covers only those courses directly related to the employee's present job. Other companies take a more liberal position, paying for general education, but with an annual cap.

Today, that's changing. With businesses emphasizing recruitment and retention in an economy with nearly full employment, employers are acutely aware of two things: (1) educational assistance is expected by savvy employees, and (2) over the past years, tuition has been increasing faster than the rate of inflation. Accordingly, more organizations are offering extended educational opportunities to their employees and, to control the escalating costs, are providing options for campus classrooms, such as courses on the Internet and long-distance learning.

Hewitt Associates, a consulting firm in Lincolnshire, Illinois, recently surveyed nearly five hundred companies relative to their educational reimbursement policies. Its findings included the following:

- ▲ sixty-four percent reimburse for tuition, books, registration fees, and lab fees.
- ▲ sixty-three percent require a grade of C or better in order to grant reimbursement.
- ▲ five percent pay for classes in advance.
- ▲ thirty-three percent allow employees to take classes as soon as they start work, 24 percent require a six-month waiting period, and 20 percent require a one-year wait.
- ▲ seventy-four percent do not require a minimum time for employees to stay on the job after the course is completed.

Hewitt's survey also revealed that 46 percent of the companies set an annual dollar maximum, with a median of $3,000 for undergraduate courses and $3,600 for graduate courses.

These median figures may strike some companies as low:

▲ At Detroit's Michigan Consolidated Gas Co., the annual tuition payment cap is $5,250.

▲ QUALCOMM, headquartered in San Diego, offers an annual educational allowance of $5,200 per employee.

▲ Sprint, whose world headquarters is in Westwood, Kansas, offers $5,250 per year if employees stay at least that long.

▲ InoTech, a systems and network management firm based in Fairfax, Virginia, prepays employees up to $7,500 for tuition and books after they've been employed for ninety days. The company pays 100 percent for an A or B grade and 50 percent for a C. Employees at every level are encouraged to take courses with the number and scheduling of classes left up to the employee, as long as productivity does not suffer as a result.

▲ Minnesota Life Insurance Co. reimburses up to $4,000 annually. Employees are paid in full for a grade of C or better.

Some businesses require written contracts with employees who are educated at company expense. The contracts outline the amount to be prepaid or reimbursed, any required grades or length of stay, and any other conditions, such as course restrictions.

Beyond Succession Planning

Traditional succession planning involves grooming future leaders to occupy designated positions, with one or two people targeted for each senior management position. Unfortunately, fewer than 30 percent of senior management positions are filled by individuals initially identified as replacements. A more viable approach may be the acceleration pool, a process that provides a constant supply of high-potential candidates for nonspecific jobs. With the focus on skill and knowledge development, participants are invited to attend special executive programs, conferences, and high-impact training programs, or to receive instruction through virtual teams and web-based self-study. Specific learning objectives are established to keep the focus on application, rather than on course completion. Accordingly, using measurable standards, pool members are evaluated on how well they apply the training concepts on the job. Mentors and executive coaches provide ongoing feedback as well as coaching.

Companies usually select members for acceleration pools based on job performance, competency development, and job-experience growth. Where utilized, assessment center results can be a factor. While employees may be in the pool for as long as fifteen years, depending on when they enter, there's no guarantee that those selected for the pool will be permitted to remain. Members may be dropped if they aren't meeting their development goals or may opt out if the work demands, travel, or relocation requirements are too great.

Acceleration pools do not presume that employees outside the pool lack potential for growth or development; rather, the presumption is that those in the pool will be accelerated in their development.

Best Practice: QUALCOMM

QUALCOMM, the six thousand–plus employee telecommunications giant headquartered in San Diego, is committed to continuous education and training. The company offers its employees more than 250 course modules online—including basic word processing, technical design, and engineering—and more than one hundred classroom-based courses. The online offerings allow employees to take courses during off hours—e.g., in the evenings, on weekends, and while traveling—and greatly reduces the company's training costs. If QUALCOMM was to limit its training to centralized classroom workshops, flying in employees from five states as well as Israel, it would cost the company millions of dollars. Instead, online training slashes the cost by 50 to 70 percent.

QUALCOMM's employees do not hesitate to take advantage of the generous course offerings. In 1999, for example, employees logged 94,000 hours of classroom training and tens of thousands of hours more online. QUALCOMM also encourages employees to obtain MBAs through San Diego State University and master's in electrical engineering degrees through the University of Southern California's distance learning program.

QUALCOMM's extensive training program is divided into four categories: technical code division multiple access, computer training/engineering, manufacturing, and professional management. Some of the courses are classroom-based, others are online, and some are offered both online and in the classroom. This dual mode of training is in recognition of employees' distinct learning schedules and styles. The courses are developed by learning specialists who track the needs of various business units. Most of the courses are voluntary; others are at the suggestion of supervisors who feel that certain employees could benefit from training in specific skills.

Basically, then, employees are able to choose from among a host of options and decide which courses will enhance their knowledge base or help them achieve their career goals. Signing up is as easy as logging on to the corporate intranet, scanning through course offerings, selecting ones that are interesting, and enrolling. After completing a course, employees complete online evaluations.

The payoff of all this training is that, according to a QUALCOMM human resources specialist, it "gives us a competitive advantage. It offers enormous benefits for QUALCOMM and all the company's employees. It has played a large role in defining the company and leading to our success."

QUALCOMM was honored by *Workforce* magazine as one of 2000's ten most outstanding HR departments. See Exhibit 9–1 for additional training and educational practices.

Exhibit 9–1. Additional Training and Educational Practices.

Here is a sampling of how other companies approach continued learning:

▲ J.P. Morgan & Co., the New York investment company, is unusually progressive in its employee development. Employees are routinely promoted into positions for which they are not yet quite ready. The reasoning behind this is that qualified candidates may soon lose interest and move on, whereas those employees not quite ready for a promotion are challenged to learn.

▲ McBer and Company, an international consulting company, conducts weekly computer games to ensure that all computer-shy employees learn how to become computer-literate.

▲ The Learn and Earn Program at ipd Co., an auto parts manufacturer, pays employees for preparing reports on what they have learned from reading books, listening to tapes, or attending seminars.

▲ Johnsonville Foods, a Wisconsin sausage maker, encourages employees to attend any company-sponsored training workshop, regardless of its applicability to their current jobs.

▲ Intel Corporation, the giant computer chip maker with seven U.S. site offices, requires all employees to attend seven seminars focusing on corporate culture, values, and business ventures during their first year of employment.

▲ Allstate Insurance Co. promotes a lifelong learning atmosphere through its commitment to retrain each employee
every four to five years.

▲ At Conners Communications, a New York public relations
firm, employees can take "quickie" training sessions of fifteen to thirty minutes in duration covering various topics.

▲ Employees select the topics they want to learn more about
at the Industrial Controls Group of Allen-Bardley, a Milwaukee auto parts manufacturer.

MENTORING

Mentoring can be defined as a developmental, helping relationship
whereby one person invests time, ability, and effort in enhancing
another person's growth, knowledge, and skills in preparation for
greater productivity or future achievement. Mentoring relationships can be situational, informal, or formal. Situational relationships are short, isolated incidences involving a casual transfer of
information or ideas from one person to another. Informal mentoring involves personal relationships in which one person voluntarily shares expertise or knowledge with another. Formal mentoring
programs are structured, sanctioned by the organization, and focus
on helping one or more individuals achieve specific goals. Accordingly, effective mentoring programs may be one-on-one, group, or
team-to-team endeavors.

Mentoring can help to attract and keep talented employees,
reduce turnover, and increase productivity. It also accelerates employee contributions to company productivity. At Coopers & Lybrand in Detroit, for example, of the original one hundred
employees in the corporate mentoring program, as of 1998 only
three had left the company.

Here's what some mentees have said about their mentoring
program experiences:

▲ "I'm contributing much more to our work team effort than I
was just six months ago. I've been able to turn my whole
attitude around. I'd give him [the mentor] credit for that, but
he wouldn't accept it. He'd say I did it, he only helped, but
without that help I doubt if I'd have made it. The mentoring
experience has changed my life for the better."

▲ "I never dreamed that a highly successful executive could

care so much about what would happen to me. I hope I can repay him by making good use of all those special insights he provided."

▲ "I've learned to trust more and to take charge of my own future through her help."

Now read what some mentors have reported:

▲ "Mentoring has added another dimension to my leadership skills. Going the extra mile was just an interesting expression until I was trained to function as a mentor."
▲ "When I help my mentees achieve something special and important to them, I feel I've made a powerful investment in our organization's most valuable asset—its people."
▲ "Becoming a mentor helped me to stop thinking of my work group as just a group. The very personal one-on-one investment in another person helped me to see each one as an individual and then our team as a synergy of harmonies, and as cooperative, unique individuals. I like this."

These representative comments illustrate how mentoring is a symbiotic relationship; that is, both mentees and mentors benefit.

Mentees also have greater visibility to more senior people and obtain guidance from executives they normally wouldn't have access to. Moreover, those professionals who have had mentors reportedly earn between $5,000 and $22,000 more annually than those who have not. Organizations benefit in additional ways: Mentoring builds a stronger company team and promotes a sense of unity.

Mentoring Programs

As stated, mentoring programs can be one-on-one, group, or team to-team. Personalized, one-on-one mentoring has the greatest potential for trust and sharing, but it's not as practical as group or team mentoring. Having one executive mentor a group of four to six employees is by far more cost-effective. In addition, participants can learn from their peers as well as from their mentor. And having senior teams mentor junior teams exposes mentees to more than one set of skills and experiences.

Mentoring programs typically cost anywhere from $400 at the low end to $5,000 per participant. This includes fees for outside consultants' training materials, advice on "matching," and training of both mentor and mentee. Training of mentees in addition to mentors is considered critical for success. Mentee training incorporates career assessment to identify goals, as well as guidance on what they can realistically expect as a result of the program. Mentor training entails conveying what their role consists of, the amount of time and energy required, and the importance of confidentiality.

Candidates for mentoring programs are selected on the basis of their executive potential. In addition to their skills and knowledge, mentors are chosen on the basis of availability, accessibility, interest, and rapport with potential mentees. Pairing up mentees with mentors can be accomplished in several different ways. Typically, matching assignments are made on the basis of defined needs of the mentees and the interests of the mentors. Sometimes, mentors and mentees are given several choices from which to choose. Hewlett-Packard in Palo Alto, California has matching receptions, where mentees can interact with mentors before making a selection. The program manager screens the requests and, in the event one mentor receives many more requests than the others, matches those that are most practical geographically. At Texas Instruments in Dallas, however, employees are encouraged to find their own mentor, by looking through a list of people who have identified themselves as senior advisers and selecting accordingly.

Exactly how mentors and mentees communicate, and for how long, varies considerably depending on the established objectives and learning styles of the mentees. Generally, mentoring programs last about a year. That's not to say, however, that informal relationships don't continue long after. Mentors and mentees usually meet every two weeks or once a month. If face-to-face meetings are impractical on a regular basis, they may communicate by audio- or videotapes, phone, fax, or e-mail biweekly or monthly, and then meet quarterly. Meetings usually last about two hours. In addition, any time mentors come across an article or hear something relevant to the mentees' goals, it can be conveyed immediately, instead of waiting for a formal meeting.

Mentors are encouraged to familiarize themselves with the approach to learning preferred by their mentees. Some need examples, some need to talk, and others need to experiment with different methods of accomplishing tasks. Regardless of the preferred methodology, mentees need to discover their own path to becoming effective. And mentors need to practice active listening, offer information and ideas, and provide frequent feedback.

Here's an example of how one company uses mentoring. At Fuller Company, of Bethlehem, Pennsylvania, increasing concern arose over the number of professional employees who were leaving after only one to three years. To combat high turnover, HR established the Targeted Employee Development Program, a mentor-team program. Potential leaders were targeted by management and coached through the development of critical leadership and technical skills. Within three years, Fuller reduced its turnover to less than 2 percent. Many of the original mentees are now the mentors for current participants.

Another example of a company that uses mentoring programs is Trevira, a division of Hoechst Celanese that develops polyester fibers in North and South Carolina. A few years ago, the company realized that a number of managers were scheduled to retire, without replacements ready to step in. Accordingly, Trevira developed a yearlong mentoring program that included a "learning group," consisting of one mentor and a half-dozen mentees. The mentor provided perspective and insight on the corporation's culture, politics, and how decisions were made. Mentees controlled the meeting times and frequency. Mentees met as a group or individually with the mentor, at their option. The program produced the desired results in that graduates of the program progressed into management positions.

RECOGNITION PROGRAMS

The importance of employee recognition and its link with retention is indisputable. Despite acknowledging its importance, some organizations still resist programs geared toward keeping employees satisfied and interested in staying aboard—that is, convincing employees that you really appreciate their efforts and contributions. Typically, obstacles such as cost, concern about measuring results, and uncertainty as to what incentives to offer are given. Since we are living in an extremely materialistic age, you might assume costly gifts, generous bonuses, or stock options head the list. Retention bonuses, for instance, are commonly offered to entice employees to stay, especially when a company is going through a transitional stage. These may be based on salary percentages or flat-rate figures, typically ranging from $1,000 to $40,000. But bonuses alone don't usually work for long. Companies have to learn what's important to each employee, and it isn't always money.

While no one would suggest that employees don't enjoy receiving monetary rewards, it appears that what a company gives is not as important as how the award or recognition is presented.

Personal and Public Recognition

Hands down, employees report that what really matters to them is personal attention and public recognition. It speaks volumes for an employee to be acknowledged for special achievements in front of peers, or to be recognized by upper-level management in a personal way. Sometimes this can be as modest as a handwritten note from the CEO, or it may be a more grand form of recognition such as an airplane-pulled banner with a thank-you message from the boss.

Starbuck's Warm Regards recognition program exemplifies this point. The program was developed to highlight outstanding achievement embodying the principles, mission, and goals of the company. Specific awards include "The MUG" (Moves of Uncommon Greatness); "BRAVO," which recognizes partner (read: employee) achievements; and "The Spirit of Starbucks," honoring passion and action.

One company that turns personal and public recognition into an art form is Disney. The next time you visit Disneyland in Anaheim, California, take a look at the windows in the shops on Main Street, U.S.A. Painted on them are the names of cast members (read: employees) who have made significant contributions to the organization. Not only can honored cast members point to their own window with pride, they are actually given a replica of the window during a formal ceremony. One recipient of a "window" is Renie Bardeau, photographer and photo archivist at Disneyland for nearly forty years. Asked how he felt upon receiving the award, he responded, "I was elated, awed, dumbstruck—and it was completely unexpected. At Disney, no job is menial. And the great thing about Disney is that, sure, they're a big company and a big profit machine, but they still take time out to recognize their people. It really shows they have their values in the right place."

Employees who are recipients of public recognition for their achievements echo the sentiment that it makes them feel valued and appreciated and less likely to leave and go elsewhere. When John Reimnitz, a senior statistical analyst for the Lincoln, Nebraska–based research company The Gallup Organization, received the company's "Mountain Top Award," he was thrilled. The prestigious award is given to an elite few regarded as the highest performers in the company's worldwide organization of three thousand employees. Reimnitz commented, "Receiving an award like this helps make the sacrifices worthwhile—it's nice to know that you're valued. It's really nice to know you're making a difference." It's interesting to note that Reimnitz also received a trip to Los Angeles to attend the People's Choice Awards, but he says he got the most satisfaction from receiving the award itself. Reimnitz also confided that he's received offers for other positions paying more, but, he said, "Money can only go so far."

Low-Cost Recognition

There are many expensive ways to show employees you appreciate what they do, but there are also many inexpensive and cost-free ways of accomplishing the same objective. When these acknowledgments are doled out publicly, they become especially memorable. For example, spring little surprises on your employees, such as having a catered breakfast for your staff for no particular occasion, and then tell everyone how glad you are to have them on your team. Also, consider letting each department hold a weekly drawing for small prizes, like a gift certificate to a local restaurant or free movie tickets. Or try doing something similar to New York City's Tavern on the Green restaurant. Its Tavern All Stars program invites all employees to nominate one manager and six line professionals for recognition each quarter. A secret committee chooses the winners, who receive a $75 gift certificate and an engraved brass star. At the end of the year, a special celebration is held.

There are also effective statements that convey appreciation. Rather than merely saying "good job," be specific. Say, "Joe, as a result of the way you handled the Springer account, they're recommending our firm to manage the accounts of another company like theirs. Thanks—you really made a difference. In fact, we couldn't have done it without you." Combining this kind of verbal recognition in front of Joe's peers at, say, a luncheon in his honor, would really make a lasting, positive impact.

Bob Nelson, author of *1001 Ways to Reward Employees*, offers these additional no-cost/low-cost tips:[2]

- ▲ Volunteer to do an employee's least desirable task for a day.
- ▲ Wash the employee's car in the parking lot during lunch.
- ▲ Post a thank-you note on the employee's office door.
- ▲ Answer the person's phone for a day.
- ▲ Make a photo collage about a successful project showing the employees who worked on it, its stages of development, its completion, and its presentation.
- ▲ Create a "yearbook" that contains everyone's photo and best achievement of the year. Put it in the reception area for applicants to review.
- ▲ Develop a "Behind the Scenes" award for those employees whose actions are not usually in the limelight.
- ▲ Name a part of the office after an employee and put up a sign.

Tangible Rewards

For employers wanting to give employees more substantive, tangible rewards, there's a limitless supply from which to choose. Just about anything you select will do—cash, gift certificates, merchandise, shopping sprees, travel, debit cards, or a host of other possibilities—as long as these incentives are given to employees for specific performance or productivity related to your business's objectives, and as long as employees understand the specific reason for the reward. For some examples of incentives, see Exhibit 9–2.

Employees catch on quickly: Demonstrate goal-oriented behaviors, and you receive a reward. Once the link between performance and prize is established, employees tend to view the organization more as a business partner and less as a boss. The company provides employees with the right tools with which to reach their goals; if successful, they are rewarded.

The partnership approach works, assuming you are consistent in your efforts. But problems are practically guaranteed if you give one employee a weekend in Vermont for meeting a particular goal and another a pair of movie tickets for meeting similar objectives in another department. Just as policies and procedures should be consistently applied throughout an organization, so should recognition programs. Even employees who are content and feel they are being treated fairly are likely to rebel if they find out someone else is getting more. That's human nature, plain and simple.

One method of dealing with potential problems in this regard is to establish reward levels. Identify specific goals and objectives which, if met, entitle employees to a particular reward or choice of rewards. This way, employees understand from the outset that not all acts are of equal significance or generate equivalent recognition.

Exhibit 9–2. Incentives.

Here's a sampling of specific incentives provided by some companies:

▲ At the Dallas-based T.G.I. Friday's, a chain of more than five hundred restaurants, the company's top workers, regardless of position, can choose to work at any Friday's restaurant around the world.

▲ Computer System Development, an Albuquerque, New Mexico–based computer consulting company, offers awards of vacations, computers, and horses (the latter in keeping with its western heritage).

▲ Once a year the top innovators at 3M are inducted into the company's Circle of Technical Excellence. This is the most prestigious honor bestowed by the company.

▲ NetManage, the Cupertino, California software manufacturer, rewards virtually all staff members with a company-paid vacation to a resort when sales goals are reached.

▲ Dierbergs Family Market, a supermarket chain with sixteen stores in the St. Louis area, rewards its associates (read: employees) who take an "Extra Step" in meeting customers' needs by giving them gift certificates, balloons, candy, movie passes, and lunch with the CEO. The number of "Extra Step" actions associates take qualifies them for the CEO's Silver, Gold, President's, or Chairman's Club, with additional gifts at each level. Apparently, Dierbergs' program works: In an independent survey of retailers in large market areas throughout the United States, the supermarket chain was rated number one in customer satisfaction. It also won the 1997 Arthur Andersen Award for Best Business Practices for Motivating and Retaining Employees.

▲ Peer recognition is practiced at the U.S. Office of Personnel Management in Washington, D.C. A "special performer" receives an engraved plaque called the Wingspread Award. The recipient holds on to the award until he or she determines that there is another deserving employee. Then the award is passed on.

▲ Carlson Marketing Group opens its Dayton, Ohio, distribution center to award recipients for a two-minute shopping spree. After walking through the warehouse and noting where particularly desirable prizes are located, award recipients make a mad dash down the aisles, game-show style. On average, employees accumulate about $3,500 worth of merchandise.

▲ When a branch of PSS/World Medical is selected for the annual audit, employees are thrilled. If the CEO and other senior staff determine, after completing the "blue ribbon tour," that the branch passes the one hundred–item checklist, the employees at the top-scoring branch for the year receive $3,000 each. Employees at the second-highest scoring branch receive $2,000 each, and so forth, down as far as the number-ten branch, where each employee receives $500.

▲ Employees at the Phelps Group marketing agency compete for a $100 award at their weekly staff meetings. All they must do is answer one question from the employee handbook.

▲ Outstanding performers at Shulman Associates in Boca

Raton, Florida, are given airline tickets for a Christmas getaway in the Bahamas.

▲ Acapulco Restaurants in Long Beach, California, presents employees with the President's Award plaque and a check of up to $2,500 for an act of outstanding service. The items are presented to the recipient by the company president. Employees are also eligible for numerous other rewards, including breakfast prepared by the management staff, for a job well done.

▲ Employees who exceed goals by a considerable margin at Nordstom Inc., the department store chain, receive the Pacesetter Award. As a Pacesetter, the employee receives a certificate; a new business card that says "Pacesetter"; an evening of dinner, dancing, and entertainment; and a 33 percent discount on all Nordstrom merchandise for the following year.

▲ At Marion Laboratories in Kansas City, Missouri, employees are given an additional week of paid vacation between Christmas and New Year's if production meets specified goals.

▲ Citibank has a Service Excellence Award that rewards employees at all levels, except senior management, for providing outstanding customer service. Recipients receive a gift certificate for up to $500 in merchandise.

▲ To express appreciation to her staff for meeting crucial deadlines, a manager at The Gap, Inc., headquartered in San Bruno, California, treats everyone to gift certificates from a spa for either a facial or a massage.

▲ Each month, high-performing groups at First Chicago receive the Service Products Group Performance Award. It includes a group outing, e.g., dinner or the theater, as well as a plaque for the group. Winning team members are also eligible to receive round-trip airfare for two to any destination in the United States, plus $500.

▲ Radisson Hotels has a program that awards points to employees for being on time, providing good service to guests, improving quality in hotel operations, reaching department profit and production goals, and referring new employees. Employees can choose from among standard merchandise gifts, such as TVs, or more practical items, including free childcare or bus passes.

▲ At The Travelers Corporation, the insurance company in Hartford, Connecticut, marketing employees earn points for every dollar they save on work-related airfare, hotel bills, and meals. The two people collecting the most points by year's end win a weeklong vacation.

Award Choices and Costs

According to Workforce Subscriber Studies, the average cost of award per employee increased from $71 in 1994 to $190 in 1998. In 1994, 22 percent of all awards cost less than $25, 29 percent cost between $25 and $49, 27 percent cost from $50 to $99, and 22 percent cost more than $100. In 1998, 13 percent of all awards cost less than $25, 22 percent cost between $25 and $49, 27 percent cost from $50 to $99, and 38 percent cost more than $100.

According to a 1999 survey conducted by Incentive Marketing Association and Ralph Head & Affiliates, Ltd., this money was typically spent on the following, in descending order: apparel, plaques and trophies, gift certificates, writing instruments, watches and clocks, desk accessories, electronics, food and beverage, sporting goods, and jewelry.

There are several web sites that provide guidance as to what to give, including www.incentivemag.com, which offers ideas for award programs and information about the rewards industry, and www.ara.org, a membership-based site for the American Recognition Association, which permits nonmembers to access articles about award program design. Additional web sites include Incentivemarketing.org, Recognition.org, giftcertificates.com, and giftpoint.com.

Employers can also contact various service providers for information about their products or services. Here are seven such providers:

1. Award Concepts, Inc. (www.members.aol.com/awardcon/homepage.html) has products that include custom jewelry, heirloom gifts, and lifestyle gifts. The cost is thirty dollars and up.
2. Bennett Brothers, Inc. (www.bennettbrothers.com) has a Choose-Your-Gift catalog with more than fifty gifts at each of thirteen different price levels, ranging from $16.00 to $1,000.
3. Hammacher Schlemmer (www.hammacher.com) offers a selection of items for personal care, sports and leisure, the home and office, gardening, pets, and electronics. Volume discounts are available.
4. Incentive Concepts (www.inconltd.com) has a wide array of items, including sound products, home entertainment units, and aerobic ski machines. Prices vary.
5. Lands' End Corporate Sales (www.landsend.com/corpsales)

offers classic Lands' End clothing and luggage, as well as gift certificates. Prices begin at $25.

6. National Association for Employee Recognition (www.recognition.org) is a two hundred–member nonprofit organization focused on recognition program administrators and managers. The web site offers previous conference highlights, upcoming events, and recognition-related articles from past newsletters.

7. Tiffany & Company (www.tiffany.com) can provide fine giftware, crystal, china, and jewelry. Prices vary.

Best Practices: The McDonald's Corporation

McDonald's sought to implement a recognition program that would in part focus on improved employee satisfaction, thereby contributing to a higher rate of retention. In addition, the fast-food chain was committed to showing its employees that they are the company's most valuable asset. While each store already had some sort of recognition process in place, e.g., employee of the month awards, there was a lack of continuity and connection with meeting company goals.

The result was a new recognition program entitled Speedee Bucks, an incentive program targeting a diverse group of employees. McDonald's tested the program in 1996 in one Midwest region. The system was so successful that it was quickly expanded to more than ten regions throughout the United States.

The underlying concept of the program is to reinforce the idea that performance is tied to the success of the company. When employees meet specific service goals, they are immediately given a certain number of vouchers called Speedee Bucks. For example, if a crew meets its drive-through order goal, Speedee Bucks representing, say, one dollar, are awarded. Once an employee accumulates a minimum dollar amount in value, the Speedee Bucks can be redeemed for cash, logoed merchandise, or gift certificates from participating retailers. Working in tandem with the consulting firm Incentives Inc. and focus groups, these retailers—including Foot Locker, Blockbuster, and Kmart—were selected to match the lifestyle and demographic profile of the employees.

While cash is an option in redeeming Speedee Bucks, surprisingly, it is not the first choice of most employees. In fact, during the regional testing, cash came in sixth place, representing only 7 percent of total voucher redemption. The top six redemption choices, in order, were: Wal-Mart, JC Penney, Foot Locker, Blockbuster, Famous Barr (a local Midwest retailer), and then cash. Since the pilot program, even the small number of Speedee Bucks redeemed for cash has been falling.

Employees endorse the program because they essentially control how much is earned and can choose their own awards. Managers and store owners appreciate its ease of administration: Incentives Inc. creates the Speedee Buck vouchers, contacts the retailers in connection with the gift certificates, fills employees' orders, and keeps records for the corporate office. All managers have to do is identify those employees eligible to receive the Speedee Bucks. Of course, they must also put up the money for the purchase of Speedee Bucks for distribution. But there are no hidden costs: If store owners pay Incentives Inc. $20,000, they receive $20,000 worth of Speedee Bucks.

Managers as well as store owners also have flexibility in the amounts and occasions for which awards are issued. This is important since each McDonald's location has different concerns and employee-related problems. For example, if a particular store is experiencing especially high turnover, the manager could decide to award all employees reaching the three-month mark an additional $25 in vouchers.

McDonald's believes that the primary reason for the success of the Speedee Bucks program is that employees are instantly rewarded for their accomplishments and receive public recognition. In addition, the employees can effectively control how much they accumulate and, therefore, the awards. Some employees cash in each voucher as soon as it's earned, regardless of the amount. Others prefer to save them to redeem larger certificates. That's their choice. Employees have been known to finance their Christmas shopping with earned Speedee Bucks; others have funded vacations.

Overall, then, the Speedee Bucks recognition program works because it offers management and employees simplicity, value, flexibility, and choice.

The program is a measurable success. Both customer and employee satisfaction scores have increased since the program started. One owner of several restaurants reported a 30 percent reduction in turnover after the Speedee Bucks program was implemented. Other store owners report that employees are anxious to work extra shifts in order to earn more vouchers. This indicates that store owners and managers are doing a credible job in ensuring that employees understand the goals and objectives they are expected to accomplish, and that employees are, in fact, meeting them.

As a result of the success of the program at the restaurant level, McDonald's has made it available to regional and corporate staff, with some modifications. The premise of the corporate staff program is the same, but the choices are different. Rather than receiving a Speedee Buck, employees receive vouchers in increments ranging from $25 to $200. Also, the retailers are different— Nordstrom, American Airlines, and Ritz-Carlton, among others.

To counter arguments that the program is mercenary and that employees only perform to acquire vouchers, Incentives Inc.'s president notes, "What's measured gets moved, what gets rewarded gets done, and people do things for their sets of reasons—not yours."

SUMMARY

Organizations recognize that talent retention must be a crucial business objective if they are to remain competitive. Retention programs work especially well in environments where employees understand and work toward business as well as financial objectives, not just operational goals. In such open work environments, employees are hired more for attitude than aptitude. More innovative work environments, designed to inspire creative thoughts and activities, provide flexible settings that allow for choices, and choice is empowering.

One of the best methods for retaining top talent is to ask employees for their suggestions. Successful suggestion programs encourage ideas from employees at every level and provide quick feedback to those who submit a productive idea.

Perhaps the group that generates the greatest challenge when it comes to retention is younger workers. Forty-five million strong, this thirty-five-and-under group expects to balance fulfilling careers with familial responsibilities, in addition to actively pursuing personal interests. The youngest of these workers—those born after 1977—are starting to make a distinct mark on American businesses. What sets this group of workers apart is the huge advantage they have when it comes to information technology. They've grown up with it, are comfortable with it, and expect it to prevail in the workplace.

Many employers view training as an important component of

retention. Traditional training, e.g., technical training, is generally viewed as critical to career growth by both employers and employees. Strategic training—that is, giving employees the skills and knowledge needed to become more invested in the business—also benefits both the company and employees.

To ease some of the expense associated with traditional classroom training, and to make workshops more accessible to employees, computer-based training has grown in popularity. By some estimates, CBT is a $1.5 billion industry. Many organizations are also offering extended educational opportunities to their employees through tuition reimbursement for on-campus classes as well as courses on the Internet and long-distance learning.

Concern over filling management positions has led to increased interest in the acceleration pool, a process that provides an ongoing supply of high-potential candidates for nonspecific jobs. Companies usually select members for the acceleration pool based on job performance, competency development, and job-experience growth.

Another aspect of retention is mentoring—a developmental, helping relationship whereby one person invests time, ability, and effort in enhancing another person's growth, knowledge, and skills in anticipation of greater productivity or future achievement. Mentoring relationships can be situational, informal, or formal. Mentoring has proven effective in attracting and retaining talented employees, reducing turnover, and increasing productivity.

The importance of employee recognition and its link with retention is indisputable. Personal and public recognition is considered most important to employees, and there are numerous low-cost as well as substantive methods for publicly acknowledging an employee's work. Of importance is that the incentives are given to employees for specific performance or productivity related to the business's objectives. Once the link between performance and prize is established, employees tend to view the organization more as a business partner and less as a boss.

NOTES

1. *Retention Management* (New York: American Management Association, 1997).
2. Bob Nelson, *1001 Ways to Reward Employees* (New York: Workman Publishing, 1994).

CHAPTER 10

Balancing Work with Personal Life

"Can we ever have too much of a good thing?"
—Miguel de Cervantes

Here's a true story. Two sales clerks working in a popular clothing store were talking. One turned to the other and said, "As of tomorrow, I'm changing my hours. I don't like this schedule. It interferes with my weekends, and I'm getting home too late at night. I'm missing some of my favorite shows." The other replied, "What are you talking about? I thought they told us we had to work these hours when we were hired." "That's true," said the first clerk. "But they're desperate for help. So I went in and told them they either switch my hours or I'd have to leave. They gave me what I wanted. You should try it. It's cool."

Cool or not, stepping outside of traditional Monday through Friday, 9 to 5 work schedules has become the new norm. Employees are looking for alternatives because of their collective desire to improve the balance between work and family. And in the current tight labor market, they're getting what they want. Like it or not, if you want to snare and keep top performers, you must offer flexible work schedules.

Just about anything goes, including full-time work that can embrace any of the twenty-four hours in a day, part-time schedules, job sharing, flextime, and compressed workweeks, to name some of the more popular work arrangements. And of course there's telecommuting, or virtual work, which has become the alternative work option favored by increasing numbers of workers.

THE NEED FOR FLEXIBILITY

Michael Losey, president and chief executive of the Society for Human Resource Management, was recently quoted in *The New York Times* as saying, "It used to be, 'We start at 8:30 and end at 5, and this is the color shirt you wear.' Now it's, 'What about flextime? What about alternative work schedules?' "

Employees can make demands like these because there are 1 million to 2 million fewer workers than there are jobs. Hence, businesses seeking to attract employees have little choice but to accommodate their scheduling demands.

For example, during tax season, H&R Block hires some two hundred students skilled in computers to troubleshoot problems. Many of these students don't need to work: They're living at home, have enough money to get by, and wouldn't have to worry about student loan repayments for several years. Accordingly, H&R Block must come up with offers that are irresistible—and that usually means flexible scheduling. Students who really aren't interested in working often reconsider after the company guarantees that it will accommodate whatever schedule the student chooses, even if that schedule varies from week to week.

Working for a company that encourages work/personal life balance is increasingly important to employees who are busier than ever juggling car pools to soccer practices and orthodontist appointments, caregiving an elderly parent or grandparent living at home, and attending classes in pursuit of a degree to enhance their career goals. That's in addition to the usual running around most of us do at the end of our workday—to pick up the dry cleaning, go food shopping, and buy gifts for children's birthday parties. In addition to all of this, more parents—women and men alike—are declaring that they want to be with their children for longer than ten minutes in the morning and an hour at night. The idea of "quality time" is wearing thin.

Many employers have become attuned to employees' needs and are trying to comply. While this may be for altruistic reasons in some instances, more often the decision to respond to work/personal balance issues is driven by bottom-line implications: A high employee satisfaction quotient translates into high morale that, in turn, impacts productivity. Companies maintaining concierge services or physicians on-site, for example, are making a bona fide attempt to help employees keep pace with their runaway lives.

But that kind of effort alone doesn't seem to be enough. Employees are no longer willing to allow employers to dictate when they must be at work. As such, there is a definite trend toward employees either spending less time at the office or having greater flexibility in determining work schedules.

Take Michelle, age 23, for instance. After working for just two weeks as an administrative assistant in a public relations firm in Manhattan, she was taken aback when her boss, Jack, a forty-six-year-old manager, informed her that she was expected to be at her desk, looking as if she were busy, even if she didn't have anything to do. This confrontation originated the previous day when, at around 3:30, Michelle had completed the tasks that she had been assigned for that day. Jack was in a meeting and she didn't want to disturb him, so she left him a note on his desk. The note read, "The files you asked me to work on are finished and on my desk. See you tomorrow. Have a good afternoon."

When she came in the next morning, Jack angrily confronted her, demanding to know where she had gone. Michelle responded, "I don't see how that's any of your business, but if you must know, I had a facial." "How could you leave work in the middle of the afternoon to have a facial?" Jack demanded. Michelle was annoyed. "What is the problem? I finished all my work before I left." That's when Jack responded, "I don't care if you have absolutely nothing to do. Just sit at your desk and look as if you're working on something! I don't want you leaving before 5!"

Michelle was quiet for a moment and then replied, "That's not how I see things, Jack. If you have something you want me to do, fine. But I'm not going to just sit there doing nothing. I have a life outside of this place. I agreed to put in a full week's work, but I assumed I would have some say as to what those hours would be. Besides, when I was hired, I was told that the company had flexible hours. So what gives?" "Some departments do have flexible hours, Michelle, but not this one. Call me old-fashioned, but I believe in an honest day's work for an honest day's pay. Besides, there's always work that can be done." Michelle stared at Jack. "I don't know what honesty has to do with this, and besides, I really don't know what you're talking about. Here's the deal, though. I thought I'd have flexibility in setting my hours. You're telling me I don't. I can't and I won't work under these conditions. I'm resigning."

What Workers Want

In a National Survey on Evaluation of Work-Life Efforts by Work & Family Connections, Inc., employees identified the work schedule options that are most significant to them. The list included tele-commuting, flextime, a compressed workweek, part-time hours, and job sharing. Clearly, today's workers want greater work schedule flexibility to create a better balance with their personal lives.

And businesses are responding out of necessity, to attract and retain top performers. Companies are scrambling to be recognized as family-friendly by publications such as *Working Mother*, *Fortune*, and *Business Week*. The criteria for selection by these magazines varies, but here's a sampling from *Business Week*'s "Best Companies for Work and Family" employee questionnaire:

▲ Can you vary your work hours or schedule to respond to family matters?
▲ Is your supervisor flexible when it comes to responding to your work-family needs?
▲ Do you feel comfortable taking time off from work to attend to family matters?

The president of First Tennessee Bank, which has been ranked on the "Best Companies" list of all three aforementioned magazines, maintains that the bank's status is largely because it puts employees ahead of shareholders. This reflects the results of surveys conducted at each branch of the bank: Employees whose needs are met provide better service to customers, and customers who are satisfied with the service they receive tend to stay with the bank. Indeed, First Tennessee has been able to boast of the highest customer retention rates of any bank in the country.

First Tennessee responded to its employees' need for greater flexibility in their schedules. Accordingly, it instituted a reduced-time work program with full benefits. Eighty-five percent of the employees who switched from full- to reduced-time work admitted that they would have quit otherwise. This translated into a savings of $5,000 to $10,000 per nonmanagerial employee, and $30,000 to $50,000 per executive.

First Tennessee even has a vice president and manager of family matters.

Other companies are equally committed to helping their employees achieve a balance between work and personal life. SAS Institute, in the top ten of *Fortune*'s "100 Best Companies to Work For" three years running, certainly fits this description. The company offers an environment designed to help employees balance work with their personal lives. Full-time work is thirty-five hours, and every white-collar employee has the opportunity to create a flexible work schedule. SAS also offers its employees numerous ways to unwind and relax, including a full gymnasium, coed workout areas, single-sex workout areas, soccer fields, baseball diamonds, and pool tables. It even offers free laundering of athletic wear overnight, delivered the following morning to the employee's locker. All of this saves employees money and the time that they would have to expend in an effort to fit in one more activity after a full day at work.

Work/Personal Life Programs

Work/personal life balance programs can succeed only if management supports them and encourages their use. For managers like Jack, who had to confront his assistant, Michelle (see above), this can be difficult, since the basic tenet of work/personal life balance conflicts with his own views and work ethic. And yet, there's enough research linking profitability to work/personal life issues that managers—even those who resist—may have no choice but to get on board with the concept.

You can encourage management support of your company's work/personal life balance program through proper training. Eli Lilly, the Indianapolis-based pharmaceutical company, is committed to training its supervisors and managers in work/life balance issues. During part of a weeklong session at "Supervisor School," attendees are first made familiar with the company's work/life program expectations, are taught the business rationale for work/life initiatives, and then learn guidelines for implementation. The training, then, focuses on two critical components: (1) the value of the work/life program, and (2) how to help employees take advantage of it. During the training, attendees analyze various scenarios involving employees who require work schedule flexibility. Then they take performance-management training to help them focus on results. All in all, Eli Lilly treats work/life balance as it would any other business initiative.

Another company that focuses on work/personal life issues is the Phoenix Home Life Mutual Insurance Company, located in Hartford, Connecticut. There, supervisors are trained in work/life issues during ten three-hour sessions. Part of the training involves role-playing during which participants can apply the skills learned during their sessions. As at Eli Lilly, managers are presented with real-life issues. For example, one role-playing scenario involves a unit where the primarily single staff wanted the option of taking three-day weekends, ten weekends a year. Throughout these scenarios, emphasis is placed on the value of work/life programs and how these programs contribute to increasing productivity.

Eastman Kodak also trains its managers in work/personal life balance issues as they relate to the company's liberal program of flexible work arrangements. Essentially, employees can opt to work any schedule, as long the hours meet with the approval of the employee's supervisor and don't adversely affect business operations. Together, managers and employees work on a proposal to support the employees' selection. If approved, employees start the new schedule on a trial basis. At the end of the trial period, the manager and employee again assess the schedule to determine whether it should continue.

As part of their performance measurement system, Eastman Kodak evaluates its managers on how well they resolve work/personal life balance issues. In fact, part of the managers' variable compensation is dependent on how effectively they support alternative scheduling. Employees, too, rate their supervisors in terms of how helpful they have been in explaining work/life options.

Changing Role of Men

Here's a typical household scene from thirty-something years ago:

▲ 7:30 A.M.: Donna prepares breakfast for her family, makes lunches for the kids, checks everyone's homework, and sends the kids off to school. Alex grabs his briefcase, kisses Donna good-bye, and heads out the door for a day at the office.

▲ 7:30 A.M. to 3 P.M.: Donna makes beds, washes dishes, cleans clothes, straightens up the house, shops for food, picks up her husband's suits from the cleaners, takes the dog to the vet, attends a PTA meeting, runs other assorted errands, and arrives home in time to greet the school bus.

▲ 3 P.M.: Donna gives the kids snacks, finds out what happened at school, and then proceeds to start her afternoon "taxi service," driving her kids and their friends to and from various activities.

▲ 5 P.M.: Donna prepares a nutritionally balanced dinner and even bakes a pie for dessert.

▲ 6 P.M.: Alex arrives home and is greeted warmly by his wife, martini in hand to help him unwind from a trying day at work. The family then sits down to Donna's delicious home-cooked dinner.

▲ 7 P.M.: Donna washes the dishes while the kids do home-work, and Alex relaxes in front of the TV, reading the news-paper.

▲ 9 P.M.: Donna makes sure the kids are washed and ready for bed. She tucks them in and reads them a story.

▲ 9:30 P.M.: Donna goes into the living room to spend some time with Alex, only to find that he's fallen asleep.

OK, maybe that's not the way it was all the time, and not in every household, but you have to admit this scenario illustrates traditional male/female roles way back when. Certainly, it's the way we saw things on popular television shows.

Now let's join Donna and Alex at the beginning of the twenty-first century for a variation of what's going on in many of today's dual-income households.

▲ 7 A.M.: Donna and Alex are both up and dressed for work. They wake up the kids and hand them an instant breakfast bar and an apple, along with money to buy lunch at school. "Mary, don't even think about missing the bus this morning because there's no way either one of us can drive you to school," warns Donna. "I've got an important meeting at 9 that I'm not ready for, and Dad has to drop your sister off at her early morning preschool session, so let's go! Oh, and don't forget you have play rehearsals after school to-day, so take the late bus home."

▲ 7:30 A.M.: Mary grabs her backpack and barely makes the bus. Donna kisses the children, grabs her briefcase, and gets into her car. Alex grabs his briefcase and his youngest daughter, Kathy, and gets into his car for the trip to her preschool's early morning program before heading to the office. Donna and Alex each put in a full day at work, as an attorney and manager respectively.

▲ 6 P.M.: Donna picks up Kathy from preschool. Alex picks up take-out food for dinner. Mary lets herself in and is doing home-work (OK, she's really on the phone with her best friend and watch-ing TV, but the minute her parents walk in the door she's doing her homework).

▲ 6:30 P.M.: Everyone sits down for a delicious dinner of pizza and garlic knots. There's some talk about everyone's day, but the conversation is short-circuited by Donna's announcement that she needs to work on a project she brought home. "Alex, could you clear the table, give Kathy a bath, and get her to bed?" Mary chimes in with "Who's driving me to the library? I need to work on my social studies report. And by the way, has anyone done the laundry lately? I haven't seen my favorite blue sweater in about a week."

▲ 10 P.M.: Mary is back from the library (her friend's mother drove them). Kathy is in bed, Donna is still working, and Alex collapses in front of the TV and lasts for all of fifteen minutes before nodding off.

In this modern scenario, while Donna and Alex both need more help than they can provide for each other, what they really need is time. Enter flexibility on the part of the employer. But not just for Donna. Traditionally, flexible work schedules were requested by and accommodated women struggling to balance work and family responsibilities. Today, with both parents working in about 51 percent of all families (according to a survey conducted by Simmons College Graduate School of Management, for Bright Horizons Family Solutions of Cambridge, Massachusetts), and with more women achieving professional status, men are taking a more active role on the home front, with everything from household chores to child-rearing tasks. Despite the concierge and other helpful services provided by some companies, however, lack of time is still a core issue. Fully 70 percent of both men and women maintain that they do not have sufficient time to spend with their families, according to the Families and Work Institute, a nonprofit research group based in New York. And in a recent study conducted by the Heldrich Center for Workforce Development at Rutgers University, 97 percent of both men and women reported that the ability to balance work and family is the most important aspect of a job, ranked ahead of job security, quality of work environment, and relationships with coworkers.

According to yet another study by the Families and Work Institute, men's participation at home has increased in the past twenty years from 1.8 hours to 2.3 hours each workday. Yet men still work longer at the office: 50.9 hours if they have children under age 18, compared with women with children under 18, who typically log in 41.4 hours.

Since men are taking on more responsibilities at home, but are still working longer hours at the office, they should avail themselves of the work/personal life balance programs being offered by an increasing number of employers. But many men are hesitant to do so. They're more likely to tell the boss, "I have a meeting," rather than "I'm going to see my daughter's school play." There are myriad reasons for this, including concern that they will be perceived less seriously by management and colleagues. In general, their identities are still tied more closely to work than are women's.

The availability of work/personal life programs for men should be trumpeted as loudly as those for women. From a purely practical standpoint, you don't want your male workers to be preoccupied with personal issues to a point that it interferes with their ability to concentrate. And you certainly don't want to lose a valuable employee who discovers that one of your competitors is more tolerant of flexible scheduling for male workers.

Companies are starting to respond to the logic of these arguments. About 1990, Apple Computer promoted family-friendly policies in the hope of attracting top female performers. It quickly discovered that its predominantly male workforce was just as interested in such programs. Other companies are reaching out to their male employees as well, For example, Texas Instruments, Marriott International Inc., Merrill Lynch, and Johnson & Johnson all offer fatherhood seminars that have proved to be resoundingly successful with working fathers. Companies such as Merrill Lynch are also promoting flexible scheduling options, including telecommuting and flextime, in addition to extended unpaid leave, for men as well as women.

Both men and women also need greater day-to-day flexibility to, say, duck out for a couple of hours to attend a parent-teacher conference or pick up a sick child from school. Rewarding and promoting the deserving employees who avail themselves of such alternatives signals to your workforce that management encourages a balance between work and their personal lives.

GUIDELINES FOR ESTABLISHING FLEXIBLE WORK OPTIONS

In their book *Creating a Flexible Workplace*, Barney Olmsted and Suzanne Smith recommend an eight-step process for introducing flexible work options.[1] For maximum effectiveness, establish a cross-function management task force consisting of representatives from top management and all segments of the company that will be affected by the changes. This task force should be responsible for the design and monitoring of the program.

Olmsted and Smith lay out these guidelines:

1. *Gain support for the program.* The task force should survey the entire workforce, from top management down, to identify their

values and needs in relation to flexible work schedules, as well as analyzing existing schedules.

2. *Set up the program's administration.* The administrators will be responsible for implementing the specifics of the program developed by the task force. Assign responsibility for overall coordination, and the development of technical assistance for supervisors and employees, to someone with an in-depth knowledge of the organization and a thorough understanding of the program's objectives. Additional staff may be needed, depending on the scope of the program.

3. *Design the program.* The task force may design the specific components of the program along with a supporting subgroup. Part of this process includes reviewing current work schedules to determine compatibility with the defined objectives.

4. *Develop resource materials.* Resource materials will help program participants understand just how the new work options will be implemented. They include a detailed program description, educational and technical assistance materials, and training.

5. *Announce the program.* Don't wait for employees to hear about the new options through the grapevine and then leave it up to them to approach their managers for more information. Publish information in newsletters, post notices on bulletin boards, and transmit details via the intranet and through any other means available.

6. *Promote the program.* Many programs are underutilized because of employee fear that participation will negatively affect their career paths. Employees must be reassured that opting for one of the new work alternatives will not aversely affect their goals, aspirations, or earning potential.

7. *Evaluate the program.* An evaluation process should be built into the program's design in an ongoing attempt to answer questions such as: Has the program achieved its desired effect? What are the financial ramifications? Do these exceed projections? What are the problem areas? Are there any unanticipated benefits? How have the organization's employees reacted? What else needs to be done?

8. *Fine-tune the program.* Use information gained during the evaluation process to recommend whatever may be needed to fine-tune those portions of the program requiring adjustment. In addition, establish a process for obtaining feedback from managers and employees on an ongoing basis.

In addition to these eight steps, I'd like to add two more:

1. *Be flexible.* If your original plan doesn't work, don't scrap the entire idea of optional work plans. Ask the task force to review the steps taken and analyze what may have gone wrong. Maybe you were trying to pattern yourself after a company that is not as similar in composition or objectives as you first thought. Not all alternative arrangements function well in all work environments.

2. *Be patient.* Even if the program you develop will clearly benefit everyone in the organization, changes are sometimes slow to catch on. The program may initially be met with suspicion or resistance, but be persistent as you continue to point out the program's benefits.

As Jerome Rosow, president of the Work in America Institute in Scarsdale, New York, stated in Olmsted and Smith's book, "New work schedules, when carefully chosen, designed, and executed, are among the best investments an employer can make. The cost is small, the risk is low, and the potential return is high. Best of all, they benefit all parties involved."

TELECOMMUTING

Also known as remote access work, going virtual, flexplace, at-home work, telework, or satellite office work, the concept of telecommuting has been around since the 1970s, but it did not gain popularity until over a decade later, with the explosion of personal computers and facsimile machines. Today, telecommuters—people who are employed by a company but work all or part of the time at home—make up one of the fastest growing components of the labor market.

Initially, employees taking advantage of telecommuting were mostly women with childcare or eldercare concerns. Employees with long commutes also opted for virtual work. But now, as telecommuting continues to gain in popularity and acceptance, more employees, even those without travel or caregiving responsibilities, are saying, "Me, too."

Several companies recently described the rationale and necessity for such practices.[2] One Long Island, New York–based company, Symbol Technologies, reported that approximately seventy-five out of their two thousand employees now telecommute. Said

Bob Blonk, senior vice president of human resources, "If employees with suitable situations have a work station at home, then the company supports telecommuting. The competition for good people is so intense that we really have to be more accommodating, and that's what telecommuting is really about."

Yes, that is what telecommuting is about, and more. Robert Zimmerman, a partner of Zimmerman-Edelson, a small New York public relations and marketing firm, adds, "The role of the workplace has been dramatically redefined because of the pressures of personal life. We have no choice but to be more responsive to the needs of our staff, and this sometimes means allowing them to create more flexible work arrangements because of responsibilities at home. The reality is that nothing replaces the synergy of an office environment in which people work together, sharing ideas and information. But in today's world, telecommuting is an essential option."

Maria Redman, a vice president of human resources at European Bank of America, which started a work-life program in 1998, discusses the benefits of telecommuting: "When you can retain good employees, you end up saving the company an incredible amount of money." Not only that, but according to director of work-life strategies at Bell Atlantic, Fred Jenkins, "By promoting the idea that we value the individual and [allow] flexibility in work arrangements, we gain more focused employees because they don't have to bring personal issues into the workplace. By recognizing that they have options, they are empowered, and satisfied employees are less likely to leave. There is strong evidence that our policy is working toward our goal of retaining good employees."

Advantages of Telecommuting

Most companies agree that there are numerous advantages to having some employees work at home, at least part of the time. Reduced utility and office space leasing costs, as well as increased productivity, are two of the most common reasons cited for hiring telecommuters.

Increasingly, employers also report that this work option has proved to be an effective recruitment tool, not only because it attracts employees but because it allows the employer to expand its recruiting base beyond the convenient commutation area. In addition, organizations have been able to utilize the services of people who might not be capable of traveling to work, including the elderly and those with certain disabilities. Employers with virtual workers also report less absenteeism, since such employees are often able to work at home even if they are not feeling well. AT&T indicates that employees working at home put in an average of an hour more per day than those who work in the office.

That's because telecommuters tend to work in spurts. For example, one at-home worker, Anne, usually starts working at around 8:30 A.M. and continues until 11:30 A.M. After taking a break to run some errands, she grabs a bite, then continues working for an hour or so until 2:30 P.M. After picking up her kids from school and driving them to soccer and dance, Anne resumes working from 4:30 to 6 P.M. Then, after preparing and eating dinner, Anne continues working for another three hours. All together, that's 8½ hours of work. The schedule works well for her. She likes moving back and forth between work and her personal life. At the same time, Anne has demonstrated to her employer that she's a responsible worker. This is a win-win combination.

Like Anne, many employees applaud a telecommuting arrangement. Parents who want to work as well as care for their children can more readily manage both. In addition, at-home workers report an ability to perform their duties more efficiently without the typical office interruptions, and they enjoy the freedom derived from working "off-hours." Other benefits include not having to commute and the luxury of wearing whatever they want while working.

Here's how some virtual workers describe their telecommuting experiences:

▲ "On nice days I throw on my most comfortable pair of jeans and work out on the deck. I take my laptop, cell phone, lunch, and a carafe of coffee. I feel productive without feeling stressed out. The hours fly by. I love it."

▲ "I get to go to the market early in the morning and am still 'at my desk' before 9. I'd never be able to do that if I worked in the office with a two-hour commute each way."

▲ "Once I fell asleep in my home office. When I woke up, my first reaction was, 'I'm going to be in trouble for dozing off!' Then I realized there was no one there to catch me! I felt incredibly liberated and went back to work."

▲ "For me, virtual work represents freedom. But not to go wild and do whatever I want. In fact, just the opposite. I'm so grateful for being able to work at home that I feel extra responsible about getting my work done. I don't want to give my company a reason to take this away from me!"

▲ "I no longer have to pay the kid next door to walk and play with my dog!"

Telecommuting Arrangements

There are several possible telecommuting arrangements. Most telecommuters live within striking distance of their offices, working at home several days a week and then going in to the office for the balance. When they do go in, they usually share someone else's office. This system is sometimes referred to as "hoteling," whereby employees reserve space for the times they'll be at the office. This technique helps the employer save on office space, while at the same time giving virtual workers some sense of having a traditional workspace. Others who live hundreds or even thousands of miles away may still travel to the office, although understandably less frequently. For instance, a systems analyst living in Miami telecommutes from her home to the European American Bank in New York. Three or four days each month she flies up for face-to-face meetings; otherwise, she participates in meetings by phone.

Some companies offer a combination of casual and formal telecommuting arrangements. At the high-tech firm Lucent Technologies, for example, certain employees can opt for a virtual work arrangement whereby they work at home only when there's bad weather or a family illness. Employees with formal arrangements, on the other hand, telecommute all the time; they do not have an office on Lucent premises and rarely even visit the company. Their entire link to the office is through Lucent's technology. About 20 percent of Lucent's 150,000 employees have a formal telecommuting arrangement.

If your employees telecommute exclusively or most of the time, here are four tips that can maximize the effectiveness of the arrangement:

1. Have them initiate periodic updates with people they haven't communicated with in a while.
2. Have them take personal responsibility for keeping information well organized and available.
3. Have them keep abreast of technology and skill upgrades.
4. Monitor their conduct at work to make sure they don't bring any "bad" habits from home into the office.

Drawbacks of Telecommuting

But there are drawbacks, as well, for both telecommuters and their managers. Some at-home workers complain of a sense of isolation, longing for the ability to interact and brainstorm with coworkers. They also miss sharing successes and failures, progress and barriers, as well as challenges and breakthroughs. E-mail, faxes, and phone calls just aren't adequate. Many complain of having to eat lunch alone. Others worry about the self-discipline required to meet deadlines and miss having a supervisor to tell them how they're doing. As one telecommuter put it, "I'm out of the loop."

Then there's concern over how working at home is perceived by others. Despite our society's increased number of at-home workers, friends and neighbors still assume that if you're home, you can't be at work. Interruptions by well-intentioned callers and visitors are not only disruptive but can raise doubts in the minds of telecommuters as to whether what they are doing is legitimate work.

And some, admittedly, yield to the temptations of a refrigerator, television, and list of household tasks requiring attention while their work suffers.

Furthermore, not everyone can adjust to the nontraditional style of virtual work. To be successful at telecommuting, workers must have the ability to stay focused and be disciplined, flexible, honest, self-assured, independent, and motivated. In addition, they should have a keen understanding of their personal strengths, preferences, and style of working, since they alone are responsible for completing assignments. They also must be willing to convert part of their home to an office environment. In addition, not all kinds of work can be performed at home. Generally, positions that supervise large groups of workers are not suited to telecommuting. Also, jobs requiring the use of heavy equipment can't be performed at home. Work that is best suited includes writing papers, reviewing documents, developing company events, preparing presentations and analyses, design, marketing, and sales.

For managers working in the traditional office setting, the greatest drawback is the lack of direct control over an employee's work. Many express concern over not knowing when employees start working each day, how many hours they actually work, and what time they stop at day's end. To offset these concerns, telecommuters may be required to sign in and out with a supervisor by telephone or e-mail. In addition, employees using a computer may be required to track the hours worked through computer-generated time reports that indicate log-on and log-off times. AT&T, for instance, requires telecommuting employees to sign an agreement stipulating location, hours, assignments, output, equipment to be provided by the employer, reimbursable expenses, and how many times each day they'll check voice-mail messages received at the main office.

Another concern involves possible misuse or theft of computers and other electronic equipment. If an employer provides a telecommuter with equipment, that person should agree, in writing, to return the equipment either upon request or automatically upon termination. Depending on applicable state laws, failure to return the equipment at the agreed-upon time could constitute authorization for the company to withhold monies otherwise due the employee.

Unsupervised and unauthorized access to confidential data is also a concern. Telecommuters should be required to sign a confidentiality agreement that covers access, use, and dissemination of confidential information.

Here are comments from managers expressing discomfort with telecommuting arrangements:

▲ "I was told that I have to start measuring my employees' work by standards other than time, that I have to stop managing time and start managing projects. I said, 'What does that mean? All of a sudden, time doesn't matter? They can send in the work whenever they want? Spend as little or as much time as they please to finish an assignment?' I don't think so!"

▲ "I called one of my telecommuting employees the other day at around 10:30 and she wasn't there. That bothered me. I guess I assume if she's not at her desk when I call, then she's off doing something personal. I don't get to do that here in the office. Why should she?"

▲ "I feel out of touch with what he's doing. I see the end result, but have no sense of the process. Maybe that shouldn't be important, but it is—to me, anyway."

▲ "I've been bothered ever since she told me she works at home in her pajamas. I don't need the image of one of my employees working on a report dressed in night clothes at 1 in the afternoon."

Telecommuting Training

Many of the managers who feel ill at ease with telecommuting employees are from the era of "in-office work is the only real work" philosophy. They need help in making the transition to accepting virtual work as meaningful. In this regard, proper training is required to analyze the ways in which the relationship between themselves and their employees will change. Training should include new ways to measure productivity and performance as well as how to enhance "lack of face" communication. In addition, managers require assistance to help shift their role from activity-based management to results-based management.

It is also important to convey to participating supervisors that the traditional methods they have been using, in terms of their management and communications style, are not inadequate. The purpose of telecommuting training is not to introduce a new way to manage. It is, instead, a new means of viewing the relationship between managers and workers who are now, part or all of the time, virtual. For example, supervisors should be taught to emphasize managing by objectives, not whether employees are at their desks when managers think they should be.

It is also important to hold team training: telecommuters and their managers together. Each group needs to ask questions of the other, voice concerns about the new working relationship, and discuss mutual expectations. These forums also allow managers and employees to iron out details of the new arrangement, such as which days the employees will telecommute, how often they will call or e-mail the manager, how often the employees will check for phone and e-mail messages, and during which core hours they can be reached.

Merrill Lynch provides virtual work training for its managers. The program is divided into three parts: (1) telecommuter training, (2) supervisor/manager training, and (3) team training. The last segment allows telecommuters and their managers to work together on issues that may affect the new working relationship. Merrill Lynch also offers a precursor to formal training called "process consultation," whereby managers are given a heads up on potential problem areas.

Arthur Andersen also offers training, covering such topics as communication with telecommuters and ways to lead telecommuting teams.

One other aspect of training should be considered—that is, educating other staff members to understand the impact telecommuting will have on their jobs and the organization overall. This includes senior management right down the ranks to all the in-office employees. Topics to be addressed may include who is telecommuting and why; how telecommuting will affect productivity, cost, and customer satisfaction; as well as what changes, if any, will be implemented as a result.

Staying Legal

In order to be equitable in determining who can telecommute and the conditions under which virtual work is acceptable, legal experts urge employers to establish clearly defined guidelines. This includes defining those specific jobs and activities that can and cannot be performed effectively at home. It also means establishing criteria that employees must meet in order to qualify for telecommuting, such as a clean record with no outstanding disciplinary problems or no record of disciplinary problems within the past year. You may also decide that employees must have worked for the company for at least a year, giving you an opportunity to evaluate their work and determine if, in fact, they can work independently at home.

Companies considering telecommuting work arrangements for some employees should consult with legal and tax experts regarding employee classifications, local zoning regulations, and insurance requirements. With regard to the latter, even though most telecommuting work is sedentary, and it is therefore unlikely that an employee will be injured while working at home, a telecommuter who is injured may be eligible for workers compensation. This can occur even though the employer has no control over the conditions in the employee's home. Some employers go so far as to require an inspection of the employee's workspace at home before telecommuting privileges are granted. To minimize workers compensation risks, telecommuters should be required to contact their managers immediately if injured while working at home.

ADDITIONAL ALTERNATIVE WORK OPTIONS

Not all workers feel the need to work at a traditional, full-time job. Increasingly, employees are demanding and attaining alternatives to full-time work in addition to telecommuting, such as flextime and compressed workweeks. And a growing population of employees is opting for part-time work or job sharing. As part of their attempt to both recruit and retain qualified workers, it is increasingly evident that businesses must offer telecommuting and additional alternatives to the traditional work schedule. While not all arrangements work equally well in every environment, an increasing number of organizations are willing to test diverse work options and are reporting positive results.

Data from the 1997 National Study of the Changing Workforce provide us with information on some workplace options and their prevalence:

▲ Sixty-eight percent of companies allowed workers to change their starting and quitting times periodically.
▲ Twenty-four percent allowed workers to change starting and quitting times daily.
▲ Fifty-seven percent permitted workers to alternate between full-time and part-time status while in the same position or level.
▲ Thirty-eight percent had job sharing.
▲ Fifty-five percent allowed employees to work at home occasionally.
▲ Thirty-three percent let workers work off-site on a regular basis.
▲ Eighty-eight percent gave time off for school or childcare functions.
▲ Eighty-four percent permitted workers to return to work gradually after childbirth or adoption.

Flextime

Flextime, the first alternative work arrangement to gain acceptance, was implemented at a Hewlett-Packard plant beginning in 1972. Since then, it has gradually been gaining in popularity, as more private- and public-sector organizations now offer flextime as an alternative work arrangement.

There are three forms of flextime: (1) the gliding schedule, which allows workers to vary arrival and departure times; (2) variable schedules, which require a specified number of working hours without set schedules; and (3) compensatory time arrangements, which allow employees to apply overtime to future time off.

Employers may vary the amount of flexibility granted workers in establishing their schedules according to the specific needs of the organization and the employees concerned. Here's a sampling of professions and the proportion of full-time workers with flextime schedules:

University teachers:	65 percent
Computer scientists:	59 percent
Executives, managers:	42 percent
Technicians:	31 percent

Salespeople: 30 percent
Administrators: 23 percent
Health service workers: 18 percent

Flextime offers employees a better balance between work demands and those of home, school, or outside activities. It also helps relieve transit and commuting problems. In addition, given a voice in the scheduling of their workday, employees tend to feel involved in the company's decision-making process. This, in turn, may strengthen employer-employee relations. Employees are also able to schedule work more in tune with their own "internal clocks," that is, they can choose to work during those hours when their skill and response levels are most keen.

Benefits to the employer include extended hours of coverage or service, which reduces or eliminates the need for overtime; reduced tardiness, absenteeism, and turnover; an expanded and improved recruitment pool; and improved work performance attributable to enhanced employee morale. As a system, it is also adaptable to many situations and can be implemented in a variety of circumstances, although it tends to function best in work environments that promote independence and self-motivation. It is least effective in assembly-line work or situations in which the work must be accomplished in a short time span.

As with any system, flextime has some drawbacks. The number one problem has less to do with the employees than with supervisors who are uncomfortable with having workers on the job, unsupervised, during noncore hours. A sufficient level of discomfort may compel some supervisors to put in longer hours themselves in order to make certain that work is being accomplished during noncore hours. Other concerns include difficulty in scheduling meetings, not having key employees available when needed, and employee abuse of flextime. In addition, overhead costs may be increased by keeping facilities open for longer periods of time.

Compressed Workweeks

Following close on the heels of flextime in the early 1970s was the idea of the compressed workweek. This alternative arrangement allows employees to work the required full-time schedule in fewer than five days. Essentially, then, total hours in compressed systems are held constant, with employees simply working more hours in each full day and fewer days per week or biweekly period. The most popular schedule remains four ten-hour days in a typical office environment. In companies with twenty-four-hour operations, shift workers typically work twelve-hour compressed schedules. There are numerous options available,[3] including:

▲ *The Du Pont.* Named after the company where it originated, the Du Pont's most notable feature is seven or eight straight days off during every twenty-eight-day rotation. Usually there is a maximum four-day or four-night stretch of work and a short twenty-four-hour break between three day shifts and three night shifts. Most employees love having a guaranteed "mini-vacation" every month. On the other hand, fatigue is a big drawback to this arrangement.

▲ *The 2-3-2.* This schedule is sometimes referred to as EOWEO: every other weekend off. Employees follow a fourteen-day pattern of two-days-on, two-days-off, three-days-on, two-days-off, two-days-on, and three-days-off. Workers know that they'll have a three-day weekend off every other week and won't be required to work more than three night shifts in a row. On the other hand, they never get more than three days off in a row, and the changing shift makes it difficult for workers to adjust from days to nights and back again.

▲ *Four On, Four Off.* In this arrangement, employees work four days or nights and then have four days or nights off. At some companies, workers stay on nights for as long as twenty-four days; others switch off every eight days. This schedule allows workers ample time to recover from their shift. However, because there are only seven days in a week and the schedule has an eight-day pattern, workers' days off move one day forward per week, so there's no consistency.

The compressed workweek has received mixed reviews from both employees and management. Positive votes come from employees reacting favorably to the longer periods of personal time that compressed workweeks allow. As one fan of the compressed workweek put it, "It seems like I'm home more than I'm at work." Employees also prefer commuting during nonrush hours and saving money by not working five days. In addition, many workers reportedly accomplish more in a given day during those hours when phone calls from customers or clients are less likely to cause interruptions. Moreover, being able to select an alternative work schedule is empowering to employees, adding to their overall job satisfaction and motivation to do a good job.

Employers have reported that the compressed workweek is an effective recruitment tool. Some improvement in rates of absenteeism, tardiness, and turnover has also been reported. In some instances, productivity has improved.

Success has mostly been with younger workers, however. Older workers seem to prefer traditional schedules. (As one thirty-four-year-old production worker from Techneglas Inc. put it, "It's because the old people don't have a life.")

Some workers and managers alike have complained about the excessive fatigue brought by lengthy workdays. This is troublesome to older employees, young singles with active social lives, and employees with families. Long-term effects on health are also of concern. Both factors can adversely affect creativity, attention to safety, and productivity. Some employees also observe that when they are away from work for three straight days, they feel "out of the loop."

As a consequence, while many long-term users of the compressed workweek have nothing but praise for the system, others have tried and abandoned it.

Companies that are considering this alternative work arrangement should make certain that state laws do not prohibit a compressed workweek. Some states require the payment of overtime compensation for hours worked in excess of eight hours on any given day.

Part-Time Work

Traditionally, candidates completing job applications have been asked to check off one of two boxes for their desired work schedule: full-time or part-time. The latter usually referred to schedules of up to twenty hours per week that rendered those individuals ineligible for benefits. It also generally applied to nonexempt-level employees—usually women with childcare responsibilities or students.

As employment concepts continue to change, the term *regular part-time* has expanded in meaning and scope. The traditional part-timer still exists in many industries, but now, increasingly, the term refers to varying levels of employees, male and female, on a reduced work-time schedule, entitled to many of the privileges and benefits available to full-time workers. The trend is also spreading up through the ranks, as many professionals are being granted part-time work arrangements.

These changes clearly indicate a redirection in thinking as employers come to realize that there is a great deal of competition for qualified candidates striving to balance family, job responsibilities, and outside interests.

In this regard, employers increasingly customize part-time jobs to accommodate the needs of valuable employees. That is, when employees with specialized skills opt to not work full-time anymore, customizing part-time jobs is a viable option. For example, when Jeffrey, a full-time computer specialist, decided to return to college for a second degree, he felt it would be easiest to just quit his job. He planned on taking twelve credits at school and knew he wasn't driven enough to balance the responsibilities and headaches of a full-time job with a full schedule at school. He enjoyed his work but didn't need the money (his wife earned enough and they had no children). When he tendered his resignation, his manager, who didn't want to lose him, asked if Jeffrey would consider a part-time schedule. Jeffrey thought it over and asked if he could set his own hours. "Yes," was the reply, if Jeffrey would commit to a mutually agreed upon number of hours each week. While both Jeffrey and the company had to make some compromises, all told this situation ended as a win-win situation: Jeffrey was able to free up most of his schedule to devote to school, and the company salvaged a valuable employee.

Job Sharing

Job sharing can be defined as an arrangement in which two employees divide the responsibilities of one full-time job. It is distinguishable from regular part-time employment in that it applies to positions that cannot be separated into two definitive part-time jobs. While the concept of job sharing has been around for more than thirty years, only since the mid-1980s have organizations such as Quaker Oats Co. and Levi Strauss & Co. started viewing it as a viable work arrangement. And while initially viewed as a female-related issue, job sharing is now seen as a solution to the needs of many employees, including parents, older workers, and students.

According to a survey of work/family benefits by Hewitt Associates of Lincolnshire, Illinois, 37 percent of employers offer job-sharing arrangements to their employees. In many instances, job sharing has been pivotal in companies' retention of valuable employees.

Numerous employer benefits are derived from job sharing, including the broader range of skills brought to the position, the retention of valuable workers who might otherwise leave, a higher level of energy, and reduced absenteeism. In addition, job sharing virtually eliminates the need for employees to take care of personal business while on the job. Also, any time one partner terminates, the job is still half filled. There's also the added benefit of having the job filled at all times. Rarely is it left uncovered because of vacation or illness.

The key to success with this alternative work arrangement is cooperation and ongoing communication between the two workers sharing a job. A typical arrangement might be as follows: Employee A works all day Monday and Tuesday, and employee B works all day Thursday and Friday. On Wednesday, the two overlap, with employee A coming in at 9 A.M. and working until 1 P.M., and employee B starting at noon and working until 4 P.M. Another possible arrangement is daily job sharing: Employee A works each day from 9 A.M. to 1 P.M., and employee B comes in at 1 P.M. and works till 5 P.M. Or, to ensure some overlap, employee B could work from 12:30 P.M. to 4:30 P.M. Regardless of the arrangement, job sharers should talk with one another every day.

That having been said, employers should not assume that job sharers know how to communicate with one another. Two people sharing a job, jointly responsible for projects, probably have different views about how the work should be accomplished. Accordingly, they must learn how to negotiate, be flexible, and recognize the other worker's contributions. Barney Olmsted, former codirector of San Francisco–based New Ways to Work, put it this way: "... any job can be shared, but not every employee can share a job. It takes work, trust and communication, not only between partners, but also with coworkers, supervisors and clients. It's particularly important to continually communicate about individual responsibilities and current schedules."[4]

While the idea of overlapping schedules is appealing from the standpoint of ensuring continuity and flow, it could create a logistics problem for employers: Where do you put both of them when they're in at the same time? While some employers resolve this dilemma by providing job sharers with an office that has two desks and two computers, this isn't always practical.

There are additional drawbacks to job sharing: Twice as much payroll and personnel record keeping is required, and clients or customers may complain about the inability to deal with the same person consistently. The issue of benefits can also create some problems: Employers may offer pro-rated benefits to each partner or elect to divide a single package.

Organizations looking into job sharing should conduct a full analysis, including consideration of the job's requirements and responsibilities; an assessment of each partner's skills, abilities, shortcomings, and interests; a clear definition of how matters of salary and benefits are to be handled; and a schedule that is acceptable as well as workable for all concerned.

Best Practice: Eddie Bauer

Eddie Bauer, the casual-lifestyle clothing retailer with 12,000 employees, headquartered in Redmond, Washington, believes that encouraging its associates (read: employees) to balance work with their personal lives will result in a maximally healthy and productive workforce. Consequently, the $1.5 billion company has implemented more than twenty Work/Life benefits programs since 1994 and continues to do so today. Its efforts have resulted in numerous awards, including *Working Mother* magazine's "Top 100 Companies for Working Mothers" in 1996 and 1997 and *Fortune*'s "100 Best Companies to Work For" in 1998.

The company's programs are all founded on nine key objectives:

1. Helping associates manage their physical and mental health
2. Helping associates care for and positively interact with dependents
3. Making work more flexible
4. Supporting associates through their financial life cycle
5. Saving associates time
6. Recognizing and rewarding associates
7. Supporting associates' outreach to the community
8. Ensuring ongoing career development
9. Keeping associates informed

Eddie Bauer's programs are available to all associates classified as regular status, thus excluding associates hired for seasonal employment. Some of the programs, however, such as the New Mother's Room, are available only in the corporate office and not in the stores. Information concerning these programs is conveyed via brochures, employee orientation, the internal Eddie Bauer web site, the company's biweekly newspaper, and bulletin boards.

Here's a sampling of Eddie Bauer's Work/Life benefits programs:

▲ *Home & Health Postpartum Visits Program.* The company pays for a registered pediatric nurse to visit an employee's newborn baby at home. The nurse examines the mother and baby and provides a variety of information pertaining to issues such as infant care, bonding, nursing, and postpartum depression. Eddie Bauer is said to be the first company nationally that offers a fully funded postpartum program.

▲ *New Mother's Room.* A lactation room in the company's corporate office allows nursing mothers to express milk in private.

▲ *Balance Day.* In addition to vacation, holidays, and personal days, Eddie Bauer allows associates to take an additional "call in well" day off, for any reason.

▲ *Outdoor Experience Allowance.* This program was established to encourage associates to engage in outdoor activities and adventures, including golf, skiing, group white-water rafting, and hiking trips. Eddie Bauer pays for half of the activity or event.

▲ *Customized Work Environment.* The company makes every effort to accommodate flexible work schedules customized to meet individual associates' needs. Options include flextime, compressed workweeks, job sharing, telecommuting, and part-time work.

▲ *Childcare and Eldercare Referrals.* In recognition of its associates' responsibilities for the care of elderly parents in addition to their children, the company's childcare and eldercare referral program supplies information and provides assistance on a variety of topics such as the best childcare facilities and housing issues for aging parents.

▲ *Kid Care Backup.* When children of associates are mildly ill and parents cannot remain at home with them, Eddie Bauer provides on-site medical care, covering 50 percent of the cost.

▲ *On-site Services.* Eddie Bauer strives to make the integration of work and personal life as seamless as possible for its associates. That's why its corporate headquarters offers a variety of services such as laundry and dry cleaning, takeout dining, postal service, newspaper stands, and massages. During income tax season, it even provides tax preparation assistance.

Why does Eddie Bauer do all this? The numerous tangible benefits of these programs, including fewer sick days, less absenteeism, and lower healthcare costs, translate into a content workforce. This means associates are less likely to seek employment elsewhere, giving the company less to worry about with regard to retention and consequently recruitment. And by keeping on top of associates' level of satisfaction through an annual survey, asking associates if Eddie Bauer is helping them balance work with their personal lives, the company can continually gauge their programs' level of success.

SUMMARY

Increasingly, employers are becoming attuned to their employees' need for a better balance between work and their personal lives. Not only are more workers seeking employment with companies that are empathetic to their need for greater balance, but employees want to determine their own work schedules. As such, employees have defined those work schedule options that are most important to them and have sought cooperation on the part of their employer. The list includes telecommuting, flextime, a compressed work-weeks, part-time hours, and job sharing.

Since businesses must continue to attract and retain top performers, they are, in fact, responding to such employee demands by establishing flexible work schedule programs. These programs can succeed only if management supports them. One of the most significant ways of encouraging management support for work/life programs is through training sessions that focus on their value.

Traditionally, flexible work schedules were requested by and designed to accommodate women needing to balance work and family responsibilities. Today, with both parents working in 51 percent of all families and more women in professional positions, men are taking a more active role on the home front while simultaneously working longer hours at the office. Accordingly, the number of male workers taking advantage of the benefits offered by flexible work schedules is on the rise.

Employers interested in establishing flexible work options would do well to establish a cross-function management task force to implement certain steps: gain support for the program; set up the program's administration; design the program; develop resource materials; announce, promote, and evaluate the program; and fine-tune it. In addition, they need to be flexible and patient while allowing the program to gain support.

Telecommuting is one of the fastest growing forms of flexible work. Most companies agree that there are numerous advantages to having certain employees work at home, at least part of the time. Reduced utility and office space leasing costs, as well as increased productivity, are among the most common reasons cited for hiring telecommuters. Employers with telecommuting workers report less absenteeism. And many employees appreciate a telecommuting arrangement. Parents who want to work and provide home care for their children can more readily manage both. At-home workers can also complete their tasks without typical office interruptions as well as work "off-hours." Then there's the benefit of not having to commute and being able to wear whatever they choose.

Drawbacks for telecommuting employees include a sense of isolation and being "out of the loop." There's also concern regarding colleagues' perception of at-home work.

Not everyone can make the adjustment to a nontraditional work style such as telecommuting. To be successful, telecommuters must have the ability to stay focused and be disciplined, flexible, honest, self-assured, independent, and motivated. They must also convert part of their home to an office environment. Drawbacks for managers include a lack of direct control over an employee's work, concern over possible misuse of computers and other electronic equipment, and unauthorized access to confidential data.

Team training can help managers and employees confront potentially divisive issues, voice concerns about the new working relationship, and discuss mutual expectations.

In addition to telecommuting, other popular work options include flextime, compressed workweeks, part-time work, and job sharing. Flextime allows employees to vary arrival and departure times, compressed workweeks permit workers to put in the required full-time schedule in fewer than five days, part-time refers to a reduced work-time schedule, and job sharing is an arrangement in which two employees divide the responsibilities of one full-time job. While not all arrangements work equally well in every environment, an increasing number of organizations are willing to test diverse work options and are reporting positive results.

Notes

1. Barney Olmsted and Suzanne Smith, *Creating a Flexible Workforce* (New York: AMACOM, 1994).
2. *The New York Times*, September 12, 1999. "Telecommuting: Bye, L.I.R.R. Ciao, L.I.E."
3. *Shiftwork Alert* (Cambridge, Mass.: Circadian Technologies Inc.) as cited in *Workforce*, July 1997.
4. *Workforce*, December 1998.

CHAPTER 11

Eye on the Future

"As a society, we have been moving from the old to the new. And we are still in motion. Caught between eras, we experience turbulence. Yet, amid the sometimes painful and uncertain present, the restructuring of America proceeds unrelentingly."

—John Naisbitt, Megatrends

O ver the past several years, there has been a preponderance of gloom and doom for employers in the nation's newspaper headlines concerning the current labor picture. Here's a sampling: "U.S. Jobless Rate Drops to 30-Year Low", "High-Tech Grads Get Multiple Offers", "Fast Times for Engineering Graduates", "Worker Shortages Loom", "Employers Hustle to Fill Job Rolls", "The Stream of Labor Slows to a Trickle", and "Is Anybody Out There?" It's downright depressing!

According to the Department of Labor, the current economic expansion and incredibly tight labor market are projected to continue, at least through 2008. Baby boomers are starting to retire and there is a shortage of younger workers, many of whom view the workplace differently than their predecessors, particularly in regard to the balance between work and their personal lives. To attract and retain top performers, employers are offering every kind of perk imaginable, in addition to generous compensation and benefits packages. High-tech skills command particularly high salaries and incentives. Some companies are so desperate for workers they're giving away new cars. And in some industries, signing bonuses, once reserved for top executives, are now demanded by employees at all levels.

What's going on in Madison, Wisconsin, illustrates the prevailing recruitment and retention picture. Early in 2000, the city had an unemployment rate of just over 1 percent.[1] That figure was second only to one other U.S. town, Columbia, Missouri, and indicates that just about everyone in Madison who can work has a job.

At one local company, Berbee Information Networks Corporation, employees enjoy stock options, company-provided Palm Pilots, cell phones, and a thousand dollar bonus to help with the down payment on their first homes, as well as company-installed and maintained high-speed digital network lines in their homes for those wishing to work from there. Jim Berbee recently took his workforce of 220 employees and their families to Disney World. He provides free bagels and muffins on Fridays, and free sodas all the time. Employees can use the office copiers for personal use, an auto-repair service comes to the employee parking lot once every two weeks to do oil changes and tire rotations, and there's dry-cleaning delivery four days a week. Employees have responded to these perks: The company boasts a 94 percent retention rate. The problem for Berbee is expansion: The company is growing so fast, it has, at the time of this writing, more than one hundred job openings. That's nearly 50 percent of the entire workforce. "We're losing ground every week," moaned Berbee.

Other businesses in Madison are hurting as well. Entry-level jobs are commanding starting salaries at nearly double the federal minimum wage. One nearby resort flies in summer help from Lithuania, Zimbabwe, Russia, and New Zealand. Some companies are so desperate they are paying people just to come in and fill out a job application.

There was a time when employers would dream of a full employment economy. But that dream wasn't in the context of rapid expansion and growth, a combination that's hurting businesses across the United States.

If finding workers isn't hard enough, once found, businesses are discovering that these employees often lack the adequate skills, knowledge, attitude, and motivation to do an effective job. Consequently, employers are, in too many instances, forced to compromise the standards of the job or tolerate substandard performance (training may take too long).

Comments such as these between a cashier and a coworker are representative: "You're not going to believe this. I went on this job interview where the manager said I'd have to use a register that didn't tell you how much change to give back to a customer. He said I should be able to figure it out! Oh, and get this: He wanted me to work on Saturdays!" "What did you do?" asked her coworker. "I walked out, of course. I wasn't gonna get paid enough to think! And I certainly wasn't going to give up my weekends for some stupid job! I have a life!''

So much for the old regime where there were bosses and employees, and the bosses had some measure of authority over the employees. It's hard to exercise authority over a population of free agents and free spirits. Employee ownership rules supreme!

In this buyers' market, where employers have become the sellers, what can companies do to ensure at least minimal skill levels and a positive attitude toward working? And what are the trends employers should anticipate so they can compete and succeed in tomorrow's labor market?

PARTNERING WITH EDUCATIONAL INSTITUTIONS

In Chapter 2, you read about how some companies are competing for top talent by developing school/business partnerships. For example, Seaman's Furniture Co., based in Long Island, New York, is a member of the Half Hollow Hills School and Business Partnership Advisory Board. The board's mission is to expose students to the work environment.

In this connection, companies have long known about the correlation between education and work. Educational requirements have always figured into most job requirements, with college degrees deemed essential to the performance of many tasks. In recent years, especially after Congress passed the School-to-Work Opportunities Act in 1994, companies became increasingly interested in developing formal business/education partnerships, beginning as early as kindergarten and continuing through the 12th grade. The Act grants seed money to states for the purpose of implementing school-to-work plan programs. The National School-to-Work Office, a joint effort between the Departments of Education and Labor, now administers the grants and coordinates communication between the states and local partnerships. And organizations such as the National Employer Leadership Council help companies to customize their participation in school-to-work activities, strengthening what the council calls the "education supply chain." As stated by John Clendenin, retired CEO of BellSouth, "The bottom line in America's fight for long-term competitiveness ultimately will be won or lost not in the halls of Congress, not in the boardrooms around the world, but in America's classrooms."[2]

One of the most efficient ways for an organization to launch a business/educational partnership is through job shadowing. In such a program, individual students spend time with business representatives and go through a typical day on the job. The students learn firsthand what working is like. More important, they can determine whether the skills they have acquired thus far in school are preparing them adequately for work.

To emphasize the importance of job shadowing, February 2 has been set aside as National Groundhog Job Shadow Day. Notes General Colin Powell, chairman of America's Promise–The Alliance for Youth, and a member of the National Groundhog Job Shadow Day Coalition, "Once experienced, I think business will see the benefits, both for their community's youth and for the future of their companies, and we will see job shadowing continue throughout the year." Additional information about National Groundhog Job Shadow Day can be obtained online at www.jobshadow.org.

Bell Atlantic is an excellent example of a business committed to partnering with schools. The company sponsors eleven technology education centers in New Jersey that prepare students for jobs in the telecommunications industry. Their success rate is impressive: Bell Atlantic hires 80 percent of the graduates coming out of the program, with the rest finding jobs elsewhere. "We're saving untold tens, if not hundreds, of thousands of dollars in training and retraining by hiring them," says Stephen Heller, manager of education programs for the company.[3]

The seeds of Bell Atlantic's efforts were sown in 1995, when a judge ordered that the Newark, New Jersey, school district be taken over by the state because of mismanagement. State-appointed superintendent Dr. Beverly Hall identified the need for school/business partnering, and Bell Atlantic was one of the companies that rose to the challenge. Lucent Technologies and the Ford Foundation also pitched in. They granted $15 million for seven elementary schools to "help better prepare teachers so youngsters will be more successful in high school," says Hall. In addition, every student completing high school and meeting certain criteria receives a $6,000 scholarship. Prudential Mutual Life Insurance Co. set up a million-dollar challenge: It would match the donations of any other organization that invested in the Newark school system. And Anheuser-Busch adopted a school after one of its executives participated in the district's Principal for a Day program.

Similar efforts were initiated in Rochester, New York. In 1997, a group of businesses decided to form the Rochester Business Education Alliances, a consortium that holds the school system to the highest standards. "We need to be competitive and we need high standards," says Robert S. Legge, president of Legge & Co., an HR consulting firm. The consortium, which includes Kodak, Xerox, and Bausch & Lomb, came up with a Certificate of Employability as a supplement to the high school diploma. Students document that they have met specific requirements in the areas of academics, applied learning competencies, attendance, and citizenship. Near the end of their senior year, students' portfolios are reviewed by a committee composed of school staff and business representatives to determine whether the student has earned the certificate.

The result of programs such as these is that everybody wins. Additional information about school/business partnerships can be obtained by contacting the Committee for Economic Development (www.ced.org) and the National School-to-Work Office in Washington, D.C. (202-401-6222).

IT Worker Shortages

The Information Technology Association of America (ITAA) has projected that the current shortage of IT specialists will rise to a staggering figure of 1.6 million by the year 2005. This shortage encompasses four key IT categories: computer scientists, computer engineers, systems analysts, and computer programmers. Included in these categories are numerous job titles, such as database administration associate, information systems operator/analyst, interactive digital media specialist, network specialist, programmer/analyst, software engineer, and technical support representative. Add to the above-stated figure the anticipated business demand for information systems growing at a rate of 30 percent per year (according to META Group, an international research and consulting organization), coupled with the BLS's estimate of 1.3 million new IT opportunities through 2008, and, potentially, you are facing a technological nightmare.

But experts offer a means of triumphing over the seemingly insurmountable odds against adequate IT staffing. The solution, they assert, lies in nurturing greater business/academic alliances. If companies seek to develop the workforce needed to meet future business demands, they must invest more time, money, and resources into our schools, colleges, and universities. Unfortunately, too many companies focus exclusively on immediate recruitment and retention efforts, rather than on building a new workforce by establishing consortia, internships, and training programs.

Those that do, however, are reaping rewards for their efforts.

Take Microsoft, for example. In 1998, the software giant launched its ambitious Microsoft 2000 program, a corporate/educational partnership that set out to provide exemplary ideas for other companies eager to promote the growth of IT. Some of its components were as follows:

▲ Sponsoring the Making College Count In-School Presentation Program, providing 50,000 high school seniors at 250 schools with tips on how to succeed in college and in business

▲ Donating $350,000 to Green Thumb Inc., a nonprofit organization that trains qualified unemployed workers, senior citizens, and people with disabilities in certain technical tasks, in a cooperative effort with Productivity Point International, Inc., a technical education center

▲ Establishing the Microsoft Authorized Academic Training Program, which trains instructors at high schools, colleges, and universities across the country

▲ Cosponsoring low-rate loans for technical training at Microsoft Authorized Technical Education Centers

▲ Providing an online career aptitude guide to disseminate information about IT career options, with questions that help students and others define their own work style and abilities (www.microsoft.com/skills2000)

Another company committed to partnering with educational institutions in the quest for IT workers is Hartford Financial Services Company, which established Hartford Technology Services in 1998 and became involved in a consortium with local business leaders. Together, they work with several area colleges and universities to identify the future training needs of businesses, then help put together college programs that will prepare students to meet those needs.

Northrup Grumman is another company that is partnering with schools to help place IT workers. Says Alysia Vanitzian, corporate director for employee development at the Los Angeles–based company, "We're employing information technology interns from colleges and universities in an effort to acquaint them with our company and industry, and with the types of projects available here. Because we're competing with more 'glamorous' industries and companies, this is one way we can establish a comfort level with future employees."[4]

Yet another example of partnering for IT is Stream International. It works closely with Brookhaven and Richland colleges, both part of the Dallas Community College District. The company provides its own course—which is 40 percent lecture and 60 percent hands-on training in the latest technology—instructors, and teaching materials. The program is geared for people who may lack computer skills but who possess the required aptitude and communications skills. As students wind down in their training, Stream courts those under consideration for employment.

Educational Institutions

Companies such as those cited above, along with the many others involved in business/educational partnerships for IT and other fields, recognize that the most effective partnership programs work with all types of educational institutions. In fact, many prefer working with community colleges rather than four-year colleges: Community colleges generally are located near partner businesses, making frequent on-site interaction easy and cost-effective, and lower tuition costs at community colleges allow corporate dollars to go further than they would at expensive universities.

Some businesses are committed to starting business/educational relationships at the elementary school level. Consider what took place in southern Illinois a few years ago. Employers were struggling with a severe labor shortage and didn't know how to combat it. Along came Betty Musgrave, a tech-prep director and school-to-work coordinator with the Franklin-Williamson Regional Office of the Illinois State Board of Education. Through her efforts, educators, employers, and local governments in southern Illinois joined forces and formed the Mid-South Partnership Coalition, a school-to-work program that begins in elementary school and continues through secondary and postsecondary education, right up until students land jobs. Soon after its formation, several hundred employers teamed up with fifty school districts, nearly two dozen high schools, two community colleges, and one state university in an attempt to resolve the region's labor shortage problem.

According to Musgrave, "There was a real gap between what's being taught in the schools and what skills are truly needed in the workforce."[5] She believes the gap was due, in part, to the fact that many teachers had never been outside the academic environment or experienced, firsthand, the business world. Introducing these teachers to representatives from businesses—people who actually perform the jobs the students will be vying for—helped educators fulfill their objectives.

Musgrave believes the cooperative effort gives teachers a clearer vision of how their work in the classroom will help students after graduation and helps employers appreciate the program's long-range investment qualities.

The region's coalition has gained attention nationally. It has been the recipient of the Society for Human Resource Management (SHRM) Education Excellence Award, received funding from the U.S. Department of Education under the School-to-Work Opportunities Act, and has served as a model for the state's other school-to-work programs.

Government Support

The U.S. government has played an increasingly active role in promoting partnerships, especially when it comes to hiring IT workers. With regard to the latter, and in response to demands made by the ITAA and other concerned industry groups, the Departments of Education, Commerce, and Labor have issued reports, generated publicity, sponsored major conferences, provided funding, and launched incentive programs to address the issue.

For example, the President's Educational Technology Initiative encourages the advancement of technological literacy among all students. The program consists of Four Pillars, or goals:

1. Modern computers and learning devices will be accessible to every student.
2. Classrooms will be connected to one another and to the outside world.
3. Interesting, educational software will be an integral part of the curriculum.
4. Teachers will be ready to use and teach with technology.

Other government initiatives include expanding industry involvement in school-to-work programs. For instance, the Departments of Education and Labor are providing some $6 million in grants for industry groups that expand private-sector involvement in school-to-work projects. With this incentive, many students will be able to acquire the academic and vocational learning needed to pursue high-skill, high-salaried jobs in any industry, including IT. The Department of Education also has established a $2 billion Technology Literacy Challenge fund, to be distributed over a five-year period.

For further help, businesses can turn to the Workforce Investment Partnership Act of 1998. Its purpose is to help match employers' needs with workers' abilities. Students select jobs from lists provided by local employers. They then receive vouchers to pay the tuition for training. Training courses are short and concentrated. Counselors steer trainees toward occupations that are likely to have slots available by the time the training is complete. For additional information, contact the Department of Labor Employment and Training Administration (www.doleta.gov.) or the National Association of Counties (202-396-6226) for a list of state job-training liaisons.

The following are additional resources that provide information to employers interested in developing business/educational partnerships:

▲ American Federation of Teachers (www.aft.org)
▲ American Vocational Association (703-683-7424)
▲ National Association of Partners in Education (www.napehq.org)
▲ National Employer Leadership Council (www.nelc.org)

Best Practice: Colgate-Palmolive Company

Pals Around the World (PAW), a collaborative effort between Colgate-Palmolive employees from its world headquarters in New York and the Rutgers University Center for Mathematics, Science, and Computer Education, was developed to create a global learning experience for students. Through the use of videoconferencing, e-mail, fax, and the Internet, children are connected to the global community as a means of improving their communications and math skills.

The pilot program joined elementary-aged schoolchildren from two locations, Perth Amboy, New Jersey, and Juncos, Puerto Rico, via the technological tools identified above. The students exchanged information about themselves and their communities over a period of several months. Each group visited Colgate sites near their respective schools and met with teachers and Colgate representatives. During these meetings, they learned interactive lessons about, not surprisingly, oral hygiene.

This effort ties in with the company's Colgate Bright Smiles, Bright Futures: Global Oral Health Education Program. This is a partnership endeavor among governments, dental professionals, educational professionals, schools, and communities. Over the past forty years, Colgate has provided oral-health education programs to school-aged children around the world. Since 1994, the program has reached more than 46 million children in more than eighty countries, enabling them to recognize the benefits of oral-health education and preventive treatment. As the program expands, Colgate plans to include other sites and educational institutions.

Colgate's commitment to partnering with educational institutions involves these other initiatives:

▲ *Onward Bound.* The purpose of this program is to teach children the value of diversity, responsibility, and trust. Sponsored by the company's Manhattan location, Colgate volunteers pair up with inner-city youths for a weekend of "roughing it" through the streets of New York City. The objective is to work as a cooperative team, developing and applying the skills needed to meet various challenges. These challenges include canoeing up the Hudson River, hiking blindfolded through the streets of lower Manhattan, sleeping outdoors on the deck of a ship, and scaling a rock face at the Cloisters.

▲ *Everybody Wins!* This is a private, not-for-profit organization devoted to promoting children's literacy and increasing their prospects for success in school and work. As one of the program's corporate partners, Colgate is committed to its success. Every week, Colgate employees volunteer to read in the Power Lunch program. Also, each week, Colgate employees from the New York world headquarters go to a local school to read, talk, and share lunch with a student. In addition to helping children hone their reading skills, the Colgate volunteers become mentors and thus serve as positive role models for these children.

▲ *Shadow Day.* The concept of job shadowing, described above, has been utilized at Colgate since 1990. Shadow Day partners children from inner-city schools with Colgate employees for a day. At Colgate, students experience a typical day at work by observing their partners. This gives students an opportunity to get the feel of a particular workplace culture, including the behavioral and interpersonal skills needed to succeed in business.

▲ *Colgate Women's Games.* Billed as the largest U.S. track and field meet for girls and young women, Colgate created the games in 1974 as a solution to the dearth of after-school activities for females. The attempt was a success: In the 1998-1999 season, for example, more than 11,000 athletes participated in weekly events at Pratt Institute in Brooklyn, New York, competing to run in the finals held at Madison Square Garden. All participants receive ribbons and medals, and the finalists are granted trophies in addition to educational grants-in-aid. To date, seventeen former Olympians and U.S. record holders have participated in the Colgate Women's Games. As impressive as this is, Colgate is quick to point out that the event is about more than athletics. Competitors leave the event with increased self-confidence. And many alumnae have used the resulting scholarship monies to become educators, lawyers, and businesswomen. Most important, they go on to be responsible mentors and involved members of their communities.

TRENDS

Freedom and nonconformity: These two terms have begun to permeate the American workplace. They are at the heart of phrases such as "I can work at home if I want to," "I got bored so I left," and "I'm a free agent." That last one is interesting and, to some degree, exemplifies the philosophy of many workers today: no routines, no dress codes, no set hours of work, no commuting, and no ties to office politics because, in many instances, there is no office. One person described what being a free agent means: "The free agent has a much better lifestyle. They're not necessarily going to make as much money as I might, but they can go snowboarding; they can decide when they want to work and when they don't want to work. It's an incredible lifestyle. I can't really think of a better way to spend your life."[6]

Some people think we're on the verge of a free-agent revolution. However, according to a study by the Economic Policy Institute, more than 60 percent of those considered free agents earn less than regular full-time workers in comparable jobs. In addition, there are no benefits, stock options, or paid vacations, nor is there protection under federal employment laws. In addition, there are expenses, like office equipment, Social Security and Medicare taxes, accountants, and attorneys, if necessary, not to mention office supplies, Internet services, and travel. How "free" can free agents afford to be?

The flattering description of free agents cited above should be contrasted with this warning from a self-defined free agent, who notes the downside of being your own boss: "It's a very hard, grueling lifestyle. . . . And you don't have control over the downtime between assignments. You may want two months off but get five, or want five months off and get only six weeks. You can't do it if you're not a self-driven person who's happy being lonely. You'll always be an outsider; you'll never be accepted as a full member of the team."[7]

The emergence of free agents is just one trend. There are additional economic, technological, and social trends that promise to impact how companies will manage their employees over the next decade. Here are some specific employment trends that have been identified by SHRM's "Workplace Visions" (Number 6-1999) as having a potential effect on workplace recruitment and retention issues.

Economic Trends

The key word on the economic employment front is *globalization*. Many of the largest U.S. corporations are projected to have more employees working outside the United States than inside. Currently, Ford employs 54 percent of its workers outside the country; IBM employs 51 percent. And one-fifth to one-third of employees at General Electric, PepsiCo, and General Motors work outside the United States. Smaller businesses are expected to expand globally as well.

This means businesses will need to find employees who not only possess the necessary tangible skills for a given job but also a host of critical intangible attributes needed to work abroad. The latter include the ability and temperament to embrace and adapt to the culture of another country, such as a different standard of living. It also means being able to adapt to another culture's sense of time. In his book *A Geography of Time*, social psychologist Robert Levine takes his readers on a fascinating journey through different cultures and how they view time.[8] He ranks the pace of life in thirty-one countries, informing us that the overall pace of living is fastest in Switzerland and slowest in Mexico. For example, in Japan, which ranked number four on Levine's list (following Ireland and Germany), speed is a highly regarded virtue: "Wasting time is frowned upon. A worker who moves too slowly, no matter whether the task actually requires speed, commits the ultimate sin in the Japanese workplace: not giving one's all." Garr Reynolds, an American who works in Japan, concurs:

> ". . . the Japanese believe they should appear to be busy at the office whether they are actually busy or not. One way to appear busy is to do things quickly: for example, jogging

the 10 feet to the copy machine; pounding the keyboard of your PC as you compose a routine letter; bolting out of your chair every time your superior calls your name. To be and/or appear to be busy is a virtue in this society, and appearing to be doing things quickly, and with an element of panic, suggests to others that you are indeed busy and therefore a good employee."[9]

Another economic trend has to do with foreign-owned companies. Currently, they employ 5 percent of all U.S. workers and 12 percent of U.S. manufacturing workers in the United States. European companies account for the largest percentage of foreign-owned companies in the United States, but Asian ownership is growing at a faster rate. The amount of investment by U.S. companies in other countries is even greater: In 1996, the value of U.S.-owned business assets in foreign countries was 26 percent greater than the amount of foreign-owned business assets in the United States.

"Electronic immigration," made possible by multimedia interconnectivity, will allow businesses to employ a labor force around the world without physically moving workers from their present locations. This could result in resentment from home-country workers and raise significant questions concerning compensation and benefits.

Technological Trends

Technological innovations will enable us to access people and information at unprecedented levels and speeds. These include expanded Internet power and usage; advances in artificial intelligence software; and the arrival of simpler, cheaper information appliances that will replace the PC for most home uses. The types of appliances will include smart phones, high definition TV, cable modems, networked computers, robots, and wearable computers.

Technologies such as data mining will impact how businesses focus their resources on the most receptive audiences, as increasing numbers of organizations use data mining to obtain information on current and potential users of their products and services. Opponents of data mining cite privacy concerns relating to the collection and dissemination of huge databases of personal information.

Concern over the potential abuse of data mining leads to other technology-related issues. There is, for example, increased worry over how technology will compromise the security of intellectual property. From breaches of e-mail systems to the release of rapidly transmitted computer viruses, data security remains an elusive concept.

Technology is going to impact how we view time. Continuous operations are becoming common, as consumer demand and technological innovation allow organizations to provide services twenty-four hours a day. Customer service will have to be available around the clock to accommodate clients who live in widely varying time zones.

Such technological trends could well result in higher stress levels. Companies such as Toyota, Toshiba, and Fujitsu are designing automobiles with multimedia systems that allow riders to access the Internet, listen to e-mail, and issue voice commands. This means that employees will be able to work anywhere, anytime. The result will be a lengthened workday and perhaps increased stress. And once employees will rarely be away from work influences, the current push for a greater balance between work and personal life will be negated.

These technological advances will require an especially well-trained workforce to operate and maintain the complex computers and machines. As a consequence, business investments in education will become more important than ever.

Social Trends

Diversity is in the HR forefront and promises to remain a priority through the next decade and beyond. The global composition of a diverse workforce will mesh nicely with expanding U.S. markets.

Workplace intergenerational tension is anticipated between Generation Xers and Ys, and baby boomers. Different work ethics and priorities are likely to clash over issues such as work schedules, incentives, and the composition of benefits packages. Providing a balance between work and personal life will remain a priority for employers striving to make the workplace more accommodating in order to attract and retain a productive workforce. It is likely that employers will offer innovative programs unlike anything currently available.

Genetic information is expected to impact the workplace in two significant ways: (1) the ability to associate certain diseases with genetic mutations will significantly affect employer-sponsored health plans, and (2) the linkage between genes and behaviors will impact job placement. Some twenty states already have laws regulating employer use of genetic information, and groups are lobbying for a federal law to address the issue.

Employment Trends

The use of contingent workers is expected to grow. As such, salary and benefits discrepancies between contingent and regular employees are likely to lead to legislative protection for the contingent workforce.

The most rapid employment growth will occur in highly paid professional occupations. Jobs requiring a college degree are expected to grow especially fast. This projection is in contrast with another prediction: that a preponderance of abundant jobs and huge salaries is expected to encourage students to opt out of college before graduating. Schools are also losing valuable faculty members attracted to the greater financial benefits of working in business. These changes are causing concern about the future worth of a college degree.

Shareholders may have greater input in employment-related issues than in the past. Since company policies on matters such as affirmative action, sexual harassment, and workplace safety can expose a company to costly litigation, shareholders may insist on a greater say in a company's decision- and policy-making process.

Alternative work options will continue to grow in popularity, with telecommuting heading the list. Companies will continue to support employees who want to work at home, but concerns about liability and workers compensation issues will still impact alternative arrangements.

Employees will also demand a greater financial stake in the companies for which they work. This interest can take a number of different forms, including ESOPs, stock options, stock purchase plans, stock bonuses, 401(k) plans, and profit sharing. While receiving part of one's compensation through stock is inherently risky, as long as the economic environment remains stable, employees will be increasingly interested in ownership-based benefits. This will be particularly important because real worker wages are expected to remain relatively flat. Strong wage growth in high-tech fields will be countered by wage restraints imposed by competition from the offshore labor used by many U.S.-based companies. In addition, new immigrants willing to work for low wages will stifle wage growth, as will the increased compensation paid to executives.

Future unionization attempts will target nontraditional

sources, such as doctors, welfare-to-work participants, and contingent workers. Unions have also seized on the income gap between high-tech workers and executives, as compared with the average worker.

Finally, healthcare costs will continue to rise. This will tempt some employers to eliminate employee healthcare coverage altogether or to increase the employees' share of the costs. It is unlikely that this will occur, however, as long as the labor market remains tight and employers need to rely on generous healthcare packages as a recruitment and retention tool.

More information concerning employment trends, in terms of projections for tomorrow's jobs, appears later in this chapter.

Additional Trends

There are a number of additional trends employers should anticipate and prepare for.

▲ *The concept of global compensation will increase.* Saturated domestic markets and the opportunity for extensive growth and expansion will increasingly result in global compensation and benefits programs. Successful programs will depend on how well HR is able to factor in trends, values, and outlooks in the major geographic regions of the world in which the companies function, in relation to those of the United States. In this regard, those companies that avoid a "one-size-fits-all" approach are more likely to attract and retain top performers.

▲ *Autonomous work units will flourish.* Many organizations will reorganize into smaller groups. These independent suborganizations will create greater opportunities for teamwork and total telecommuting. Many workers tend to stay with smaller business teams because they feel more a part of what's happening and are more likely to witness firsthand that their work makes a significant difference. Suborganizations, then, may help organizations resolve retention issues.

▲ *The emphasis will be on location.* Companies will move their facilities to locations that are more likely to enhance the quality of life for their employees. These sites are expected to be healthier, quieter, safer, and smaller and will hopefully attract qualified workers.

▲ *Outsourcing will grow in popularity.* People will be allowed to leave their core employer to join the outsourced contractor and vice versa. There will be dual-employment relationships, similar to dual citizenships. The goal is to develop loyalty between core employees and outsourcing contractors. It is expected that the opportunity to outsource will serve as a recruitment and retention tool.

▲ *Electronic commuting will increase.* The number of people working from home, a remote location, or at several different offices will rise dramatically. E-mail will be our connection with coworkers, suppliers, and customers.

▲ *"Stay for pay" will be offered to reduce turnover.* Employers will target retention periods and offer top performers cash incentives. For example, an employer will offer an employee a bonus equal to 150 percent of his or her pay if that person agrees to remain with the company for a certain number of years.

▲ *Significant new job categories will emerge.* There is, for example, a growing market for entertainment software (worldwide entertainment software revenues grow 38 percent a year, as compared with movie box-office revenues growth of 7.7 percent). Also, "virtual-company angels" are starting to make their mark. These are independent contractors who provide counseling services to home offices in computing, accounting, office management, and legal matters.

▲ *Significant job losses will hit certain occupations.* Those occupations with the largest projected job losses will include secretaries (other than legal and medical) and typists, bookkeepers, accounting and auditing clerks, and farmers.

▲ *Consortia will mushroom.* Project-oriented consortia designed to tackle the global market will become more common in virtually every industry. Companies, even those in different fields and those that normally compete, will work as one for the duration of a single project and then go about their separate businesses.

▲ *Virtual management will prevail.* Technology and telecommuting will enable increasing numbers of employees on both a national and international level to form virtual teams to work on a variety of tasks without physically meeting.

▲ *The HR function will be revamped.* HR professionals will spend most of their time dealing with the same strategic and operating issues as do others involved with running the business. They will need a sound working knowledge of various business matters, such as how to impact revenue growth, productivity, and customer satisfaction, and will need to focus on building organizational capabilities.

▲ *Hiring for attitude, training for skills will prevail.* As a result of the continued tight labor market, increasing numbers of employers will have no choice but to hire people lacking essential skills. Accordingly, training will become critical to survival. While initially, performance and productivity may suffer, ultimately the investment in training will pay off in growth and profitability.

▲ *Workforce planning will be vital to boosting economic growth.* This means supplementing homegrown talent with workers from abroad. Some organizations will circumvent visa restrictions by shifting work abroad and then using virtual work teams to manage projects from the United States.

WHERE THE JOBS ARE

Career planning is not what it used to be. Not so long ago, you went to school, got a job that often became your career, moved up the ranks, and retired with a gold watch. Now, as a result of corporate restructuring and new technologies that have eliminated some jobs while creating many others, we are being called on to effectively manage our own careers. This does not just mean selecting one career, but multiple careers. Experts predict that on average, Americans will select five or six different careers before retiring. Indeed, many of these careers will be in areas that don't even exist now but are in the process of emerging from major trends in business or society. Identifying such trends will itself be considered one of the career skills of the future.

Employees are being advised by career counselors to see themselves as a package of skills to which various titles can be applied. They are increasingly encouraged to commit to a lifetime of learning new skills, to develop analytical abilities, and to be flexible and creative. Above all else, they are urged to be proactive about their careers. Employers, on the other hand, are assessing economic, business, and social trends, seeking ways to profit from them.

Projections about Tomorrow's Jobs

Let's look at some of the projections as to where tomorrow's jobs are likely to be found. According to the Department of Labor, the five jobs projected to have the largest percentage increase between 1998 and 2008 are computer engineers (108 percent), computer support specialists (102 percent), systems analysts (94 percent), database administrators (77 percent), and desktop publishing specialists (73 percent). Some of the fields and occupations that are expected to flourish include genetics, microbiology, Internet marketing, home healthcare, foreign trade, entertainment, physical therapy, sales, and telecommunications.

The Department of Labor predicts the types of jobs Americans will perform based on long-term trends:

▲ The way Americans prepare meals has changed dramatically. Meals eaten at home rely increasingly on the purchase of prepared or partially prepared foods. Food stores have hired more staff to respond to the need for convenience with such features as delis and salad bars. Fast-food and carryout restaurants, as well as restaurants delivering food to the home, have both diversified and multiplied. The growth in meals eaten outside of the home, the result of both a long-term trend and the recent economic boom, has also led to a sharp increase in employment at eating and drinking establishments. This trend can be expected to continue as children, brought up in homes where little cooking is done, grow up lacking traditional culinary skills.

▲ Increases in the percentage of women who work outside the home have contributed to the growth in retail services as well as retail products. Greater spending power and limited free time have inspired the growth of stores that provide convenience—from catalog shopping to greater emphasis on customer service to personal shopper services.

▲ Childcare is increasingly being "contracted out" to daycare centers and nannies. The childcare industry is projected to add 164,000 jobs through 2006. Similar changes are occurring in the care of the increasing population of elderly persons. Residential care institutions providing twenty-four-hour, year-round personal care have multiplied, along with nursing homes and home healthcare services.

▲ Healthcare jobs have been increasing since the 1950s, more than in any other comparable industry group, because of the aging population, new technologies, and greater administrative requirements. Jobs in medical offices, clinics, and health maintenance organizations have grown rapidly as the healthcare industry strives to provide greater services in less costly ways. Nurse practitioners have increased in number as the healthcare industry encourages their use for functions formerly performed by doctors. In fact, states have increased nurse practitioners' authority, often allowing them to prescribe drugs and admit patients to healthcare facilities. Nutritionists are also growing in number, as more people grow interested in a holistic approach to health. Health-services employment is projected to increase by 3.2 million jobs by 2006.

The *Monthly Labor Review* projects growth in the following occupations through 2006 (number of jobs added by 2006):

Systems analysts:	519,600
General managers and top executives:	467,000
Registered nurses:	410,800
Secondary school teachers:	312,100
Database administrators and computer support specialists:	249,200
Maintenance repairers, general utility:	245,800
Special education teachers:	240,700
Computer engineers:	235,300
Social workers:	187,600
Food service and lodging managers:	167,700
College and university faculty:	162,300
Engineering, mathematical, and natural scientists:	155,100
Licensed practical nurses:	148,400
Financial managers:	146,400
Marketing, advertising, and public relations managers:	137,600
Computer programmers:	129,200
Sports and physical education instructors and coaches:	123,400
Lawyers:	118,400
Physicians:	117,500
Electrical and electronics engineers:	104,800
Corrections officers:	103,300
Securities and financial services sales workers:	99,600
Physical therapists:	81,100
Artists and commercial artists:	78,200

Conversely, the *Monthly Labor Review* also projects those occupations with the largest anticipated job decline: secretaries (except legal and medical) and typists, including word processors; bookkeepers, accountants, and auditors; farmers and farm workers; private household cleaners; sewing machine operators; office machine operators; and welfare eligibility workers.

New Workplace Jobs

The newly emerging workplace is creating a host of unique positions, many serving the needs of today's high-powered, high-paid workers. These include professional servants to ease their stress, personal chefs to cook their meals, personal trainers to keep them in shape, vitamin counselors to keep them healthy, and shapeware designers to help with their expanding waistlines (in case the personal trainers don't earn their keep). Indeed, many of the 150.9 million jobs that the U.S. Bureau of Labor Statistics expects will exist by 2006 bear little resemblance to their predecessors. Most traditional jobs will undoubtedly continue, but not without a period of reengineering. And with this retooling of jobs comes retraining of employees. Futurists anticipate that the least change will occur for workers in blue-collar jobs, which now account for nearly one-fourth of the nation's workforce. While subject to technological improvements that will reduce their number, these are jobs not readily automated, and therefore they will probably prevail.

Exhibit 11–1 provides a closer look at some of the new, sometimes unique, positions that are joining the ranks along more traditional jobs.

GETTING FROM HERE TO THERE

In a 1999 Best Practices Report, Watson Wyatt Worldwide offers suggestions for resolving current recruitment and retention problems. After first warning that there are no silver bullets or quick fixes, the report recommends that businesses begin by identifying their employee age distribution, assessing hiring and termination patterns, reviewing career paths, and examining the impact of aging on compensation and benefits costs. Next, it suggests that companies ask themselves some key questions as they relate to attraction, retention, performance, and costs. Some of these questions are:

- ▲ *Attraction:* How flexible is our recruitment strategy? How many openings are there today, and for what positions? How many openings do we anticipate in five years? What are the marketplace demographics for those positions? Are we digging too deep in a shallow pool of younger workers?
- ▲ *Retention:* Have we recalibrated reward systems to address

new demographic realities? Do strategic rewards and benefits support our retention strategy, e.g., portability for young workers and retirement security for older workers? Do we offer noncash awards and incentives? What is our current recognition plan? What do we recognize and how?

▲ *Performance:* Are our reward systems reinforcing business objectives? Is training aligned with needed skills and competencies? Do we offer flexible career pathing? Do we have an integrated strategy for keeping employees healthy? Is performance management linked with training objectives?

▲ *Costs:* Are we paying for age and tenure as opposed to performance? How much money are we paying or losing in turnover costs? What will be the impact of aging on our compensation and benefits costs? Are we throwing dollars at problems that are better fixed by a stronger culture?

The report goes on to suggest that employers adopt a long-term approach with a mixture of solutions, including:

▲ Revamping career paths to allow employees to move up the corporate ladder early in their careers and then partially back down as they wind down toward retirement

▲ Redesigning benefits plans to help control rapidly rising costs

▲ Linking pay plans to productivity, not tenure and age

▲ Revisiting recruitment and retention strategies to encompass leadership training, fast-track development, alternative work arrangements, retention bonuses, and noncash recognition

▲ Focusing on the link between health and productivity

Additional questions concerning the future, posed by the Department of Labor, can help employers establish policies that will address the changing times and their effect on workers' needs:

▲ How can workers get the education and training they need to keep their skills up-to-date and to ensure that they do not get stuck in low-wage jobs?

▲ What incentives will keep individuals learning over the course of their work lives to bolster their lifelong economic security?

▲ As computer networks compete with human networks in

our workplaces, who will guide and mentor new workers on the job?

▲ Technology provides flexibility in existing jobs and creates new jobs. It also can make jobs obsolete. How will employers manage this paradox?

▲ How can workers balance their needs for both lifelong economic security and the resources and time to care for their families?

▲ How can employers build on and multiply successful existing programs such as on-site childcare and eldercare and flexible work arrangements?

▲ How will workers in both traditional and nontraditional working arrangements acquire the health insurance and pension benefits they need?

▲ Will policy and decision makers in government, labor unions, private industry, schools, and communities address the changes that are inevitable and embrace the challenge of meeting future workers' needs?

A Future Timeline

This timeline represents combined predictions made by professionals in various fields as well as federal and state agencies:

▲ *2004:* The share of technology workers will peak at 9 percent of the workforce.

▲ *2006:* Of the 18.5 million jobs added, nearly one-third will be office, education, and health occupations. The health services sector will add more than 3 million jobs and will grow at more than double the economy's growth rate; cashiers and retail clerks will account for just under 1 million additional jobs; personnel supply services will make the biggest job gains; general managers and top executives, receptionists, clerical workers, and office supervisors together will account for 1.7 million new jobs; and teachers, teacher aides, and childcare providers will add 1.2 million jobs.

▲ *2013:* The size of the U.S. workforce will peak.

▲ *2020:* Annual unemployment rates will fluctuate between 3.5 percent and 6.5 percent, averaging about 4.7 percent. Significant numbers of the population will move away from the plains states and the Northeast; Florida, Texas, California, Arizona, and Nevada will be the fastest growing state economies.

▲ *2030:* One in five Americans will be a senior citizen, compared with one in eight in the mid-1990s.

▲ *2060:* Some 24 million Americans will need long-term care services, up from 9 million in 2000.

Back to the Future

Despite the futuristic tone of many of the projections cited in this chapter, especially those driven by technology, the primary themes that shape our recruitment and retention goals for the future reflect many of the same goals that have prevailed for decades. These include:

▲ Ensuring that all workers have equal employment opportunities

▲ Making certain employees understand the work they are hired to perform

▲ Providing employees with the tools needed to perform their jobs

▲ Honestly appraising employees' work performance

▲ Compensating employees fairly for the work they've been hired to perform

▲ Offering competitive and comprehensive benefits

▲ Establishing goals for career development or job advancement

▲ Enabling employees to gain additional knowledge through training

▲ Rewarding employees who effectively perform their duties and responsibilities

▲ Accommodating workers' needs to balance their jobs with caring for their families

▲ Providing employees with a safe and harassment-free environment in which to work

▲ Supplying a motivating environment

▲ Listening to employees' ideas

▲ Responding to concerns or complaints

Drucker on the Future

Since this book started with insightful projections made by Peter Drucker more than twenty years ago, it seems only fitting that it conclude with some of his views on the future. In his most recent book, *Management Challenges for the 21st Century* (New York: Harper Business, 1999), Drucker explores issues that he believes are certain to represent the major challenges of tomorrow.

Drucker states that we need to stop thinking about managing people and referring to them as employees. Instead, we should think in terms of leading them and using the term "knowledge workers." He believes that knowledge workers are the most valuable asset of any twenty-first-century organization. He states, ". . . knowledge workers must know more about their job than their boss does—or else they are no good at all. In fact, that they know more about their job than anybody else in the organization is part of the definition of knowledge workers." For example, "The engineer servicing a customer does not know more about the product than the engineering manager does. But he knows more about the customer—and that may be more important than product knowledge. The mechanic servicing an airliner knows far more about the technical condition of the plane than the airport manager of the airline to whom he reports, and so on."

Drucker acknowledges that these people are employees in the sense that they depend on the organization for promotions, appraisals, salary raises, and so on. But they are not dependent on the organization for what they know and how to apply that knowledge. Workers hold the key to succeeding or failing in their own particular job function. This is especially significant since, unlike years past, many of today's bosses have not previously held the jobs their workers hold. The depth of knowledge is not the same. Indeed, if the worker fails, so too does the organization on some level.

Knowledge workers increasingly have mobility—they can, in this tight labor market, take their product or their knowledge and leave. Accordingly, an organization's focus must be on keeping these people motivated. But not with tangible items, including money. We have known for more than fifty years that money alone does not motivate a person to perform (dissatisfaction with money, on the other hand, demotivates). Money is, as Frederick Herzberg called it, a "hygiene factor." Drucker urges corporations to look beyond offering "things" and instead treat knowledge workers as if they were volunteers: Offer them a challenge. Provide knowledge workers with information about the organization's mission, offer them continual training, allow them to apply their specific strengths to their job, let them see results, allow them to effectively manage themselves, and, says Drucker, the organization will thrive.

Another critical issue according to Drucker is what organizations perceive to be "the starting point." The starting point can no longer be the organization's own product or service, or even its known market or known end uses for the products or services. The starting point has to be what customers consider value. And what is value to the customer is often quite different from what is value or quality to the supplier. This means abandoning the prevailing concept that technology serves as a foundation for management policies. "The foundations have to be customer values and customer decisions on the distribution of their disposable income. It is with those that management policy and management strategy increasingly will have to start," Drucker states.

Drucker also identifies five phenomena that he views as certainties: (1) the collapsing birthrate in the developed world, (2) shifts in the distribution of disposable income, (3) defining performance, (4) global competitiveness, and (5) the growing incongruence between economic globalization and political splintering. He believes it is incumbent upon organizations to consider these "realities" in order to be prepared for the challenges that the next few decades are certain to raise. "Unless these challenges can be met successfully, no enterprise can expect to succeed, let alone to prosper, in a period of turbulence, or structural change and of economic, social, political and technological transformation."

A further observation of Drucker's is that "one cannot manage change. One can only be ahead of it." Accordingly, a key twenty-first-century challenge for management is to collectively become change leaders. Change leaders establish systematic methods to look for and to anticipate change, know how to introduce change both inside and outside the organization, and establish policies to balance change with continuity.

Drucker envisions a new information revolution that will radically change the meaning of information for organizations and individuals alike. He adds that this is a revolution in concepts that is driven by our need to understand the meaning of information. This is in contrast with our current emphasis on technology as being the collection, storage, transmission, and presentation of data. He believes that by examining the purpose of information, we will first redefine the tasks to be done and then redefine the institutions that do these tasks.

Will the changes that Drucker envisions come about? Perhaps. After all, he has proved insightful in the past. If nothing else, perhaps we will be better equipped to anticipate the future work environment and what we need to prevail.

SUMMARY

In this buyers' labor market, where employers have become sellers—a trend that is expected to continue at least through 2008—companies focus on ensuring at least minimal skill levels and a positive attitude toward working. One way of accomplishing this is by partnering with educational institutions.

Companies have long recognized the correlation between education and work. In recent years, companies have become increasingly interested in developing formal business/educational partnerships, beginning as early as kindergarten and continuing through 12th grade. One of the most efficient ways for an organization to launch a business/educational partnership is through job shadowing. This means that individual students spend time with representatives from businesses, experiencing a typical day on the job. The students learn firsthand what working is like; more important, they can determine whether the skills they have acquired thus far in school are preparing them adequately for a work environment.

Business/academic alliances will also help alleviate the severe shortage of IT specialists anticipated in the near future. With the current shortage expected to rise to 1.6 million by 2005, and more than 1.3 million new IT opportunities anticipated through 2008, businesses have no choice but to invest more time, money, and resources in our schools, colleges, and universities.

The U.S. government has played an increasingly active role in promoting partnerships, especially when it comes to hiring IT workers. For example, the President's Educational Technology Initiative encourages the advancement of technological literacy among all students, and the Workforce Investment Partnership Act of 1998 helps match employers' needs with workers' abilities.

Employers must also be cognizant of upcoming trends so they can compete in tomorrow's labor market. In addition to the emergence of free agents, there are numerous economic, technological, social, and employment trends with the potential to impact the workplace over the upcoming decade and beyond. Employers should be mindful, too, of projections that global compensation will increase in popularity, autonomous work units will flourish, electronic commuting will increase, "stay for pay" will be offered to reduce turnover, consortia will mushroom, and virtual management will prevail. Also, because of a continued tight labor market, increasing numbers of employers will have no choice but to hire people lacking necessary skills. Accordingly, training will become critical to survival.

Businesses may resolve current recruitment and retention problems by identifying current employee age distribution, assessing hiring and termination patterns, reviewing career paths, and examining the impact of aging on compensation and benefits costs. They should also ask themselves some key questions relating to labor attraction, retention, performance, and costs. In most instances, a long-term approach, reflecting a mixture of solutions, will yield the best results.

Compatibility is less of an issue with some of the specialized jobs projected to represent the new wave of employment, even as employers wrestle with their impact on the workplace. Jobs such as workplace concierge, corporate anthropologist, forensic accountant, and intellectual property lawyer are on the rise, as traditional occupations such as bookkeepers, auditors, and office machine operators decline in numbers. See Exhibit 11-1 for future job projections.

Despite the futuristic tone of many of the projections made, the primary themes that shape our recruitment and retention goals for the future are reflective of many of the basic goals that have prevailed for decades, such as providing employees with the tools needed to perform their jobs, establishing goals for career development or job advancement, and supplying a motivating environment.

Notes

1. David Brooks, "0%⁺ Unemployment." *The New York Times Magazine*, March 5, 2000.
2. *HR Focus*, February 1999.
3. *HR Focus*, February 1999.
4. *Workforce*, July 1998.
5. *HR Magazine*, May 1997.
6. Nina Munk, "The Price of Freedom." *The New York Times Magazine*, March 5, 2000.
7. Munk, "The Price of Freedom."
8. Robert Levine, *A Geography of Time* (HarperCollins, 1997).
9. Levine, *A Geography of Time*.

Exhibit 11–1. Future job projections.

Each category listed includes current average pay and web site resources for obtaining additional information.

▲ *Workplace concierge.* A growing number of workplace concierge businesses are springing up to serve as a single point of contact for sorting out the hundreds of details that clutter our lives. Many have contracts with a specific company to provide employees with a range of services, from travel bookings to dinner and theater arrangements. Pay: $31,000. Resource: National Concierge Association (www.conciergeassoc.org).

▲ *Corporate anthropologist.* Anthropologists are being hired in ever-increasing numbers by corporations and consulting firms. As trained observers, problem detectors, and problem solvers, they are brought in to study customer habits as a basis for designing useful products and services or to spot underlying glitches that hamper the meshing of employees from different corporate cultures. Pay: $30,000–$50,000 (starting salary). Resources: National Association for the Practice of Anthropology (www.ameranthassn.org), Society for Applied Anthropology (www.telepath.com/sfaa).

▲ *Virtual office assistant.* These are home-office assistants who help clients with any tasks customarily performed by an on-site secretary or office manager, such as word processing, database management, mail merge, Internet research, travel arrangements, and bookkeeping. Assignments and instructions are communicated through e-mail, fax, phone, and diskette. Pay: $15–$25 per hour. Resources: International Virtual Assistants Association (www.ivaa.org), Global Association of Virtual Assistants (www.gava.org).

▲ *Arbitrator or mediator.* Arbitrators and mediators are becoming more popular as employers attempt to settle adverse claims out of court through alternate dispute resolution. Pay: $150–$250 per hour. Resource: American Arbitration Association (www.adr.org).

▲ *Chef.* As more Americans eat out or bring prepared foods into the home, chefs are in greater demand, working either in restaurants or functioning as personal chefs for an individual or for a family. Pay: $18,000–$24,000 (starting salary); $30,000–$40,000 (with four to five years' experience). Resources: American Culinary Federation Inc. (www.ACFchefs.org), National Restaurant Association (www.restaurant.org).

▲ *Diversity trainer.* Increasingly, teams of workers originate from different ethnicities, backgrounds, religions, and specialties.

To make sure they work together productively to achieve common goals, a diversity trainer provides instruction, resources, and staff development plans. Some work as staff members and others as consultants. Pay: $44,000–$88,000. Resources: The DiversiTeam Associates (www.diversiteam.com), Diversity Training University International (www.diversityuintl.com).

▲ *Forensic accountant.* Forensic accountants are behind-the-scenes investigators who scrutinize accounting records for evidence of criminal conduct. They are retained by lawyers to testify in court cases involving fraud or are hired to advise companies contemplating a declaration of bankruptcy. Pay: $35,000–$40,000 (starting salary); $100,000+ (with ten years' experience). Resource: American Institute of Certified Public Accountants (www.aicpa.org).

▲ *Financial planner.* Financial planners provide money management advice to customers in several areas, including budgeting, taxes, investments, estate and retirement planning, and insurance. Pay: $30,000 (starting salary); $200,000+ (with experience). Resource: The Institute of Certified Financial Planners (www.icfp.org).

▲ *Intellectual property lawyer.* These lawyers file the appropriate protection for patents, copyrights, and trademarks. Pay: $60,000–$80,000 (starting salary); $80,000-$100,000 (midlevel); $100,000–$120,000 (senior level). Resources: American Bar Association (www.abanet.org), American Intellectual Property Law Association (www.aipla.org).

▲ *Commercial artist.* Also known as graphic artists, their work includes designing corporate logos and developing the layout of an annual report. Pay: $33,000–$100,000. Resource: Graphic Artists Guild (www.gag.org).

▲ *Environmental aroma specialist.* These people install aroma systems designed to enhance a location's ambience. Pay: $20–$25 per hour. Resource: Olfactory Research Fund (www.olfactory. org).

▲ *Pharmacoeconomist.* Because of the rapid development of new drugs and treatments in addition to rising healthcare expenditures, HMOs and pharmaceutical companies are looking for ways to cut costs. Pharmacoeconomists measure and compare the quality versus the cost of different techniques, advising companies as to which drugs and treatments to use. Pay: $75,000–$100,000 (starting salary); $250,000+ (with experience).

▲ *Herbalist.* Herbalists provide nontraditional treatments to relieve or cure many of the ailments that plague overworked Americans in today's workforce, including high blood pressure, headaches, depression, and osteoarthritis. Pay: $30–$70 per hour. Resource: American Herbalists Guild (www.healthy.net/herbalists).

▲ *Grief counselor.* These counselors help employees to cope with losses and life transitions. Some even specialize in pet bereavement. Pay: $30,000–$50,000. Resource: Association for Death Education and Counseling (www.adec.org).

▲ *Holistic nurse.* These practitioners treat employees through acupressure, biofeedback, guided imagery, massage, nutrition counseling, relaxation, smoking cessation, weight management, and AMMA therapy, which involves manipulation of acupressure points to rebalance energy in the body. Pay: $12,000–$150,000. Resource: American Holistic Nurses' Association (www.ahna.org).

▲ *Knowledge analyst.* As part marketer and part editor for web sites, knowledge analysts create web pages designed to present information in a friendly and usable manner. They also program web sites to automate certain tasks, as well as serve information to web surfers based on their individual preferences. Pay: $45,000 (starting salary). Resource: 1to1 (www.1to1.com).

▲ *E-commerce strategist.* Businesses retain these Internet-savvy marketers to bring them into the Information Age by establishing their shops online. Using marketing and technological skills, these strategists create a new distribution channel for businesses on the web. Pay: $30,000–$40,000 (starting salary); $1 million including stock options and bonuses (senior executives). Resource: New York New Media Association (www.nynma.org).

▲ *Multimedia manager.* Multimedia managers coordinate news on the Internet, where many types of media are concentrating their resources. Such managers make sure the links take surfers to the desired destinations and, in addition, decide what audio and visual effects to create. Pay: $30,000 (starting salary); $125,000 (senior managers). Resource: New York New Media Association (www.nynma.org).

▲ *Distance learning specialist.* Instead of speaking from a training room, these instructors interact with students at online conferences via a web site, videotape, or videoconference. Pay: $30,000–$70,000. Resources: Distance Education and Training Council (www.detc.org), United States Distance Learning Association (www.usdla.org).

▲ *Cybercops.* They cruise the Internet to track down corporate crimes, such as theft of trade secrets. Pay: $20,000–$120,000 (depending on the employer, with private-sector employers paying the most). Resources: National Consortium for Justice Information and Statistics (www.corp.search.org), International Association of Computer Investigative Specialists (www.cops.org).

Appendix A: Employee Benefits Glossary

Accrual of Benefits (pension plans)—For defined benefit plans, the process of accumulating pension credits for years of credited service, expressed as an annual benefit to begin at normal retirement age. For defined contribution plans, the process of accumulating funds in the individual's pension account.

Actuarial Assumptions—Assumptions made by actuaries in estimating pension costs, e.g., investment yield, salary scale, mortality rate, and employee turnover.

Actuarial Equivalent—a benefit of equal value.

Annuity—Periodic payments made for a specific term or for life.

Annuity Certain—a form of annuity under which payments are guaranteed for a specified period.

Basic Medical Benefits—Insurance that reimburses hospital and doctor charges up to stipulated limits. Additional coverage can be provided by major medical insurance.

Business Travel Accident Insurance—Insurance limited to indemnity for an accident while traveling on company business.

Cafeteria/Flexible Benefits—Plans that permit covered employees to select benefits they want from a package of employer-provided choices, some of which may involve employee contributions.

Class-Year Plan—Savings, profit sharing, or pension plans in which each year's contributions from the employer vest separately after a specified amount of time.

Coinsurance—A plan provision specifying that the plan will pay a certain percentage of eligible expenses and the covered person will be responsible for the remaining portion.

COLA—Cost of living adjustment, periodically made to benefits payable to pensioners.

Contributory Plan—A plan under which part or all of the cost is paid by the employee and any remainder by the employer.

Conversion Privilege—The right of an individual covered by a group insurance contract to purchase individual insurance of a stated type and amount, when all or part of the group insurance is canceled, without meeting any medical requirements, provided application is made within a stipulated period (normally 31 days).

Defined-Benefit Pension Plan—A pension plan that specified the benefits to be provided on retirement. The contributions are actuarially determined in amounts necessary to provide the benefit.

Defined-Contribution Pension Plan—An individual account pension plan, in which the contributions are specified by a formula. The benefits are whatever the amount accumulated in the participant's account will buy.

Early Retirement Age Pension Plan—The age when an employee is first permitted to retire and to elect either immediate or deferred income. If payments begin immediately, they are generally paid in a reduced amount.

Effective Date—The date on which a benefit plan or insurance policy goes into effect.

ESOP (Employee Stock Ownership Plan)—A plan in which a company borrows money from a financial institution, using its stock as security or collateral for the loan. The stock is placed into an employee stock ownership trust (ESOT) for distribution at no cost to employees. The employees receive the stock upon retirement or separation from the company.

Final Average Pay (pension benefits formula)—A formula that bases benefits on the credited earnings of an employee during a selected number of years immediately preceding retirement.

Flat Benefit (pension benefits formula)—A formula that bases benefits on a fixed amount rather than a percentage of earnings.

HMO (Health Management Organization)—Prepaid group medical service organization emphasizing preventive health care. Licensed by federal or state authorities, HMO's must be offered to participants in group health plans as an alternative choice for coverage.

Indexing—An automatic adjustment of benefits in the course of payment to reflect changes in a consumer price, cost of living, or other index.

Integration (of pension plans with Social Security)—The process of combining a private pension plan with Social Security in an overall scheme of retirements benefits for employees.

Joint and Survivor Annuity—An annuity that, upon the death of the pensioner, continues to be payable, in whole or in part, to a designated survivor.

Life-Only Annuity—An annuity payable as long as the annuitant lives, with all payments (except for return of any employee contributions) ceasing at death.

Long-Term Disability—A plan providing for substantial replacement of an employee's salary in the event of total and permanent disability.

Major Medical Insurance—Protection for large surgical, hospital, or other medical expenses and services. Benefits are paid, once a specified deductible is met, and are then generally subject to coinsurance. May be provided with a basic medical plan or as a single comprehensive plan.

Money Purchase Plan—Plan that involves predetermined contributions that may be a percentage of earnings or a dollar amount. The benefits paid depend on the accumulated value of the contributions in an individual's account at the time the benefit comes due.

Noncontributory Benefit Plan—A plan in which the employer pays the entire cost.

Pension—The amount of money paid at regular intervals to an employee who has retired.

Pension Trust Fund—A fund consisting of money contributed by the employers, and in some cases the employee, to provide pension benefits.

Portability—A pension plan feature that allows participants to change employers without changing the source from which benefits are to be paid.

PPO (Preferred Provider Organization)—Hospitals, physicians, and dentists who, as groups, enter into contracts with employers to provide medical care for their employees at less than the customary charges.

Rollover—A transfer of funds from one qualified plan to another.

Savings Plan—An employer plan to systematically accumulate capital for employees through contributions from the employees that are supplemented by the employer.

Severance Pay—Normally a lump sum payable on involuntary termination of employment.

Step-Rate Pension Formula—A method of integrating private pension plan benefits with Social Security retirement benefits.

Stock Purchase Plan—A program under which employees buy shares in the company's stock.

Term Life Insurance—Insurance which has no cash or surrender values. It is pure insurance.

Variable Annuity Plan—Benefits that vary according to changes in cost of living, the investment portfolio, or some other index.

Vesting—A pension plan provision that gives participants the right to all or part of their accrued benefits after a specified period, even if employment under the plan terminates before retirement. Employee contributions are always fully vested.

Workers Compensation—Each state has its own workers compensation law, providing cash payment or medical care to cover health services for workers injured on the job and rehabilitation services. All benefits are totally employer financed.

Appendix B: Legal Issues

"Even when laws have been written down, they ought not always to remain unaltered."

—*Aristotle*

As an HR practitioner or manager, you may believe that your concern with recruiting and retaining top performers precludes employment legal issues; that is, that workplace law is for the company's attorneys to be concerned about. But as you search for the best possible employees to work for your company and struggle to create a retention environment after their hire, it is possible that your lack of familiarity with equal employment opportunity (EEO) legislation and related issues could result in a lawsuit.

While no one expects you to be as knowledgeable as an attorney, realize that the arena of workplace law is undergoing numerous changes that directly impact your role in recruitment and retention. Laws are more central to employee-related decisions, employees are more savvy then ever when it comes to their legal rights, employee lawsuits have escalated in number and scope, globalization exposes business to new laws, and technical advances, (e.g., expanded Internet use) set new legal standards and raise privacy concerns. These matters concern you additionally because personal liability is on the rise, and employers are increasingly held financially responsible for the actions or the failure to act on the part of their employees.

Here are some examples of recent, specific legal changes in the workplace. At the beginning of 2000, the Equal Employment Opportunity Commission (EEOC) issued guidelines providing undocumented workers with protection against discrimination and described expanded remedies available to them (www.eeoc.gov).

The Department of Labor (DOL) and the Department of Health and Human Services issued guidance on new protections for breast cancer patients under the Employee Retirement Income Security Act (ERISA) (www.dol.gov/dol/pwba/public/pubs/finalq&a.htm). The EEOC revised its guidelines on employer liability for harassment by supervisors (www.eeoc.gov).

Experts predict additional changes in the near future, including an increase in age and disabilities litigation, additional family and medical leave legislation, and amendments to the Fair Labor Standards Act concerning comp time. There is also legislation entitled the Teamwork for Employees and Management (TEAM) Act that may be implemented, enabling greater employee involvement, without placing employers in jeopardy of being found to have created a company-dominated union. In addition, it is likely that either Title VII of the Civil Rights Act of 1964 will be expanded or new legislation will be introduced to protect individuals at a federal level from sexual-orientation discrimination.

All of this means that employers must stay current with regard to federal, state, and local actions that affect employment policies and programs. In addition, knowing how to head off lawsuits, making the most of employment contracts, understanding compensation-related legal implications, and being familiar with employee rights and employer obligations when it comes to Internet use will better enable you to function in a legally defensible work environment.

A little bit of knowledge can go a long way, especially if it means heading off costly lawsuits or maintaining peaceful employer/employee relations—two important factors in any labor market.

FEDERAL LEGISLATION

Consider the following scenarios:

▲ You're having a hard time filling a position when in walks the perfect candidate. The only problem is that she's clearly pregnant, and you want to know if she intends to continue working after having the baby.
▲ One of your top performers informs you of his conversion to a religion that requires him to alter his current work schedule drastically.

▲ A minimally qualified applicant strikes you as the better choice over one who exceeds the requirements of the job. The former is a white male, and the latter, an Asian-American woman, has what you would describe as a "bad attitude."

▲ Two of your best employees develop a romantic relationship that ends badly. The woman in the relationship supervises the work of her former lover, who now claims he was coerced into having the relationship and believes he was the victim of sexual harassment.

▲ An otherwise qualified applicant for a hard-to-fill position requires accommodation for his physical disability.

▲ An employee who was always an outstanding performer has started slipping somewhat in her performance. Given her age, you think she might be working "past her prime" and want to suggest early retirement.

Would you know what to do in these instances? Just as important, would you know what *not* to do? You would if you were familiar with key EEO federal legislation. These are just a few of the types of situations employers confront regularly in the workplace. A wrong decision could quickly result in a costly and time-consuming lawsuit. One way of skirting legal disaster is having familiarity with workplace laws.

The following highlights of fair employment laws and categories of discrimination represent selected federal statutes, rules, and regulations. Employers are urged to obtain a copy of each of these laws, which unless otherwise noted are available from the Equal Employment Opportunity Commission (EEOC), Department of Labor, 1801 L Street, NW, Washington, D.C. 20507 (202-663-4900). In some instances, booklets outlining the key provisions of these laws, in addition to employer responsibilities and employee rights, are also available. State and local laws may differ and should also be considered.

Discrimination and Employment Rights

Civil Rights Act of 1964

This is probably the best known piece of civil rights legislation and the most widely used, in that it protects several classes of people and pertains to numerous employment situations. Title VII of this Act prohibits discrimination on the basis of race, creed, religion, sex, or national origin in all matters of employment, from recruitment through discharge. The criteria for coverage under Title VII includes any company doing business in the United States that has fifteen or more employees. Title VII does not regulate the employment practices of U.S. companies employing U.S. citizens outside the United States. Violations are monitored by the EEOC.

Violators of Title VII are generally required to "make whole." This includes providing reinstatement, if relevant, and back pay. Jury trials are not allowed.

Plaintiffs in Title VII suits generally need not prove intent; rather, they may challenge apparently neutral employment policies having a discriminatory effect.

The EEOC's 1980 Guidelines on Sexual Harassment have become an important aspect of the Civil Rights Act of 1964. Sexual harassment is defined as "unwelcome sexual advances, requests for sexual favors, or other unwanted verbal or physical conduct of a sexual nature that is made a term and condition of employment, or used as the basis for making employment decisions; or which creates a hostile, intimidating or otherwise offensive work environment."

There are two types of sexual harassment. *Quid pro quo harassment* involves rewards or threats; sex is made a condition of employment. *Hostile environment harassment* involves regular and repeated offensive conduct that interferes with an employee's ability to work. Examples of hostile environment conduct include offensive jokes, vulgar language or gestures, sexual slurs and innuendoes, suggestive comments, unwanted physical contact, leering, stalking, sexual pictures, and graffiti.

Both men and women may be victims of sexual harassment; consequently, members of both sexes may sue for violation of Title VII.

The EEOC Guidelines state that employers are absolutely liable for acts of sexual harassment if they are committed by a supervisor or manager. If the acts are committed by rank-and-file employees or nonemployees, such as customers or vendors, employers are liable only if they know or should have known about the situation and failed to take appropriate action. On the other hand, corporate officials, supervisors and managers, HR professionals, individuals who falsely claim sexual harassment, and other employees who spread unproved allegations or gossip relating to sexual harassment may face personal liability.

Executive Order 11246

Because Title VII did not immediately have the desired impact against discrimination, a series of executive orders were issued by the federal government. The best known, E.O. 11246, contains an EEO clause that requires companies doing business with the federal government to make a series of commitments. Three of the most significant mandates are as follows:

1. *Practice nondiscrimination in employment.* When a company does business with the federal government, it is on the basis of a contract; should the company discriminate in employment practices, it would effectively be violating its contract. The ramifications of this could be severe, including contract cancellation and debarment, meaning that the government would no longer do business with that company.

2. *Obey the rules and regulations of the Department of Labor.* This includes a requirement that companies allow periodic checking of their premises by DOL representatives to ensure compliance with the other two commitments listed here.

3. *Attain affirmative action goals.* This commits a company to hiring, training, and promoting a certain percentage of qualified women and minorities. The actual percentage is based on the number of women and minorities in a specific geographic location, referred to as a Standard Metropolitan Statistical Area (SMSA). Employers should contact the Office of Federal Contract Compliance Programs (OFCCP) to determine the most recent requirements for separate affirmative action plans pertaining to different establishments.

Affirmative action guidelines can be obtained by contacting the U.S. Department of Labor, OFCCP, 200 Constitution Avenue, NW, Washington, D.C. 20210 (202-219-6666). The OFCCP has also published a Compliance Manual that outlines the specific steps followed by its field staff in reviewing and monitoring affirmative action plans.

Age Discrimination in Employment Act of 1967

The federal Age Discrimination in Employment Act of 1967 (ADEA), as originally written, protected workers from ages 40 to 70. A 1978 amendment permitted jury trials, which gives claimants greater profitability. Effective January 1, 1987, Congress unanimously approved, and President Reagan signed into law, H.R. 4154, amending the ADEA by extending its protection to workers beyond the age of 70. Now, most private-sector and federal, state, and local government employees can seek redress for discrimination in matters of pay, benefits, or continued employment regardless of how old they may be. The Act also pertains to employees of employment agencies and labor organizations, as well as to U.S. citizens working outside the United States.

However, the ADEA contains an exemption for bona fide executives or high-level policy makers who may be retired as early as age 65, if they have been employed at that level for the preceding two years and meet certain criteria, including exercising discretionary powers on a regular basis; having the authority to hire, promote, and terminate employees; and having as a primary duty management of an entire organization, department, or subdivision. (Contact the EEOC for detailed guidelines.)

The general criterion for coverage under the ADEA is employment of at least twenty employees. Labor organizations employing at least twenty-five workers are required to comply. Part-time employees are included when calculating coverage.

The following guidelines should help you avoid age discrimination suits:

▲ Language in HR policies and procedures manuals, employee handbooks, orientation publications, and any other company-issued written material should be age-neutral.
▲ Employment application forms should not require applicants to provide their date of birth. (Some state laws also prohibit requiring graduation dates on application forms.)
▲ Interviewers should ask only age-neutral questions.
▲ Apply the same salary guidelines when hiring older workers as you would when hiring younger applicants. Do not try to justify a lower salary because an older worker is receiving a pension or Social Security.
▲ Do not deny older workers training or promotional or transfer opportunities.
▲ Make certain that the basis for all disciplinary action, including termination, is poor work performance, supported by comprehensive written performance appraisals and documentation or other "good cause"—not age.

The average age of an ADEA plaintiff is between fifty and fifty-nine. Now that more than a quarter of baby boomers have turned fifty, employers must be even more vigilant in avoiding age discrimination lawsuits.

Rehabilitation Act of 1973

Section 501 of this federal law prohibits discrimination against persons with disabilities by contractors doing business with the federal government when the contracts total $2,500 or more per year. In addition, government contractors who do business totaling $50,000 or more per year and have fifty or more employees must prepare an affirmative action plan to comply with the Act, although hiring goals, promotion goals, and timetables are not required under this plan. In addition, Section 504 requires employers receiving federal financial assistance to take affirmative action in hiring and promoting qualified workers with disabilities.

The Act protects "any person who (1) has a physical or mental impairment that substantially limits one or more of the person's major life activities, (2) has a record of such an impairment, or (3) is regarded as having such an impairment." Included in this definition are former drug addicts and recovering alcoholics. Current drug or alcohol users are not protected. Victims of acquired immune deficiency syndrome (AIDS) and AIDS-related conditions are also covered by this Act.

An employer's obligation extends to making a reasonable effort to accommodate the person's disability, as long as such accommodation does not create an undue hardship. Undue hardships are determined by considering such factors as the size of the organization, the type of work involved, and the nature as well as cost of such accommodation. For example, job restructuring might be required if the person with the disability can perform the essential functions of the job but requires assistance with one remaining aspect of the work, such as heavy lifting. Others aspects of job restructuring may include modification of procedures, providing readers or interpreters, or modification of equipment. Any adjustment, including alterations to facilities, that does not create an undue hardship may be required.

Many resources are available to assist in modifying facilities and equipment to accommodate workers with disabilities, such as the Job Accommodation Network, West Virginia University, 918 Chestnut Ridge Road, Suite 1, PO Box 6080, Morgantown, WV 26506-6080 (800-526-7234).

An individual's physical fitness for work must be determined by a qualified physician. Any negative findings should be phrased in specific, objective, job-related terms. The results of the examination must be shared with the applicant. If the applicant can perform the job being interviewed for, the fear that employment will aggravate an existing condition is a weak basis for denying that person employment. You are on stronger ground if the condition is degenerative. If the applicant can do the present job but probably not the next job in the promotional chain, employment may be denied if you can document that promotion is the normal pattern in that particular job family.

Americans with Disabilities Act of 1990

Going beyond government contractors, President George Bush in 1990 signed landmark legislation prohibiting all employers, including privately owned businesses and local governments, from discriminating against employees or job candidates with disabilities. Exempt are the federal government, government-owned corporations, Native American tribes, and bona fide tax-exempt private membership clubs. Religious organizations are permitted to give preference to the employment of their own members. In addition, the law requires every kind of establishment to be accessible to and usable by persons with disabilities. This legislation, entitled the Americans with Disabilities Act of 1990 (ADA), pertains to employers with fifteen or more employees and is monitored by the EEOC.

Under the ADA, the term *disability* is defined the same way as in the Rehabilitation Act of 1973—that is, as a physical or mental impairment that substantially limits an individual's major life activities. The definition also encompasses those with a history of impairment and individuals perceived as having an impairment. Examples of disabilities that are covered include impaired sight and hearing; muscular conditions such as cerebral palsy and muscular dystrophy; diseases like cancer, AIDS, diabetes, and epilepsy; cosmetic disfigurements; emotional disturbances; stuttering; smoke sensitivity; tension; and depression. In fact, there are over one thousand different impairments that are covered by this Act. Current users of illegal drugs or alcohol are not protected by the ADA. Also, people with contagious diseases or those posing a direct threat to the health or safety or others are not covered by the Act. In addition, the ADA specifically excludes homosexuals, bisexuals, transsexuals, transvestites, individuals with sexual behavior disorders, compulsive gamblers, kleptomaniacs, and pyromaniacs.

Under the ADA, employers are required to make a "reasonable accommodation" for those applicants or employees able to perform the "essential" functions of the job with reasonable proficiency. Reasonable accommodation includes job restructuring, allowing part-time or modified work schedules, making reassignments, hiring additional workers to aid employees with disabilities in the performance of their jobs, and installing new equipment or modifying existing equipment. An accommodation is considered unreasonable only in those instances where undue physical or financial hardship is placed on the employer. Such hardship is determined according to the overall size of an organization in relation to the size of its workforce, its budget, and the nature or cost of the required accommodation.

Essential functions are loosely defined as tasks that are "fundamental and not marginal," according to the Senate report on the ADA. Employers are encouraged to conduct a detailed review of each job to determine just which functions are essential. This should include an assessment of the amount of time devoted to each task.

Pregnancy Discrimination Act of 1978

The Pregnancy Discrimination Act of 1978 (PDA) recognizes pregnancy as a temporary disability and prohibits sex discrimination based on pregnancy, childbirth, or related conditions. Women must be permitted to work as long as they are capable of performing the essential functions of their current job. Likewise, pregnant applicants may not be denied equal employment opportunities if they are able to perform the essential functions of the available job. The Act prohibits mandatory pregnancy leaves of any duration unless a similar requirement is imposed on male employees with disabilities that impair their job performance. If an employer insists on establishing special rules for pregnancy, such rules must be dictated by business necessity or related to issues of health or safety. The PDA further mandates that an employer permit an employee on maternity leave to return to her job on the same basis as other employees returning after an illness or disability leave.

An important concern related to pregnancy discrimination has to do with fetal protection. Whether an employer may bar women of childbearing age from jobs that involve toxic substances, X rays, lead exposure, or the like is an issue that has been addressed by the EEOC in a series of fetal protection guidelines. The guidelines require the employer to determine first if exposure to a workplace hazard poses a substantial risk of harm to an employee's potential offspring. To accomplish this, the employer should rely on scientific evidence of the risk of fetal or reproductive harm from exposure and the minimum period of time required for exposure to cause harm. Then, the employer should assess its policy to determine whether there is a reasonable alternative that would be less discriminatory than exclusion, such as a temporary transfer to another nontoxic job or wearing a personal protection device.

Religious Discrimination Guidelines

The EEOC guidelines define religion and religious practices as "moral or ethical beliefs as to what is right and wrong which are sincerely held with the strength of traditional religious views. . . ." In 1972, Congress amended that portion of Title VII pertaining to religion in the workplace by expanding the definition to include an individual's right to "all aspect of religious observance and practice, as well as belief, unless an employer demonstrates that he is unable to reasonably accommodate an employee's or prospective employee's religious observance or practice without undue hardship on the conduct of the employer's business." This amendment placed the burden on employers to prove their inability to reasonably accommodate an individual's religious practices.

As with accommodating persons with disabilities, what would constitute an undue hardship depends on a number of factors, including prohibitive cost. Undue hardship must be provable by the employer before it can be considered a relevant factor.

In some cases, employees able to meet a job's work schedule at the time of hire can subsequently become involved with particular religious practice and, as a result, are no longer able to do so. In such instances, employers should make good-faith attempts to accommodate religious-based scheduling requests. Such accommodation might include adjusting work schedules, implementing flexible working hours, or responding to other viable employee suggestions that will integrate the employees' religious needs with the needs of the company.

Certain work assignments might also require some adjustment if an employee raises a religious objection. For example, a foreign work assignment to a country where prevailing religious practices conflict with the beliefs of an individual might be the basis for that employee's request to work at a different location. Every effort should be made to accommodate such a request.

Balancing an employee's religious beliefs with an organization's dress and grooming practices can also become an issue. When the safety of the employee or others is at stake, the employee may be required to conform to company policy in spite of any religious convictions. If, however, safety is not a factor, the employer should make a reasonable effort to accommodate religious-based attire and grooming.

It should be noted, however, that religion and work should be kept separate, meaning that employers have the right to require "quiet and unobtrusive" observance of religious practices on the part of employees.

National Origin Discrimination Guidelines

The EEOC's Guidelines on Discrimination Because of National Origin preclude denial of employment opportunity because of an individual's ancestry; place of origin; or physical, cultural, or linguistic characteristics. There are four main areas pertaining to employment:

1. Citizenship requirements may not be valid if they have the purpose or effect of discrimination on the basis of national origin.
2. Selection criteria that appear to be neutral on first glance may have an adverse impact on certain national groups.
3. Speak-English-only rules may be considered discriminatory when applied at all times.
4. Ethnic slurs may be considered national origin discrimination and must not be tolerated.

Civil Rights Act of 1991

The Civil Rights Act of 1991 went well beyond the Civil Rights Act of 1964's Title VII "make-whole" remedies of back pay and reinstatement. Under the 1991 Act:

▲ Coverage has been extended to U.S. citizens employed at a U.S. company's foreign site.
▲ The burden of proof is placed on employers to show lack of discrimination.
▲ Jury trials are permitted.
▲ Awards of compensatory and punitive damages are permitted in cases of intentional discrimination.
▲ Victims of intentional sex discrimination are permitted to seek compensatory and punitive damages up to $300,000.
▲ Victims of race discrimination are permitted to seek unlimited damages. (This has prompted some companies to require nonunion employees to submit discrimination claims

to binding arbitration. Companies can also request that job applicants give up the right to sue as a condition of employment.)

▲ A "glass ceiling" commission has been established to develop policies for the removal of barriers to women and minorities seeking advancement.

▲ "Race norming," or the practice of adjusting test scores by race, is banned.

Overall, then, the Civil Rights Act of 1991 seems to favor employees over employers.

Pay and Benefits

Fair Labor Standards Act

The Fair Labor Standards Act (FLSA) of 1938 establishes the minimum wage, maximum hours, and overtime pay provisions that employers must provide for covered employees. An employee may be exempt or nonexempt. Individuals who are exempt from the provisions of the FLSA include workers in bona fide executive, administrative, professional, and outside sales positions. All others are referred to as nonexempt: They are the employees covered by the FLSA's minimum wage and maximum hour provisions.

The FLSA requires employers to pay nonexempt employees no less than the prevailing minimum hourly wage. In addition, any nonexempt employee required to work in excess of forty hours per week must be compensated at a rate of not less than one-and-one-half times the worker's regular rate. In the public sector, the FLSA permits employers to provide compensatory time off instead of overtime compensation. Like overtime pay, however, compensatory time off must be provided at a rate of not less than one-and-half hours for each hour worked over forty hours weekly.

The actual work performed by employees, not their job titles, determines exemption status. With most positions, there is no question as to the exemption status. However, some jobs fall into a gray area and are not as easily categorized. To assist with exemption classification, the Department of Labor offers a series of requirements that must be met before classifying someone as exempt. These requirements appear in both a short and long test that help evaluate the four employee classifications recognized by the FLSA: executive, administrative, professional, and outside salespersons. Since the tests include minimum salary requirements that are not frequently updated, such requirements should not be relied upon for determining exemption status. A more reliable gauge is the specific duties performed coupled with the job responsibility. The degree of independent judgment required and the extent of managerial authority are also key criteria.

A copy of the Department of Labor's guidelines can be obtained by writing to the Employment Standards Administration, Wage and Hour Division, 200 Constitution Avenue, NW, Washington, D.C. 20210.

Employers who violate the FLSA are liable for the amount of unpaid minimum wages, unpaid overtime compensation, interest, and reasonable attorney's fees, and may be liable, at the court's discretion, for an additional amount as liquidated damages for willful violation of the Act. Willful violation of the FLSA may also subject employers to criminal penalties.

The FLSA was amended by the Equal Pay Act of 1963. This amendment protects against wage and salary discrimination on the basis of sex.

Employee Retirement Income Security Act of 1974

The Employee Retirement Income Security Act of 1974 (ERISA) governs employer-sponsored pension and welfare benefits plans. ERISA applies to all employers engaged in commerce, with the exception of churches and federal, state, and local governments. ERISA establishes participation and vesting provisions for pension plans, imposes minimum funding standards for certain pension plans, and imposes fiduciary standards of conduct, reporting requirements, and disclosure requirements on employers as well as plan administrators. In addition, ERISA's preemption clause overrides conflicting state laws that relate to employee benefits plans.

Among other stipulations, ERISA's reporting and disclosure provisions require plan administrators to provide employees with summaries of their benefits plans within ninety days of participation; updates of the plan summary every five years if there have been any changes; statements of participants' deferred vested benefits at the time of job termination, retirement, or upon specific request for a statement; and statements of participants' total accrued benefits, including the percentage vested, when they leave the job, retire, take a one-year break from service, or request a statement.

The Internal Revenue Service is responsible for enforcing the vesting, participation, and funding requirements under ERISA. The

Department of Labor is responsible for enforcing the fiduciary requirements.

Health Insurance Portability and Accountability Act

The Health Insurance Portability and Accountability Act (HIPAA) offers improved protections for employees, primarily in the areas of portability and continuity of health insurance coverage, by imposing new requirements on employers and insurers. The law amends ERISA, the Public Health Service Act, and the Internal Revenue Code in that it limits exclusions for preexisting medical conditions, provides for rights that allow individuals who lose coverage or have a new dependent to enroll immediately in health coverage plans, guarantees availability of health insurance coverage for small employers, and guarantees renewability of health insurance coverage in both small and large group markets.

Equal Pay Act of 1963

The Equal Pay Act of 1963 (EPA) requires equal pay for men and women performing substantially equal work. The work must be of comparable skill, effort, and responsibility, performed under similar working conditions. Coverage applies to all aspects of the employment process including starting salaries, annual increases, and promotions. This law protects women only. Others who feel they are being discriminated against in matters of pay may claim a violation under the provisions of Title VII. The criterion for coverage under the Equal Pay Act is at least two employees.

Unequal pay for equal work may be permitted in certain instances, however, as when wage differences are based on superior educational credentials or extensive prior experience. However, this pay difference should diminish, and ultimately disappear, after a number of years on the job.

An important issue related to equal pay is comparable worth. Several states have implemented programs for comparable worth pay, whereby employers are required to compare completely different job categories. Those held predominately by women (e.g., nursing and secretarial) must be compared with those occupied predominately by men (e.g., truck driving and warehouse work). Point systems determine the level of skill involved in the job, as well as the economic value of each position. If the female-dominated jobs are deemed comparable, pay adjustments are required to reduce the difference in wages.

The important distinction between comparable worth and equal pay is that in order to claim violation of the EPA, identical job classifications must be compared. Therefore, if a woman accountant believes that she is not receiving a rate of pay equal to that of her male counterpart—a male accountant performing substantially equal work—she may have sufficient cause to claim violation of the EPA. On the other hand, comparable worth compares different job categories. For example, if a female clerk-typist believes that her work is of comparable worth to that of a male custodian working for the same employer, she might sue on the basis of sex discrimination. Since there is currently no federal law that deals specifically with comparable worth, she would sue for violation of Title VII.

Companies are urged to voluntarily assess their hiring practices and work toward minimizing designated female or male categories.

Family Medical and Leave Act of 1993

The Family Medical and Leave Act of 1993 (FMLA) provides eligible employees with up to a total of twelve weeks' leave during any twelve-month period for the birth of a child or placement of a child for adoption or foster care, or when an employee has a serious health condition or is caring for a spouse, child, or parent with a serious health condition. To qualify, employees must have worked for at least twelve months and not fewer than 1,250 hours in the past year, and they must give thirty days' notice of the leave, when practical. Employers can require a doctor's certification to substantiate the employee's request to tend to family medical problems (these forms are available from the Department of Labor). Employees can also be required to use up all of their accrued vacation, personal, or sick leave before taking unpaid family leave. Employers can deny leave to salaried employees within the highest-paid 10 percent of the workforce, if such leave would create undue hardship for the company. Upon returning to work, employees are entitled to the same job or one that is equal in status and pay, as well as continued health and other benefits.

The FMLA covers private businesses with fifty or more employees, state and federal employees, public agencies, and private elementary and secondary schools. The Act may not interfere with collective bargaining agreements, more generous company policies, or less restrictive state or local laws.

The Department of Labor offers a Fact Sheet on Family and

Medical Leave Act and a Compliance Guide to Family and Medical Leave Act (www.dol.gov).

THE IMPACT OF WORKPLACE LEGISLATION ON RECRUITMENT AND RETENTION

In looking for new hires or when making decisions concerning employees, make certain that you are not denying anyone equal employment opportunity, either inadvertently, out of some well-meaning yet misguided sense of what is best for the company, or because of personal bias. Returning to the scenarios presented early in this Appendix, let's look at the relevant legislation and what you should and should not do in each instance:

▲ You're having a hard time filling a position when in walks the perfect candidate. The only problem is that she's clearly pregnant, and you want to know if she intends to continue working after having the baby.

Relevant legislation: Pregnancy Discrimination Act of 1978

What not to do (not an inclusive list): Don't ask when the baby is due. Don't ask if she plans on working after the baby is born. Don't ask if she has made any childcare arrangements in the event that she does plan to return to work. Don't ask if she is experiencing a "normal" pregnancy. Don't discuss her family, e.g., other children or her husband. Don't have her sign a statement committing to continued work after the baby is born.

What to do (not an inclusive list): Treat her as you would any other applicant. Remember that while you are not obliged to hire her because she is pregnant, the law precludes you from rejecting her for the same reason. Consider her skills and what she will bring to the job as compared with other qualified candidates (if there are any).

▲ One of your top performers informs you of his conversion to a religion that requires him to alter his current work schedule drastically.

Relevant legislation: Congress's 1972 amendment of that portion of Title VII of the Civil Rights Act of 1964 pertaining to religion in the workplace

What not to do: Don't ask him the name or nature of his new-found religion. Don't ask for proof that the religion is "legitimate." Don't try to talk him out of converting. Don't threaten him with dismissal if he does not adhere to his current work schedule. Don't give him time to reconsider his decision. Don't ask other employees to talk with him about his decision. Don't tell him he has to choose between work and religion.

What to do: Try to make a reasonable accommodation for his religion. This may include offering alternative work arrangements, such as telecommuting, flextime, a compressed workweek, or reduced hours in the form of a part-time job or job sharing. (See Chapter 10 for detailed information concerning alternative work arrangements.)

▲ A minimally qualified applicant strikes you as the better choice over one who exceeds the requirements of the job. The former is a white male, and the latter, an Asian-American woman, has what you would describe as a "bad attitude."

Relevant legislation: Title VII of the Civil Rights Act of 1964 and the EEOC's Guidelines on Discrimination Because of National Origin

What not to do: Don't hire the Asian-American woman hoping her attitude will improve once on the job. Don't reject the preferred candidate because he is a white male.

What to do: As an employer, you have the right to select whoever is deemed best qualified to perform the duties and responsibilities of a given job. You are not required to select the *most* qualified person; rather, you are required to select someone meeting the minimum requirements of the job. While you should never hire anyone failing to meet job-related tangible or intangible criteria, it is always a good idea to review your organization's affirmative action goals and work environment in terms of diversity before making any hiring decisions.

▲ Two of your best employees develop a romantic relationship that ends badly. The woman in the relationship supervises the work of her former lover, who now claims he was coerced into having the relationship and believes he was the victim of sexual harassment.

Relevant legislation: The EEOC's 1980 Guidelines on Sexual Harassment

What not to do: Don't assume sexual harassment can be experienced only by women. Don't laugh at the employee's claims. Don't try to convince the employee to drop his charge of sexual harassment.

What to do: Conduct a thorough investigation. Your findings may result in transfer or termination of the supervisor, transfer of the employee, or no change in the job status of either person.

▲ An otherwise qualified applicant for a hard-to-fill position requires accommodation for his physical disability.

Relevant legislation: The Americans with Disabilities Act of 1990

What not to do: Don't ask questions about his disability. Don't make assumptions about what he can and cannot do because of his disability. Don't decide for him what accommodations will enable him to perform the job.

What to do: Ask (generally on the application form), "Can you perform the tasks required to carry out the job for which you have applied with or without accommodation?" Make a "reasonable accommodation" if he is able to perform the "essential" functions of the job with reasonable proficiency. This may include job restructuring, allowing a modified work schedule, or modifying existing equipment.

▲ An employee who was always an outstanding performer has started slipping somewhat in her performance. Given her age, you think she might be working "past her prime" and want to suggest early retirement.

Relevant legislation: The Age Discrimination in Employment Act of 1967

What not to do: Don't tell her she did a better job when she was younger. Don't tell her you think her performance started to deteriorate when she turned sixty-five (or whatever her age is). Don't leave articles on her desk about how taking ginkgo biloba might improve short-term memory and offset early Alzheimer's disease. Don't point out how her younger colleagues produce more work in a shorter period of time. Don't threaten her with early retirement if her work doesn't return to her previous level of performance.

What to do: Determine if there are issues within or outside the workplace that are impacting her work (this might best be handled through an Employee Assistance Program). Discuss her interests and aspirations as they pertain to work. Discuss alternative work assignments or mentoring.

Make certain, too, that your requirements are job-related and not arbitrarily set. With regard to education, this means ensuring that there is valid, objective documentation for job criteria. If high school is required, it must be relevant to the job. The same holds true for college degrees. However, since degrees are usually required for higher-level positions with fewer tangible requirements, the guidelines are also less tangible. For example, degree requirements are permitted when the consequences of employing an unqualified person are grave, especially when public health or safety is involved. Positions demanding a great deal of judgment often have degree requirements, as well as those demanding knowledge of technical or professional subject matter.

Finally, check your employment practices for possible systemic discrimination.

While requiring a college degree for a higher-level position is relatively safe, the burden of proof may still be on employers to show job-relatedness. The less tangible the reason is, the more difficult this can be. It is often wiser to state "degree preferred" or "degree highly desirable." Even better, spell out exactly what knowledge and skill level you are seeking. That way, applicants who have additional years of experience or have attended college without receiving a degree are not locked out of consideration. You are helping yourself as well as such candidates by broadening the field of choice.

Be careful about changing educational requirements. If you have an opening with specific requirements and find someone for the job who does not quite meet them, do not lower the requirements or hire the applicant. You are leaving yourself wide open to discrimination charges by other applicants. Also, if the opening has a set of educational requirements and an applicant meets them, but in retrospect the requirements are not deemed stringent enough, you are asking for trouble. If you want to change them once set, reevaluate the entire job in relation to the specific duties. Only then can you properly determine whether the educational requirements warrant adjustment.

As with education, requirements for previous work experience should be job-related. The standards should never be arbitrary, artificial, or unnecessary. The more complex the job, the more reasonable it is to have experience requirements. However, if you have not required specific experience in the past and the job has not changed substantially in its level of responsibility or specific duties, do not start now. The new requirements can have a greater negative impact on women and minorities than on white males. The greater this disparity between past and current job requirements, the greater the burden will be on you to prove the necessity for such requirements.

Be careful, too, about asking for specific years of experience. It is difficult to prove that four years of experience is not adequate but that five years is. It is also difficult to justify preference for someone with a little more experience as opposed to just enough. As with degrees, then, it is best to say that five years' experience is preferred—not required. Remember, not only is it unwise from an EEO standpoint to ask for a specific number of years' experience, you may also preclude yourself from hiring the best candidate when measured by other criteria.

Finally, be aware of your organization's affirmative action goals, and take them into consideration when weighing the qualifications of women and minorities as compared with white males. Full compliance with affirmative action goals is your objective, and every effort should be made to achieve this end whenever you have an opening.

If, after considering all of these factors and assessing both the tangible as well as intangible qualifications of the candidates, you determine that the most suitable person for the job is someone who happens to be a white male, go ahead and make that person a job offer. However, if the credentials of two candidates—one a white male and the other a minority member or a woman—are essentially the same, and your affirmative action goals have not been adequately met, you are urged to hire the minority member or the woman.

LITIGATION PREVENTION

Both the number of employment lawsuits and the monetary awards being won by employees are escalating. The median employment-related damages award that employees walk away with is approximately $205,000, with a median punitive damages award of about $200,000. Cases that settle before trial can be expensive too: While some 58 percent settle for less than $50,000, roughly 37 percent settle for between $50,000 and $500,000, and about 5 percent settle for more than $500,000. Typically, it costs more than $100,000 just to go to court to defend yourself against charges of workplace discrimination. Even if you "win," you are not likely to recover any of that money. Also, there is lost time, productivity, employee morale, and customer perception to consider. While the federal sentencing guidelines "reward" employers that make a reasonable attempt to comply with the law by reducing fines or sentences, your overriding goal should be to prevent lawsuits, not win them.

Alternate Dispute Resolution

Some organizations try to reduce legal risks by purchasing employment practices liability insurance (EPLI), but that isn't going to prevent problems from occurring in the first place. Alternate dispute resolution (ADR) is one strategy that many HR managers are adopting instead to settle employment disputes before they become lawsuits.

ADR prevents employment disputes from reaching the court system. Policies generally depend on either internal or external mediation or arbitration. Mediation involves an expert hired to assist the parties in settlement; arbitration involves a decision maker who is appointed to make a binding decision. Costs for arbitration and external mediation procedures are around $3,000, including administrative fees of another $1,500 or so, plus negotiated hourly fees. ADR policies can be either voluntary or mandatory, although the latter is generally frowned upon. Mandatory arbitration ADR policies—that is, when policies are made a condition of employment—are opposed by the American Bar Association and prohibited by the National Association of Securities Dealers. Some employers avoid using a mediator altogether and designate a peer review panel coupled with an internal complaint resolution process. Generally, complaints are heard and decided within six weeks. An employee dissatisfied with the decision can later file a formal complaint with the EEOC. The EEOC, however, may be less inclined to pursue a complaint that has already been resolved by ADR. Still other companies establish a "company court" with a designated person rendering a decision, usually within two weeks of the hearing.

There are many advantages to ADR. Besides the financial savings, the process allows employers to focus on trouble spots in the company without publicity. In addition, it sends a message of fair dealing and trustworthiness to employees. Employees also appreciate not having to wait months or years for resolution.

On the other hand, the advantages of ADR policies can have one significant unintended consequence. An effective ADR program may actually encourage employees to bring complaints that might otherwise not have been brought. This results in an increase in the number of employment-related disputes and costs associated with maintaining the program. ADR opponents also argue that the primary reason for the program is to deprive injured workers of their right to a jury trial and to override expanded remedies provided by the courts.

Successful ADR programs incorporate the following principles:

1. The ADR process should be carefully explained to prospective employees during the application and interview process.
2. The employee handbook should clearly describe ADR, including its purpose and uses.
3. Employers should make certain their ADR agreements are enforceable under state arbitration statutes and modeled after the Union Arbitration Act.
4. The process should be well publicized at the outset and receive senior management's support.
5. All complaints should be treated confidentially, with concessions and admissions leading to settlement without outsiders becoming aware of the details.

Employers are advised to consult with an attorney specializing in labor and employment law before establishing an ADR program.

Guidelines for Reducing the Risks of Litigation

Reducing potential liability is the responsibility of all employees in an organization. While there is no absolute way of preventing applicants or employees from bringing a lawsuit against your company, there are cost-saving guidelines that will help minimize the chances:

▲ *State your company's commitment to equal employment.* A standard statement informing applicants and employees of your EEO policy lets everyone know that you do not tolerate discrimination on the basis of race, creed, religion, sex, national origin, age, disability, veteran status, or status in any other group protected by federal, state, or local law.

▲ *Make certain your hiring criteria are objective, uniformly applied, and consistent in effect.* By applying job criteria across-the-board that do not have a greater negative impact on any one group, you are demonstrating fair employment practices.

▲ *Show job-relatedness.* Every criterion you set, each question you ask, and every decision you make should be job-related.

▲ *Require applicants to attest to truthfulness on the employment application.* For example, have them sign a statement that says: "I certify that the information contained in this application is true and complete to the best of my knowledge. I understand that any misrepresentation or omission of fact in this application will be cause for refusal of employment if employed termination from [organization]." This type of statement enables you to freely terminate someone you discover has lied on the application.

▲ *If you conduct physical examinations or drug tests, have applicants sign a statement.* The statement could read: "I understand that any offer of employment with [organization] is contingent upon my passing a required physical examination. I further acknowledge that it is the policy of [organization] that all applicants submit to a drug test. I understand that the purpose of this drug test is to determine or rule out the presence of nonprescribed or prohibited controlled substances."

▲ *Focus on making sound hiring decisions that properly match an applicant's skills, knowledge, and interests with a job's duties and responsibilities.* This should lead to fewer terminations and ultimately fewer legal claims, since firing is the act that triggers many lawsuits.

▲ *Conduct employment reference checks.* While this is not always easy or even possible to do, making the effort may reveal important information that can influence your decision to extend a job offer. Obtain permission to conduct reference checks from applicants in the form of a statement similar to the following: "I authorize and request that my current and all former employers and those people I have listed as references furnish [organization] with information about my employment record, including a statement of the reason for the termination of my employment, work performance abilities, and other qualities pertinent to my qualifications for employment; hereby releasing them and [organization] from all liability and responsibility arising from any information provided."

▲ *Develop an employment-at-will disclaimer.* Employers seeking to preserve the right to fire at will should include a disclaimer on their application form and in their employee handbook. Here's a sample: "I agree to comply with the policies, rules, regulations, and procedures of [organization]. I understand that I do not have a Contract of Employment with [organization], that my employment will be at will and is not for a definite duration, and that my employment can be terminated, with or without cause or notice, at any time, at the option of either [organization] or myself."

▲ *Think like a juror.* To avoid actions that generate lawsuits, think about how a juror would interpret your actions. For example: Did the employee know what the employer expected of her? Did the employer follow policies and procedures known to the employee? Did the employer treat all employees consistently, reasonably, and fairly?

▲ *Treat all employees equally.* Most lawsuits alleging any form of discrimination are based on failure to treat employees equally. This includes overt discrimination and other, more subtle forms, such as stereotyping, patronizing, and favoritism. Note that while "equal treatment" does not mean "same treatment," it does mean ensuring that each employee has the same opportunity for consideration as every other.

▲ *Respect an employee's legal rights.* These include civil rights, the right to a safe workplace, the right to refuse to perform illegal acts without fear of retaliation, the right not to be defamed, the right to nonharassing treatment, the right to participate in certain union activities, the right to compensation according to the Fair Labor Standards Act, and the right to certain benefits under the Employee Retirement Income Security Act (ERISA). Some employees may have additional rights as a result of written or implied contracts, e.g., based on the language in employee handbooks.

▲ *Honestly appraise employees.* Negative performance appraisals are difficult to write, but they can save you a lot of trouble later on. It's hard to justify termination on the basis of poor performance with a file filled with glowing reviews (and don't even think about back documentation). If an employee exhibits performance problems, then identify the problems, document them, and together set goals for improvement. If, ultimately, you end up terminating the employee, an unjust termination lawsuit will be difficult to sustain if the reasons for firing are sufficiently documented.

▲ *Take allegations seriously and act promptly.* Whether allegations are of sexual harassment or other forms of misconduct or illegal acts, responding quickly and appropriately will often diffuse a situation and preclude a lawsuit.

Responding to a Lawsuit

In spite of your best efforts and intentions, you may find yourself involved in an employment-related lawsuit. While many such lawsuits are frivolous, they still require a response to the allegations. According to the Society for Human Resource Management (SHRM) *White Paper*, there are immediate steps employers should take upon being sued:

1. *Review the charge for procedural flaws.* When plaintiffs fail to follow procedures properly, the charges are often dismissed.
2. *Ensure that the complainant's HR file is kept intact.* All records relating to the lawsuit should be kept until the complaint is resolved.
3. *Guard against retaliatory action.* Employees are protected by law against retaliation when filing discrimination lawsuits.
4. *Conduct your own investigation.* Go on a fact-finding mission to ferret out all relevant facts.
5. *Conduct an honest appraisal of the facts.* You may then decide to settle rather than attempt to defend yourself against the charge.
6. *Prepare an official response.* This "statement of position" is used by the EEOC to evaluate the employee's claim. However, be aware that it may also be used against the employer later on.
7. *Prepare for a mediation conference.* New EEOC procedures encourage use of an investigator to mediate a settlement between the parties, wherever possible.
8. *Anticipate an EEOC on-site investigation.* The EEOC often conducts an on-site fact-finding investigation, including witness interviews.
9. *Anticipate settlement negotiations.* If no settlement has been reached by the time of the EEOC investigation, the EEOC investigator will probably initiate negotiations.
10. *Identify relevant policies and procedures.* Determine which policies and procedures are both the source of the charge and the ones that will help in your defense.
11. *Identify relevant training.* Assuming a discriminatory act did occur, determine what training will ensure that it does not continue and is not repeated.

EMPLOYMENT CONTRACTS

Chapter 1 discussed the growing concern over how workplace loyalty is becoming increasingly scarce. As loyalty between employers and employees continues to erode, employment contracts grow in popularity. Once reserved for executives, these agreements are increasingly available to middle managers as well. HR practitioners and managers need to understand the scope and impact of these contracts so they can be maximally effective in their recruitment and retention efforts.

What Employment Contracts Cover

By definition, employment contracts are documents that express an agreement between employers and employees regarding such matters as compensation, bonuses, vacations, medical leave, stock options, and termination. These contracts can also include confidentiality agreements, noncompete clauses, and nonsolicitation agreements, although each of these additions can stand alone as a separate contract.

Confidentiality agreements typically preclude employees from disclosing to outsiders company proprietary information or trade secrets during or after their employment. The term *confidential* generally applies to any business or technical information possessed by the company that is not known to the public and that gives the company an advantage over its competitors. Often there's a provision in the agreement that once the information becomes public through legitimate means, then the obligation to maintain confidentiality is gone. Confidentiality agreements are commonplace in the information technology field or other fields in which employees deal with sensitive financial information or trade-secret type information, such as patents, formulas, or technology codes. These agreements can also protect customer lists and inventions or other tangible improvements made to the company's current or planned lines of business.

Noncompete clauses—also called restrictive covenants— typically prevent former employees from competing with their prior employer for a limited period of time, in a limited geographic area. Not all states allow noncompete agreements. For example, California refuses to enforce noncompetes unless they are entered into as part of the sale of a business. In states where they are permitted, noncompete clauses are enforceable if reasonable in terms of time and distance, and designed to protect a legitimate business interest. Such claims are generally limited to a year or two and restricted in geographic scope to the area in which the company is actually doing business.

Noncompete clauses can include one or two nonsolicitation

agreements: (1) a nonsolicitation-of-customers agreement, meaning that for a limited period of time after employees leave, they won't solicit the former employer's customers or prospective customers; and (2) a nonsolicitation-of-employees clause, which means that for a limited period of time after employees leave the company, they won't attempt to hire away former colleagues.

An effective employment contract describes the employee's position, specifies the duration of the contract, and identifies agreed-upon compensation and benefits. Reference to compensation typically includes when the employee is eligible for a raise or bonus. If it's a long-term contract, there may be built-in increase levels at certain points. If you put in a timeline for bonuses or raises, you should also include criteria for those increases. Termination stipulations are also commonly outlined—that is, whether termination can be by either party at will, or whether the employee can't be fired for whatever period of time the agreement covers unless he or she has provided cause, such as theft.

Benefits of Employment Contracts

Employment contracts can be beneficial to both employers and employees. Employees feel more secure about matters like equity ownership, benefits, and salary; employers know they have set boundaries for compensation and other matters. In addition, contracts can protect a business against false claims of wrongful termination.

Another way that employment contracts benefit both employers and employees is that businesses can encourage top-level employees to stay with the company for a certain period of time by offering deferred cash or retirement benefits. An employment contract can spell out what is required for the employee to realize the deferred cash or benefits, as well as ensure that the deferred payment does not inadvertently become subject to ERISA regulations. Compensation plans for a select group of management or highly compensated employees, known as "top hat" compensation plans, are exempt from many ERISA requirements. Unlike rank-and-file workers, top hat employees are exempted because the law assumes that these select employees, by virtue of their special status, have sufficient influence over plan design not to require the protection of ERISA regulations. For example, a top hat benefit could provide monthly payments to a senior vice president upon retirement, provided that this executive remains with the company until the age of 65. If employment ends before that time, the employee forfeits the payments. Businesses have discretion in determining which of its senior executives are to be given these benefits and the amount that they will be paid, although both the Internal Revenue Service and the Department of Labor require that top hat employees earn a certain minimum salary per year.

Considering an Applicant with an Employment Contract

If you are considering hiring an applicant who is currently working or has worked in your industry, determining whether that person previously signed an employment contract can lessen the chances that you will become part of a lawsuit or can make such a lawsuit more defensible in court. These lawsuits are usually disputes over corporate raiding—attempts to target key employees. The company that's losing a valuable worker may claim that the hiring company is misappropriating its trade secrets, justifying a temporary restraining order or preliminary injunction. The outcome is likely to depend on factors such as the departing employee's knowledge of confidential, proprietary information; the safeguards the prior employer has taken to protect its confidential information; the caution exercised by the hiring company to avoid misusing trade secrets held by the new employee; and the evidence, if any, that the new employer acted with harmful intent.

Here are a few suggestions that can help preclude employment contract–related headaches:

1. Ask if the person signed a noncompete or confidentiality agreement at any time during employment. If the answer is yes, ask to see a copy of the agreement, and have an employment attorney review it to determine exactly what the employee may do under the agreement.

2. Discuss the kinds of confidential information to which the applicant was exposed. Make clear to the candidate that you do not want this information used at your company in the person's new position. Instruct the candidate not to bring any documents from the former company. If prohibited by the employment agreement, advise the applicant to refrain from soliciting the former employer's clients to defect to your company.

3. Do not sign an employment contract with the applicant until after employment with the prior company has terminated.

4. If a customer of the other company does business with your organization after the new employee starts work, it's a good idea to have the customer sign a statement that the employee did not solicit the company's business.

COMPENSATION-RELATED LEGAL IMPLICATIONS

Consider this scenario: Thirteen months ago, you hired a highly qualified vice president of operations. You developed a mutually agreed-upon, formula-based bonus plan, the bonus to be awarded at the end of his first year, citing last year's earnings as an example of what he could hope to receive. Unfortunately, earnings at the time his bonus was calculated were at an all-time low. Disheartened, he tendered his resignation and brought legal action against the company, claiming to have been misled into believing he would earn a good deal more money. He said he would rescind his resignation and drop the lawsuit if the company gave him the bonus he thought he should have earned. Otherwise, he would take legal action and demand a comprehensive severance package. While you hated to lose such a valuable employee, you also resented the position he was forcing you into.

Did the employee have a legitimate claim against the company? Would you have given him an additional bonus if it kept him from leaving? What were the company's obligations with regard to severance pay?

Incentive Compensation

There are three types of incentive compensation plans: (1) discretionary, (2) fixed figure, and (3) formula-based. With a discretionary plan, employers decide how much of a bonus they want to give an employee. Employees work, not knowing exactly how much to expect. If the company seems to be doing well, they're likely to assume a big bonus is coming their way. Unfortunately, the result is often disappointing, sometimes leading to lawsuits, as employees realize what they hoped to see in their paychecks isn't what they actually got. Such cases are usually tried as breach-of-contract or broken-agreement cases, even when there is no written agreement: Expressed and implied agreements are often binding. For this reason, experts generally discourage discretionary plans.

In fixed figure plans, a person knows exactly how much of a

bonus he or she is to receive. For example, at the time of hire the employer says, "Your salary will be $65,000. You will also be entitled to receive a bonus of between $15,000 and $20,000 at the end of your first year." These plans tend to yield the smallest number of lawsuits. Occasionally, there are disputes over specific language, such as what "the end of your first year" actually means.

Formula-based plans are sometimes tied to the person's performance; other times they tie in with the value of the company's stock. When based on simple mathematical calculations, this type of plan is generally straightforward and fair. For example, the employer may say to the employee, "For every dollar rise in the stock price, you will receive a $1,000 bonus. The bonus will be based on the stock price on December 31." The only time formula-based plans may yield lawsuits is when there are miscalculations or miscommunications concerning the formula. Of course, there is a risk involved with this type of bonus plan: Depending on the basis for the formula, e.g., company stock value, employees could earn a tremendous sum of money or very little. For this reason, experts recommend setting minimums and maximums. Better yet, tie bonuses in with performance.

"Creative" Compensation

With employees working longer hours in increasingly nontraditional ways, there's greater probability of lawsuits. Consider, for example, what appears to have happened at Taco Bell in 1998 (the case was settled so there is no court case to cite). *Newsweek* reported that the fast-food restaurant failed to pay its employees properly by not paying them for overtime. Allegedly, managers coaxed workers into cleaning up the store on days off in exchange for free pizza parties, rather than money. This is illegal, since the FLSA says you've got to pay nonexempt employees their regular wages for the first forty hours of work, and time-and-a-half when they work more than forty hours. Another company tried to pay its workers with beer instead of money, reasoning that the beer had a value equivalent to their hourly wages. The law is very clear in this regard: Employers are not permitted to barter.

Even if employees work over forty hours voluntarily, without any expectation of additional pay, you must pay them.

Even when workers perform some of their duties off-site, as is the case with a growing number of telecommuters, they must be compensated for all hours worked. If they are nonexempt and entitled to overtime pay, then it doesn't matter where that overtime work is performed.

To protect yourself against lawsuits, communicate in writing to nonexempt employees that they are not permitted to work beyond their regularly scheduled forty-hour workweek unless advance approval is obtained from their manager. Many experts recommend that a statement to this effect be included in the handbook given to employees at the time of hire.

Severance Pay

By definition, severance pay is compensation that an employer gives to an employee in a "not for cause" termination, e.g., a layoff or downsizing. It is not generally paid to employees who leave employment voluntarily, except by mutual agreement in an employment contract.

While severance pay is not required by law, about twenty states require that employers pay severance if that has been their practice or if they have agreed to do so orally or in a written policy, such as an employee handbook. Therefore, the decision whether to pay severance in the first place is voluntary, but having made a policy of severance, you may be mandated to continue.

Many employers provide severance pay to terminated workers unless they are being fired for cause. A recent survey revealed that 90 percent of employers with one thousand or more employees and almost half of employers with one hundred or more workers have some sort of severance payment plan. These employers pay severance to gain a reputation for maintaining a fair and generous workplace, to attract good workers, as part of employment contracts, or simply in the spirit of good employment practices.

Severance pay is generally calculated on the number of years of service. Typically, this translates into paying one to two weeks for every year the employee has been with the company. Some employers also continue health insurance for as long as the severance pay continues. Most require departing employees to sign a release stating that in order to receive the payment, they must promise not to sue the employer for wrongful discharge or discrimination.

This practice dates back to the 1980s when early retirement, layoff, and downsizing incentives became common. Such practice involved an enhanced severance package paid to employees in exchange for signing waivers promising not to sue for employment discrimination. Employers were generally worried about age discrimination lawsuits under the Age Discrimination in Employment

Act, since older workers were usually involved in these early retirement and downsizing programs. This practice of severance incentives continues today. However, a 1998 U.S. Supreme Court
decision determined that an employee was not obliged to return
incentive severance pay in order to sue for age discrimination.
This, the Court held, was in violation of the Older Workers Benefit
Protection Act (OWBPA) of 1990. Since that decision, federal
courts have applied the high court ruling to other categories of discrimination suits, such as that of a woman who was out of work on
disability only to be fired the day she returned. She was given a
severance incentive and signed a release of all claims, but neverthe-
less she then sued under the Family Medical and Leave Act, claiming that she hadn't had enough time to consider the offer. The
employer insisted that her failure to return the severance payment
precluded the lawsuit. However, the Supreme Court ruled that she
wasn't required to return the severance incentive because she
hadn't had enough time to review the offer.

Experts recommend that employers draft all of their severance
agreements to comply with the requirements of OWBPA. This includes putting the severance agreements in writing and using simple and clear language without misleading information. Every
claim that the employees are expected to waive should be specified, and employees should be encouraged to consult with an attorney before signing. In addition, they should be given twenty-one
days to decide whether to sign the waiver. If the severance is connected to a termination program offered to a group of employees,
that time period should be forty-five days. Finally, employees
should be given seven days after the waiver is signed during which
they can revoke the decision.

Under certain circumstances, even informal severance practices may be considered employee welfare benefits plans under
ERISA. This is often the case where employers have followed a
consistent practice in applying eligibility criteria in addition to a
specific benefits formula in awarding severance pay. Also, if the
severance plan requires administrative involvement for a benefits
payout over time, ERISA will probably be involved. A onetime
lump sum payment is generally not considered an ERISA plan, because it requires no procedures for receiving ongoing benefits.

If a plan is found to be ERISA-governed, then the severance
plan must be in writing. It must describe how payments will be
made, provide for one or more named fiduciaries to manage and
control the plan, provide a funding policy, provide a procedure for
amending the plan, and provide for participants to be given sum-

mary plan descriptions. In addition, there must be a claim procedure, and the administrator must file a Form 5500 with the Department of Labor.

EMPLOYER INTERVENTION IN EMPLOYEE LIVES

Cyberspace Privacy Issues

Have any of these scenarios taken place where you work?

- ▲ Upon entering a colleague's office, a female employee notes that the coworker quickly clicks off his computer screen, but not before she sees a graphically posed naked woman.
- ▲ A supervisor walks by an employee's cubicle, glimpsing stock quotes on his computer screen.
- ▲ A manager goes online to revise the company's home page only to discover that an employee has added proprietary material to the page.
- ▲ An employee with an ax to grind, for receiving what he perceived as an inadequate pay raise, accesses employee HR files and then e-mails other employees' current salaries via the intranet.

A national study on high-tech workplace behavior, *Technology & Ethics in the Workplace*,* revealed that nearly half of America's workers engage in unethical and perhaps illegal actions related to cyberspace. Examples of behavior considered by employees to be acceptable include playing computer games during work, using e-mail for personal use, shopping online, and copying company software for home use. A large percentage of employees, however, draw the line when it comes to sabotaging systems and data or accessing private computer files without permission.

Cyberspace invites us to view sexually explicit material, read sports scores and statistics, go shopping online, check stock market quotes, enter chat rooms, and e-mail messages to friends. This is all done in the privacy of a one-on-one relationship with our computer. But do employees have the right to use computers for these

*Survey by the American Society of Chartered Life Underwriters (CLU), Chartered Financial Consultants (ChFC) and the Ethics Officer Association (EOA). Results reported in June, 1998.

purposes while at work? Many employers are finding themselves in the awkward position of being forced to deal with Internet situations such as these, and they don't know how to respond. While employers recognize their potential liability for what their employees do while on company property, it's not always clear when they are violating workers' privacy. With regard to e-mail and the Internet, the conflict is between the employer's interest in controlling their use and the employees' rights to protect personal communications. It's an interesting dilemma: The computers are owned by the company, so the company believes it has the right to control the use of its property by employees. On the other hand, employees feel that e-mail and Internet use are their personal forms of communication. If they want to spend their lunch hour on the computer, the company should not prevent them from doing so. Further, if an employee wants to send a private e-mail, the company should not be permitted to access the message.

The fact of the matter is that employers have a right to control on-the-job employee e-mail and the use of the Internet because of potential exposure to legal liability. Areas of exposure include:

▲ *Privacy.* Employers may have legal responsibilities to protect data pertaining to customers, employees, and others from disclosure. Interpretation, use, and disclosure may be impacted by the Federal Communications Privacy Act. Employers, therefore, need to develop policies to alert employees that their time and usage may be monitored for business purposes. Consent to such monitoring should also be obtained. The combination of informing employees and requesting their consent works to defeat any legitimate expectation of privacy.

▲ *Sexual harassment.* One of the most common problems emanating from employee abuse of the Internet is sexual harassment. This can occur when employees view or even download sexually explicit materials, potentially creating a hostile environment.

▲ *Other forms of discrimination.* While not as common as sexual harassment, other forms of hostile environment discrimination can result from Internet use. For example, the use of the Internet for transmitting racial epithets and jokes could lead to a lawsuit.

▲ *Theft.* Removing software or hardware, stealing company time by playing computer games, or using confidential company information in a subsequent job all constitute theft.

▲ *Licensing.* Application software is generally licensed rather than sold, and copying or transmitting such software is generally prohibited under the terms of the license. If employees copy, upload, or transmit licensed software, the employer may face liability for breach of the license agreement.

▲ *Copyright.* Employees may violate copyright laws by copying and reposting original text from web pages, as well as sound and graphics files.

▲ *Trade secrets.* Employers may be exposed to liability if employees sell trade secrets, take them to another job, or unwittingly transmit them over the Internet without recognizing their confidentiality.

▲ *Fraud.* Fraud may include sending messages under another employee's name or gaining access to another employee's password and files. It might also take the form of an employee's use of the employer's Internet access to promote his or her own product.

To prevent potential legal liability, organizations are installing filtering and blocking software to prevent employee access to specific computer sites. In addition, experts recommend monitoring devices that provide information on each individual employee's use of the computer system. These devices report exactly which web sites were visited, what e-mail messages were sent, how long the user was online, or whether the employee attempted to access a blocked site. Other programs provide employees with a number of cautionary messages that appear on their screen.

The trend in cases involving cyberspace usage by employees so far has been to uphold employers' rights more than employees'. Typically, employers have discovered employees engaged in electronic activities considered inappropriate. Upon being issued a reprimand, employees have replied, "You have no right to do that. We were doing that on our own time, so it's our personal business." They may then turn around and sue for invasion of privacy.

For example, two employees, John and Mary, were romantically involved and used the company's e-mail system to send romantic and sexually explicit notes to one another. During a routine system maintenance, the systems administrator came across several of these messages. Soon, word of the relationship spread throughout the company. John's wife filed for divorce. John, in turn, sued the company for invasion of privacy.

While there have been some cases in which employee suits have been upheld and damages awarded, as previously stated, the trend is to allow the employer to control what happens at the worksite.

Acceptable Use Policy

Because of potential liability issues like those cited above, more businesses are developing an "acceptable usage policy." Experts recommend that the policy begin with a statement that Internet, intranet, and other computer tools are owned by the company. Whether you state that these tools are intended to be used solely for business purposes is your choice. Note that such a statement can be problematic: While it may be that productivity problems have escalated with use of the Internet, a claim can be made that there are no greater time losses resulting from computer usage than from other forms of nonproductive activity. Going a step further, it can be maintained that "downtime" leads to effective and creative thinking.

Your policy should also include a description of acceptable uses of the Internet, intranet, e-mail, and other computer systems, as well as a ban on unacceptable activities. These may include solicitation of noncompany business for personal gain and the viewing or transmitting of obscene, degrading, or derogatory materials.

Also, include notification about security, privacy, confidentiality issues, and copyrights, as well as a statement that employees and their online activities are subject to monitoring. Clearly identify your rights as the employer and what disciplinary action will be taken for inappropriate or illegal use. Be as specific as you can in this regard. You may, for example, decide that it's reasonable to prohibit computer game-playing on company time, but that game-playing during lunch hours is acceptable.

Include reference to the fact that the policy may be amended or modified by management at any time.

Make sure employees clearly understand the contents of your acceptable use policy. This is typically accomplished in training sessions during which employees can ask questions and employers can obtain signatures acknowledging an understanding of the policy's contents. Also, include the policy in your employee handbook and HR policies and procedures manual, as well as publishing it online.

Employee Lifestyles and Appearance

A young man hired as a teller for a large commercial bank in a New York suburb showed up for his third day on the job wearing a red polyester suit and a tie with cartoon characters on it. The branch manager was completely taken aback. The man had dressed conservatively during his interview, and during the first two days of work he had worn navy blue and gray suits. Disturbed by his appearance, she called me and demanded to know if she could terminate the teller for inappropriate attire. When I suggested she talk with him before resorting to such drastic measures, she responded, "I'm too upset. Besides, I can't be that close to a man wearing red polyester!"

I decided to go in to talk with him at the bank branch. While we'd never met before, he was easy to pick out. We chatted a bit about his job and where he wanted to go careerwise. It wasn't long before he volunteered information germane to my mission. "I guess you're wondering why I'm wearing this suit," he said. "Well, just look around. Everyone at the bank is dressed in dark, dreary colors. I thought I'd bring a little life into the place with this suit. What do you think?" I told him that I understood his thinking, but that perhaps he would want to save the suit for non-work-related occasions, given the conservative nature of the banking industry. He responded, "Sure, but it's too bad. You've got to admit, my suit really stands out!"

He made my task easy. Had he insisted on his right to wear what he wanted, our discussion would have led to dress codes, and while the bank had a policy on dress and grooming, I wondered about the effect the dictate would have had on his work performance and future with the bank, or what would happen if he refused to comply.

How far can employers intrude when it comes to matters such as their employees' dress, grooming habits, or lifestyles? The laws are beginning to favor employee freedom over employer mandates.

In a recent survey, more than 62 percent of U.S. employers claimed to have a formal dress code; another 30 percent responded that they had an unwritten dress code. While in the past, employers dictated how their employees were to dress, and the employees, for the most part, complied, dress codes today have been adjusted to reflect employee preferences, as well as many U.S. discrimination laws.

Examples of employee preference abound. One involves a valued attorney who quit his firm when the employer rescinded its casual dress policy by reinstituting a policy of wearing only suits and ties. The law firm reversed its hasty decision, but too late for the return of this important employee. Many other examples involve candidates who have chosen one company over others because of their policies excluding casual attire.

Such examples are unfortunate, but not as costly as those involving discrimination. Recently, the First Amendment and Title VII of the Civil Rights Act of 1964 have been invoked against both public and private employers on dress code issues. For example, in one case, the 6th Circuit Court of Appeals allowed an African-American employee to sue her private employer because of the company's objections to her "eye-catching hairstyles." The worker, who was disciplined, alleged racial discrimination since white women wearing identical hairstyles were not reprimanded.

Generally, employers are on safe ground if they can link their concerns to business necessity. For example, if a company wants an employee to stop wearing a nose ring and a pink mohawk, it will have a better chance of "winning" if the employee has customer contact and the nature of the business is inherently conservative. Your case is also going to be stronger if you can document customer concern, as opposed to speculating about that concern. On the other hand, if the employee doesn't have client contact and the employer is creating some form of dress standard out of personal preference for a particular type of look, the company can anticipate litigation awarding damages to the employee.

In matters of appearance or attire, employers should first ask themselves: "Is this safety-related?" This might be the case with loose-fitting clothing or dangling jewelry because these items could get caught in equipment. Employers should next consider. "Is this job-related?" Generally, the answer to this question is no. The third issue employers should raise is: "Is the dress or appearance code we seek to impose in any way discriminatory?" For example, a grooming code that prohibits men from wearing facial hair could have an adverse impact on African-Americans because more African-American males than members of other ethnic groups have a skin condition that limits their ability to shave. It could also impact others who wear beards for religious reasons, like the two Sunni Muslim policemen who sued the Newark, New Jersey police department because they were required to shave. (Increasingly, private employers are changing their antibeard policies, allowing them for religious or medical reasons.)

Next, employers should ask: "Does the dress or appearance code reflect a stereotype?" This might be the case in a restaurant where the uniform for men consists of a tailored shirt and pants, but the uniform for women entails a revealing blouse and short skirt. This does not mean, however, that employers may not require different grooming and dress standards for men and women, as long as the policy does not benefit one gender to the detriment of the other gender, and as long as it is enforced without discrimination.

If you are going to institute a dress code, be sure to distinguish among business, casual business, and casual attire. You can, if you choose, identify specific articles of clothing that are unacceptable, such as jeans, sneakers, sandals, work boots, T-shirts, shirts with photos or writing, halter or tube tops, shorts, and bathing suits. You can stipulate that facial hair must be neat and trimmed; fingernails must be neat, clean, and trimmed; and perfume, if used, must be used sparingly, but discontinued if the scent bothers anyone.

Another area where employers need to tread softly is sexual orientation. In some states, sexual orientation is a protected classification, like race, sex, and national origin. Even in those areas of the country where it's not a protected classification, it's an issue that in almost all cases is unrelated to the working environment, and thus is an area that an employer should simply avoid when possible.

Office romances are an area where employers actually can get involved to a limited extent. An employer can prohibit individuals engaged in a personal relationship from being in a direct reporting line. The rationale is business related: You don't want a personal relationship to interfere with work. Enforcing a "no office romance" rule, however, is going to be more difficult.

Index